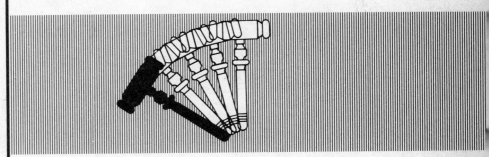

CASENOTE LAW OUTLINES

CIVIL PROCEDURE

John B. Oakley
Professor of Law
University of California, Davis
co-author: *An Introduction to the Anglo-American Legal System* (with Bodenheimer & Love)
chair: AALS Section on Civil Procedure (1979-80)

and

Rex R. Perschbacher
Professor of Law
University of California, Davis
co-editor: *Cases and Materials on Civil Procedure* (with Crump, Dorsaneo & Chase)
author: *California Trial Technique*

Published and Distributed by:
CASENOTES PUBLISHING CO., INC.
1640 Fifth Street, Suite 208
Santa Monica, Calif. 90401
(213) 395-6500 · FAX (213) 458-2020

ISBN 0-87457-179-0

With the introduction of Casenote Law Outlines, Casenotes Publishing Company brings a new approach to the legal study outline. Of course, we have sought out only nationally recognized authorities in their respective fields to author the outlines. Most of the authors are editors of widely used casebooks and/or hornbooks. Those who are not casebook editors have published extensively in respected legal journals, and some have written treatises cited by courts across the nation in opinions deciding important issues on which the authors have recommended what the "last word" on those legal issues should be.

     What is truly novel about the Casenote Law Outlines concept is that each outline does not fit into a cookie cutter mold. While each author has been given a carefully developed format as a framework for each outline, the format is purposefully flexible. The student will therefore find that each outline is not alike. Instead, each professor has used an approach appropriate to the subject matter. An outline on Evidence cannot be written in the same manner as one on Constitutional Law of Contracts or Torts, etc. Accordingly, the student will find similar features in each Casenote Law Outline, but they may be handled in radically different ways by each author. We believe that in this way the law student will be rewarded with the most effective study aid possible.

     We continually seek law student and law professor feedback regarding the effectiveness of our publications. As you use Casenote Law Outlines, please do not hesitate to write or call us if you have constructive criticism or simply would like to tell us you are pleased with the approach and design of the publication.

     Best of luck in your studies.

                CASENOTES PUBLISHING CO., INC.

CASENOTE LAW OUTLINES -- SUPPLEMENT REQUEST FORM

Casenotes Publishing Co., Inc. prides itself on producing the most current legal study outlines available. Sometimes between major revisions, the authors of the outline series will issue supplements to update their respective outlines to reflect any recent changes in the law. Certain areas of the law change more quickly than others, and thus some outlines may be supplemented, while others may not be supplemented at all. In order to determine whether or not you should send this supplement request form to us, first check the printing date that appears by the subject name below. If this outline is less than one year old, it is highly unlikely that there will be a supplement for it. If it is older, you may wish to write, telephone, or fax us for current information. You might also check to see whether a supplement has been included with your *Casenote Law Outline* or has been provided to your bookstore. If it is necessary to order the supplement directly from us, it will be supplied without charge, but we do insist that you send a stamped, self-addressed return envelope. If you request a supplement for an outline that does not have one, you will receive the latest *Casenotes* catalogue.

If you wish to request a supplement for this outline:

#5040, CIVIL PROCEDURE, FIRST EDITION ▸ 1991, by Oakley and Perschbacher

please follow the instructions below.

• **TO OBTAIN YOUR COMPLIMENTARY SUPPLEMENT(S),** *YOU MUST FOLLOW THESE INSTRUCTIONS PRECISELY IN ORDER FOR YOUR REQUEST TO BE ACKNOWLEDGED.*

1. **REMOVE AND SEND THIS ENTIRE REQUEST FORM:** You *must* send this *original* page, which acts as your proof of purchase and provides the information regarding which supplements, if any, you need. The request form is only valid for any supplement for the outline in which it appears. *No photocopied or written requests will be honored.*

2. **SEND A STAMPED, SELF-ADDRESSED, FULL-SIZE (9" x 12") ENVELOPE:** *Affix enough postage to cover at least 3 oz.* We regret that we absolutely cannot fill and/or acknowledge requests unaccompanied by a stamped, self-addressed envelope.

3. **MULTIPLE SUPPLEMENT REQUESTS:** If you are sending supplement requests for two or more different *Casenote Law Outlines,* we suggest you send a return envelope for each subject requested. If you send only one envelope, your order may not be filled immediately should any supplement you requested still be in production. In that case, your order will not be filled until it can be filled completely, *i.e.,* until all supplements you have requested are published.

4. **PLEASE GIVE US THE FOLLOWING INFORMATION:**

Name: _____   Telephone: (_____) _____-_____

Address: _____   Apt.: _____

City: _____   State: _____   Zip: _____

Name of law school you attend: _____

Name and location of bookstore where you purchased this *Casenote Law Outline:* _____

_____

Any comments regarding *Casenote Law Outlines?* _____

_____

CASENOTES PUBLISHING CO., INC., 1640 Fifth Street, Suite 208, Santa Monica, CA 90401
(213) 395-6500 • FAX (213) 458-2020

CASENOTE LAW OUTLINES

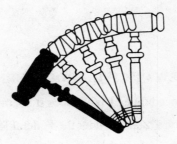

CIVIL PROCEDURE

DEDICATIONS

By John Oakley

I dedicate this work to my wife, Freddie, with thanks for her patience and counsel in traversing the many fields of procedure we have encountered in twenty-two years of marriage. I also acknowledge with thanks the many contributions to my knowledge of civil procedure that I have gained from colleagues and students during the sixteen years I have been privileged to teach at King Hall, the law school of the University of California at Davis.

By Rex Perschbacher

I dedicate this work to my King Hall civil procedure tutors: Alan, Jon, Michael, Debbie, Chantal, Felicia and Craig. My work on this outline would not have been possible without the encouragement and editorial assistance of my wife, Debbie; research help on the index from Carolyn Broesamle ('93); and the excellent staff assistance of Ms. Saralee Buck and Ms. Helen Forsythe.

TC

TABLE OF CONTENTS

CHAPTER 5: PLEADING

CHAPTER 6: JOINDER OF CLAIMS AND PARTIES

CHAPTER 7: DISCOVERY

CHAPTER 8: PRE-TRIAL PROCEDURE AND DISPOSITIONS — ALTERNATIVES TO TRIAL, PRE-TRIAL CONFERENCES, DISMISSAL, DEFAULT JUDGMENT, AND SUMMARY JUDGMENT

CAPSULE OUTLINE

CO

CAPSULE OUTLINE

AUTHORS' NOTE: The purposes of a capsule outline are to guide and to remind, not to instruct. By compressing the master outline's discussion of each topic into a few lines, a capsule outline shows you the relationships between topics, directs you to the pages of the master outline at which a discussion in depth may be found, and serves as a checklist by which to review your memory and comprehension of the master outline. It is a mistake to assume that you can learn Civil Procedure simply by reading the highly qualified and abbreviated headings and summaries that constitute this capsule outline.

In order to allow you to use the capsule outline as an annotated table of contents, you will find heading-by-heading page references to the master outline. The numbering and lettering of the major headings and all subheadings are identical in the capsule outline and the master outline, but the text of the capsule outline's headings has been occasionally revised and compressed in the interest of brevity. Subheadings have been included only to the degree necessary to present an organizational overview of the most important subordinate topics discussed in the master outline.

INTRODUCTION: The selection of the particular court where a case is tried involves consideration of the validity of judgments, service of process, choice of law, venue, discretionary doctrines for refusing jurisdiction, and methods for attacking a plaintiff's choice of forum.

CO

CO

CO

CO

CHAPTER 3: MINIMUM CONTACTS ANALYSIS 3-1

INTRODUCTION: "Minimum contacts" is the nebulous term that the Supreme Court has used to describe the relationship that a state must have with a particular defendant in order for the state's assertion of territorial jurisdiction over that defendant to be consistent with the Constitution's guarantee of due process of law.

I.   **HISTORICAL BACKGROUND** 3-1

  A. **The original terms of the Constitution did not authorize federal regulation of state court territorial jurisdiction.** 3-1

  B. **The Fourteenth Amendment required state courts to conform to federal due process standards.** 3-1

  C. **In the 1878 case of *Pennoyer v. Neff,* the Supreme Court declared that due process generally required personal service of process on the defendant within the territory of the forum state.** 3-1

  D. **The 1905 *Harris v. Balk* case significantly expanded the use of quasi-in-rem jurisdiction as a fallback method for states to allow residents to sue non-residents who could not personally be served with process with the state.** 3-2

  E. **The economic growth of the United States prompted many states to adopt "long-arm" statutes further stretching the boundaries of *Pennoyer* by serving process within the forum state on a fictitious agent of an out-of-state defendant.** 3-2

II. **THE BIRTH OF MINIMUM CONTACTS DOCTRINE IN *INTERNATIONAL SHOE*** . . . 3-3

  A. **The 1945 *International Shoe* case upheld process mailed out of state.** 3-3

  B. **In *International Shoe,* the Supreme Court announced the new concept of "minimum contacts" as the due process standard for state court personal jurisdiction over an out-of-state defendant. The ultimate test for minimum contacts is whether the relationship between the defendant, the forum, and the litigation is such that the forum's assertion of personal jurisdiction over the defendant is consistent with "fair play and substantial justice."** 3-3

III. **FURTHER DEVELOPMENT OF MINIMUM CONTACTS DOCTRINE** 3-4

  A. **The constitutional law of state court territorial jurisdiction since *International Shoe* has consisted of a gradual working out of the idea of minimum contacts.** 3-4

appointed a resident agent for unrestricted service of process in the forum state; the defendant is an individual domiciled in the forum state; the defendant is a non-resident individual who has appointed a resident agent for unrestricted service of process in the forum state; or the defendant is a non-resident individual served with process while voluntarily present in the forum state. General jurisdiction may also exist over a foreign corporation or non-resident individual who have not appointed resident agents, if such defendants have engaged in continuous, systematic, and substantial general business activity in the forum state. 3-15

Step 4. *Power* to exercise specific jurisdiction? 3-16

a. General jurisdiction (Step 3) may be distinguished from specific jurisdiction (Steps 4 and 5) by thinking of general jurisdiction as based on "maximum contacts." If the purposeful contacts fall short of the "maximum contacts" threshold, the question remains whether these contacts amount to the mysterious quantum of "minimum contacts" that, in the context of a particular lawsuit, will suffice for specific jurisdiction. 3-16

b. The modern approach to specific jurisdiction distinguishes the penultimate question of whether there are the minimum contacts necessary for jurisdictional power (Step 4) from the ultimate question of the reasonableness of exercising that power (Step 5). . 3-16

c. The problem of "relatedness." Whether "minimum contacts" exist depends on whether the defendant's purposeful contacts are sufficiently related to the subject-matter of the litigation. The Supreme Court has not yet ruled on how direct a relationship there must be between the defendant's contacts and the plaintiff's cause of action in order for the contacts to qualify as minimum contacts. The soundest approach at present is to resolve doubt by finding sufficient "relatedness" to permit the analysis to proceed to Step 5. 3-17

Step 5. Is it *reasonable* for the forum to exercise specific jurisdiction? 3-19

a. Minimum contacts analysis entails a qualitative weighing of the contacts to determine whether under all the circumstances it is reasonable for the forum state to exercise jurisdiction. 3-19

b. When the weight of the purposeful contacts of the defendant with the forum state is so great that the forum has general jurisdiction over the defendant, it is *per se* reasonable for the forum to exercise its jurisdiction. 3-19

c. When the defendant's purposeful contacts qualify as "minimum contacts" but are insufficient for general jurisdiction, a number of additional factors are relevant to whether it is reasonable for the forum to exercise specific jurisdiction over the defendant. These "reasonableness factors" include the burden on the defendant; the forum state's interest in adjudicating the dispute; the plaintiff's interest in obtaining convenient and effective relief; the interstate judicial system's interest in obtaining the most efficient resolution of controversies; the shared interest of the several states in furthering fundamental substantive social policies; and whether the litigation will affect the procedural and substantive policies of other countries by subjecting a foreigner to the jurisdiction of American courts. 3-19

d. Operation of reasonableness factors in the marginal case 3-21

(1) If there is doubt at Step 4 whether minimum contacts exist, the plaintiff can invoke the reasonableness factors to help meet her burden of proof of the existence of the forum's jurisdictional power. 3-21

(2) If the outcome of Step 4 clearly establishes that minimum contacts exist, the defendant must meet a heavy burden of "compelling" proof in order to establish at Step 5 that it would be unreasonable for the forum state to exercise specific jurisdiction. 3-21

CO

INTRODUCTION: Federal jurisdiction is one of the most complex and demanding fields of study in all of American law. There are two major categories of cases eligible for trial in federal court: "federal question" litigation in which federal jurisdiction is based on the characteristics of the issues, and "diversity" cases in which federal jurisdiction is based on the characteristics of the parties. "Removal jurisdiction" allows a defendant under certain conditions to invoke federal jurisdiction over a diversity or federal question case, even if the plaintiff has chosen to file the suit in state court. "Supplemental jurisdiction" extends the jurisdiction of the federal courts to other claims and parties that are appropriately connected to federal question and diversity litigation. It is quite possible for a case that qualifies for federal jurisdiction to be filed in the wrong court. Federal venue rules vary for diversity and federal question cases, and you must also be familiar with federal rules governing changes of venue. Our last topic is the *Erie* doctrine. It provides, roughly, that state law, not federal law, is the substantive law to be applied in federal lawsuits unless Congress has specified to the contrary. Mastery of the *Erie* doctrine and its application to federal changes of venue is essential to understanding how the choice between a federal or state forum may affect the outcome of a lawsuit.

CO

III. **NOTICE PLEADING REQUIREMENTS — THE COMPLAINT. Federal or notice pleading also has distinctive formal and substantive elements, both different from those found in code pleadings. Under Federal Rule 8, the elements of a federal pleading are simple. A federal pleading stating a claim for relief must contain (1) a jurisdictional statement showing the court it has jurisdiction of the subject matter; (2) a short and a plain statement of the claim showing that the pleader is entitled to relief; and (3) a demand for judgment.** 5-4

    A. **Formally, under federal or notice pleading, ultimate facts are not required. Only a short and plain statement of the claim is necessary.** 5-4

    B. **Federal rules pleadings also have a substantive aspect. It is still necessary for the pleader to give grounds or show that she is entitled to relief. The test is that a complaint should not be dismissed for failure to state an adequate claim unless it appears beyond doubt that the plaintiff can prove no set of facts in support of the claim which would entitle him to relief.** 5-4

IV. **Under state systems in general and under the Federal Rules in particular, there is a category of claims, properly categorized as disfavored claims, that must be pleaded with greater than usual factual specificity. These claims are identified in Federal Rules 9(b) and 9(g).** 5-4

    A. **Rule 9(b) requires that in making allegations of fraud or mistake, the pleader must state the circumstances constituting fraud or mistake with particularity. Federal Rule 9(g) also provides that special damage claims must be specifically stated. For these disfavored allegations, the federal pleader must add factual information similar to that required of a code pleader.** 5-4

    B. **However, the general requirements of notice pleading otherwise apply to fraud claims. Only the facts of the particular allegation must be stated specifically.** 5-5

    C. **The similar requirement in special damage claims applies to those unusual damages that do not ordinarily occur as a result of the standard claims.** 5-5

    D. **Although the Federal Rules officially recognize only the additional pleading requirements in Rules 9(b) and 9(g), federal judges have judicially created special pleading rules requiring greater specificity or factual detail in a variety of settings, including "big" cases; in *pro se* pleadings; and in certain civil rights cases. The propriety of judicially-created extraordinary pleading requirements is subject to considerable debate.** 5-5

    E. **Alternate and Inconsistent Allegations. The Federal Rules, and modern Code-pleading rules, tolerate the pleading of alternate and inconsistent allegations.** 5-5

    F. **Form of Pleadings. The elements of a caption, style of paragraph number, and other matters of form are governed by Federal Rule 10 and the local rules of trial courts.** 5-5

V. **ANSWERS. In federal court, the answer contains three distinct elements: first, admissions and denials of the allegations in the complaint, ordinarily on a paragraph-by-paragraph basis; second, new matter, that is, affirmative defenses available to the party; and, third, other defenses often of a preliminary nature. In federal practice only, the answer may contain a counterclaim or cross-claim making affirmative allegations of liability owed to the answering party.** 5-6

    A. **Under Federal Rule 8(b), defendant's answer must admit or deny the allegations of the complaint. If the defendant is without knowledge or information sufficient to form a belief as to the truth of one of the allegations of the complaint, defendant can cite this lack of information or belief as the basis of a denial.** 5-6

    B. **Affirmative defenses are provided for in Federal Rule 8(c). It requires that in responding to a pleading, a defending party should affirmatively set forth a laundry list of defenses. Affirmative defenses are matters which are not principally a denial or rebuttal of any of**

CO

INTRODUCTION: Joinder doctrines govern how and how many claims and parties may be joined
together in a single lawsuit. Modern American civil procedure encourages "liberal joinder" of both claims

and parties in order to dispose efficiently and consistently, at just one trial, of all claims with common issues or between common parties.

CO ▶

CO

CHAPTER 7

CO

CO

CO ►

D. Recent court decisions have somewhat reined-in overly-zealous judges who have attempted to force the parties to participate in mini-trials or summary jury trials or to compel jurors from the court's standard jury list to serve as jurors in a summary jury trial. Court-enforced alternatives to litigation have been restricted to annexed arbitration procedures which are not final and binding and to the regular use of settlement conferences with a settlement conference judge. Both of these procedures allow the parties to avoid or reject the private resolution and to insist upon taking the case to trial, although substantial burdens may accompany this process. 8-3

II. **PRE-TRIAL CONFERENCES AND PRE-TRIAL ORDERS.** The movement in the past decade to give judges greater tools and encouragement to manage all aspects of litigation is particularly prominent with regard to pre-trial procedure. 8-3

A. Both Rule 16 regarding pre-trial conferences and its companion, Rule 26(f), providing for a discovery conference, allow the parties or the judge supervising the litigation to bring together all parties either at regular intervals or a specific time before trial to resolve pending matters of discovery and procedure; to consider settlement or other early disposition of the case; and to simplify the legal and factual issues for trial. 8-3

B. Rule 16 was amended in 1983 to expand its terms to conform with the practice that had evolved under the narrower terms of old Rule 16. 8-3

III. **RULE 41 VOLUNTARY AND INVOLUNTARY DISMISSALS** 8-5

A. **Voluntary Dismissal.** Under Rule 41(a), plaintiff's may, for a variety of reasons, seek to dismiss actions at a pre-trial stage before any decision on the merits. 8-5

B. **Involuntary Dismissal.** Under Rule 41(b) there are two types of involuntary dismissal. . 8-6

1. In the usual case, where an action is yet to be tried or will be tried by a jury, Rule 41(b) allows dismissal for plaintiff's failure to prosecute the action in an effective or procedurally proper manner. 8-6

2. In cases tried to the court, Rule 41(b) dismissals may also operate in the manner of a non-suit. 8-7

IV. **SUMMARY JUDGMENTS** 8-7

A. **Purposes of Summary Judgment.** Under the Federal Rules the pleadings frame the dispute in very general terms, and the competing factual contentions of the parties are developed through the discovery process. The motion for summary judgment is the device used to detect and dismiss claims and defenses that are either factually unsupported or, on the established facts, are insufficient as a matter of law. 8-7

B. **Standard for Granting Summary Judgment.** Rule 56 authorizes summary judgment when the trial court finds an absence of a genuine issue as to any material fact. It is not enough for the party opposing a motion for summary judgment to rely upon discovery material that shows merely the *possibility* that favorable evidence may be introduced at trial. The Supreme Court has recently interpreted the summary judgment standard as a pre-trial version of the standard for granting a directed verdict. In ruling on a motion for summary

CO

CO

CHAPTER 10

CO ▶

INTRODUCTION: Correcting judicial error takes foresight, skill, and persistence. The mechanics of appeal are similar in most courts, but appellate policy and philosophy varies widely. The appellate courts of the federal system and the state of California illustrate the extremes of variation.

CO

CHAPTER 11   **CHAPTER 11: ENFORCEMENT OF JUDGMENTS** 11-1

INTRODUCTION: A valid judgment is enforceable, but in most cases enforcement requires further proceedings to coerce a recalcitrant defendant into paying or otherwise complying with the judgment.

CO

CO

CO

A. Each of the states and the federal system has its own system of preclusion. Problems are relatively simple when a federal court judgment is applied to other federal court proceedings and when a state court judgment is applied to other proceedings within the same state. However, when inter-system preclusion is sought, the problems are more complex.   . . 12-12

B. Interstate Enforcement of Sister-state Judgments. The United States Constitution's full faith and credit clause and the accompanying full faith and credit statute, 28 U.S.C. § 1738, require that each state give full faith and credit to the public acts, records, and judicial proceedings of every other state. 12-12

C. Preclusive Effect of State Court Judgments in Federal Court. The Supreme Court has read the full faith and credit statute as requiring that the federal courts must enforce the judgments of state courts and give them the same preclusive effect that the states from which the judgments emerged would give them. 12-12

D. Preclusive Effect of Federal Judgments in State Court. This area is unregulated by statute, but the federal courts have, through a series of decisions, read the Supremacy Clause of the Constitution to require states to give preclusive effect to federal court judgments. . 12-12

E. Preclusive Effect of Federal Judgments on Federal Court. Federal courts must give effect to the judgments of other federal courts by virtue of the federal court registration statute, 28 U.S.C. § 1963. 12-12

1

OVERVIEW OF CIVIL PROCEDURE

▶ # CHAPTER SUMMARY

OVERVIEW OF CIVIL PROCEDURE

INTRODUCTION: In this chapter we describe what Civil Procedure is, how it fits into the standard law school curriculum, and why it is commonly perceived as a more challenging subject than the basic courses in substantive law. We discuss what is and isn't covered in most law school courses on Civil Procedure, and tell you the sequence of topics that you will find covered in this outline. We conclude the chapter by noting the special importance of the Federal Rules of Civil Procedure as the dominant model of procedure in modern American courts.

WHAT IS CIVIL PROCEDURE?

1

I. **WHAT IS CIVIL PROCEDURE AND WHY DOES IT SEEM SO DIFFICULT?**

   A. **Civil Procedure deals with the system set up by the government of a particular society for the submission and official resolution of civil disputes. It is a set of procedural rather than substantive rules of law.**

   1. *Substantive law* consists of rules of primary conduct governing how individuals, entities (such as corporations and public agencies), and the government itself are supposed to act and interact. The substantive law either governs primary conduct directly or specifies ways in which individuals by agreement can set up self-governing rules.

      a. Rules of substantive law that create rights and impose duties directly, by force of law, are obligatory regardless of whether the persons regulated by the law have agreed to be bound by it.

      Examples of such non-volitional substantive rules of law are the entire law of torts, and the massive body of modern tax and regulatory statutes.

      b. Other rules of substantive law don't impose duties directly but confer powers upon people privately to create legally enforceable rights and duties by voluntary agreement.

      Examples of this sort of do-it-yourself substantive law are the rules governing contracts and the making of wills.

   2. *Procedural law,* including that part we call Civil Procedure, prescribes and administers the process for enforcing the rights and duties specified in the substantive law.

   B. **What *IS NOT* Covered in Civil Procedure**

   1. *Criminal Procedure.* Civil Procedure doesn't deal with all the rules of procedural law. For starters, we don't deal with the procedural rules of the criminal justice system, which are covered in — you guessed it — "Criminal Procedure."

   2. *Administrative Law.* We also don't deal with the process by which administrative agencies implement statutes by promulgating quasi-legislative regulations and then enforce those regulations through quasi-judicial prosecution and adjudication of violations. These issues are dealt with in the course called "Administrative Law." There are many important intersections between Administrative Law and Civil Procedure. The law requires some civil disputes to be submitted to the processes and forums of the administrative legal system before the dispute is eligible to be submitted to decision by a formal court of law in the form of a petition to review the administrative decision.

   3. *Evidence and Trial Practice.* An important part of old-fashioned civil adjudication in a formal court of law is the conduct of trials, both in terms of trial advocacy and in terms of the law of evidence governing what information may be presented to the trier of fact. These subjects are particularly important when the trier of fact is that body unique to formal, court-of-law adjudication: the jury. Although these subjects are logically part of the topic of Civil Procedure, they are so important and so specialized that at most law schools the law of evidence and the skills involved in selecting and presenting a case to a jury are dealt with in separate courses.

C. **What *IS* covered in Civil Procedure, as organized and explained in this outline? Civil Procedure deals with just about every other aspect of judicial adjudication of civil disputes, that is, the process for resolving civil disputes about rights and duties under the substantive law through formal adjudication by courts staffed by judges. Every state and the federal government has a more-or-less old-fashioned court system for judicial adjudication of civil disputes. The following headings track the chapter-by-chapter organization of this outline's discussion of how that system operates. Each heading begins with the chapter title and author, and then presents a thumbnail sketch of the content of the chapter.**

1. OVERVIEW OF CIVIL PROCEDURE (Oakley).

2. CONTROLLING THE CHOICE OF FORUM: JURISDICTION, PROCESS, AND CHOICE OF LAW (Oakley). The first factor a plaintiff must consider in choosing a forum is whether it will have the "jurisdiction" to render a "valid" judgment. In Chapter 2, we introduce you to the concepts of jurisdiction and the validity of judgments. We spell out a six-step analytical framework for resolving problems of validity and jurisdiction. We pay special attention in this chapter to the requirement that the parties to a valid judgment have received proper notice and service of process. We discuss choice of law and venue doctrines that affect choice of forum, and we conclude with a review of the various motions and other means by which a defendant can attack the plaintiff's choice of forum.

3. MINIMUM CONTACTS ANALYSIS (Oakley). In Chapter 3, we continue our analysis of validity and jurisdiction by considering the federal constitutional law that limits the territorial jurisdiction of state courts over non-resident defendants. "Minimum contacts" is the legal buzzword used to describe the relationship that a state must have with a defendant in order for the state's assertion of territorial jurisdiction over that defendant to be consistent with the fourteenth amendment's guarantee of due process of law.

4. FEDERAL SUBJECT-MATTER JURISDICTION AND RELATED DOCTRINES AFFECTING CHOICE OF A FEDERAL FORUM (Oakley). In Chapter 4, we conclude our analysis of validity and jurisdiction by introducing you to the federal court system. This is our longest chapter. We discuss the constitutional context of the federal courts and their limited powers, the basic structure of the court system Congress has created, the rules and policies governing the two major categories of original federal subject-matter jurisdiction ("federal question jurisdiction" and "diversity jurisdiction"), the special features of federal removal jurisdiction by which a defendant can choose a federal forum even though the plaintiff has elected to file suit in state court, and the additional constraints on choice of a federal forum posed by federal venue rules. We take you very carefully through the multi-faceted facts and law of the *Erie* doctrine that controls whether state or federal law governs a case litigated in federal court on the basis of diversity jurisdiction, and we conclude with a five-step analytical framework for answering modern "*Erie* problems."

5. PLEADING (Perschbacher). In Chapter 5, we turn from choice of forum to what a plaintiff must do in her chosen forum in order properly to present a dispute for the forum's resolution. There are basically two pleading systems found in modern American courts. The older "code pleading" system requires more factual detail than the "notice pleading" permitted under the Federal Rules of Civil Procedure and the parallel rules of the many state court procedural systems that are modeled on the Federal Rules. We discuss the sequence of pleadings, standards for the truthfulness of pleadings, amendments of pleadings, and attacks on pleadings.

6. JOINDER OF CLAIMS AND PARTIES (Oakley). A hallmark of modern civil procedure is "liberal joinder," whereby pleaders are allowed to join together groups of claims and parties that may ultimately result in literally thousands of claims being litigated at once. There are many fine points and technical distinctions. In Chapter 6, we guide you through

the maze with numerous examples and illustrations that are carefully keyed to the relevant Federal Rules of Civil Procedure. Closely tied to the law of liberal joinder are the supplemental doctrines of "pendent" and "ancillary" federal subject-matter jurisdiction. We discuss the scope of the supplemental jurisdiction of the federal courts and provide you with a detailed checklist of how supplemental jurisdiction relates to each particular Federal Rule on joinder of claims and parties.

7. DISCOVERY (Perschbacher). In Chapter 7, we deal with the formal process by which parties may obtain litigation-related information from their adversaries and other witnesses. The major issues are the scope of discovery, the limitations necessary to protect the adversary process, the comparative features of the major discovery devices, and the problem of abuse of the discovery process.

8. PRE-TRIAL PROCEDURE AND DISPOSITIONS: ALTERNATIVES TO TRIAL, PRE-TRIAL CONFERENCES, DISMISSAL, DEFAULT JUDGMENT, AND SUMMARY JUDGMENT (Perschbacher). Chapter 8 covers the variety of procedural mechanisms by which civil disputes otherwise eligible for full-scale litigation may be resolved without the great economic and social expense of adversarial trial. The most important alternative to trial is negotiated settlement, but even if the *substance* of a dispute cannot be settled, the parties may be able to agree on an alternative *method* of dispute resolution such as arbitration, mediation, or some other form of abbreviated or advisory fact-finding. After reviewing the various "Alternative Dispute Resolution" or "ADR" devices that the parties can employ independently of the courts, we turn to the various mechanisms judges can use to dispose of cases without formal trial. Pre-trial conferences give the trial judge a platform for monitoring the progress of attacks on the pleadings and choice of forum, for supervising the discovery process, and for narrowing the issues requiring trial in light of the evidence produced during discovery. The state of the case and the evidence may compel a voluntary or involuntary dismissal of all or part of a case. Failure to substantiate factual claims sufficiently to warrant trial may result in summary judgment ordered by the court for lack of prima facie proof. Finally, failure to comply with procedural rules may result in judgment by default.

9. TRIAL AND POST-TRIAL MOTIONS (Perschbacher). Chapter 9 begins with a brief rehearsal of the stages of a trial, from the pre-trial conference "scripting" of the trial through the selection of a jury, presentation of the case, argument to and instruction of the jury, return of verdict, and entry of judgment. We then discuss in detail the scope of the right to jury trial, especially in federal court under the seventh amendment. Finally, we consider the various means by which jury autonomy is controlled by judicial instruction, verdict forms, burdens of proof and persuasion, directed verdicts, new trials, and judgments notwithstanding the verdict.

10. APPEAL (Oakley). In Chapter 10, we address the mechanics and philosophy of appeal by looking closely at the details of the appellate process in the intermediate federal appellate courts and the state appellate courts of California. These two systems illustrate a fundamental division of American appellate courts over the purpose and timing of appeal. The federal system values appeal primarily as a means for the institutional development of the law and, accordingly, delays appeal in the ordinary case until a final judgment has been entered. The California system values appeal primarily as a means for correcting judicial error that harms individual litigants and, accordingly, permits immediate "interlocutory" review on a far more routine basis than does the federal system. We also look at the procedures employed by the Supreme Court of the United States for reviewing judgments of inferior state and federal courts.

11. ENFORCEMENT OF JUDGMENTS (Oakley). In Chapter 11, we discuss the means and mechanics of enforcing judgments. The fact that a judgment meets all the criteria for validity set forth in Chapter 2 does not guarantee that a plaintiff who has succeeded in winning a judgment will be able to gain any practical benefit from its enforcement.

Although some judgments are self-enforcing, most judgments require the further step of proceedings to enforce the judgment in order to coerce a recalcitrant defendant into payment or compliance.

12. **PRECLUSION DOCTRINES: RES JUDICATA AND COLLATERAL ESTOPPEL** (Perschbacher). Chapter 12 discusses the preclusion doctrines that give effect to a judgment by precluding relitigation of any factual and legal disputes resolved by the judgment. There are three problematic dimensions along which the scope of preclusive effect must be measured. First, what is the proper scope of the issues whose relitigation is precluded? The doctrine of res judicata precludes relitigation of the same claim or cause of action as was previously adjudicated. The doctrine of collateral estoppel precludes relitigation of the same issues as were necessarily decided by the previous litigation. Second, who are the persons who are properly deemed bound by the outcome of the prior litigation? This is rarely problematic in the res judicata context, but in the collateral estoppel context difficult questions arise about "mutuality" of estoppel. Third, to what degree does the judgment of one state or federal American court preclude subsequent related litigation in a different American court system?

D. **Why is Civil Procedure a tricky and seemingly difficult course?**

1. Rules of procedural law deal with rights and duties once removed from the day-to-day conduct of life, and deal instead with the system for *enforcing* the day-to-day rules of life. This gives procedural law a rather dry flavor. It may seem that procedural law has no life of its own, as it were, no independent purpose — it succeeds or fails by how well it allows the rules of substantive law to operate, and by how just a society is created and served by the rules of substantive law. But this dim view of the intrinsic importance of procedural law overlooks the fact that justice is in part procedural. Justice requires a fair and efficient system for settling disputes about the substantive law.

2. Most of what outsiders (*i.e.*, people who haven't gone to law school or otherwise become closely acquainted with the legal system) think of as "law" is the body of substantive rules of law governing primary conduct. Since most beginning law students are outsiders, procedural law comes as a bit of a surprise. When this hidden body of law is revealed to be both pervasive and complex, new students gain a first impression of procedural law as forbidding, technical, and a bit mysterious.

3. Much of the mystery and challenge of Civil Procedure comes from comparing it to the far more intuitive rules of the substantive law. The basic rules of the substantive law are soundly based in common sense, and are strikingly similar worldwide.

   a. Virtually every civilized society features rules of law that provide, generally speaking, that promises be kept, that citizens act with reasonable care to avoid harming each other, that a person may exercise sovereignty over some sphere of personal space and material possessions free of unreasonable interference by others, and that only the state may lawfully resort to violence in order to enforce its will. These intuitively reasonable principles are the core of the law of contracts, torts, property, and crimes.

   b. Poor Civil Procedure! By contrast, there is very little that intuition recommends, with one voice across all humanity, as the core principles of dispute resolution. The single most global procedural principle is probably that "no one should be the judge of his or her own cause" — judges should be neutral and impartial. But should questions of fact be resolved by juries, by judges, or by panels of knowledgeable experts? Should parties be required to disclose their evidence to each other in advance of trial? Should every dispute be subject to adjudication in just one court, even when multiple parties from multiple places are involved? Or should the parties be given some leeway in choice of forum? Should the issues to be resolved be fixed firmly and precisely by the documents initiating the litigation, or should the scope of the litigation remain flexible as the litigation progresses?

c. There are no clear answers to these questions and most others that arise in Civil Procedure. Every procedural system strives to achieve "justice." But within any working theory of what counts as procedurally "just" there is always tension between competing goals of efficiency and fairness. We want a procedural system that "works," that decides cases reasonably quickly and inexpensively. But we also want a procedural system that "works right," that is reasonably accurate in its determination of the facts and the law, of what really happened and what the law requires in light of the true facts.

d. Because there are few clear answers to the many procedural questions that pit the concern for efficiency against the concern for fairness, most procedural systems are based as much on random chance and the dumb weight of history as on a reasoned choice among procedural alternatives. At any given time, much of the law of procedure in a given jurisdiction "just is." This makes the law of procedure frustrating. You can't just guess at it. It also makes the law of procedure much more volatile than the substantive law. There is lots of room for improvement, you can only improve it a little bit at a time, and so a little improvement is always going on somewhere in the law of procedure. The rules are always changing.

4. Our aim in this outline is to show you that despite these difficult qualities the law of Civil Procedure is lively, important, and eminently learnable. All it takes to master Civil Procedure is an open mind, a willingness to work hard (sometimes you will have to read procedural cases and rules several times in order to follow their twists and turns), and an experienced guide to help you avoid the occasional arbitrary trap and to see the many historical connections that tie the rules together.

WHY WE FOCUS ON PRACTICE UNDER THE FRCP

II. **WHY WE FOCUS ON PRACTICE UNDER THE FEDERAL RULES OF CIVIL PROCEDURE.**

A. **American law is made much more complex than the domestic law of most other countries by the unique overlap of state and federal governmental powers in the United States. Our federal system of government significantly complicates the study of Civil Procedure because the individual states are by-and-large free to run their local court systems as they see fit.**

1. This means that the same case may be governed by much different procedural and even substantive rules depending on which state is the forum for the litigation.

2. Extreme variations in state practice are curtailed by the uniform nationwide effect of the federal Constitution's demand that state courts afford litigants "due process of law," and by the occasional preemption of state law by an Act of Congress.

3. The practical scope of variation in state practice is also restricted by the tremendous influence that the Federal Rules of Civil Procedure have had in reforming and harmonizing the procedural systems of state courts.

B. **Although we constantly keep an eye on important state variations, our primary focus is on the procedural system specified by the Federal Rules of Civil Procedure. This system is, by far, the most widely followed in American courts, since it governs not only the federal courts but also the courts of the many states that have enacted rules of procedure substantially identical to the Federal Rules.**

1. In a recent survey, 25 states and the District of Columbia were found to have procedural systems modeled closely on the Federal Rules, and another 11 states had procedural systems that had been substantially influenced by the Federal Rules. *See* Oakley and Coon, *The Federal Rules in State Courts*, 61 Wash. L. Rev. 1367 (1986).

2. California, New York, and Illinois continue by and large to follow the distinctly different procedural system known as "code pleading." Other states with code-based procedural systems are Connecticut, Nebraska, and Louisiana. The remaining eight states operate substantially independently of both the Federal Rules and the code pleading models of procedure. These states with idiosyncratic procedural systems are Florida, Maryland, Missouri, New Jersey, Oregon, Pennsylvania, Texas, and Virginia.

1

2

CONTROLLING THE CHOICE OF FORUM: JURISDICTION, PROCESS, AND CHOICE OF LAW

▶ **CHAPTER SUMMARY**

CONTROLLING THE CHOICE OF FORUM: JURISDICTION, PROCESS, AND CHOICE OF LAW

INTRODUCTION: In this chapter we discuss the concept and consequences of a valid judgment, and we set forth a six-step approach for determining whether a judgment is valid. We also examine the basic rules of "choice of law" and other doctrines affecting choice of forum, and we discuss the procedural steps by which objections to a plaintiff's choice of forum are asserted and resolved. This chapter's six-step analysis of the validity of judgments deals in depth with service of process, and introduces two other bodies of complex jurisdictional law that are more fully explicated in subsequent chapters. We complete our discussion of the validity of judgments by devoting Chapter 3 to "minimum contacts analysis" of state court territorial jurisdiction, and Chapter 4 to the law of federal subject-matter jurisdiction.

OVERVIEW FROM PLAINTIFFS' PERSPECTIVE

I. **OVERVIEW FROM PLAINTIFFS' PERSPECTIVE**

A. The objective of any competent lawyer who commences litigation on behalf of a client is to secure for her client a judgment that is not only *favorable* but also *enforceable*.

B. An unenforceable judgment is a complete waste of time and money. The client must endure more litigation and more expense — the relitigation of the original claim, or the litigation of a malpractice claim against his lawyer. A plaintiff's lawyer must always *think enforceability first*.

C. In order to be enforceable a judgment must be *valid*. The principal factor in the validity of a judgment is the *jurisdiction* of the trial court to resolve the particular dispute in question against the particular parties named as defendants.

D. Skillful choice of forum involves more than finding a court with the jurisdiction to render a valid judgment. *Choice of forum* should reflect careful consideration of *choice of law*.

   1. Different American jurisdictions will apply different substantive rules of law to the very same controversy. Conduct that one jurisdiction views as no tort at all — say the non-negligent design and manufacture of the gas tank that ruptured when plaintiff's car was hit from behind — another jurisdiction might view as the "strict liability" tort of manufacturing and marketing an unsafe product.

   2. On top of crucial differences in their substantive rules of law may be a host of procedural variations among jurisdictions that can work to plaintiff's favor or disfavor given the particular facts of his case — concerning, say, the scope of discovery or standards of proof.

OVERVIEW FROM DEFENDANTS' PERSPECTIVE

II. **OVERVIEW FROM DEFENDANTS' PERSPECTIVE**

A. Defense counsel is given the opportunity to *challenge plaintiff's choice of forum* and needs to devote careful thought to whether and how to do so.

B. Unlike the plaintiff, the defendant can benefit from an unenforceable judgment if it is too late for the defendant to be sued again. In rare circumstances a plaintiff's choice to sue in the wrong court may thus inspire intelligent defense counsel to "play possum." The defendant has no affirmative duty to disclose that the plaintiff's chosen forum lacks jurisdiction.

C. If the defendant does wish to object to the plaintiff's choice of forum, the objection must generally be asserted at once in order to avoid *waiver* of the objection.

   1. Defense counsel should decide whether to assert an available objection by comparing the law of the chosen forum with the law of the alternative forums in which the case may be tried if plaintiff's choice is successfully challenged.

2. Defense counsel needs also to evaluate the cost and probability of success in challenging plaintiff's choice of forum. If the case was close to settlement before suit was filed, a serious challenge to jurisdiction may well convince the plaintiff to accept a prior settlement offer. Pursuit of a costly but unsuccessful challenge to jurisdiction, however, will merely increase the plaintiff's settlement demand.

III. JURISDICTION AND VALID JUDGMENTS

A. Definition of a Valid Judgment

1. Jurisdiction and validity are essentially two sides of the same coin.

   a. *Validity* pertains to a judgment.

   b. *Jurisdiction* pertains to a court.

   c. A court with jurisdiction over the subject-matter and over properly notified parties has the power to issue a valid judgment.

2. There is a *fundamental distinction* in law between "an act in excess of jurisdiction" and "an error in the exercise of jurisdiction." The point of the distinction is supremely important to your proper understanding of civil procedure.

   a. It is a completely separate issue whether a court *has jurisdiction* and whether a court *has made a mistake* in the conduct of litigation that is within its jurisdiction.

   b. If a court mistakenly attempts to adjudicate a case that is not within its jurisdiction, the resulting judgment is "invalid" and "void." A void judgment cannot be enforced even if it is too late to raise the issue of invalidity on appeal.

   c. Mere error in the conduct of proceedings that are within a court's jurisdiction — error "in the exercise" of jurisdiction — does not deprive the court of jurisdiction.

     (1) Erroneous judgments are nonetheless valid judgments.

     (2) The only way to avoid the enforcement of an erroneous but valid judgment is to have the judgment set aside by post-trial motion or reversed on appeal. *See* Chapters 9 and 10.

3. The jurisdiction of a court is primarily determined by two types of rules.

   a. One type prescribes the *kinds* of cases that the court is entitled to adjudicate. These are rules of *subject-matter jurisdiction.*

   b. A second type determines the location and other characteristics of the *parties and property* whose legal interests are within the control of the court. These rules are usually a function of sovereignty (governmental power), and sovereignty is usually defined geographically (by the borders of a particular state or country). Therefore, these kinds of jurisdictional rules are called rules of *territorial jurisdiction.*

4. Some of the rules governing the validity of a judgment deal with how a court must operate during the process of adjudication. These are rules of *due process.*

   a. The law's use of procedural criteria for the validity of a judgment can lead to confusion. Failure to follow the rules of due process invalidates a judgment because of errors by a trial court in the conduct of litigation that is otherwise within the jurisdiction of the trial court. As noted above, the commission of error in the course of exercising jurisdiction does not ordinarily make the resulting judgment invalid. But the procedural rules that constitute "due process" are of such overriding importance that judgments obtained in violation of these rules are not enforceable.

   b. The federal Constitution's fourteenth amendment and the constitutions of most states guarantee that no person shall be deprived of life, liberty, or property without "due process of law." Procedural rules that are essential to the fundamental fairness of trial proceedings are jurisdictional rules of "due process."

    c.   Although the jurisdictional significance of "due process" is most profound in the domain of the criminal law, it has had two sweeping effects on the validity of civil judgments. Under the Fourteenth Amendment's due process clause:

        (1) *Fair notice* to a defendant that she has been sued is required independently of the requirement that the court have territorial jurisdiction over particular parties or property.

        (2) The *territorial jurisdiction* of any state's courts over a non-resident served with process while outside the state is limited to cases in which the defendant has "minimum contacts" with that state.

B. How to determine whether a judgment is valid.

    1. *The three elements of validity.* If a court has jurisdiction, its judgment will be valid. It is generally recognized, however, that analysis of whether a court has the jurisdiction to render a valid judgment is helpfully broken up into three discrete jurisdictional subtopics: *subject-matter jurisdiction, territorial jurisdiction,* and *notice.*

        a.   *Subject-matter jurisdiction* is sometimes referred to as "competence." It deals primarily with the subject-matter of the dispute rather than the characteristics of the parties and their relationship to the court.

        b.   *Territorial jurisdiction* embraces two forms of geographically oriented jurisdiction.

           (1) *In personam* jurisdiction is party-specific jurisdiction to adjudicate claims against a particular person. The existence of in personam jurisdiction over a particular defendant depends on whether that party has, under the circumstances of a particular controversy, a sufficient territorial connection to the forum (*i.e.*, the trial court and the government, state or federal, in whose name it operates).

               (a) When a valid in personam judgment declares a defendant to be liable for some amount of damages, the judgment creates a personal liability that can be enforced against that party anywhere that party's assets can be found. This makes in personam judgments the most desirable kind for a plaintiff to obtain.

               (b) The fact that valid in personam jurisdiction can be asserted only against defendants with a sufficient territorial connection to the forum limits the power of any given forum to adjudicate the personal liabilities of all defendants a given plaintiff might wish to sue. This constrains the plaintiff's choice of forum.

           (2) *In rem* jurisdiction is property-specific jurisdiction resulting in a judgment that determines who owns particular property within the territorial control of the forum. There are two types of in rem jurisdiction.

               (a) *True* in rem jurisdiction adjudicates the ownership interests of the world at large in the property in question. The purpose of a true in rem action is to transfer ownership from all present owners en masse to some new owner, generally the state as plaintiff in a condemnation or eminent domain action.

               (b) *Quasi-in-rem* jurisdiction adjudicates the ownership interests only of particular named parties. Thus quasi-in-rem jurisdiction only settles the question of who owns the property in question as between the opposing parties to a lawsuit based upon quasi-in-rem jurisdiction. The judgment in such a lawsuit does not affect the interests any other persons, not parties to the lawsuit, might claim in the same property. There are two sub-types of quasi-in-rem jurisdiction.

i) *Type I* involves a lawsuit in which the dispute between the parties arises out of their interests in the property in question.

Example: If A believes that she owns Greenacre, a parcel of land in State X, but B, a resident of some other state, also claims an interest in Greenacre, A can bring a Type I quasi-in-rem action in a State X court of appropriate subject-matter jurisdiction and (assuming proper notice to B) can get a valid judgment determining as between A and B who really owns Greenacre.

ii) *Type II* is sometimes called "attachment jurisdiction." It involves a lawsuit in which the dispute between the parties has nothing to do with the fortuitous presence of property within the territory of the forum state that can be attached by the courts of the forum state for the purpose of holding it "hostage" to a suit against the property owner.

Example: Suppose *A* concedes that out-of-stater *B* owns Greenacre, a parcel of property located in State *X*. *A*'s cause of action against *B* has nothing to do with Greenacre, but the nature of the cause of action and *B*'s relationship to State *X* are such that under the local law of State *X* the courts of State *X* will not assert in personam jurisdiction over *B* on this particular cause of action. If for some tactical reason *A* nonetheless would prefer to sue *B* on this cause of action in a State *X* court, provided *A* can find a way for a State *X* court to assert the territorial jurisdiction necessary for a valid judgment, a Type II quasi-in-rem action against *B* may allow *A* to proceed in *A*'s chosen forum.

c. *Proper notice* is analytically separate from the existence of territorial jurisdiction. The existence jointly of territorial jurisdiction and proper notice gives a court "jurisdiction over the parties." Whether proper notice was given depends on the timing, content, and method of delivery of notice of suit.

Example: In the Type I quasi-in-rem scenario described above, in which State *X* asserts in rem jurisdiction over Greenacre to decide if *A*'s claim of ownership is superior to *B*'s, it is clear that under the local law of every state there is quasi-in-rem jurisdiction over *A*'s "quiet title" action against *B*. The only really serious threat to the validity of *A*'s judgment quieting title against *B* will be the question whether *B* was given proper notice of *A*'s action and hence had a meaningful opportunity to appear in the State *X* court to contest *A*'s claim of superior title. Under current law, notice to *B* that consisted merely of posting notice at the property and at the courthouse where *A*'s suit was filed would not constitute constitutionally proper notice to *B*, and a judgment entered without any appearance by *B* would be invalid for lack of proper notice.

2. *Why analysis of the validity of a judgment requires a six-step process.* American law is greatly complicated by the fact that legal power is shared "vertically" by overlapped federal and state systems of government. This complex system of shared power requires a six-step process for analyzing the three elements of the validity of a judgment. *Each* element of validity — subject-matter jurisdiction, territorial jurisdiction, and proper notice — must pass muster under *two* separate standards: the local law of the particular court system involved and the overriding demands of supreme federal law.

C. Summary of our six-step approach for analyzing the validity of a judgment

Step 1: Does the trial court have subject-matter jurisdiction under the local law of the court system?

Step 2: Does the trial court's exercise of subject-matter jurisdiction conflict with the federal Constitution?

Step 3: Does the local law of the court system give the trial court territorial jurisdiction over the defendant or the defendant's property?

Step 4: **Does the trial court's exercise of territorial jurisdiction over the defendant or the defendant's property conflict with the federal Constitution?**

Step 5: **Was the defendant given proper notice of the action according to the local law of the trial court system?**

Step 6: **Did the notice given the defendant meet the minimum standards of the federal Constitution?**

D. **Explication of our six-step approach**

Step 1. *The local law of trial court subject-matter jurisdiction*

   a. *State courts*

     (1) The local law of state court systems regarding subject-matter jurisdiction is generally rather simple. Most states have a trial court of general jurisdiction authorized to adjudicate all civil disputes except those in which the amount in controversy is below a certain amount and simple relief (such as damages, but not most forms of equitable relief) is sought. These petty disputes are left to a trial court of inferior jurisdiction. California conforms to this model.

     (2) A few states, such as New York, employ topical as well as monetary criteria to divide up the business of their trial courts. In such states, specialized courts are given exclusive jurisdiction over all cases of a given type, such as family law cases or probate matters. The New York model is disfavored because it reduces the flexibility of judicial administration and increases the risk of invalid judgments.

     (3) At one time many states divided their trial courts into separate systems of courts of law and courts of equity (often called "chancery" courts). Almost no states continue to have separate courts of legal and equitable subject-matter jurisdiction. Delaware is one of the rare exceptions to retain a separate chancery court. Most states do restrict the equitable jurisdiction of their inferior courts. The theory is that equitable remedies, particularly injunctions, are especially serious assertions of judicial power. Cases for equitable relief are therefore placed within the subject-matter jurisdiction of the trial court of general jurisdiction, where the trial judges will be the most experienced in the state.

   b. *Federal courts*

     (1) The federal trial courts are entirely different in jurisdictional structure from the trial courts of any state. Most controversies are within the jurisdiction of some court in a state court system. The problem is finding the right court. That's easy in California, a bit harder in New York or Delaware. But the federal government has only such powers as the Constitution gives it, leaving residual power to the states. Thus the federal courts have narrowly defined subject-matter jurisdiction.

     (2) The basic categories of federal subject-matter jurisdiction are cases in which the plaintiff is suing to enforce a right created by federal law, and cases brought by or against a citizen of a state in which the opposing party is a citizen of some other state, or of a foreign country.

     (3) The study of federal subject-matter jurisdiction is so complicated, and so important to the process of controlling the choice of forum in civil litigation, that we have devoted to it the whole of Chapter 4.

Step 2. *Federal constitutional limits on subject-matter jurisdiction*

   a. *State courts*

     (1) The Constitution itself has little to say directly about state court subject-matter jurisdiction, although basic constitutional principles such as the illegality of racial discrimination and the protection of interstate commerce and travel and the

privileges of national citizenship would nullify any state attempt to restrict access to a state court on racial grounds, or to limit the right to sue in a state's courts only to citizens of that state.

(2) Federal *statutes* do constitutionally limit the subject-matter jurisdiction of state courts in other, less obvious ways that occasionally do invalidate state judgments. These statutes sometimes confer *exclusive jurisdiction* on federal courts in some categories of cases within the subject-matter jurisdiction of the federal courts. (*See* Chapter 4.) When Congress has made a particular type of case exclusively triable in federal courts, this limits the subject-matter jurisdiction of state courts.

Example: While a state court foreclosure suit was pending against them in a Wisconsin county court, the defendant farmers filed an action invoking the exclusive subject-matter jurisdiction of a federal bankruptcy court. The subsequent state court judgment confirming the forced sale of the farmers' property under color of the foreclosure judgment was held invalid by the Supreme Court. "If Congress has vested in the bankruptcy courts exclusive jurisdiction over farmer-debtors and their property, and has by its Act withdrawn from all other courts all power under any circumstances to maintain and enforce foreclosure proceedings against them, its Act is the supreme law of the land which all courts — State and Federal — must observe." *Kalb v. Feuerstein*, 308 U.S. 433 (1940).

b. *Federal courts*

(1) The federal courts cannot be given jurisdiction beyond the limits allowed by the Constitution, as discussed in detail in Chapter 4. One of the most famous cases in American legal history is *Marbury v. Madison*, 5 U.S. (1 Cranch) 137 (1803), in which the Supreme Court first ruled that it had the power and the duty to declare unconstitutional an act of Congress. The provision held unconstitutional in *Marbury* was a part of the Judiciary Act of 1789, which authorized the Supreme Court to issue writs of mandamus.

(2) Ever since, Congress has legislated in the shadow of *Marbury*. Generally, Congress has avoided passing unconstitutional statutes dealing with federal jurisdiction. In 1982, however, the Supreme Court invalidated a judgment that as a matter of the federal bankruptcy court's "local law" had been duly authorized in 1978 by an Act of Congress. Congress had violated the Constitution, the Supreme Court held, by assigning to a Bankruptcy Court a case that under the Constitution could be assigned only to a United States District Court. *Northern Pipeline Construction Co. v. Marathon Pipe Line Co.*, 458 U.S. 50 (1982).

Step 3. *The local law of trial court territorial jurisdiction*

a. *State courts*

(1) All states provide for in personam jurisdiction to be exercised by their courts against persons served personally with process within the territory of the state, and for in rem jurisdiction to be exercised against property subject to attachment within the territory of the state.

(a) The tricky question concerning the in personam jurisdiction of a state court under the local law of that state is the scope of local law's desire to assert in personam jurisdiction against defendants who *cannot* be personally served within the territory of the state. All states authorize service of process beyond the borders of the state in some circumstances.

(b) The provision (or set of provisions) in each state's local law authorizing service of process out-of-state is called that state's "*long-arm statute*." As the image implies, "long-arm" jurisdiction is an assertion of power by a state, grounded in some act of the defendant that occurred or caused an effect within the state, that reaches beyond the borders of the state to serve process on an absent defendant.

(2) There is considerable variation in the language and effective scope of state court "long-arm statutes."

    (a) Some states, such as California, have adopted a "to the limits of the Constitution" long-arm statute that expressly declares the state's intention to assert in personam jurisdiction against one and all defendants to the limits that federal constitutional law permits. *See* Cal. Code of Civ. Proc. § 410.10.

    (b) Other states have long-arm statutes that are less broadly worded but have been construed by the states' highest courts to extend to the limits of the federal Constitution with respect to the particular categories of cases named in the statutes. For instance, Oklahoma's long-arm statute provides for in personam jurisdiction to be asserted against an out-of-stater whose actions outside of Oklahoma have caused injury inside of Oklahoma "if he regularly does or solicits business or engages in any other persistent course of conduct, or derives substantial revenue from goods used or consumed or services rendered, in this state." This statute has been construed to extend Oklahoma's jurisdiction over non-residents to the full extent permitted by the federal Constitution. *See World-Wide Volkswagen Corp. v. Woodson*, 444 U.S. 286 (1980).

    (c) Still other states have "shorter" long-arm statutes that clearly *do not* assert the in personam jurisdiction of these states against out-of-state defendants to the full extent permitted by the federal Constitution.

    (d) In states with "California-style" unrestricted long-arm statutes or their judicially-construed equivalents, analysis of the scope of in personam jurisdiction permitted by local law collapses into "minimum contacts analysis" as discussed in Chapter 3, *i.e.*, analysis of the maximum scope of in personam jurisdiction permitted to that state by federal constitutional law, predicated upon identifying the bare minimum of contacts a defendant may have with a state in order to be subject to its in personam jurisdiction.

    (e) In a state with a restricted long-arm statute it is possible that "minimum contacts" exist sufficient to subject a particular defendant to that state's in personam jurisdiction free of any federal constitutional objection, but nonetheless that defendant cannot be sued in personam in the courts of that state because of the restricted scope of its long-arm statute as a matter of local law.

  b. *Federal courts*

    (1) Federal courts freely exercise territorial jurisdiction over any party who has been served with process in a manner permitted by Federal Rule 4 while that party was present *within* the federal court's "home state," *i.e.*, the state in which the federal district court is located.

    (2) Federal Rule 4 allows federal courts to exercise *in rem* jurisdiction only insofar as that is authorized by the local law of their home states.

    (3) With the exceptions noted below, Federal Rule 4 allows federal courts to exercise *in personam* territorial jurisdiction over a party served with process *outside* the federal court's home state only to the extent that such territorial jurisdiction is authorized by the local law of the federal court's home state.

    (a) Under Rule 4(e), a special federal statute governing service of process in particular cases may override the general rule that federal courts may exercise territorial jurisdiction only to the extent provided by local state law. Such special statutes are called *nationwide service of process* statutes. They have been enacted to facilitate enforcement of various federal regulatory schemes, including many provisions of the antitrust and securities laws.

    (b) Nationwide service of process is also authorized under the Federal Interpleader Act, 28 U.S.C. §§ 1335, 2361, discussed below in Chapters 4 and 6.

    (c) Under the extremely limited circumstances discussed *infra* in Step 5 and in Chapter 6, Rule 4(f) also allows federal courts to assert personal jurisdiction beyond the scope of state law in order to permit the joinder of additional parties to an existing action.

Step 4. *Federal constitutional limits on territorial jurisdiction*

  a. *State courts*

    (1) The federal constitutional principles governing state court assertions of "long-arm" jurisdiction are collectively referred to as the law of "*minimum contacts.*"

    (2) Minimum contacts analysis is subtle and complex. We have reserved our discussion of this topic for Chapter 3.

  b. *Federal courts*

    (1) Since the federal courts can generally exercise only such territorial jurisdiction over out-of-staters as is permitted under the local law of their home states, the federal constitutional limitations on state court territorial jurisdiction embodied in the concept of "minimum contacts" (discussed in Chapter 3) also limit indirectly the exercise of territorial jurisdiction by federal courts.

      (a) If a federal court has asserted jurisdiction over a defendant by service of process out of state under the long-arm statute of the federal court's home state, pursuant to Rule 4(e)(1), and the defendant can show a lack of minimum contacts with that home state, the defendant will succeed in having the federal judgment held invalid.

      (b) It makes no difference whether or not Congress could constitutionally have subjected that defendant to the territorial jurisdiction of the district court in question, if Congress has not done so. In such a situation, all limits on the scope of territorial jurisdiction under the law of the home state — as a matter of the local law of the home state and as a matter of the federal constitutional limits on the long-arm jurisdiction of the home state — apply equally to the assertions of territorial jurisdiction by the federal district court.

    (2) Where a federal court has asserted territorial jurisdiction under the authority of a federal nationwide service of process statute, the governing constitutional concept is still "minimum contacts" (as elaborated in Chapter 3). But when Congress has authorized nationwide service of process, the governmental entity with whose territory the defendant must have "minimum contacts" is *the entire United States*, not just the territory of the federal district court's home state.

Step 5. *The local law of proper notice*

  a. *The mechanics of "service of process"*

    (1) Our criterion of "proper notice" forces you to consider whether there has been full compliance with the *mechanics* of service of process as prescribed by local law. The form and contents of the court papers served on the defendant must have been correct, and the way in which the defendant was presented with these papers must also have been correct. The papers are referred to as the *process* of the court, and the manner of their presentation is referred to as *service* of process on the defendant.

    (2) Form of process

2

(a) The papers served on a defendant at the commencement of a civil action ordinarily consist of a copy of a *summons* naming specifically the particular defendant being served and a copy of the *complaint* stating a claim against the defendant. By literally "summoning" the defendant to appear in court to answer the complaint (under modern practice the appearance consisting merely of filing a written answer with the court and serving a copy on the plaintiff's lawyer), the summons also informs the defendant of what must be done in order to avoid the entry of a default judgment.

(b) The defendant receives a copy of the summons, the original of which is ordinarily endorsed by the process server, reciting the date and other particulars of service, and filed with the court as the "return of service." The return establishes presumptively that a particular defendant has received proper notice under local law.

(3) Service of process

(a) *Personal service of process.* This is the classic form of service of process, by delivery in-hand to the named defendant. Personal service of process was required by the common law.

   i) Generally, process may be served by any adult civilian not a party to the action. Professional process-servers are available for hire by plaintiffs and are commonly used. In extraordinary cases, process may be served by peace officers employed directly by the courts (generally called marshals or bailiffs) or by ordinary police officers.

   ii) Where the defendant is an entity (such as a corporation, an association, or a governmental agency), local law will specify the officer or agent responsible for accepting personal service of process in the name of the agency.

(b) *Substituted service of process.* Local law will generally prescribe a variety of means for serving process without the difficulties and expense of personal service of process on an elusive or distant defendant.

   i) The classic form of substituted service, authorized by many jurisdictions, is service at the residence of the defendant on someone of suitable age and discretion who lives with the defendant.

   ii) Service by mail is also a common form of substituted service. Sometimes it is referred to as *"postal service"* and differentiated from substituted service because the departure from classic personal service is the method of service (by mail instead of delivery in hand) rather than the person receiving service.

   iii) Postal or otherwise substituted service of process within the forum state is often effective only if the defendant returns by mail a form acknowledging receipt of process. The defendant becomes liable for the cost of arranging for personal service of process if the defendant unreasonably fails to complete the substituted service by mailing back the acknowledgment of service.

   iv) Postal service on an out-of-state defendant is generally effective without any cooperation or acknowledgment by the served defendant.

(c) *Constructive service of process.* Constructive service of process is generally used when the location (and sometimes the identity) of a defendant is unknown, and actual delivery of process by personal or substituted service is impossible.

i) Constructive service is thus a last resort, a symbolic gesture at achieving service of process. There is no pretense under modern law that constructive service is likely actually to inform a defendant of the pendency of the suit.

ii) When constructive service is authorized but there is nonetheless available to the plaintiff a last known address of a defendant, local law generally requires (and federal constitutional law independently demands) that postal service be attempted in addition to constructive service.

iii) The most common means of constructive service are *publication* of the summons in a newspaper, or *posting* the summons at a designated location, such as the relevant courthouse or the land involved in an in rem action. When constructive service is constitutionally required, the United States Supreme Court demands publication.

b. *State courts*

(1) Technicalities of form and service of process

(a) State law rules for the form and service of process vary greatly, and the wise practitioner assumes in the absence of convincing evidence to the contrary that any technicalities in the rules governing service of process will be strictly enforced. Nit-picking technical defects in the content of process or the manner of its service may be grounds for successful objection to the trial court's territorial jurisdiction, adding avoidable delay and expense to the costs of prosecuting a claim.

(b) Although defects of process and service of process are generally deemed waived if not raised by timely objection to the trial court, they may be grounds for collateral attack on a default judgment — *see, e.g., Rogers v. Silverman,* 216 Cal. App. 3d 1114, 265 Cal. Rptr. 286 (1989) — hence our insistence that "proper notice" under local law be considered an element of a valid judgment.

i) Although the modern trend of authority is towards a rule of reason in determining the adequacy of the form and service of process, there is a tradition of rigid technicality regarding service of process that continues to color the decisions of American courts.

ii) In states where strict compliance with technical details of the rules governing the form and service of process is a condition to acquiring territorial jurisdiction over a defendant, it will generally be *irrelevant* that *actual notice* was received by an out-of-state defendant. *See, e.g., Feinstein v. Bergner,* 48 N.Y.2d 234, 422 N.Y.S.2d 356, 397 N.E.2d 1161 (1979); *Bond v. Golden,* 273 F.2d 265 (10th Cir. 1959) (Kansas law).

(2) Time limits on redressing defective service of process

(a) Involuntary dismissal

i) Some states require dismissal for lack of prosecution if process is not served within a stipulated period of time and will invalidate default judgments entered on the basis of untimely service.

a) In California, that period is three years from the commencement of the action, and is jurisdictional in the sense that a judgment entered by default or otherwise in which there was untimely service of process may be set aside. Cal. Civ. Proc. Code §§ 583.210-583.250.

b) Moreover, where there was a timely attempt at service but the defendant is confident that the manner of service was improper (*e.g.,* by substituted service at defendant's supposed residence where he

2

does not in fact reside), the defendant can allow a default judgment to enter, wait until after the three-year period makes it impossible to moot the original defective service of process by re-serving defendant in the proper manner and, simultaneously with his motion to vacate the invalid default judgment, move to dismiss the action because timely service is now impossible. *Rogers v. Silverman*, 216 Cal. App. 3d 1114, 265 Cal. Rptr. 286 (1989).

ii) Because the statute of limitations will probably bar the effective refiling of the complaint, vacation of judgment and dismissal of a complaint for failure to effect the proper and timely service of process will generally render the cause of action worthless.

(b) *Statutes of limitation*

i) Many states require effective service of process within the period prescribed by the applicable statute of limitations. Obviously, failure to serve process within the stipulated period bars litigation of the cause of action. *See, e.g., Walker v. Armco Steel Corp.*, 446 U.S. 740 (1980) (Oklahoma law).

ii) Since timely but improper service is deemed by most states to count as no service at all, even for statutes of limitations purposes, a successful challenge to the content of process or the manner of service of process can effectively bar litigation of a cause of action if proper service of process can no longer be accomplished within the time allowed by the statute of limitations. *See Ellis v. Great Southwestern Corp.*, 646 F.2d 1099 (5th Cir. 1981) [reversing a district court dismissal where initial service was ineffective and later service of process was untimely under the Arkansas statute of limitations, but only because the district court erred in choosing to apply Arkansas law rather than Texas law].

c. *Federal courts*

(1) Form of process

(a) Federal Rule 4(a) requires that the clerk issue a summons upon the filing of the complaint. Rule 4(b) prescribes the simplest conceivable form for the summons, as illustrated by the model summons set forth as Form 1 of the Appendix of Forms accompanying the Federal Rules.

(b) "Insufficiency of process," *e.g.*, a defect in the form of process under the Federal Rules, is a defense that is waived if not properly asserted at the earliest appearance of defendant in opposition to the action. *See* Rule 12(b)(4) and Rule 12(h)(1).

(c) Defects in the form of process do not invalidate a default judgment by a federal court unless the notice afforded to the defendant fell short of the minimum required by federal constitutional law.

(2) Service of process

(a) By whom

i) Federal Rule 4(c)(2)(A) provides that any person not a party to an action, and at least 18 years of age, may serve process on a defendant. When service of process requires physical delivery of process to some person, service is ordinarily accomplished by a professional process server. When substituted service by mail ("postal service") is used pursuant to Rule (4)(c)(2)(C)(ii), there is no restriction on who may make the service — even the plaintiff can mail the papers to the defendant. Ordinarily the plaintiff's attorney or someone employed by that attorney physically mails the documents and executes the affidavit of service of process by mail.

    ii) Rule 4(c)(2)(B) provides for service by a United States marshal or by a specially appointed process server when the plaintiff is a pauper or a merchant seaman, when the United States is the plaintiff, or when the court orders service by the marshal or a special appointee upon a showing that this is necessary to accomplish proper service of process.

(b) Methods of service

    i) *Federal incorporation of state law.* The most universal "method" of service authorized by the Federal Rules is to effect service in the manner authorized by state law for the courts of general jurisdiction of the state in which the federal district court is located. The incorporation of state law makes available to the federal plaintiff the whole range of methods of service available under state law — personal service, substituted service, and constructive service — on whatever terms and conditions are prescribed by state law. The following classes of defendants may be served with federal process in accordance with state law:

        a) Competent adult individuals pursuant to Rule 4(c)(2)(C)(i).

        b) Infants and incompetent adults pursuant to Rule 4(d)(2).

        c) Entities, including corporations and unincorporated associations such as partnerships, whose members are subject to suit under a common name, pursuant to Rule 4(c)(2)(C)(i).

        d) State governments and governmental agencies pursuant to Rule 4(d)(6).

        e) Non-residents pursuant to Rule 4(e).

    ii) *Additional methods of serving federal process within the forum state.* In addition to the right to serve process in the manner permitted by state law, federal plaintiffs can elect to serve process under independent federal procedures that are cumulative to the methods of service of process available under state law. These methods of service are valid and support valid judgments, even if they conflict with state law. *See Hanna v. Plumer,* 380 U.S. 460 (1965).

        a) *Competent adult individuals* are subject to personal service of process under Rule 4(d)(1). Although delivery "in hand" is desirable, it is not required if the defendant is being evasive. Touching the defendant and attempting to hand her the papers will suffice, as will leaving them in the immediate visible proximity of the defendant. Postal service is authorized by Rule 4(c)(2)(C)(ii). Substituted service of process on a cohabitant is authorized by Rule 4(d)(1). The process must be left at the defendant's "dwelling place or usual place of abode with some person of suitable age and discretion then residing therein." Substituted service of process on an agent is also authorized by Rule 4(d)(1). This method of substituted service involves personal service of process on an agent authorized either by appointment (voluntary act of the defendant) or by law (when the defendant commits certain acts, such as doing business in the forum state, without first appointing an agent for service of process).

2

b) *Corporations, partnerships and similar entities* are subject to personal service of process under Rule 4(d)(3). The person "personally" served as representative of the entity must be someone who routinely "stands in the shoes" of the entity or is in charge of its activities in the forum state — "an officer, a managing or a general agent." When personal service is made under Rule 4(d)(3) it does not matter that the officer or manager actually served is not the person whom state law deems to be the entity's agent for service of process. Rule 4(d)(3) also authorizes substituted service of process on any person, regardless of managerial status, who is authorized by law or appointment to receive process on behalf of the entity.

c) *Federal governmental defendants* are subject to service under Rule 4(d)(4)-(5) by serving the United States Attorney (or the U.S. Attorney's formal designate) for the district in which suit has been filed and sending a copy by registered or certified mail to the Attorney General (when the United States has been sued) or to the defendant officer or agency.

d) *State governmental defendants* are subject to service under Rule 4(d)(6) by serving the chief executive officer of the entity.

iii) *Additional methods of serving federal process outside the forum state*

a) *Within 100 miles of the place of trial.* Under Rule 4(f), parties impleaded under Rule 14 or required to be joined under Rule 19 may be served with process according to the service-within-the-forum-state procedures of Rule 4(d)(1)-(6), even if service occurs outside the forum state, provided service occurs within 100 miles of the place of trial. This curious "100-mile bulge" provision has special significance in litigation along the Atlantic coast, where the states are far more crowded together than in the west. For instance, Rule 4(f)'s 100-mile bulge permits service in much of New Jersey and Connecticut on parties joined under Rule 14 or Rule 19 to litigation filed in New York City's federal courts, the Southern and Eastern Districts of New York.

b) *Nationwide.* A number of important federal statutes, such as the Securities Exchange Act of 1934 and the Federal Interpleader Act, provide for "nationwide service of process" in actions brought under those acts. In such an action non-residents of the forum state may be served with the process of the federal court even if they are beyond the reach of the forum state's local long-arm statute.

c) *In foreign countries.* If a non-resident lives in a foreign country rather than simply some other state, Rule 4(i) authorizes numerous methods for effective service, including personal service on individuals and entities, postal service (provided a signed receipt is executed), any method of service specially ordered by the court, or any method of service prescribed by the law of the country of service. *Take note*, however, that if the foreign country is a signatory of the *Hague Service Convention*, discussed at the end of this step, the Convention prescribes the exclusive means for effective service in that country.

(c) Technicalities of form and service of process

i) Federal policy emphasizes substantial rather than formal justice. Rule 1 decrees that the Federal Rules are to be "construed to secure the just, speedy, and inexpensive determination of every action." Technical nit-picking will not render ineffective a service of process substantially in compliance with the Federal Rules.

ii) Defects in the form of service of process that cause actual prejudice to the objecting party may be raised by appropriate motion to dismiss, and under extreme circumstances disclosing flagrant disregard for the Federal Rules, such a motion may be granted. Where actual notice has occurred, dismissal is unlikely. Rule 4(h) allows liberal amendment of both the form of process and the proof of service.

iii) Where the "defect" in service of process is so palpable as to suggest disregard of the Federal Rules, a resulting judgment will be invalid despite the fact that the improper service conveyed actual notice.

Example: The United States sued a business corporation and also sued personally its three owners — a father and two sons. The father and one son were served personally with process at the time of service on the corporation. Service was attempted on the other son by leaving a copy of the summons and complaint with his father and brother at the family's place of business. Substituted service at a defendant's place of business rather than place of residence is unauthorized by Rule 4(d)(1). Therefore, the son who was not present at the place of business when his father and brother were served did not himself receive proper service of process. When the ensuing default judgment was about to be enforced against the unserved son's personal assets, the district court permitted that defendant to collaterally attack the default judgment by a Rule 60(b)(4) motion. The district court declared the default judgment void. *United States v. Wahl*, 406 F. Supp. 1396 (D. Mich. 1976), *rev'd on other grounds*, 583 F.2d 285 (6th Cir. 1978).

(d) Time limits on redressing defective service of process

i) Federal Rule 4(a) imposes on the plaintiff the duty of "prompt service" of process on the defendant. Rule 4(j), added by Act of Congress in 1983, mandates dismissal of the action (without prejudice) if without good cause service of process has not been accomplished within 120 days of the filing of the complaint. This makes it possible that delay in achieving effective service of process will result in an originally timely action being barred by the statute of limitations upon refiling.

a) Rule 4(j)'s good cause exception permits escape from dismissal where a timely attempt at service of process was rendered ineffective by some technical defect. The standard for establishing good cause is likely to be rigorous, however. Rule 4(j) was adopted at the same time as Rule 4(a), which shifted responsibility for assuring service of process from the United States marshal to the party asserting the claim. Together these rules reflect a clear congressional policy favoring prompt service of process and argue against lenient exceptions from Rule 4(j) mandatory dismissals. There is some authority, however, that an attempted but defective service of process may toll the statute of limitations applicable to the refiled complaint. *United States v. Wahl*, 583 F.2d 285 (6th Cir. 1978).

b) Where the defect in service of process is raised by appearance and meritorious Rule 12(b)(5) objection (discussed later in this chapter), the normal procedure is for the district court to quash service of process rather than to dismiss the action. This avoids limitations problems except in those jurisdictions where service of process is a prerequisite to commencement of an action for limitations purposes. *See Walker v. Armco Steel Corp.*, 446 U.S. 740 (1980) (Oklahoma law).

(e) The Hague Service Convention

   i) The normal provisions for "long-arm" service of process under local law are suspended when service on an out-of-state defending party requires the serving party to "transmit a judicial or extrajudicial document for service abroad." The Hague Service Convention is a multilateral treaty ratified by 32 countries, including the United States. As a treaty it is the law of the United States, with a force equivalent to an Act of Congress. Its terms control over any inconsistent state law or Federal Rule.

   ii) The Convention requires that service within a signatory country take place by serving documents on a central authority set up by each signatory country for the purpose of accepting the process of a foreign court and forwarding it to its residents. The terms of the Convention are mandatory and exclusive. Any non-conforming service of process that is within the scope the Convention will be held ineffective. *See Volkswagenwerk Aktiengesellschaft v. Schlunk*, 486 U.S. 694 (1988).

Step 6. *Federal constitutional standards for proper notice*

   a. *Unified standard for state and federal courts*

   (1) The federal Constitution contains *two* "due process" clauses. The fifth amendment applies to the federal government and its court system. The fourteenth amendment applies to the states and their courts. With respect to the notice that must be given to a civil defendant before a court can issue a valid judgment enforceable against that defendant's person or property, the two due process clauses impose on state and federal courts an *identical constitutional standard*.

   (2) At one time there was considerable confusion about the kind of notice required by due process.

      (a) The first case to hold that Fourteenth Amendment due process principles limited the powers of state courts to render valid in personam judgments was *Pennoyer v. Neff*, 95 U.S. 714 (1878) (discussed at greater length in Chapter 3).

         i) *Pennoyer* appeared to endorse differential notice standards for assertions of in personam as opposed to in rem jurisdiction, insisting that in rem jurisdiction be initiated by the attachment of the relevant property *prior* to any other judicial proceedings, and reasoning that this requirement of prior attachment would serve to give notice to the defendant whose property was attached of the need to defend the property against the claim of the plaintiff. In an in personam action, the *Pennoyer* Court demanded personal service of process within the territory of the forum state prior to any other judicial proceedings, with allowance for substituted or constructive service of process in exceptional situations.

         ii) *Pennoyer*'s strict standards for personal service of process generally assured that in most suits either (a) there would be no personal jurisdiction against a particular defendant, or (b) the fact of personal service of process on that defendant would serve simultaneously both (i) to confer on the court the power to assert personal jurisdiction over the defendant and (ii) to provide to the defendant actual notice of the suit in which the court now had jurisdiction to proceed.

      (b) Gradually, *Pennoyer's* standards for personal jurisdiction were watered down by courts coping with twentieth century conditions of an integrated national economy, instantaneous channels of communication, and convenient interstate travel.

i) Eventually, *Pennoyer's* constitutional test for the scope of state court personal jurisdiction was replaced by that of the second seminal personal jurisdiction case (discussed in Chapter 3), *International Shoe Co. v. Washington*, 326 U.S. 310 (1945), which articulated standards for personal jurisdiction in terms of "minimum contacts" with the forum state rather than actual presence in the forum state at the time of service of process.

ii) This de-emphasis of service of process as the criterion for personal jurisdiction created doubt whether there was any constitutional need for a particular form of process when personal jurisdiction could be shown to exist without personal service of process on a defendant within the territory of the forum state.

iii) In the meantime, nagging questions were accumulating about the notice defendants were receiving prior to default judgments predicated on in rem jurisdiction. It became increasingly artificial to view the seizure of property, especially intangible property such as bank accounts and other forms of debts attached by garnishment of the debtor or real property attached by posting notices at the courthouse and somewhere on the property, as inherently likely to provide notice to the defendant in time to avoid loss of the property by default judgment.

(3) These problems were resolved by the Supreme Court's decision in *Mullane v. Central Hanover Bank & Trust Co.*, 339 U.S. 306 (1950).

(a) In a statutory proceeding to settle trust accounts on a periodic basis in which the statute required only notice by publication, the Court said that it was immaterial whether the proceeding was conceived of as an exercise of in rem as opposed to in personam jurisdiction. A state had undoubted power to settle periodically the host of conflicting present and contingent claims to the interest and principal of trusts administered by financial institutions within the territory of that state, regardless where the various persons with interests in the trust accounts might by residing. The issue was not one of due process constraints on the scope of state court jurisdiction to affect the interests of out-of-state beneficiaries of the trusts, but rather one of how that undoubted power was fairly to be exercised. Thus, *Mullane* definitively segregated the issue of proper notice to defendants from the issue of a state's power over the property of those defendants.

(b) *Mullane*'s test for notice sufficient to satisfy the Constitution's due process standards for valid judgments is "notice reasonably calculated, under all the circumstances, to apprise interested parties of the pendency of the action and afford them an opportunity to present objections .... The means employed must be such as one desirous of actually informing the absentee might reasonably adopt to accomplish it."

i) *Defendant's name and address are known.* Here *Mullane* demands a serious effort at actual notice, not necessarily by personal service of process when that is not jurisdictionally demanded, but at least by ordinary mail to the last known address of the defendant.

ii) *Defendant's name is known but not her address or present location.* Here, *Mullane* adopts a rule of reason that weighs the interests of the defendant at stake in the litigation against the cost and likely success of discovering the defendant's whereabouts and the likelihood that the defendant's interests may adequately be represented by other parties with similar interests who have received actual notice.

    iii) *There are defendants of unknown number, identity, and location who may be affected by a judgment.* Here *Mullane* permits notice by publication, not because such notice is likely actually to inform the absent defendants, but because it is the best notice reasonably practicable under the circumstances.

  b. *Recent case law on due process standards for proper notice.* In two recent cases the Supreme Court invalidated default judgments because *Mullane*'s constitutional standard for proper notice had not been satisfied by service of process that fully complied with the notice standards of local law.

    (1) In *Greene v. Lindsey*, 456 U.S. 444 (1982), a class of public housing tenants in Kentucky collaterally attacked default judgments obtained against class members by public housing officials who gave notice of eviction proceedings in strict compliance with a Kentucky statute (similar to the laws of at least 10 other states) permitting service in an eviction action by merely posting process on the door of the premises at issue, if the sheriff serving the process found neither the defendant nor any relative over 16 years of age at home when the sheriff went to the premises to serve process. There was no requirement of a second attempt at personal service at a different time of day, or of backup service by mail as required by the "nail and mail" statutes of some other states applicable to similar actions. The Supreme Court held that the judgments were invalid for lack of constitutionally sufficient notice under *Mullane*.

    (2) In *Mennonite Board of Missions v. Adams*, 462 U.S. 791 (1983), the underlying proceeding was an Indiana county's "tax sale" of real property to satisfy unpaid taxes on that property. The issue was whether due process required a reasonable effort by the county to provide actual notice of the tax sale to a publicly recorded mortgagee of the property. Under local law the only notice provided was by certified mail to the last known address of the delinquent taxpayer, by posting notice at the county courthouse, and by publishing notice in the local newspaper. The Supreme Court invalidated the resulting tax deed, holding that when a mortgagee is identified in a mortgage that is publicly recorded, constructive notice by publication must be supplemented by notice mailed to the mortgagee's last known available address, or by personal service. Unless the mortgagee is not reasonably identifiable, constructive notice alone does not satisfy *Mullane*. In a useful illustration of the balancing of investigatory cost against the interests at stake, the Court declared that a recorded address of only "Wayne County, Ohio," was enough to warrant an attempt at actual notice to the mortgagee by mail to that address. The Court did not indicate, however, what (if any) further effort at notice would have been required if notice so addressed had been returned undelivered.

E. The Effect of a Valid Judgment

  1. Within the same jurisdiction

    a. *General principles.* A *valid* judgment is regarded as having conclusively established the existence or non-existence of the right to relief claimed by the plaintiff, subject only to whatever right of appeal may exist. Once the process of appeal has run its course or the time for an appeal has expired, a judgment is *final*. (*See* Chapter 10.) The validity of a final judgment ensures that it will be *enforceable* within the jurisdiction that has rendered it.

    (1) Enforceability does not assure actual enforcement — you can't get blood from a turnip, and you can't get money damages from a "judgment-proof" defendant,

i.e., someone who has no assets. (See Chapter 11 for more on the "execution" of a judgment.)

b. In personam judgments may be enforced against any assets of the defendant, wherever found, and whether or not they have any relationship to the facts giving rise to the judgment.

c. In rem judgments may be enforced only against the property that was attached as the basis for the court's jurisdiction. The effect of an in rem judgment is supposed to be exhausted by the transfer of title to the attached property or by the entry of a judicial decree establishing conclusively the relative rights of the parties to title to the attached property. This is certainly true where the judgment was by default. Where the defendant has appeared to defend against the plaintiff's claim, however, the trend of modern authority is to give preclusive effect to the determination of issues by the contested in rem judgment.

(1) In quasi-in-rem cases the title to the property is generally transferred to the sheriff or some other officer of the court, who sells the property under color of the judgment and distributes the proceeds according to the judgment.

(2) In the unusual case where the property sells for more than the amount of the judgment, the excess is given to or held for the benefit of the defendant.

(3) Where the property sells for less than the amount of the judgment, the plaintiff must sue again for the remainder. In jurisdictions in which no preclusive effect is given to an in rem judgment, all issues may be freely relitigated in the successor lawsuit.

d. *Enforcement* of in personam and in rem judgments *compared*

Examples: In a quasi-in-rem action in a State X court predicated on attachment of Greenacre, D's ranch located in State X, a default judgment is entered holding D liable to P for $400,000 for breach of a fiduciary duty D owed to P arising out of their business venture in State Y.

(1) Pursuant to the State X judgment, Greenacre is sold at a sheriff's sale to T, the high bidder, for $350,000. If P wishes to obtain damages from D in excess of $350,000, P must sue D again in a jurisdiction in which D is subject to in personam jurisdiction, or in which D has further property subject to attachment for purposes of quasi-in-rem jurisdiction.

(2) This makes it clear why P would prefer to gain in personam jurisdiction over D, if P can do so in a jurisdiction whose law is favorable to P. An in personam judgment can be enforced against any property of D. An in rem judgment can be enforced only by disposition of the property that was attached as the basis for jurisdiction. Almost certainly State Y would have the power to assert in personam jurisdiction over D. P must be suing elsewhere because State Y's law is unfavorable to P.

(3) Suppose P discovers that D also owns Redacre, another ranch in State Y. P has Redacre attached and again asserts the breach-of-fiduciary-duty cause of action against D. If State Y's prior judgment was "in rem" (or quasi-in-rem) rather than "in personam," P must litigate the entire cause of action again. If D is found liable but this time P's damages are determined to be $500,000, the $350,000 already recovered will be credited to D, and Redacre will be auctioned off by the sheriff in an attempt to raise the remaining $150,000. D cannot reduce the damages to $400,000 by relying on the valuation of P's damages at that amount in the prior lawsuit, because an in rem judgment cannot have effect beyond the property upon which it was based (except for possible issue preclusion, discussed below). Similarly, if this time the jury decides that P's damages are only $300,000, the previous damages are a full credit for that amount, and having received full satisfaction P can litigate the claim no further.

2

e. *Preclusion* doctrines. As more fully discussed in Chapter 12, the law of res judicata establishes that a valid judgment may be given preclusive effect in other litigation involving the same claim or similar issues. Validity is a condition of preclusive effect.

(1) Traditionally, quasi-in-rem judgments were accorded no preclusive effect, on the theory that the authority of the court extended exclusively to disposition of the property at issue. Modern preclusion doctrine as set forth in § 32 of the *Restatement (Second) of Judgments* urges courts to give issue-preclusive effect to quasi-in-rem judgments in which the defendant has entered a "limited appearance" to contest the claim of the plaintiff.

(2) A "limited appearance" is one in which local law allows the defendant to appear in the action to defend her interest in the attached property by contesting the merits of the plaintiff's claim. Ordinarily any appearance by a defendant that is not a "special appearance"—questioning only the existence of jurisdiction—is deemed to be a general appearance that waives any objection of the defendant to the personal jurisdiction of the trial court. (*See* the discussion of special appearances below in the section on direct attacks on the choice of forum.) A "limited appearance" in a quasi-in-rem action is an appearance to contest the merits in which the liability of the defendant is limited to loss of the attached property.

(3) Issue preclusion requires that there actually have been contested litigation. Thus the trend toward giving preclusive effect to contested quasi-in-rem adjudications following entry of a limited appearance has no application to default judgments in quasi-in-rem actions. These remain judgments whose only effect is to dispose of the property that was attached as the basis for jurisdiction.

(4) In jurisdictions that do not allow limited appearances, the defendant's appearance to contest the merits of the claim of the plaintiff converts the exercise of quasi-in-rem jurisdiction into in personam jurisdiction, and the resulting judgment establishes a personal liability of the defendant in whatever amount the court determines. The value of the property initially attached is irrelevant to the enforceability of the full amount of the ensuing judgment in personam.

2. In other jurisdictions

a. *General principles.* Within the United States, the full faith and credit clause of the Constitution (Art. IV, § 1), the full faith and credit statute (28 U.S.C. § 1738), the supremacy clause of the Constitution (Art. VI), and related principles of comity and preclusion, make valid in personam judgments enforceable throughout the length and breadth of the land. The out-of-state enforcement of in rem and quasi-in-rem judgments is limited to the determination of ownership of the property in question, and to such collateral issue preclusion as may be permitted by the law of the state rendering the judgment.

b. *Sister states.* The full faith and credit clause requires that each state give "full faith and credit" to the valid judgments of other states. The accompanying statute adds that a sister state judgment is to be given the "*same* full faith and credit" by the courts of the enforcement state as it would be given by the courts of the judgment state. Thus, the effect of a judgment is to be determined by the law of the judgment state. This means that the scope of a judgment — in rem or in personam — and its preclusive effect must be determined by the law of the judgment state even if, under the same circumstances, a more comprehensive judgment would have been rendered had the cause of action been litigated in the courts of the enforcement state.

c. *Federal courts.* The full faith and credit statute requires the federal courts to give the same effect to a state judgment as would the courts of the judgment state. Obviously federal courts fully and freely enforce the valid judgments of other federal courts, since they are all part of the same court system subject to the common supervision of the

United States Supreme Court. This process of system-wide enforcement is facilitated by an Act of Congress (28 U.S.C. § 1963) providing for the registration in any federal district of the final judgment of any other district, and requiring that the district of registration enforce such a judgment as if it had been rendered by that district.

d. *Federal judgments in state courts.* Curiously, the full faith and credit statute does not mandate that state courts give the same effect to judgments of federal district courts as they must to the judgments of sister states. This gap has been remedied, however, by the development of unchallenged doctrine that under the supremacy clause of the Constitution, state courts are bound to give full effect to the judgments of the courts of the superior federal sovereign. For all practical purposes, then, full faith and credit principles apply equally to federal court judgments when state courts are asked to enforce them.

e. *Foreign courts.* The practice of international comity underscores the importance of the full faith and credit clause as a source of national unity and cohesiveness in American law. It would be woefully wrong to assert or imply that the judgments of American courts, state or federal, are given no effect by foreign courts. They routinely are respected and enforced. But this is a matter of the case-by-case discretion of the foreign government whose courts are asked to enforce an American judgment. Absent an overriding treaty obligation, foreign governments are free to decide in particular circumstances to withhold enforcement of the domestic judgments of other countries. This is a world apart from the constitutionally binding effect of state and federal court judgments on the courts of sister states within the American union.

IV. CHOICE OF LAW INFLUENCES ON CHOICE OF FORUM

A. **Interstate Choice of Law. Variation among American jurisdictions in the law they will apply to a given controversy both inspires and constrains conflict between the parties over the choice of forum.**

1. Substantive law

a. Constitutional constraint. The due process clause of the fourteenth amendment and the full faith and credit clause of Article IV of the Constitution operate in tandem to limit state court choice of law to the law of a state that has *"significant contacts"* with the parties and the controversy giving rise to litigation.

(1) This is a very weak constraint. It prevents a forum from applying its own substantive law to a dispute only if the dispute has arisen between parties wholly unconnected to the forum and is based on events wholly unconnected to the forum. Such disputes will arise infrequently.

(2) A more significant constraint on forum-shopping is the non-constitutional doctrine of *forum non conveniens*, discussed later in this chapter. A plaintiff may be able to find a forum with favorable law, "significant contacts," and jurisdiction over the parties. But if that forum's relationship to the controversy is insubstantial in a pragmatic sense — the parties reside elsewhere and the injury occurred elsewhere — it may appear to the forum's courts to be a waste of judicial time and taxpayers' money to adjudicate the case.

b. Range of choice of law rules. Generally, the forum must choose between applying its own substantive law and the law of some other state with significant contacts to the parties and the dispute. There are three major approaches, which may dictate the choice of vastly different rules of substantive law to resolve the very same controversy.

(1) The "vested rights" approach looks to the law of the place where a right was acquired (*"lex loci contractus"*) to determine the validity of a contract, and to the

law of the place where injury occurred (*"lex loci delicti"*) to determine whether there has occurred a breach of contract or commission of a tort.

(2) The "interest analysis" approach looks to the competing governmental interests of the various states with significant contacts to the parties and the dispute.

(3) The "most significant relationship" approach looks to the relative significance of the contacts of the various interested states and applies the law of the state with the most significant contacts.

2. Procedural systems

    a. Very limited constitutional regulation

        (1) States have wide latitude in adopting procedural systems, subject only to the background constitutional requirement that litigants receive "due process of law."

        (2) In practice "due process" operates at the level of detail, occasionally invalidating a state procedural rule for lack of fairness to an adversely affected party.

        (3) States are free to choose whether to model their procedural systems on the Federal Rules, to follow the code pleading model, or to adopt some idiosyncratic blend of procedures.

    b. Forum-state procedure always governs

        (1) There is no "significant contacts" test governing choice of procedure. If a court has territorial jurisdiction over the defendant and chooses to exercise that jurisdiction despite a forum non conveniens objection, it will always apply its own procedural rules.

    c. The substance/procedure distinction

        (1) The guaranteed application of the forum's procedural law creates great forum-shopping incentives when procedural rules will have a clear impact on the outcome of a lawsuit.

        (2) The classic illustration is the statute of limitations. For choice of law purposes this is regarded as procedural. In a tort suit, for instance, a forum's choice of law rules may require that the substantive law of the place where the tort occurred be applied to a lawsuit in the forum for damages arising out of tortious injury suffered somewhere else. But even if the lawsuit would be barred by the statute of limitations of the state where the tort occurred, the longer statute of limitations of the forum state will be applied, and the lawsuit will go forward. *See Sun Oil Co. v. Wortman*, 486 U.S. 717 (1988).

    d. Differences in procedural systems

        (1) It is true, as a generalization, that most states conform roughly to a "national" system of civil procedure modeled on practice under the Federal Rules of Civil Procedure. But don't be misled by this generalization into neglecting the impact of choice of forum on the procedure governing a lawsuit.

        (2) While the Federal Rules are indeed the dominant model, many significant state variations exist. As indicated by the list at the end of Chapter 1, the non-conforming states are among the most populous in the country.

B. Intrastate Choice of Law

1. If a case is within the concurrent jurisdiction of both the state and federal courts, there is a choice to be made not only among the various state courts that may be able to adjudicate the case, but also between the state and federal courts sitting in any of the states in which suit is possible. To the extent that different rules of law may be applied to the same case depending on whether it is being litigated in a state or federal court, there is an opportunity for intrastate forum-shopping.

2. Intrastate forum-shopping is primarily a problem in cases that qualify for federal jurisdiction because of the *diversity of citizenship* of the parties. The choice between state and federal law in a diversity case is governed by the famous case of *Erie Railroad Co. v. Tompkins*, 304 U.S. 64 (1938).

    a. Under *Erie,* federal courts exercising diversity jurisdiction must apply the same substantive rules of law as state courts. Disparities between state and federal practice with regard to procedural matters continue to provide important forum-shopping incentives as between federal and state courts sitting within the borders of the same state. Because so many of the most populous states do not follow the federal model of civil procedure, on a per capita basis a litigant's choice between a federal or state forum will have significant procedural consequences in over half of all civil actions filed in the United States in which diversity jurisdiction could be invoked.

    b. Diversity jurisdiction and the *Erie* doctrine are discussed at length in Chapter 4.

V. OTHER CONSTRAINTS ON CHOICE OF FORUM

A. Venue

1. Venue rules are non-jurisdictional rules for allocating judicial business on a geographical basis among the various courts or departments of a particular system of trial courts. They are non-jurisdictional because they are merely administrative rules designed primarily for the convenience of parties. It is the defendant's burden to object if the plaintiff has filed suit in a court of improper venue, and absent objection the case may proceed to a valid judgment.

2. State venue rules

    a. State venue and forum-shopping. Generally, contests over proper venue within the court system of a particular state are motivated by the relative convenience to the parties of the venues in question. The same procedures and substantive rules will apply regardless of the outcome of an intrastate venue dispute. Venue selection can have important practical consequences, however. The social characteristics of residents of a particular judicial district may influence the outcome of a jury trial. For instance, a jury composed predominantly of rural, low-income, or unemployed people might set at a lower amount the damages to be paid for causing the wrongful death of a 20-year old female pre-law college student than would a jury composed predominantly of urban professionals.

    b. Basic venue principles. There is almost always some form of geographic relationship between a lawsuit, its parties, and the designated venue(s) for trial.

        (1) Venue based on the geographic status of the parties to the litigation. Examples are venue rules permitting suit to be brought where the defendant resides, where the defendant was served, or (generally restricted to cases in which the defendant is a non-resident) where the plaintiff resides.

        (2) Venue based on the geographic status of the events giving rise to the litigation. Examples are venue rules permitting suit to be brought where the tort occurred or the cause of action arose or the contract in issue was entered into.

        (3) The *local action* rule limits the venue of certain actions involving real property to the county or other judicial district in which the land is located.

            (a) Local actions are actions involving ownership of, possession of, or injury to real property. All actions which are not local actions are classified for venue purposes as transitory actions.

2

      (b) Almost all states retain the local/transitory action distinction for purposes of their state court venue rules, and limit the venue of a local action to the county in which the relevant property is located regardless of the venue choices that would apply were the action regarded as transitory. But venue in a local action remains waivable and subject to transfer.

      (4) Plaintiff's choice. Sometimes state law suspends the normal rules of proper venue and allows the plaintiff to choose to file suit in any court of the state that has proper subject-matter jurisdiction. This unfettered choice of venue is typically permitted in actions against non-resident defendants, for whom no particular state court is likely to be more or less convenient than any other.

  3. Federal venue rules

      a. Federal venue and forum-shopping. The *Erie* doctrine looks to the state in which a diversity case is originally filed to determine the substantive law to be applied in the case. Federal venue rules are fairly narrow and may rule out a plaintiff's choice of a federal forum within certain states that would otherwise be attractive to the plaintiff based on their territorial jurisdiction and choice of law.

      b. Because the practical importance of federal venue rules is greatly affected by the *Erie* doctrine, and because federal venue is a constraint on choice of forum necessarily secondary to the constraints imposed by the rules of federal subject-matter jurisdiction, we present our detailed explication of the rules of federal venue in Chapter 4, as an adjunct to our discussion of federal subject-matter jurisdiction.

B. Discretionary Refusal to Exercise Jurisdiction: Forum Non Conveniens and Other Doctrines

  1. Even when possessed of subject-matter jurisdiction and territorial jurisdiction in a case laid in the proper venue and brought against properly notified parties, an American court, state or federal, is free to invoke the doctrine of *forum non conveniens*. This doctrine permits a court to refuse to exercise jurisdiction because the forum has no interest in the controversy and it may more conveniently be litigated elsewhere.

      a. Some of the most influential forum non conveniens cases are decisions of the United States Supreme Court applying federal common law to decide whether federal courts should exercise jurisdiction. *See, e.g., Piper Aircraft Co. v. Reyno*, 454 U.S. 235 (1981). It is important to remember, however, that forum non conveniens may be applied in each state according to its own view of the common law. The doctrine of forum non conveniens is not required or regulated by the federal Constitution.

      (1) Under modern law, simple changes of venue from one federal district court to some other, more convenient federal district court are governed by the federal inter-district transfer statute, 28 U.S.C. § 1404. (We discuss § 1404 as part of our discussion in Chapter 4 of federal subject-matter jurisdiction, *Erie*, and federal venue.)

      (2) When a federal court is confronted by the claim of a defendant that the court of some foreign country is a more convenient forum, § 1404 does not apply, and the federal common law of forum non conveniens governs. This was the case in *Reyno*, involving the crash of an American-built airplane in Scotland. In light of the facts that the defendant owner and operators of the aircraft, the decedents, and their heirs were all British subjects, the Supreme Court decided in *Reyno* that claims against the American manufacturers of the airplane and its components should be adjudicated in the courts of Scotland.

      b. Under the common law fashioned by the Supreme Court in *Reyno* and similar cases and widely followed by American state courts, the *fundamental prerequisite* for a forum non conveniens refusal to exercise jurisdiction (by dismissing or staying the case pending adjudication elsewhere) is the *availability of an alternative forum*. Forum non conveniens should not be used to deny the plaintiff an opportunity to sue, somewhere, for some form of legal redress.

c.   It is no bar to a forum non conveniens motion that the law applicable to the plaintiff's claim in the alternative forum may be less favorable to the plaintiff than in the plaintiff's chosen forum. Thus forum non conveniens motions are a powerful defense against plaintiffs' forum-shopping.

d.   Where defendant can show the availability of an arguably more convenient forum, the court in which plaintiff has filed suit will generally give considerable deference to plaintiff's initial choice of forum. Nonetheless, the court may decide that the presumption in favor of plaintiff's choice of forum is overcome by the clear inconvenience of the forum chosen. This is especially true when nothing would seem to recommend the forum chosen by plaintiff — the legally disputed events occurred elsewhere, and the parties are resident elsewhere — except for the forum's favorable law and its jurisdictional power over the defendant.

2. Other doctrines of discretionary refusal to exercise jurisdiction

a.   In general. At common law, other doctrines than forum non conveniens could be invoked to block the exercise of a court's jurisdiction. Chief among such subsidiary doctrines of refusal to exercise jurisdiction were the local action rule and various doctrines of immunity from service of process. The modern view is to treat such doctrines as special applications of the policy of forum non conveniens.

b.   *Local actions.* The importance of restricting discretionary refusal to exercise jurisdiction to the conditions specified by the doctrine of forum non conveniens is especially great in the application of the ancient common law venue doctrine, the local action rule. If forum non conveniens principles are followed, an action will not be dismissed under the local action rule unless there is an alternative forum available to the plaintiff.

(1) Local actions (previously defined in our discussion of state court venue) had to be tried at common law in the locality in which the relevant real property was located. When applied as a venue rule within the court system of a single state, the local action rule is relatively harmless. It restricts proper venue to just one judicial district, but that is a waivable objection, change of venue is generally permitted, and the place of venue does not affect the choice of the law to be applied to the case.

(2) When the local action rule is made the basis for refusal to adjudicate a claim against a defendant who is subject to the territorial jurisdiction of the forum state, solely because the claim involves real property in some other state, the local action rule can become the vehicle for injustice. If the state where the land is located happens to have a limited "long-arm" statute which does not reach the defendant, who resides in the forum state, invocation of the local action rule might leave the plaintiff with no forum in which the defendant can be called to account. Proper analysis of interstate local action questions as a special application of the forum non conveniens doctrine makes clear that an action should not be dismissed on local action grounds unless the defendant consents to suit in the forum where the property is located. The leading case is *Reasor-Hill Corp. v. Harrison*, 249 S.W.2d 994 (Ark. 1952).

c.   Immunity from service of process

(1) To avoid interference with the administration of justice

(a) In the era when the principal means of gaining territorial jurisdiction over non-resident individuals was to serve them with process if they could be found temporarily within the borders of the desired forum state, the fear of unwanted

2

service could be a major deterrent against travel to states within which hostile plaintiffs might be lurking.

(b) This disincentive to travel in states in which an individual did not want to be sued threatened disruption of the orderly adjudication of existing litigation already within the jurisdiction of a particular forum's courts. Therefore, most courts extended immunity from service of process to attorneys, parties, and witnesses coming to and going from a state for the purposes of participating in court hearings or related proceedings.

(c) Mechanical immunity rules make little sense in the modern world of long-arm statutes and service of process by mail. Many modern courts now apply immunity rules discretionarily, in the interests of justice, as another special application of the doctrine of forum non conveniens.

(2) As a sanction for the use of *fraud and deceit* to effect service of process

(a) Trickery is generally tolerated when used to get an elusive defendant to expose herself to personal service of process. A particularly outrageous strategem may so shock the conscience of the trial court that, upon timely motion, service of process will be quashed.

(b) In tolerating trickery, courts generally draw the line at the state line. Trickery used to induce a defendant to enter the forum state, where personal service then occurs, is almost always grounds for quashing the service of process. This is probably required as a matter of federal constitutional law if defendant has no contacts with the forum state other than his fraudulently induced presence at the time of personal service.

Example: Unable otherwise to accomplish personal service on *D*, *P* arranges for a fraudulent phone call to *D*'s residence advising *D* that *D*'s child has been admitted to the emergency room at a stated hospital. When *D* rushes into the hospital in search of her child, she is served by *P*'s process server. Although this may stretch the tolerance of some courts, most will uphold the service so long as *D* did not come to the hospital from another state.

ATTACKING THE CHOICE OF FORUM

VI. ATTACKING THE CHOICE OF FORUM

A. "Direct attack" During Trial and Appeal of the Cause of Action

1. *Grounds for attack in the trial court.* The following headings summarize the various grounds available to the defendant to attack the plaintiff's choice of forum by motion in the trial court. Where a Federal Rule expressly authorizes such a motion, it is identified in brackets. Some grounds are subject to hair-triggered waiver rules that require objection to be made immediately upon the defendant's appearance in the action. We begin with the most easily waived objections to choice of forum and work towards those objections that a defendant may delay until the later stages of the litigation.

   a. Insufficiency of process, *i.e.*, insufficiency of the form and content of the process served on the defendant. [Rule 12(b)(4).]

   b. Insufficiency of service of process, *i.e.*, insufficiency of the manner in which service of process was accomplished. [Rule 12(b)(5).] Although formally a motion to dismiss the action, a Rule 12(b)(5) motion is also correctly referred to as a "motion to quash" service of process.

   c. Lack of territorial jurisdiction. The Federal Rules expressly authorize a motion to dismiss for lack of jurisdiction over the person. [Rule 12(b)(2).] Lawyers and judges often refer (incorrectly) to Rule 12(b)(2) motions as "motions to quash service of process." There is no expressly denominated motion for challenging in federal court an assertion of in rem jurisdiction. The Federal Rules authorize in rem jurisdiction over non-residents by incorporating state law attachment procedures into the service-of-process provisions of Federal Rule 4(e). Therefore, the logical method for challenging the power of the court to assert in rem jurisdiction is by motion to quash the service of process under Rule 12(b)(5).

d. Improper venue. [Rule 12(b)(4).]

e. Inconvenient forum. [A common law motion not expressly provided for by the Federal Rules.]

f. Failure to state a claim upon which relief can be granted. [Rule 12(b)(6).] If the legal sufficiency of a complaint (*see* Chapter 5) turns on a controversial choice of law issue, a Rule 12(b)(6) motion is one way for the defendant to attack the plaintiff's choice of law theory at the outset of the action, possibly forcing the plaintiff to seek voluntary dismissal of the action under Rule 41 (*see* Chapter 8) in order to avoid claim preclusion if the trial court rules in the defendant's favor as to the law to be applied. If the choice of law issue is not apparent on the face of the complaint, it can be presented by motion for summary judgment under Rule 56 (*see* Chapter 8), although decision of such a motion is likely to be deferred until after the discovery process.

g. Failure to join necessary parties (*see* Chapter 6). [Rule 12(b)(7).]

h. Lack of subject-matter jurisdiction. [Rule 12(b)(1).] In the event the defendant has invoked federal subject-matter by removing the case to federal court, the plaintiff may move to dismiss for lack of subject-matter jurisdiction under Rule 12(h)(3). If the removal was procedurally improper, the plaintiff can move to remand by statutory motion under 28 U.S.C. § 1446(c).

2. Preservation and presentation of objections

a. The *special appearance* rule

(1) The common law historically regarded an appearance in an action as a submission to the jurisdiction of the court whose process had been served on the summoned defendant. The only way to contest the jurisdiction of the court over the person or property of the defendant was to allow a judgment to enter by default, after the failure of the defendant to appear in response to the summons, and then to collaterally attack the validity of the default judgment by resisting its enforcement. *See* Chapter 11.

(2) The "code pleading" reform of American civil procedure in the 1850's led to the widespread adoption of the device of the "special appearance." A defendant who properly enters a *special appearance* is permitted to object to the territorial jurisdiction of the trial court without consenting to that jurisdiction by the very fact of appearing in court. Any other form of appearance in a code pleading jurisdiction is considered to be a *general appearance*.

(a) General appearances have the effect of irreversibly waiving any objections to the power of the court over the defendant, just like any appearance did earlier in the history of the common law.

(b) Although intended to be a remedial and liberalizing reform of procedure, special appearance rules are frequently applied in rigid and unforgiving fashion to penalize incautious attorneys who seek to object to jurisdiction but raise some other, non-jurisdictional objection as well, thereby converting an intended special appearance into an inadvertent general appearance. Appearances by attorneys are binding on their clients, so this kind of mistake waives a client's right to object to defects of service of process and territorial jurisdiction, regardless of the merit a properly entered objection might have had.

(c) Attorneys should regard the entering of a special appearance as "risky business" to be undertaken with great caution. The *only* objection presented to the trial court upon the defendant's special appearance should be a *motion to quash service of process*. Such a motion may be based on any reason sufficient under local law or federal constitutional law to deprive the trial court of jurisdiction over the person of the defendant or (in an in rem action) over the property of the defendant that has been attached by the plaintiff.

  i) Jurisdictions vary as to what, if any, matters can as a matter of local law be raised during the defendant's special appearance in addition to the motion to quash service of process. *See Goodwine v. Superior Court*, 63 Cal.2d 481 (1965). It is *reckless and foolish*, however, to present anything beyond the motion to quash service of process at a special appearance, unless local law expressly declares that certain other objections are waived unless presented during a special appearance. If you are free to raise the other objections at a later date, it makes no sense to assume any risk of converting a special appearance into a general appearance by asserting the other objections jointly with your motion to quash.

  ii) Because special appearance is allowed solely by grace of state law, there is no presently recognized federal constitutional basis for arguing your way out of a slip-up that converts a special appearance into a general appearance at the cost of your client's meritorious objection to the trial court's territorial jurisdiction.

b. Procedure for timely objection under the Federal Rules

(1) *Objections waived if not asserted at once.* There are a number of grounds for objecting to the plaintiff's choice of forum that Federal Rules 12(g) and 12(h) require to be asserted in the defendant's first appearance in response to the complaint. This is not a special appearance rule. These objections can be asserted in combination with any other objections either by Rule 12 motion or simply by asserting them in the answer if no Rule 12 motion was previously filed. But whatever the nature and timing of defendant's initial response to the complaint, these objections are waived if not included in that initial response.

  (a) Lack of personal jurisdiction. [Rule 12 (b)(2).]

  (b) Improper venue. [Rule 12 (b)(3).]

  (c) Insufficiency of process. [Rule 12 (b)(4).]

  (d) Insufficiency of service of process [Rule 12 (b)(5).]

(2) *Objections timely throughout trial.* These objections may be asserted at the convenience of the defendant at any time before or during trial.

  (a) Issues of law essential to legal sufficiency of the complaint (*see* Chapter 5). [Rule 12 (b)(6).]

  (b) Failure to join an indispensable party (*see* Chapter 6). [Rule 12 (b)(7).]

(3) *Objection timely throughout both trial and appeal.* The objection that the trial court lacks subject-matter jurisdiction may be asserted at any time during the litigation of a case, from the time of the first appearance of the defendant until the last moment before the judgment becomes final after the exhaustion of all appeals. [Rules 12(b)(1) and 12(h)(3).]

3. Appeal of choice of forum issues

a. Only the objection of a lack of subject-matter jurisdiction can be raised for the first time on appeal. (Some courts have also permitted the objection of failure to join an indispensable party to be raised for the first time on appeal.)

b. All other grounds for direct attack on the choice of forum can be appealed only if first raised by timely objection to the trial court. If the trial court sustains the objection and dismisses the case, the order of dismissal can be appealed in the normal fashion of any order that ends proceedings in the trial court. But if the trial court overrules the objection, difficult questions of appealability can arise.

   (1) In a court system that allows appeal only from final judgments, the action must proceed to judgment in the trial court before there is an opportunity to appeal the trial court's denial of defendant's motion attacking the choice of forum. This is the general mode of appeal in the *federal court system.*

   (2) In a court system that allows appeal as of right of "interlocutory" rulings (a ruling that stops short of a final judgment in the case), the ruling must be appealed immediately or the right to appeal is waived. California follows this model to a limited degree by allowing interlocutory appeal as of right of orders granting motions to quash service of process or staying actions on grounds of inconvenient forum, as well as orders granting or denying motions to quash the attachment of property.

   (3) In a court system that allows its appellate courts to exercise discretionary interlocutory review of trial court rulings, adverse rulings on motions to dismiss or quash may be submitted for appellate review at the option of the unhappy party. If the appellate court decides to grant interlocutory review, that will be the only appeal allowed. But if discretionary interlocutory review is denied or not sought, the trial court's overruling of an objection to choice of forum is an error that can be corrected by appeal of the trial court's final judgment. *In most respects, this is the California model* for appellate review of trial court rulings on objections to choice of forum.

B. "Collateral attack" by Separate Proceeding Attacking the Validity of a Prior Judgment

  1. Motion to vacate the judgment

    a. Modern procedure allows a trial court upon proper motion to set aside a previously entered judgment that is void for lack of territorial or subject matter jurisdiction, even though an appeal was not taken and is now untimely, or the appeal has already been concluded. Such proceedings under Federal Rule 60(b)(4) or similar state rules are substitutes for traditional suits in equity to set aside unenforceable judgments, and hence are regarded (loosely) as a form of "collateral attack" on a judgment by proceedings independent of the "direct" litigation leading to the entry of the judgment and its review by the normal processes of appeal.

     (1) Rule 60(b) proceedings are a procedural improvement over equitable suits to set aside judgments, because a Rule 60(b) motion reopens proceedings in the lawsuit whose judgment is being attacked, and generally will be heard by the judge who presided over the previous proceedings and entered the challenged judgment. It takes less time and expense to bring the judge "up to speed" and to focus on the crucial issues affecting the validity of the previously entered judgment.

    b. A Rule 60(b)(4) or similar motion is most frequently used when the void judgment was entered by *default.* Any jurisdictional defects in a *contested* judgment entered after an appearance by the defendant will generally have been waived if not presented to the trial court, or have been ruled upon by the trial court subject only to correction on appeal.

c. A special problem is presented when a claimed lack of subject-matter jurisdiction is raised by motion to vacate the judgment after a contested case has run its full course at trial and on appeal.

(1) Subject-matter jurisdiction is not supposed to be established by consent or inaction, but on the other hand there is a need for some degree of finality of judgments after the appellate process is over.

(2) Many courts (including the federal court system) indulge in the fiction of a conclusive presumption that a contested judgment (any judgment other than a default judgment, *i.e.*, one entered after the defendant has entered an appearance) must have resolved any controversy over the existence of the trial court's subject-matter jurisdiction.

(a) If no appeal can now be taken, this presumed resolution of the jurisdictional issue is accorded *res judicata* effect.

(b) Courts that use this fiction to foreclose collateral attack on the subject-matter jurisdiction of contested judgments generally make exceptions where necessary to preserve particularly important public interests. Such courts permit collateral attack of a contested judgment for lack of subject-matter jurisdiction when state courts have exercised jurisdiction over a controversy exclusively subject to federal jurisdiction, or where the judgment would infringe a state's sovereign immunity.

(3) Some courts allow a judgment to be collaterally attacked for lack of subject-matter jurisdiction, even if the defendant appeared and contested the claim, unless the issue of subject-matter jurisdiction was actually contested and resolved in the process of rendering the judgment.

2. Independent judicial proceedings

a. In two circumstances the validity of a judgment may be collaterally attacked by independent proceeding commenced in the same jurisdiction as rendered the judgment under attack.

(1) The jurisdiction may be one that does not permit motions to vacate judgments to be brought as a continuation of the lawsuit in the original trial court, requiring instead that the judgment be collaterally attacked by the traditional means — an independent suit in equity seeking to have the judgment set aside or to restrain the enforcement of the judgment by appropriate injunction against the prevailing party or the officials charged with enforcing judgments.

(2) The party seeking relief from the judgment may not have been named as a party to the original proceedings and, hence, may lack standing to reopen those proceedings by moving to vacate the judgment.

b. Such collateral attacks on a judgment by independent proceedings in the same jurisdiction are functionally identical to collateral attack by Rule 60(b)(4) or similar motion and are governed by the same basic principles recited above.

c. Regardless whether the jurisdiction rendering a putatively invalid judgment may permit collateral attack on that judgment in its own courts by motion or independent suit, it may be convenient to withhold attack on the validity of a judgment until the judgment-winner seeks to enforce it in some other jurisdiction. *See* Chapter 11.

(1) The opportunity for successful collateral attack on judgments rendered by sister states or the federal courts is severely limited by the principles of the full faith and credit and supremacy clauses of the Constitution, previously discussed under the heading of "Effect of a Valid Judgment."

(2) These principles require the court in which a foreign judgment (*i.e.*, a judgment from some other American court system) is being attacked to give that judgment the *same effect* as it would be given if the collateral attack were being maintained in the court system that rendered the judgment.

(3) With respect to those judgments most frequently subject to collateral attack — default judgments and judgments that may be invalid for lack of subject-matter jurisdiction — collateral attack by resistance to enforcement is an important element of the law governing choice of forum. As we pointed out at the beginning of this chapter, the point of litigation is to get a valid judgment. The threat that a judgment may be rendered unenforceable by successful collateral attack colors the entire progress of litigation from service of process to appeal of judgment.

2

MINIMUM CONTACTS ANALYSIS

▶ **CHAPTER SUMMARY**

MINIMUM CONTACTS ANALYSIS

INTRODUCTION: As promised during Chapter 2's analysis of the validity of judgments, we present in this chapter a detailed guide to federal due process limitations on state court territorial jurisdiction. "Minimum contacts" is the nebulous term that the Supreme Court has used to describe the relationship that a state must have with a particular defendant in order for the state's assertion of territorial jurisdiction over that defendant to be consistent with due process of law.

There is current controversy about the scope of minimum contacts analysis. This is sure to be a *major* topic of discussion in every civil procedure course until the law is settled. In 1977, the Supreme Court appeared to say that due process required *all* assertions of state court territorial jurisdiction to be justified by minimum contacts analysis. *Shaffer v. Heitner*, 433 U.S. 186. In 1990, a splintered Supreme Court, speaking without a majority opinion, retreated from its 1977 holding. The Justices were unwilling to hold that due process demands "minimum contacts" when a state court asserts territorial jurisdiction on traditional grounds that were a familiar basis for jurisdiction when the fourteenth amendment (and its due process clause) were added to the Constitution in 1868. *Burnham v. Superior Court*, ___ U.S. ___, 110 S.Ct. 2105.

Whether or not minimum contacts analysis applies across the board, or only to the assertion of state court territorial jurisdiction based on non-traditional grounds, an understanding of minimum contacts remains of fundamental importance to the mastery of American civil procedure. The "non-traditional" grounds of state-court territorial jurisdiction that indisputably must still pass constitutional muster according to minimum contacts analysis include all state long-arm statutes, and all assertions of "in rem" or "quasi-in-rem" jurisdiction directed against the interests of non-residents of the forum state. We conclude this chapter with a 5-step approach for resolving minimum contacts problems.

HISTORICAL BACKGROUND

I. **HISTORICAL BACKGROUND**

 A. **There was no provision in the original Constitution of 1789 authorizing the federal courts to regulate assertions of state court territorial jurisdiction. Federal courts had no authority to redress arbitrary or unfair conduct by state officials.**

 B. **This situation was fundamentally changed in 1868 when the fourteenth amendment was added to the federal Constitution. This was one of the "Civil War amendments" that were added to the Constitution expressly to increase federal power over states and to decrease state power over individuals. The fourteenth amendment prohibits states from depriving anyone of "life, liberty, or property" without "due process of law."**

 C. **In the landmark case of *Pennoyer v. Neff*, 95 U.S. 714 (1878), the Supreme Court announced a comprehensive set of due process principles governing the validity of state court judgments.**

 1. "Due process" principles distinguished from "full faith and credit" principles

 a. Prior to *Pennoyer*, the Supreme Court had begun to develop federal constitutional standards for the validity of state court judgments through its interpretation of the full faith and credit clause of the Constitution. A determination by the Supreme Court that a judgment was invalid merely *permitted* sister states to refuse to enforce that judgment. It did not *compel* sister states to refuse enforcement. The "invalid" judgment *could still be enforced* by any state choosing to do so — the state rendering the judgment, as well as any other state that might disagree with the Supreme Court's standards of validity.

 b. *Pennoyer* took full faith and credit principles and made them due process principles. As such, they became constitutional preconditions to the enforcement of *any* judgment by *any* state — even by the state whose courts had rendered the judgment. After *Pennoyer,* every state court and every state court litigant had to be alert to the standing possibility that a judgment perfectly valid under state law might be invalid under federal law and hence unenforceable under the due process clause.

3

2. *Pennoyer's* criteria for validity distinguished sharply between judgments in personam and judgments in rem. But *Pennoyer's* central theoretical premise applied to both in personam and in rem jurisdiction: the jurisdiction of a court was a function of its *physical power* over the person or the property in question.

    a. Judgments in personam were the major concern of *Pennoyer* because they could be enforced nationwide under the full faith and credit clause. States were given considerable leeway in asserting personal jurisdiction over their own residents. But when it came to asserting personal jurisdiction over residents of other states, *Pennoyer* insisted on personal service of process *within the borders of the forum state*.

    b. Judgments in rem were the principal safety valve available to a state to protect the interests of its residents in prosecuting claims against non-residents who were careful to remain outside the state. In personam jurisdiction could not be obtained over an absent non-resident, but if the non-resident owned property within the state, *Pennoyer* allowed for attachment of the property upon complaint of the plaintiff. The attached property could then be the basis for a judgment in rem or quasi-in-rem on any claim against the defendant, but with the effect of the judgment limited to disposition of the attached property.

    c. *Pennoyer* also fashioned some other safety valves to allow necessary litigation to proceed against non-residents even if they had no property in the state and could not personally be served with process within the state.

        (1) Marriage was a "status" over which a state had power by virtue of the residence within the state of either partner to a marriage. Thus, divorces could be granted without an abandoned spouse having to go to some distant forum where personal service of process might be possible.

        (2) Agents of non-resident individuals could be empowered to accept service of process on behalf of their principals, and the appointment of such agents could be required by states as a condition to permitting non-residents to do business within the state. To like effect, domestic corporations created by a state and foreign corporations permitted to do business within a state could be required by state law to designate means for effective service of process on some officer or agent personally present within the state.

D. **The case of *Harris v. Balk*, 198 U.S. 215 (1905), significantly expanded the use of quasi-in-rem jurisdiction as a fallback method for states to allow residents to sue non-residents who could not personally be served with process within the state.**

    1. Under *Harris v. Balk*, any form of debt or other intangible property could be attached (by a process called "garnishment") through personal service of process on the garnishee, *i.e.*, the person present within the territory of the forum state who happened to be indebted to the non-resident defendant.

    2. Since most of us are owed many debts at any one time — wages by our employers, deposits by banks, the value of travelers' checks and insurance policies by the issuing companies — the ability to seize intangible assets became principally a question of deciding when the garnishee, often a major corporation with multiple offices, was properly deemed "present" within the forum state in which the plaintiff wished to bring suit.

E. **As the economy of the United States grew more and more integrated in the decades after *Pennoyer*, pressure mounted to allow in personam suit on any cause of action against a non-resident that arose from the non-resident's activities within the forum state. There were two common scenarios that caused recurrent stretching of the boundaries of *Pennoyer*.**

    1. A foreign corporation or non-resident individual would transact some sort of business within a state, by mail or by intermediary or sometimes by sending a full-fledged agent temporarily

into the state. The problem would be that the corporation or individual had not qualified legally to do business within the state by filing registration papers and appointing an agent within the state on whom process might be served in personam in the name of the non-resident. If a resident of the state later sought to sue the foreign entity or individual for damage suffered as a result of the sale or deal in issue, *Pennoyer* would seem to make in personam jurisdiction impossible. But many states adopted early "long-arm" statutes that subjected out-of-state business enterprises to suit by treating any act that constituted "doing business" in the state as automatically "appointing" a state officer — generally the Secretary of State — as the out-of-stater's "agent" for service of process within the state.

3

2. With the development of the private automobile came a new class of tort litigation against an uncommonly elusive class of defendants — the out-of-state driver who might stay at the scene of an accident to exchange identification, but who would be well beyond the state line before process could be served. The device of fictitious appointment of an agent was already working well in the business setting. It was soon extended to out-of-state motorists by long-arm statutes that treated driving on a state's highways as automatically appointing the Secretary of State to be the out-of-state driver's in-state agent for service of process in suits arising out of use of the state's highways.

THE BIRTH OF MINI-
MUM CONTACTS
DOCTRINE IN *INTER-*
NATIONAL SHOE

II. THE BIRTH OF MINIMUM CONTACTS DOCTRINE IN *INTERNATIONAL SHOE*

A. ***International Shoe Co. v. Washington,* 326 U.S. 310 (1945), involved a claim for unpaid employment taxes asserted by the State of Washington against International Shoe Company, a Delaware corporation with its principal place of business in St. Louis, Missouri, and with secondary manufacturing and distribution establishments in several states other than Washington.**

1. The company had painstakingly arranged its sales operations in those states in which it maintained no formal place of business so as to avoid the conclusion that it was "doing business" in these states within the meaning of contemporary state long-arm statutes. The company paid commissions on orders solicited by roughly a dozen salesmen residing in Washington, but structured the transactions so that all sales were completed only upon acceptance of orders in St. Louis, and all billing was made from a place of shipment outside of Washington.

2. The State of Washington had served notice of its suit to collect the employment taxes from International Shoe by serving process on a local salesman and by mailing a copy of the papers to company headquarters in St. Louis. The company maintained that this was an attempt by a state to exercise in personam jurisdiction beyond its borders in contravention of *Pennoyer*. The salesman served within the state had not been expressly authorized by the corporation to be its agent for service of process, and the corporation's activities within the state did not constitute the "doing of business" of the sort sufficient to allow the state to treat the salesman as an implied agent of the corporation.

B. **In ruling against the International Shoe Company, the Supreme Court declared *Pennoyer's* standards for the validity of in personam judgments to be unworkable as applied to "long-arm" jurisdiction over defendants not really present in the state when served with process. The *International Shoe* Court refused to continue confusing symbol and reality by asking whether corporations were "present" or whether some individual was another's unknown "agent." Instead the Court developed the new concept of "minimum contacts."**

1. Although, historically, jurisdiction in personam was grounded in the court's physical power over the person of a defendant who had been arrested and brought before the court, in the modern era "personal service of summons or other form of notice" is adequate to bind a defendant to answer a claim or suffer a default judgment. Generalizing from this

development, the Supreme Court declared in *International Shoe* that "due process requires only that in order to subject a defendant to a judgment in personam, if he be not present within the territory of the forum, he have certain *minimum contacts* with it such that the maintenance of the suit does not offend 'traditional notions of fair play and substantial justice.'" (Emphasis added.) Due process forbids a state "to make binding a judgment in personam against an individual or corporate defendant with which the state has no contacts, ties, or relations."

2. For an individual defendant, who is indeed personally present in just one place at one time, presence within the forum state might alone be a sufficient "contact, tie, or relation." *International Shoe* carefully qualified its demand for minimum contacts with the proviso: "if he [the defendant] be not present within the territory of the forum."

3. For a corporation, whose "presence" anywhere is always fictitious, *International Shoe* clearly indicates that "minimum contacts" furnish the only meaningful test for determining whether state court personal jurisdiction is consistent with the demands of due process. "Those demands may be met by such contacts of the corporation with the state of the forum as make it reasonable, within the context of our federal system of government, to require the corporation to defend the particular suit which is brought there."

III. FURTHER DEVELOPMENT OF MINIMUM CONTACTS DOCTRINE

A. *Ad Hoc Development of Doctrine.* **The constitutional law of state court territorial jurisdiction since *International Shoe* has consisted of a gradual working out of the idea of minimum contacts. The Supreme Court's decisions have provided a series of illustrations of circumstances that do or do not amount to minimum contacts, but the accompanying explanations have tended to be conclusory and occasionally inconsistent. No seamless theory has emerged.**

B. *Extension to In Rem Jurisdiction.* **In *Shaffer v. Heitner,* 433 U.S. 186 (1977), the Supreme Court held that *International Shoe* governs in rem as well as in personam cases.**

1. *Shaffer* completely repudiated the *Pennoyer* approach to jurisdictional analysis. There were two fundamental conceptual mistakes in the *Pennoyer* framework for due process analysis of state court territorial jurisdiction.

    a. *Pennoyer* erred in assuming that jurisdictional power had to rest on the mutually exclusive sovereignty of the states. This error had already led to *International Shoe*'s formulation of minimum contacts analysis for determining whether an assertion of in personam jurisdiction was consistent with due process.

    b. *Pennoyer* erred in distinguishing conceptually between the interests at stake in an assertion of in personam jurisdiction as opposed to in rem jurisdiction. Interests in property are simply the interests of persons in property. The due process clause gives the defendant the same rights in an in rem or quasi-in-rem case as in an in personam case. Hence an in rem judgment in the absence of minimum contacts is just as invalid as an in personam judgment.

2. *Shaffer* concluded that "*all* assertions of state court jurisdiction must be evaluated according to the standards set forth in *International Shoe* and its progeny." (Emphasis added.) As discussed below, the thrust of *Shaffer* has since been blunted by *Burnham v. Superior Court,* ___ U.S. ___, 110 S.Ct. 2105 (1990).

C. **Focus on *Defendant's* Contacts. In determining whether the requisite "minimum contacts" exist, the purposeful contacts must be those of the defendant, not the plaintiff.**

1. The essence of the inquiry is "the relationship between the defendant, the forum, and the litigation." *Shaffer, supra.*

2. A total lack of pre-litigation contacts between the plaintiff and the forum will not defeat jurisdiction over the defendant. The plaintiff's pre-litigation contacts with the forum, while "not, of course, completely irrelevant to the jurisdictional inquiry," enter into the calculus only at the secondary stage of determining whether the quantity and quality of the defendant's purposeful contacts make it reasonable, under all the circumstances, to subject the defendant to the territorial jurisdiction of the forum state. *Keeton v. Hustler Magazine*, 465 U.S. 770 (1984).

3. Ordinarily, the basis of the forum's power to render a binding judgment *against the plaintiff* is self-evidently the plaintiff's purposeful act of invoking the jurisdiction of the forum by electing to file suit there. Although this purposeful act would support a minimum contacts-based theory of jurisdictional power over plaintiffs, the Supreme Court has never endorsed such a theory.

    a. In a pre-*International Shoe* case, the Supreme Court held that the plaintiff's invocation of the forum's jurisdiction over the defendant constituted "consent" to the forum's assertion of jurisdiction over the plaintiff with respect to a counterclaim. *Adam v. Saenger*, 303 U.S. 59 (1938). As discussed below in our analysis of consent-based jurisdiction, the Supreme Court has persisted since *International Shoe* in treating consent as a waiver of the need for minimum contacts rather than as itself a form of purposeful contact.

    b. The Supreme Court has held that minimum contacts need *not* exist between *absent class plaintiffs* and the forum state in order for a judgment in a class action seeking predominantly money damages to be binding on the absent and out-of-state members of a plaintiff class who have not expressed any consent to the jurisdictional power of the forum state. Because lesser burdens are placed on absent class-action plaintiffs than on out-of-state defendants, due process requires only that absent class-action plaintiffs receive (1) the best practicable notice of the suit and an opportunity to participate in its litigation; (2) the opportunity to "opt out" of the class litigation; and (3) adequate representation of their interests by the named plaintiff. *Phillips Petroleum Co. v. Shutts*, 472 U.S. 797 (1985).

D. *Purposefulness* of the Contacts. **The defendant's contacts with the forum state must have been "purposefully established" rather than "random," "fortuitous," "attenuated," or "unilateral."** *Hanson v. Denckla*, **357 U.S. 253 (1958);** *Burger King v. Rudzewicz*, **471 U.S. 462 (1985).**

1. The purposeful activity must have been motivated by a desire to secure the "benefits and protection" of forum law. The need for purposefulness is sometimes referred to as the "purposeful availment" requirement, based on the language of *Hanson v. Denckla*, that "it is essential in every case that there by some act by which the defendant purposefully avails itself of the privilege of conducting activities within the forum state, thus invoking the benefits and protections of its laws." Purposefulness always exists when the defendant has "purposefully directed" its activities at residents of the forum state, but it remains undecided whether "purposeful direction" is a necessary element of purposefulness.

2. Merely altruistic behavior, such as a divorced father's permitting a child to spend more time with her mother in the forum state than was required under a separation agreement, and paying for her travel there "in the interests of family harmony and his children's preferences," is not purposeful activity of the sort that may establish "minimum contacts." *Kulko v. Superior Court*, 436 U.S. 84 (1978).

3. A defendant may establish the requisite purposeful contact with the forum state without physically entering it. *Burger King v. Rudzewicz, supra*.

    a. Physical presence in the forum state is, however, an especially important form of purposeful contact given heavy weight in determining the overall reasonableness of the forum's exercise of jurisdiction over the defendant. *Burger King, supra*.

b. As discussed below under the heading of "Transient Jurisdiction," the voluntary physical presence of an individual within the forum state when served with process is such a significant purposeful contact that it alone constitutes the "minimum contacts" needed to justify territorial jurisdiction. *Burnham v. Superior Court, supra.*

4. The "stream of commerce" problem: purposefulness has been an especially troublesome component of minimum contacts analysis in products liability cases. There is often a rather attenuated connection between the manufacture and sale of the injury-causing product in some other state, and the circumstances of its presence in the forum state at the time of injury. Courts have generally permitted the forum state to assert jurisdiction over a non-resident manufacturer if the defendant purposefully cast its product upon the "stream of commerce" by which it eventually flowed into the forum state. There is as yet no precise definition of the "stream of commerce" and its relationship to territorial jurisdiction.

a. In *World-Wide Volkswagen v. Woodson*, 444 U.S. 286 (1980), the Supreme Court declared in dicta that delivery of products into the stream of commerce "with the expectation that they will be purchased by consumers in the forum state" would be a sufficiently purposeful contact to support the territorial jurisdiction of the forum state in a products liability suit.

c. In *Asahi Metal Industry Co., Ltd. v. Superior Court*, 480 U.S. 102 (1987), an evenly split Court failed to muster a majority in support of either of two inconsistent theories of purposefulness in the stream of commerce context.

(1) The four-Justice plurality opinion of Justice O'Connor argued that "purposeful availment" requires more than mere "awareness" by a manufacturer that the stream of commerce into which the manufacturer has placed its product may or will sweep that product into the forum state. The manufacturer must have "purposefully directed" its product toward the forum state. Relevant to this determination is whether the defendant has indicated an intent or purpose to serve the market in the forum state by, for example, "designing the product for the market in the forum state, advertising in the forum state, establishing channels for providing regular advice to customers in the forum state, or marketing the product through a distributor who has agreed to serve as the sales agent in the forum state."

(2) The four-Justice plurality opinion of Justice Brennan disagreed that "purposeful availment" required any act or intent beyond the defendant's placing its product in the stream of commerce. "The stream of commerce refers not to unpredictable currents or eddies, but to the regular and anticipated flow of products from manufacture to distribution to retail sale. As long as a participant in this process is aware that the final product is being marketed in the forum state," the requisite minimum contacts exist.

(3) Justice Stevens was the wild card in *Asahi*, remaining formally uncommitted to either plurality but indicating in an opinion joined by two of the Brennan group that a defendant's mere awareness of the flow of its product into the forum state ought to suffice for minimum contacts jurisdiction if the size of the flow is substantial, such as the 100,000 units of the defendant's product delivered annually to the forum state according to the facts of record in *Asahi*.

E. **"General" versus "Specific" Jurisdiction**

1. "Fair play and substantial justice" will in some circumstances allow a state to adjudicate a claim against a defendant that has nothing to do with the defendant's contacts with the forum state. *Perkins v. Benguet Consolidated Mining Co.*, 342 U.S. 437 (1952); *Burnham v. Superior Court, supra.* When a state has this power to adjudicate any cause of action against a defendant, no matter how unrelated to the defendant's contacts with that state, the state has *"general jurisdiction"* over the defendant.

3

2. When the nature of a defendant's contacts and due process concerns for "fair play and substantial justice" limit the adjudicatory power of a state to only such causes of action as arise out of or are related to the defendant's contacts with the state, the state has *"specific jurisdiction"* over the defendant. A defendant's single purposeful contact with the forum state can in appropriate circumstances support specific jurisdiction to adjudicate a lawsuit arising directly from that single contact. *McGee v. International Life Insurance Co.*, 355 U.S. 220 (1957).

3. General jurisdiction over a *corporate defendant* requires *continuous, systematic and substantial general business contacts*.

    a. Only two Supreme Court cases have dealt directly with these criteria. *Perkins v. Benguet Consolidated Mining Co., supra; Helicopteros Nacionales de Colombia, S.A. v. Hall*, 466 U.S. 408 (1984). In both cases the Court's opinion was closely tied to the particular facts at hand, and failed to announce comprehensive guidelines.

        (1) *Perkins* upheld general jurisdiction over an inactive corporation whose principal place of business was in the forum state.

        (2) *Helicopteros* held that equipment purchases exceeding a total of $4,000,000 over a seven-year period were insufficient contacts with the forum state to justify general jurisdiction over an alien corporation. The Court's apparent emphasis that mere purchases were involved has led some commentators to conclude that *purchases* as opposed to *sales* should be analyzed differently in deciding whether corporate business activity in a state is sufficient in magnitude to support general jurisdiction.

    b. In a third case, the Supreme Court declared that general jurisdiction requires a substantially greater degree of contacts than the bare minimum that may justify specific jurisdiction over a lawsuit arising out of the corporation's forum-related activity. *Keeton v. Hustler Magazine, supra*. The defendant foreign corporation was a magazine publisher. Its purposeful contacts with the forum state consisted of the sale of about 15,000 copies of its magazine in the forum state each month. Although these facts were sufficient for the forum state to have specific jurisdiction over the publisher, the Supreme Court made it clear that they would not support general jurisdiction. Although the publisher's contacts were continuous and systematic, they were not substantial enough for the forum to have general jurisdiction.

    c. Standard instances of continuous, systematic and substantial general business contacts supporting general jurisdiction over a corporate defendant are:

        (1) *incorporation* in the forum state (*i.e.*, it is a "domestic" corporation); and

        (2) maintaining in the forum state a *resident agent* for unrestricted service of process (*see Bendix Autolite Corp. v. Midwesco Enterprises*, 486 U.S. 888 (1988)).

    d. When a corporate defendant is a "non-resident" or "foreign" corporation, meaning that it is not incorporated in the forum state, and the foreign corporation has not appointed an agent for service of process, the issue may arise whether its level of general business activity is nonetheless so continuous, systematic and substantial that the state may assert general jurisdiction over it despite its failure to appoint a resident agent for service of process.

        (1) There seems little doubt that a state may assert general jurisdiction over a foreign corporation that maintains its *principal place of business* in the forum state. (A corporation's principal place of business is an important part of the law governing federal subject-matter jurisdiction based on diversity of citizenship. The idea of a corporation's principal place of business is discussed more fully in Chapter 4.)

        (2) When a forum state is not a foreign corporation's principal place of business, there is considerable uncertainty concerning the level of business activity of the foreign

corporation in the forum state that is needed to justify an assertion of general jurisdiction over the foreign corporation.

   (a) Some states have asserted general jurisdiction based on a level of corporate business activity that is "substantial" in an absolute sense — such as sales revenue in the state of a million dollars a year — but that is trivial relative to the corporation's nationwide volume of business. For many nationally active corporations, such a low threshold for state court general jurisdiction exposes them to the possibility that a plaintiff could choose among almost any of the fifty states and obtain territorial jurisdiction there to adjudicate against these corporations any claim whatsoever, regardless of where it arose or whom it involved as parties and witnesses. The Supreme Court has recently indicated, however, that the interstate commerce clause supplements the due process clause in limiting state court general jurisdiction over foreign corporations. *See Bendix Autolite Corp., supra.*

   (b) The effective range of plaintiff forum-shopping in suits against corporations that do significant levels of business in every state is also cut down by the restricted long-arm statutes of some states, and by the probability that a state court will invoke the doctrine of forum non conveniens to dismiss a suit brought by an out-of-state plaintiff on an out-of-state cause of action.

e. Actual assertions of general jurisdiction over foreign corporations are rare. Although state courts frequently claim to be asserting general jurisdiction, in most cases the defendant's contacts with the forum are sufficiently related to the cause of action that specific jurisdiction exists, and the existence of general jurisdiction is not necessary to sustain the validity of the resulting judgment.

4. General jurisdiction over individual defendants

a. The conventionally accepted basis for general jurisdiction over an individual is domicile (or "citizenship") in the forum state.

   (1) The concept of domicile and its relation to citizenship are discussed in greater detail in Chapter 4, since the state of domicile (and hence citizenship) of the parties to a lawsuit is often crucial to the existence of federal jurisdiction.

   (2) Many courts use the terms "residence" and "domicile" interchangeably, but you should be aware that when a court refers to "residence" in the context of territorial jurisdiction, what is meant is the place that the individual presently considers "home" rather than some place of merely temporary residence.

b. A non-resident individual may be subject to general jurisdiction by virtue of an appointment of a resident agent for unrestricted service of process. Forum law may require such an appointment in light of the individual's business activities in the forum, subject to the constraints of the interstate commerce clause. *See Bendix Autolite Corp., supra.*

c. The *Burnham* case, discussed below, held that the physical presence of an individual in the forum state when served with process is a sufficiently substantial connection to the forum state to permit the adjudication of *that particular lawsuit*, even if the circumstances of the defendant's presence in the state when served with process have no relation whatsoever to the contentions of the lawsuit. This is not, strictly speaking, an instance of general jurisdiction. True general jurisdiction is based on an affiliation to the forum so substantial that it *alone* justifies the forum's power to try *all* claims against the defendant by *all* suitors.

F. The Relevance of Consent. Implied consent requires purposeful contact, but express consent is construed as a waiver of the need for purposeful contact.

1. The old "implied consent" cases are easy to accommodate to minimum contacts analysis.

3

a. In these cases, some act by the defendant — selling a product for use in the forum state, or driving a car in the forum state — was deemed sufficient to "appoint" some stranger (such as the Secretary of State) as defendant's "agent" for service of process within the forum state.

b. Under minimum contacts analysis, it is easy to see that the acts that used to trigger implied consent to the involuntary appointment of an in-state agent for service of process were what we would now call *purposeful contacts* with the forum. It is the nature and quality of these purposeful acts that justify the forum state's assertion of jurisdiction over the defendant, and there is no longer any need for some ritual of fictitious appointment of an agent on whom service of process can be made within the boundaries of the forum state. The purposeful contacts with the forum state give that state jurisdictional power over the defendant; all that remains is for that power to be exercised fairly by, *e.g.*, giving the defendant proper notice of the action.

2. When a defendant who has no (other) contacts at all with the forum state has expressly consented to be sued in the forum state, the Supreme Court has made clear that the defendant's consent alone is sufficient to confer on the forum state the power to render a valid judgment.

a. The Supreme Court has treated consent as an *exception* to the general requirement that states can exercise territorial jurisdiction only on the basis of the defendant's minimum contacts with the forum.

b. Because a defendant's consent must have been freely given, rather than obtained by duress or a contract of adhesion, *see The Bremen v. Zapata Off-Shore Co.*, 407 U.S. 1 (1972), it is theoretically possible to treat freely given consent as simply another form of purposeful contact amounting to "minimum contacts" with the forum state. Coerced consent would not be purposeful and, hence, could not be relied upon as basis for territorial jurisdiction.

c. Such a theory of voluntary consent as itself constituting "minimum contacts" is not currently the law. The Supreme Court treats freely given consent as *waiving* the need for minimum contacts rather than as *satisfying* the need for minimum contacts.

G. **Divisible Divorce. The special treatment of domestic relations cases ordained by *Pennoyer* has continued to this day. *Pennoyer* avoided conflict between its limitation of personal jurisdiction to states with physical power over the defendant (or the agent or property of the defendant) and fundamental fairness to abandoned spouses by stipulating in dicta that marriage was a state-created civil status, from which it followed that the state that created a marriage had the power to dissolve the marriage even if the defendant in the divorce proceeding was by then a non-resident who could not be served with process within the state granting the divorce. *Pennoyer* did not address the property and custody consequences of divorce, and this soon led to the phenomenon of "divisible divorce." The modern components and a brief sketch of the rules pertaining to "divisible divorce" are as follows:**

1. *Dissolution.* A valid judgment dissolving a marriage may be granted by the state of domicile of either spouse even if the defendant lacks minimum contacts with the forum state.

a. *Pennoyer* permitted a state to grant a divorce without service of process on the non-resident defendant, but the Court there seemed to assume that the forum state would be the state in which the marriage had occurred and in which the spouses had been jointly domiciled until their separation. It was many decades before the Supreme Court established that either spouse could acquire his or her own separate domicile after a spousal separation and bring suit there for a valid divorce based solely on the plaintiff's newly acquired domicile in a forum totally foreign to the defendant. *Williams v. North Carolina*, 317 U.S. 287 (1942).

b. Modern law recognizes that the state of domicile of the complaining spouse has jurisdiction to grant an annulment or judicial separation as well as a divorce.

2. *Support.* The obligation to provide financial support or alimony to a former spouse is a classic personal obligation. The power of the state of present domicile of either spouse to dissolve the marital status — without regard to the defendant's lack of minimum contacts with that state — does not extend to awarding marital support.

   a. A judgment imposing such an obligation is invalid unless the defendant has minimum contacts with the forum state. *Kulko v. Superior Court, supra.*

      (1) Most states have long-arm statutes that reach as far as federal due process will allow to assert personal jurisdiction over non-resident defendants in marital support cases.

      (2) In states without long-arm statutes that reach to the limits of the Constitution, quasi-in-rem jurisdiction may be invoked if the defendant has both minimum contacts with the forum and possesses property subject to attachment within the forum. (As discussed in Chapter 2, a quasi-in-rem judgment can be enforced only against the attached property.)

   b. Where the spouse suing for support has remained in the state of marital domicile, it is clear that the previous purposeful contacts of the defendant with the forum state as the state of former domicile and spousal cohabitation will constitute the minimum contacts needed to support personal or quasi-in-rem jurisdiction in an action for marital support regardless of where the defendant is presently domiciled.

3. *Property.* The power of the state of present domicile of either spouse to dissolve the marital status does not extend to dividing marital property any more than it extends to awarding marital support.

   a. A court with personal jurisdiction over both former spouses ought to have the power to render a binding final judgment dividing the marital property and determining the respective interests of each spouse in that property. Unfortunately, the law falls short of the desirable.

     Example: In *Fall v. Eastin*, 215 U.S. 1 (1909), the Supreme Court held that the state where real property is located does not have to give full faith and credit to the judgment of another state's court with personal jurisdiction over both parties ordering a conveyance of real property from one former spouse to the other as part of a comprehensive division of marital property.

   b. *Fall* is a fading echo of the local action rule in its old role as a limitation on state court territorial jurisdiction. (*See* the discussion of the local action rule in Chapter 2.) *Fall* is sure to be overruled sooner or later. In the meantime, a court with personal jurisdiction over both parties can render an assuredly binding judgment dividing marital property only with respect to all personal property and so much of the real property as is located within the forum state. While the judgment may purport to govern the disposition of real property located in other states, its enforcement as to this property will depend on the comity of the courts in those states. ("Comity" is discretionary respect for the judgment of a court of another governmental system.)

4. *Custody.* The validity and enforcement of judgments determining child custody was long one of the sorriest areas of modern civil procedure. Cloudy constitutional law and diverse state practices and philosophies created a climate in which former spouses dissatisfied with current custody rights were encouraged to take children to other states in breach of existing custody decrees and sometimes only after obtaining physical power over the bodies of their children by outright kidnapping. It was an expensive and emotionally wrenching crapshoot whether any given state in which a child was presently domiciled would give full faith and credit to a prior custody decree of another state in which the child had previously been

domiciled. Determinations of domicile, always fact-oriented and subject to controversy, were made even more uncertain by differing views over the relationship of a child's domicile to that of the parents, especially when the parents lacked a common domicile. The morass has been substantially drained by the widespread enactment by states of the Uniform Child Custody Jurisdiction Act, followed by congressional enactment of the Federal Parental Kidnapping Prevention Act of 1980, 28 U.S.C. § 1738A. The latter statute requires states to give full faith and credit to custody determinations of a sister state provided that at the time of the custody determination the sister state was the "home state" of the child, as statutorily defined to exclude domicile acquired by a parental attempt to evade the terms of an earlier custody determination. *See Thompson v. Thompson,* 484 U.S. 174 (1987).

5. *Federal courts.* Even when all the other requisites exist for the exercise of jurisdiction based on diversity of citizenship between the parties, by long-standing prudential rule the federal courts will not grant divorces, award alimony, divide marital property, or determine child custody matters. There is unsettled law on the extent to which tort and contract suits for breach of custody and support obligations can be adjudicated by federal trial courts on the basis of diversity jurisdiction.

BURNHAM AND TRANSIENT JURISDICTION

IV. *BURNHAM* **AND TRANSIENT JURISDICTION: NEW QUESTIONS ABOUT THE FUTURE OF MINIMUM CONTACTS DOCTRINE**

A. *International Shoe* **involved a corporate defendant, an imaginary person, for which any attribution of "presence" was necessarily symbolic. Do the minimum contacts principles of *International Shoe* also limit state court territorial jurisdiction over individuals? This question must be answered: "Yes . . . maybe."**

1. The answer is clearly "Yes" when the individual is served with process outside of the forum state.

2. The answer is apparently "Yes" when the individual has received personal service of process within the forum state, but in recently confronting this question the Supreme Court failed to muster a clear majority in support of "minimum contacts analysis" as opposed to other modes of analyzing whether an assertion of state court territorial jurisdiction over an individual defendant is consistent with due process of law. The testing theory for the application of minimum contacts analysis to suits against individuals has been *"transient jurisdiction."* In these cases, an individual is served with process while physically but fleetingly present in the forum state for reasons entirely unrelated to the plaintiff's cause of action.

B. **In *Burnham v. Superior Court,* ___ U.S. ___, 110 S.Ct. 2105 (1990), the Supreme Court upheld transient jurisdiction unanimously, but without a majority opinion.**

1. *Justice Scalia's opinion.* Justice Scalia's opinion announcing the judgment of the Court, joined by Chief Justice Rehnquist and Justice Kennedy and in part by Justice White, emphasized that minimum contacts analysis is simply a guide to the ultimate due process question: whether a state's assertion of territorial jurisdiction is consistent with *"traditional* notions of fair play and substantial justice." (Emphasis added.)

a. To the extent that modern "long-arm" statutes authorize state courts to assert jurisdiction in ways at odds with nineteenth century practice, minimum contacts analysis is properly used to determine if the defendant's due process rights have been violated. But when a state simply continues to assert territorial jurisdiction on grounds already well-established by tradition and common practice at the time the due process clause was ratified in 1868, "traditional notions of fair play and substantial justice" are obviously satisfied. The defendant's physical presence in the forum state when served with process was a familiar and virtually universal basis for state court territorial jurisdiction in 1868, and remains so today. It follows that physical presence must be a sufficient contact to satisfy due process, despite the lack of any relationship between that contact and the cause of action.

b. In the concluding part of his opinion, joined only by the Chief Justice and Justice Kennedy, Justice Scalia called into question the continuing validity of *Shaffer v. Heitner* by asserting that traditional procedures in widespread use when the due process clause was enacted in 1868 are immune from current due process invalidation, save (possibly) for once-prevalent procedures now abandoned by all but a very small minority of states. Justice Scalia's reasoning, although purporting to endorse the holding of *Shaffer*, is incompatible with *Shaffer*'s requirement that a highly traditional form of state court jurisdiction widely practiced in 1868, quasi-in-rem jurisdiction, be invalidated for lack of due process unless the owner of the attached property has minimum contacts with the forum state.

2. *Justice White's concurring opinion.* Justice White did not join that part of Justice Scalia's opinion that went on to declare *Shaffer v. Heitner* inapplicable to traditional court procedures that were common practice in 1868. In a brief concurring opinion signed by him alone, Justice White expressly reaffirmed *Shaffer*'s holding that the Supreme Court "has the authority under the [Fourteenth] Amendment to examine even traditionally accepted procedures and declare them invalid." While indicating that involuntary presence might make transient jurisdiction violative of due process, Justice White appears to have concluded that the purposeful presence of a defendant in the forum at the time of service is always enough to make the forum's assertion of territorial jurisdiction over the defendant consistent with due process of law.

3. *Justice Brennan's concurring opinion.* Justice Brennan's concurring opinion was joined by Justices Marshall, Blackmun, and O'Connor. Justice Brennan concurred in the Court's judgment upholding transient jurisdiction, but only after following the conventional steps of minimum contacts analysis under *International Shoe* and *Shaffer v. Heitner*. Objecting strongly to Justice Scalia's departure from the rationale of *Shaffer*, Justice Brennan deemed history and tradition relevant to — but not dispositive of — the ultimate question: whether an assertion of state court territorial jurisdiction "comport[s] with contemporary notions of due process." Assuming that service of process occurs while an individual's presence in the forum state is knowing and voluntary, that presence constitutes purposeful contact that is sufficient of itself to make the assertion of territorial jurisdiction reasonable.

4. *Justice Stevens' concurring opinion.* Justice Stevens joined none of the other opinions, noting that when *Shaffer* was decided he had not joined it because he objected to its "unnecessarily broad reach." He declared that the present opinions of both Justice Scalia and Justice Brennan shared the same vice. For Justice Stevens, history, fairness, and common sense made *Burnham* an easy case to decide without setting standards for future cases.

5. *Summary: Burnham* suggests that the Court is retreating from its insistence in *Shaffer* that *all* assertions of state court territorial jurisdiction must pass muster under minimum contacts analysis. In the meantime, *Shaffer* continues to command shaky support for its more abstract proposition that even traditionally accepted procedures must satisfy contemporary standards of due process. There is no current majority, however, ready to agree that "minimum contacts analysis" is the proper measure of contemporary due process except when a non-resident defendant has been served with process outside the forum state. Justice Brennan's retirement just weeks after *Burnham* was decided makes the current state of minimum contacts doctrine even more volatile.

V.   **STEP-BY-STEP GUIDE TO MINIMUM CONTACTS ANALYSIS**

A. **It is important to remember that, until the Supreme Court speaks, there are no guaranteed "right" answers to minimum contacts problems. There is still a great deal of flux in the precedent and policy from which your answers must be constructed. Our five-step approach to minimum contacts analysis organizes and explicates the various strands of minimum contacts doctrine previously discussed. If you follow this approach, you are unlikely to miss any relevant issue in a minimum contacts problem.**

B. **Summary of our Five-step Approach**

Step 1: Does the defendant have *any* contacts with the forum state?

Step 2: Are the contacts you have identified *purposeful* contacts?

Step 3: Are the contacts you have identified so continuous, systematic, and substantial as to justify *general jurisdiction*?

Step 4: If the forum lacks general jurisdiction over the defendant, are the defendant's purposeful contacts with the forum sufficiently related to the litigation to constitute the "minimum contacts" that confer on the forum the *power* to exercise *specific* jurisdiction?

Step 5: Granted that there exist the requisite "minimum contacts" between the defendant and the forum, under all the circumstances of the case is it *reasonable* for the forum to exercise *specific* jurisdiction?

C. **Step-by-step Explication of our Approach**

Step 1. *Any contacts?*

a.   In *International Shoe*, the Supreme Court summarized minimum contacts analysis as follows: "Whether due process is satisfied must depend ... upon the quality and nature of the activity in relation to the fair and orderly administration of the laws which it was the purpose of the due process clause to insure. That clause does not contemplate that a state may make binding a judgment in personam against an individual or corporate defendant with which the state has *no* contacts, ties, or relations." (Emphasis added.)

b.   At this step, we are just trying to get past the "no contacts, ties, or relations" stage of our analysis. Your initial inquiry should focus on the activities of the defendant that might in any way serve to affiliate the defendant with the forum. Your survey of possible contacts should be as broad as possible, leaving to future steps the decision whether to discount or discard some contacts because they lack purposefulness or relatedness to the plaintiff's cause of action.

Step 2. *Purposeful contacts?*

a.   The Supreme Court has not fully developed a theory of purposefulness. The best summary we can offer is that purposefulness is a fairness constraint on the assertion of territorial jurisdiction over a non-resident. Only fair contacts, *i.e.*, purposeful contacts, will be counted in deciding whether the defendant's conduct is such that she should be subject to the forum's jurisdiction. The dominant considerations seem to be:

(1)   *voluntary and self-serving conduct* such that the defendant's contacts with the forum resulted from actions undertaken on her own, and in her own behalf; and

(2)   *foreseeability of forum litigation* such that a reasonable defendant would have known that by engaging in her voluntary and self-serving conduct she was incurring the risk of having to defend against suit in the forum's courts.

b.   Clearly, actions taken under gun-to-the-head duress are not purposeful. The Supreme Court has not dwelt much on the subtleties of the myriad other circumstances that impair our control of our lives. This makes it important that you keep nagging questions about purposefulness in mind throughout the remainder of your minimum contacts analysis.

(1) On the one hand, contacts resulting from egregious fraud or deceit perpetrated on the defendant are likely to be deemed non-purposeful; on the other hand, contacts resulting from the defendant's bad luck or mistake or involuntary acts while voluntarily intoxicated, are more likely to be counted as purposeful.

(2) For so long as the Supreme Court continues to stress the importance of purpose-fulness without elaborating its meaning, many situations may present themselves in which the unsettled meaning of "purposefulness" will permit good faith argu-ment that an apparently affiliating contact should not be the basis for jurisdiction because the conduct giving rise to the contact was not purposeful.

3

(a) *Voluntary conduct? Hanson v. Denckla, supra,* is the case which added the concept of purposefulness to minimum contacts analysis. It provides the classic illustration of "involuntary" and hence non-purposeful conduct, which rendered jurisdictionally irrelevant a series of otherwise substantial contacts with the forum.

i) The relevant defendant was a Delaware trust company that had agreed to act as trustee of a trust established by a Philadelphia matron. The matron (the "settlor" of the trust) later moved to Florida. The trust company kept right on sending trust business by mail to the settlor, unconcerned whether her address was in Pennsylvania or Florida. Income, instructions on trust administration, revisions of the appointments of beneficiaries of the trust — all flowed between Delaware and Florida just as they had flowed between Delaware and Pennsylvania. But the Supreme Court ruled, 5-4, that the trust company could not be subjected without its consent to the personal jurisdiction of a Florida court.

ii) The extensive contacts of the trust company with Florida were deemed not purposeful because they resulted from the unilateral decision of the settlor to remove herself to Florida after the trust had been established. In this special sense, the contacts with Florida established by the trust company in continuing to do business with its client after her move to Florida were not voluntary contacts and, hence, were not purposeful contacts.

(b) *Self-serving conduct?* The classic illustration of intentional conduct that was deemed non-purposeful in light of the defendant's motivation is provided by *Kulko v. Superior Court, supra.*

i) The defendant, a resident of New York, was the divorced father of two children. The terms of the divorce had granted custody of both children to the father during the school year and to the mother during vacations. The mother had moved to California and remarried. The year after the divorce, as the couple's 11-year-old daughter prepared to leave New York to spend her Christmas vacation in California, she asked to remain in California. The father consented, bought her a one-way ticket, and sent her clothing with her. The daughter thereafter spent her vacations with her father and the remainder of the year with her mother. The couple's son, one-year older than their daughter, followed in his sister's footsteps two-years later. His move to California was arranged with and paid for by the mother without the father's knowledge or assistance, but with his retrospective consent. Shortly after the son took up residence with the mother, the mother sued the father in a California court to increase his

$3,000 per year child support obligation in light of the reversal of the earlier custody arrangement.

    ii) The California Supreme Court upheld jurisdiction over the non-resident father, relying for the requisite purposeful contact on the father's course of conduct in sending his daughter to California to live there with her mother. The United States Supreme Court reversed. "We cannot accept the proposition that [the father's] acquiescence in [his daughter's] desire to live with her mother conferred jurisdiction in the California courts in this action. A father who agrees, in the interests of family harmony and his children's preferences, to allow them to spend more time in California than was required under a separation agreement can hardly be said to have 'purposefully availed himself' of the 'benefits and protection' of California's laws." The benefits and protection of California law enjoyed by the daughter in the form of California's schools, police and the like, were "essentially benefits to the child, not the father, and in any event were not benefits that [the father] purposefully sought for himself."

  (c) *Foreseeability of forum litigation?* The Court has sometimes articulated its concern for purposefulness in terms of the "foreseeability" that the defendant will be "haled" into court, *i.e.*, that the defendant's actions might embroil the defendant in litigation in the forum state. *See, e.g., World-Wide Volkswagen v. Woodson, supra.*

    i) "Purposefulness" so conceived is seen as protecting unsuspecting defendants from being "ambushed" by burdensome suits in remote forums.

      a) If only purposeful contacts can be the basis for territorial jurisdiction, and if purposeful contacts are by definition activities connecting persons to a state in such a way that they can foresee the risk of being subjected to the jurisdiction of that state, then potential defendants may rationally choose either to avoid the risk of being sued in an undesirable forum by avoiding or ending the purposeful contact with that state, or to accept the risk of suit and insure against it as they see fit.

      b) This conception of purposefulness defines purposeful contacts as those that were (i) within the *control* of the defendant and (ii) were such that a *reasonable person would know* that the contacts might subject the defendant to suit in the forum in question. Because the defendant chose "purposefully" to act in whatever way created the contact, the defendant may justly be burdened with the foreseeable jurisdictional consequences of that choice.

    ii) The connection between "foreseeability" and "purposefulness" has been a particularly troublesome concern in products liability litigation against defendants whose products reached the forum indirectly via the "stream of commerce." As previously noted, in the 1988 *Asahi* case, the Supreme Court split 4-4 on whether the foreseeability that a component manufacturer's part would be incorporated in a product sold in the forum state, was sufficient to constitute purposeful contact between the component manufacturer and the forum state.

Step 3. *General jurisdiction?*

  a. General jurisdiction is an analytical shortcut. If you can show it exists, you don't need to examine the relationship between the defendant's contacts and a particular plaintiff's cause of action or weigh the reasonableness of permitting the forum to adjudicate that particular case against the defendant.

b. As previously discussed, there are some clear rules and some rough edges to the concept of general jurisdiction.

    (1) At this point in your analysis, you should be looking first for the clear-cut instances of general jurisdiction:

        (a) the defendant is a domestic corporation, *i.e.*, it has been incorporated under the law of the forum state; or

        (b) the defendant is a foreign corporation that has appointed a resident agent for unrestricted service of process in the forum state; or

        (c) the defendant is an individual domiciled in the forum state; or

        (d) the defendant is a non-resident individual, *i.e.*, domiciled outside the forum state, who has appointed a resident agent for unrestricted service of process in the forum state; or

        (e) the defendant is a non-resident individual served with process while voluntarily present in the forum state. (Such "transient jurisdiction" is not true general jurisdiction but the distinction is of no importance in deciding whether you need to go past Step 3 of your minimum contacts analysis.)

    (2) You should also consider whether foreign corporations or non-resident individuals with extensive business activities in the forum state might be subject to its general jurisdiction despite their failure to have appointed resident agents, where local law authorizes general jurisdiction over business concerns "doing business" in the state, as determined by the dollar volume of their sales or other evidence of continuous, systematic and substantial general business activity in the forum state.

Step 4. *Power* to exercise *specific* jurisdiction?

    a. Distinguishing general jurisdiction (**Step 3**) from specific jurisdiction (**Steps 4** and **5**)

        (1) In a loose sense, general jurisdiction is a theory of "maximum contacts." You start out first by surveying the defendant's contacts with the forum (**Step 1**) and then by sorting out the purposeful from the non-purposeful contacts (**Step 2**). If the magnitude of the purposeful contacts exceeds the threshold for general jurisdiction, you have the "maximum contacts" that permit the forum to adjudicate any claim whatsoever against that defendant.

        (2) If the purposeful contacts fall short of the "maximum contacts" threshold, the question remains whether these contacts amount to the mysterious quantum of "minimum contacts" that, in the context of a particular lawsuit, will suffice for specific jurisdiction.

    b. Distinguishing between the "power" component of specific jurisdiction (**Step 4**) and the "reasonableness" component of specific jurisdiction (**Step 5**)

        (1) The essence of specific jurisdiction is that the same contacts by the same defendant with the same forum may give that forum jurisdiction over the defendant with respect to one lawsuit but not with respect to other lawsuits against the same defendant. Variation in both the nature of the claims and the nature of the claimants can affect whether a particular lawsuit against a given defendant is or is not within the specific jurisdiction of the forum. **Step 4** and **Step 5** of our minimum contacts analysis help you to identify the relevant variables and to understand how they work.

        (2) "Power" and "reasonableness" in minimum contacts analysis

            (a) For many years the process of answering whether specific jurisdiction exists was seen as an integrated, seat-of-the-pants process of "considering all the circumstances" and deciding whether the exercise of jurisdiction would be

3

consistent with "fair play and substantial justice." A "yes" answer yielded the conclusion that "minimum contacts" existed; a "no" answer indicated that they did not.

(b) The modern approach is to break down the process into two discrete steps. The *penultimate* question concerns the existence of jurisdictional *power*; the *ultimate* question concerns the *reasonableness* of exercising that power. *See Burger King v. Rudzewicz, supra; World-Wide Volkswagen v. Woodson, supra.*

    i) First, determine whether the purposeful contacts qualify as the "minimum contacts" that give the forum state the *power*, within a federal system of territorially defined states and co-equal state sovereignty, to assert jurisdiction *in this one* case over a non-resident defendant.

        a) Such a defendant is, by definition, someone whose affairs are regulated principally by the governments of whatever other states have general jurisdiction over the defendant based on domicile or the other forms of "maximum contacts." There has to be some compelling reason for this particular forum state to exercise jurisdictional power over a defendant whose legal relations are, for the most part, not the business of that state.

        b) In determining whether the non-resident defendant's contacts with the forum state are sufficient within the framework of our federal system to give that state the power of specific jurisdiction, the focus is exclusively on the relationship between the defendant, the forum, and the cause of action.

    ii) If a court determines that the defendant's purposeful contacts constitute "minimum contacts," it must confront the ultimate question of the reasonability of exercising specific jurisdiction. The focus of analysis widens at this stage to consider not only the relationship between the defendant, the forum, and the cause of action, but also the set of additional reasonableness factors that we discuss in **Step 5**.

    iii) The Court's current terminology refers to the "power" step as the point at which it is determined whether "minimum contacts" exist. The final step of "minimum contacts analysis" grants that minimum contacts exist, but weighs whether they are a "reasonable" basis for exercising jurisdiction, all things considered. *Burger King, supra.* Thus, it is possible for minimum contacts to be found to exist, but for the exercise of specific jurisdiction to be so unreasonable that it would violate the right of the defendant to due process of law.

(c) We proceed in the remainder of **Step 4** to analyze the "power" component of specific jurisdiction: whether "minimum contacts" exist. **Step 5** deals with the "reasonableness" component of specific jurisdiction: whether the minimum contacts are, in light of other relevant circumstances, a reasonable basis for the exercise of jurisdiction.

c. The Problem of "relatedness"

    (1) Whether "minimum contacts" exist depends on whether the defendant's purposeful contacts are somehow related to the litigation over which the forum's specific jurisdiction would be exercised. The "essential foundation" of specific jurisdiction is a three-way relationship between the defendant, the forum, and the litigation. *Helicopteros Nacionales de Colombia, S.A. v. Hall*, 466 U.S. 408 (1984).

    (2) The Supreme Court has raised but not resolved the question of *how direct* a relationship there must be between the defendant's contacts and the plaintiff's

cause of action in order for the contacts to qualify as minimum contacts. "[W]e decline to reach the questions (1) whether the terms 'arising out of' and 'related to' describe different connections between a cause of action and a defendant's contacts with a forum, and (2) what sort of tie between a cause of action and a defendant's contacts with a forum is necessary to a determination that either connection exists." *Helicopteros, supra.*

(3) A host of "different connections" — not just two — may exist between a defendant's contacts and a defendant's alleged liabilities.

    (a) The most direct connection between contacts and a cause of action is, of course, when the cause of action arises directly out the contacts — when one or more of the elements of the cause of action is also a purposeful contact with the forum state.

    Example: Tourist and Victim are involved in an automobile collision in Forum. Victim sues Tourist in Forum, seeking damages for injuries caused by Tourist's negligent driving. Tourist's automobile trip through Forum is Tourist's only purposeful contact with Forum. Forum may assert specific adjudication over Tourist to adjudicate Victim's cause of action for negligent driving because that cause of action arises directly out of Tourist's purposeful contact with Forum, *i.e.*, Tourist's decision to drive on the highways of Forum.

    (b) It is easy to imagine a host of less direct but still "related" connections between a defendant, a forum, and a cause of action.

    Example: Suppose that after the accident Tourist, who is unconscious, is taken to a hospital in an ambulance. While Tourist is hospitalized, her car is stolen. The car thief injures a pedestrian while driving the stolen car. As before, Tourist's only purposeful contact with Forum is driving on its highways. The ambulance company sues Tourist for the cost of transporting her to the hospital. The pedestrian sues Tourist for the injuries caused by the car thief, relying on a Forum statute that makes the registered owner of an automobile vicariously liable for the negligence of any driver of the vehicle. Both suits are "related" to Tourist's operation of her car on the highways of Forum, but neither arises as "directly" from that purposeful contact as does Victim's suit against Tourist.

d. "Relatedness" in theory and practice

(1) *International Shoe* suggested that the quantum of purposeful contact and the degree of relatedness of those contacts should jointly be considered in deciding whether minimum contacts exist, so that few contacts would suffice only if they were directly related to the cause of action, and proportionately more contacts would be required as the relatedness of the contacts diminished.

(2) In extreme cases, the Supreme Court has approved *International Shoe's* suggestion that, in the calculus of minimum contacts, the significance of contacts varies inversely with their relatedness.

    (a) *Perkins v. Benguet Consolidated Mining Co.*, 342 U.S. 437 (1952), the leading Supreme Court case on general jurisdiction, established that entirely unrelated contacts will confer jurisdictional power on the forum when they are sufficiently continuous, systematic, and substantial.

    (b) In *McGee v. International Life Insurance Co.*, 355 U.S. 220 (1957), the Supreme Court upheld specific jurisdiction over a foreign corporation that had but a single customer in the forum state when the litigation concerned the defendant's liability on the contract of insurance it had sold to that single customer. Legions of lower court out-of-state motorist suits are analytically identical to *McGee*.

(3) The Supreme Court has remained silent since *Helicopteros, supra,* on the proper approach to the intermediate case, where the cause of action does not arise *directly* from the defendant's contacts but is (more or less) related to those contacts. The Court continues to phrase the relatedness requirement as "'arise out of or relate to,'" quoting the fence-straddling language of *Helicopteros. See Burger King v. Rudzewicz, supra.*

(4) There is great theoretical appeal to adopting *International Shoe's* suggestion that the significance of contacts varies inversely to their relatedness across the range of relatedness. But *Burnham* cautions against expecting the Supreme Court to change present practice in the name of theoretical integrity.

(5) The soundest approach at present is to classify purposeful contacts as either "related" or "unrelated," with doubtful cases classified as "related."

   (a) This requires you to ignore the reality that contacts actually exhibit graduated degrees of relatedness — you are forced to classify shades of grey as either "black" or "white."

   (b) The reason for resolving doubt in favor of "related" status is that an undue attenuation of the relationship between minimum contacts and the cause of action can still be considered at **Step 5** as a factor arguing against the reasonableness of exercising jurisdiction.

Step 5. Is it *reasonable* for the forum to exercise specific jurisdiction?

a. *International Shoe* emphasized that minimum contacts analysis entails more than a mere mechanical counting of the relevant contacts. A subjective weighing of the contacts is required in order to determine whether, in light of "the quality and nature of the activity in relation to the fair and orderly administration of the laws …, the maintenance of the … suit … involves an unreasonable or undue procedure."

b. When the weight of the purposeful contacts of the defendant with the forum state is so great that the forum has general jurisdiction over the defendant, it is *per se* reasonable for the forum to exercise its jurisdiction.

c. When the defendant's purposeful contacts qualify as "minimum contacts" but are insufficient for general jurisdiction, a number of additional factors are relevant to whether it is reasonable for the forum to exercise specific jurisdiction over the defendant.

(1) As recently summarized in *Burger King Corp. v. Rudzewicz, supra,* these "reasonableness factors" include (but are not limited to):

   (a) the burden on the defendant;

   (b) the forum state's interest in adjudicating the dispute;

   (c) the plaintiff's interest in obtaining convenient and effective relief;

   (d) the interstate judicial system's interest in obtaining the most efficient resolution of controversies; and

   (e) the shared interest of the several states in furthering fundamental substantive social policies.

(2) Explication of the *Burger King* reasonableness factors

   (a) The "burden on the defendant" factor entails consideration of a host of *relative convenience* concerns: *e.g.,* is the defendant an individual of impaired health or modest wealth, or a multi-national corporation? Is the forum easily reached

3

from the defendant's state of domicile? Will the case come to trial more quickly in the forum or in some available alternative forum? Many more illustrative concerns could be added. Virtually any factor relevant to a motion for a stay or transfer on forum non conveniens grounds may be advanced as an argument against the reasonability of an exercise of specific jurisdiction, including (for whatever weight it will be given) the unfavorable substantive law that would be applied under the forum's choice of law rules.

(b) The "forum state's interest" factor is most frequently implicated when the plaintiff is a resident of the forum state, especially if the nature of the plaintiff's injuries is likely to reduce the plaintiff to depending on public support (welfare) if compensation is not obtained from the defendant. This factor is also implicated if forum state law and choice of law rules seek to serve so important state public policy, such as the regulation of out-of-state activity that poses a severe economic or environmental threat to the welfare of forum state residents.

(c) The "plaintiff's interest" factor is by and large the counterpart to the "burden on the defendant" factor. All arguments that would be relevant in opposition to a forum non conveniens motion would be relevant here — lack of a truly available alternative forum, lack of adequate discovery or other procedural benefits in another forum, or unfavorable choice of law. (*See* the discussion of the *Reyno* case in Chapter 2, however, for a reminder that choice of law arguments carry little weight in forum non conveniens determinations.)

(d) The "interstate judicial system's interest" factor directs concern to the efficiency and federalism costs of asserting specific jurisdiction in the case at hand. If similar litigation is already pending in other states where this plaintiff could easily gain jurisdiction over the defendant, allowing the plaintiff's chosen forum to proceed with this splinter suit not only makes the litigation unnecessarily costly to the defendant but also shows disrespect for the mutual sovereignty interests of other states already engaged in resolving the same or a related dispute. For instance, if numerous suits arising from a major airplane crash are already pending in State *A*, where the defendant is clearly subject to the forum's territorial jurisdiction, why stretch to find that marginal minimum contacts are a reasonable basis for allowing this plaintiff to bring her single suit in State *Z*?

(e) The "shared interest of the several states" factor directs concern to the risk of arbitrariness in allowing one forum to advance its public policies by adjudicating a dispute touching many states and implicating no less their public policies. Just as the "burden on the defendant" and the "plaintiff's interest" factors invite countervailing arguments about the reasonability of jurisdiction in terms of private, party-oriented concerns, so do the "forum state's interest" and the "shared interest of the several states" factors invite countervailing arguments about public, forum-oriented concerns, with the "interstate judicial system's interest" factor tending also to be a counterweight to concern for the "forum state's interest."

(3) An important new reasonableness factor was introduced in *Asahi Metal Industry Co., Ltd. v. Superior Court, supra*. Despite the lack of a majority opinion on the issue of purposefulness, eight Justices in *Asahi* agreed that "the procedural and substantive policies of other *nations* whose interests are affected by the assertion of jurisdiction by the [forum] court" was an important reasonableness factor. (Emphasis in original.) Although the Court indicated that this new factor in its minimum contacts calculus of reasonableness was analogous to the previously articulated factor of the "shared interests of the several States," it is to be given

even greater weight. "'Great care and reserve should be exercised when extending our notions of personal jurisdiction into the international field.'" The difficulty of establishing that it is reasonable to assert jurisdiction over an alien defendant is further increased by the *Asahi* Court's mandate that the "burden on the defendant" factor be given special weight in transnational litigation because of "the unique burdens placed upon one who must defend oneself in a foreign legal system."

d. Operation of reasonableness factors in the marginal case

(1) *When reasonableness analysis favors the plaintiff: the burden of proof as to reasonableness at Step 4*

(a) If the outcome of **Step 4** of our minimum contacts analysis is doubtful — it is arguable whether minimum contacts exist at all, and if they do they are the bare minimum — the plaintiff can invoke the reasonableness factors to help meet her burden, as the party seeking to invoke the forum's jurisdiction, of establishing the requisite facts. "These considerations sometimes serve to establish the reasonableness of jurisdiction upon a lesser showing of minimum contacts than would otherwise be required." *Burger King, supra.*

(b) In other words, if the reasonableness factors distinctly favor trial in the plaintiff's chosen forum — that is clearly the most convenient forum, trial there imposes no significant burden on the defendant, trial elsewhere would significantly burden the plaintiff, forum state interests would be served, and other states' interests would not be offended — the Supreme Court is prepared to fudge a bit in counting up the minimum contacts required at **Step 4** of our analysis.

(2) *When reasonableness analysis favors the defendant: the burden of proof of unreasonableness at Step 5*

(a) If the outcome of **Step 4** clearly establishes that minimum contacts exist — there is no question that the defendant engaged in purposeful contact with the forum state that is directly related to the cause of action — the defendant can invoke the reasonableness factors to prohibit the forum state's exercise of specific jurisdiction only by presenting a "compelling case that the presence of [these] factors would render jurisdiction unreasonable." *Burger King, supra.*

(b) Normally the plaintiff who is invoking a particular forum's jurisdiction has the burden of proving the facts necessary to support that jurisdiction. But after **Step 4** of the process, the Supreme Court has reversed that burden. If the plaintiff carries her burden at **Step 4** of the process by proving the existence of minimum contacts, the burden at **Step 5** of the process shifts to the defendant to establish a compelling factual basis for the conclusion that the exercise of jurisdiction would be unreasonable.

FEDERAL SUBJECT-MATTER JURISDICTION AND RELATED DOCTRINES AFFECTING CHOICE OF A FEDERAL FORUM

▶ **CHAPTER SUMMARY**

**FEDERAL SUBJECT-MATTER JURISDICTION AND RELATED DOCTRINES
AFFECTING CHOICE OF A FEDERAL FORUM**

INTRODUCTION: In Chapter 2's treatment of the choice of forum, we reserved discussion of the rules of federal-subject matter jurisdiction that affect that choice. Now we fill that gap. Federal jurisdiction is one of the most complex and demanding fields of study in all of American law. It combines the subtleties of constitutional law with the technicalities of a procedural code. In most law schools, its fine points are explored in a rigorous upper-division course. But the study of federal jurisdiction begins in Civil Procedure, where students are expected to know the general doctrines and basic rules of federal jurisdiction that allow civil cases to be tried in federal trial courts. There are two major categories of cases eligible for trial in federal court: *federal question* litigation in which federal jurisdiction is based on the characteristics of the issues, and *diversity* cases, in which federal jurisdiction is based on the characteristics of the parties. Both categories feature quirky and arbitrary rules that make it foolhardy to try to "wing it" with only a general idea that federal jurisdiction exists whenever a case involves an issue of federal law or has been brought by parties from different states.

We begin our discussion of federal jurisdiction by examining its constitutional and jurisprudential context. The potential scope of federal subject-matter jurisdiction allowable under the Constitution, already rather narrow in comparison to the subject-matter jurisdiction of an ordinary state court, has been further limited in practice by legislative and judicial concern for "federalism" and the "separation of powers." Next we review the basic structure of the federal court system. Although the scope of federal jurisdiction is limited, the presence of the federal court system is nationwide. Turning to the statutory rules of federal subject-matter jurisdiction, we cover federal question jurisdiction first. Next comes the statutory scheme for diversity jurisdiction. The major issues are the differing degrees of diversity required under the Constitution and the diversity statutes, the rules for determining the states of citizenship of the parties, and the statutory criteria for a minimum amount in controversy.

Two doctrines represent special applications and extensions of the basic principles of federal question and diversity jurisdiction. *Removal jurisdiction* allows a defendant under certain conditions to invoke federal jurisdiction over a diversity or federal question case, even if the plaintiff has chosen to file the suit in state court. *Supplemental jurisdiction,* noted here but discussed fully in Chapter 6, extends the jurisdiction of the federal courts to other claims and parties that are appropriately connected to federal question and diversity litigation.

It is quite possible for a case that qualifies for federal jurisdiction to be filed in the wrong federal district court. Federal venue rules vary for diversity and federal question cases, and you must also be familiar with federal rules governing changes of venue. While defects of venue do not invalidate judgments if no objection is raised, the opportunity for a well-grounded venue objection has a significant influence on a plaintiff's choice of forum.

Our last topic is the *Erie* doctrine. It provides, roughly, that state law, not federal law, is the substantive law to be applied in federal lawsuits unless Congress has specified to the contrary. On the other hand, federal courts have wide latitude to apply their own procedural rules. Mastery of the *Erie* doctrine and its application to federal changes of venue is essential to understanding how the choice between a federal or state forum may affect the outcome of a lawsuit.

Special update: Congress enacted a number of important changes to the law of federal jurisdiction and venue in the Judicial Improvements Act of 1990, Act of December 1, 1990, Public Law 101-650, 104 Stat. 5089. This Act went into effect immediately. We have fully incorporated the new law into this outline.

**GENERAL PRIN-
CIPLES OF FEDERAL
SUBJECT-MATTER
JURISDICTION**

I.   GENERAL PRINCIPLES OF FEDERAL SUBJECT-MATTER JURISDICTION

    A.   The existence of federal subject-matter jurisdiction over a particular controversy is *the exception, not the rule.* Unlike state court systems, which have broad constitutional

authority to resolve all ordinary civil disputes, the federal courts' subject-matter jurisdiction is strictly limited in scope.

1. *Basic constitutional theory.* The Constitution provides for dual systems of government with shared sovereignty. Federal power is supreme in its sphere but limited in its scope.

   a. State governments have residual or background authority, which is qualified only by the superseding power granted to the federal government. When federal governmental power has been validly asserted, it controls over any conflicting state law pursuant to the supremacy clause of Article VI of the Constitution.

   b. Most federal powers authorized by the Constitution are not self-executing and require implementation by one of the branches of the federal government — Congress, the President, or the Courts — in order to displace state law with supreme federal law.

      (1) Which branch has implementing authority as to some particular federal power? That can present deep issues of *separation of powers.* The Constitution complicates separation of powers issues by on the one hand dividing up governmental power into legislative, executive, and judicial powers, and on the other hand allowing its allocation of these powers to overlap so as to create a system of checks and balances. The President has a veto power over Congress, the Supreme Court can hold legislative or executive action unconstitutional, the President appoints Supreme Court Justices with the advice and consent of the Senate, and so forth.

      (2) How readily should the various federal branches of government act to implement their constitutional powers, thereby displacing state law? How broadly should federal power be construed in the doubtful case? These questions present deep issues of *federalism.* The idea of federalism is that federal power, although potentially vast, should be held in check in order to maintain healthy state governments.

   c. The power of "judicial review" permits federal courts to invalidate unconstitutional Acts of Congress and Executive Orders. Because the Constitution provides only implicitly for judicial review of the constitutionality of legislative and executive action, and because it brings the only unelected branch of government into conflict with the political branches, federal courts exercise judicial review with great restraint. This tradition of "judicial restraint" carries over to the exercise of federal jurisdiction generally, as part of a spirit of caution that combines separation of powers concerns (the federal courts should keep a low profile in government except when events beyond judicial control thrust the judiciary unwillingly but unflinchingly into the spotlight) with federalism concerns (the federal government should be careful to maintain the health of state governments, and when federal power is to be increased at state expense, the initiative should come from the elected branches of the federal government).

2. *Article III and federal judicial power.* Article III authorizes Congress to create the nationwide federal trial courts and specifies the kinds of cases Congress can authorize them to try. The structure of Article III encourages political debate over the scope of federal jurisdiction but insulates federal judges from political pressure.

   a. Article III leaves to Congress the choice whether or not to create *any* lower federal trial and appellate courts and authorizes Congress to assign these courts jurisdiction in very broad categories of cases. Congress has always honored the idea of federalism by choosing to limit the scope and jurisdiction of the lower federal court system to far less than that authorized by Article III.

   b. Congress's vast power over federal jurisdiction does not extend to vast power over federal judges. Article III, § 1, guarantees the independence of federal judges, once appointed, by providing that they cannot be removed from office except by impeachment for serious misconduct, and their pay cannot be reduced.

c. Article III authorizes federal jurisdiction only in specified categories of "cases" and "controversies." This "case or controversy" requirement is in addition to the requirement that a federally adjudicated dispute fall within one of the prescribed categories.

(1) No distinction has developed in practice between the meaning of "case" and that of "controversy." But together these terms constitute a "case or controversy" requirement that excludes disputes that are "nonjusticiable" because they are unduly theoretical or speculative.

(2) Examples of the various justiciability doctrines that are rooted in Article III's case or controversy requirement are:

(a) the "standing" doctrine that requires the parties to have a concrete stake in the outcome of the case;

(b) the "mootness" doctrine that requires dismissal of a case if the actions of the parties or the simple passage of time has dispelled the controversy between the parties;

(c) the "ripeness" doctrine that precludes premature adjudication of issues where injury is threatened but is not certain to occur; and

(d) the "political question" doctrine that requires a dispute to be capable of judicial resolution without undue interference in the responsibilities of the Congress and the President.

B. **Article III's jurisdictional categories of cases and controversies fall into two groups. Some tie federal jurisdiction to the character of the *issues* in a case, others to the characters of the *parties* to the case.**

1. *Federal question jurisdiction* is the most important issue-based category of Article III. The judicial power extends to "all Cases, in Law and Equity, arising under this Constitution, the Laws of the United States, and Treaties made, or which shall be made, under their Authority." This is also referred to as the "arising under" or "federal claim" jurisdiction.

2. *Diversity jurisdiction* is the term for a cluster of party-based categories where Article III permits Congress to grant federal jurisdiction without regard to the federal nature, if any, of the issues to be adjudicated. The two most important types are:

a. "Controversies ... between Citizens of different States." This is the classic form of diversity jurisdiction.

b. "Controversies ... between a State, or the Citizens thereof, and foreign States, Citizens or Subjects." This form of diversity jurisdiction, applicable where one of the parties is a foreign sovereign or a non-resident citizen of a foreign government, is called the "alienage jurisdiction."

C. **The *Article III* grants of federal question and diversity jurisdiction have been *construed very broadly* in terms of the power given to Congress.**

1. *The federal "ingredient" test.* If Congress wants to, it can authorize federal jurisdiction of a case in which there is any possible issue of federal law that might conceivably control the outcome, whether or not the issue will actually arise, and whether or not the issue has already been determined by binding Supreme Court precedent. This extraordinarily liberal test for when a case "arises under" federal law within the meaning of Article III is called the *ingredient* test, following the language of Chief Justice Marshall in *Osborn v. Bank of United States*, 22 U.S. 738 (1824).

2. *The "minimal diversity" test.* If Congress wants to, it can authorize federal jurisdiction of a case in which there is any diversity of citizenship between any pair of parties with opposing interests, even if the parties are named as codefendants, and even if all other

parties are citizens of the same state. This extraordinarily liberal test for when there is "diversity of citizenship" within the meaning of Article III was the basis for the Supreme Court approving the constitutionality of the Federal Interpleader Act (discussed in Chapter 6) in *State Farm Fire & Casualty Co. v. Tashire*, 386 U.S. 523 (1967).

D. **The *jurisdictional statutes* Congress has enacted have been *interpreted much more narrowly* than the parallel provisions of Article III.**

1. The identical words — "arising under" and "diversity" — have been interpreted much more narrowly when transposed from Article III into a jurisdictional statute. We explore the narrow statutory meanings of these terms in later sections of this chapter.

2. The Supreme Court's philosophy in interpreting jurisdictional statutes more narrowly than Article III is to give Congress wide power to expand the role of the federal courts in American life, but to demand unambiguous evidence that this is what Congress wants.

3. This philosophy of grudging interpretation of jurisdictional statutes has been accompanied by the development of a group of judicially developed "prudential" doctrines further limiting federal jurisdiction.

   a. The various "justiciability" doctrines rooted in the constitutional requirement of a "case or controversy" — especially the law of "standing" — have been extended by the Supreme Court far beyond what the Constitution requires. Thus, the federal courts routinely refuse to adjudicate sensitive cases because, in the judges' opinion, it is unwise to do so at the present time or with the present parties.

   b. An entire body of doctrine called "abstention" represents the federal courts' systematic development of decisional law refusing to decide cases where relevant issues of state law are unsettled, where federal jurisdiction might interfere with complex state regulatory schemes, or where other state governmental interests might be offended by the exercise of federal jurisdiction.

   c. These prudential doctrines are in principle subject to a congressional override. If the Congress commands that the Court exercise federal jurisdiction in an area in which the Court has expressed the need for caution, the Court will exercise federal jurisdiction to the limit allowed by the Constitution. But since the Court habitually leaves quite vague the line between its "prudential" and its "constitutional" limits on the scope of federal jurisdiction, Congress is rarely willing to force the Court's hand.

4. Some Justices and commentators feel that the current Supreme Court's interpretive and prudential policies have turned federalism and separation of powers concerns inside out, to the point of diminishing the supremacy of federal law and ceding back federal judicial power to rival branches and subordinate levels of government. For the present time, however, judicial curtailment of the scope of federal jurisdiction — judicial activism in the name of judicial restraint — shows no sign of abatement.

E. ***Concurrent state-court jurisdiction is presumed.* Congress has the power to make any grant of federal jurisdiction over a particular category of cases exclusive of concurrent jurisdiction by the states but rarely does so.**

1. In a few types of cases where Congress is concerned that federal law be developed and federal policy be enforced in an especially urgent or consistent fashion, such as antitrust and patent cases, federal jurisdiction has been made exclusive.

2. The vast majority of civil cases eligible for trial by a federal court remain within concurrent state-court jurisdiction. Exclusive federal jurisdiction is the exception, not the rule. It requires an express statutory declaration of exclusive jurisdiction to overcome the presumption of concurrent jurisdiction. *Yellow Freight System v. Donnelly*, ___ U.S. ___, 110 S. Ct. 1566 (1990).

THE FEDERAL COURT SYSTEM

II. THE FEDERAL COURT SYSTEM

A. *Background.* One of the first items of business at the very first session of the First Congress was the Judiciary Act of 1789, which created a federal court system. Although the historical fabric of the federal courts has been filled with seams and wrinkles, Congress has never retreated from a basic policy of a nationwide federal court system endowed with relatively limited jurisdiction.

B. *Trial Courts.* The trial court of general jurisdiction in the federal system is the United States District Court.

    1. There are presently 91 federal judicial districts, all geographically defined. Every state has at least one district. Some states have as many as four districts. Only one district crosses state lines — that is the District of Wyoming, which embraces all of Yellowstone National Park, including the portions situated in Montana and Idaho. Two of the districts are located in places lacking formal statehood: the District of Columbia and Puerto Rico.

    2. Until 1976 some cases involving constitutional claims had to be heard by special "three-judge district courts." Except for some extremely rare types of constitutional cases, just one judge now presides over all district court proceedings.

    3. Per-judge caseloads have risen steadily in the district courts. The tradition of limited federal jurisdiction has made Congress hesitant to expand the numbers of federal courts and judges to keep pace with caseload and population growth. Wherever possible, judges make extensive use of federal magistrates, who are full-time deputy judges appointed by the judges of each district pursuant to an act of Congress. Many routine procedural matters are heard by magistrates, who may also conduct trials with the consent of the parties.

C. *Intermediate Appellate Courts.* Appeals from federal district courts are heard by a system of 13 United States Courts of Appeals.

    1. Twelve of these courts operate regionally. The regions are called "circuits" in deference to practice under the Judiciary Act of 1789, when the original circuit judges literally "rode circuit" as they travelled throughout the areas of their courts, holding sessions at the major towns and cities. There are presently 11 numbered "circuits" consisting of clusters of states, plus the District of Columbia Circuit.

    2. The United States Court of Appeals for the Federal Circuit, created in 1982, is the thirteenth court in the system and the only one with its jurisdiction defined in terms of the subject-matter of the appeal rather than the location of the court from which appeal has been taken. The Federal Circuit sits in the District of Columbia and hears primarily appeals involving patents, international trade, and contract claims against the United States.

    3. The various circuit courts range widely in size from the First Circuit's four judges to the Ninth Circuit's 28. All sit in panels of three except where conflicts of opinion among the judges requires that the law of the circuit be settled by a special session of all or most of the circuit's judges. This is called a hearing *en banc.*

    4. All contested final judgments of the federal district courts may be appealed as of right to a designated federal court of appeals. In addition, certain interlocutory decisions can be appealed, but, in general, federal policy disfavors "piecemeal review" and permits appellate correction of district court error only when it can be shown to have prejudiced a contested final judgment. This increases the power of federal trial judges by insulating from review many of their pleading and discovery rulings.

    5. Caseload pressure in the circuit courts has risen even more dramatically than in the district courts. As the cost of civil trials increase, the additional cost of taking an appeal becomes slight relative to the overall cost of prosecuting or defending a case all the way through trial in the district court. On the criminal side, the provision of free counsel to indigent defendants assures an appeal after virtually every conviction. The resulting flood of appeals has brought with it "screening" procedures which filter out seemingly routine, low-merit appeals for decision without oral argument and sometimes without a full opinion.

D. *The Supreme Court.* **The Supreme Court is the only federal court that the Constitution required Congress to establish.**

1. Congress controls the number of Supreme Court Justices. It originally set the number of Justices at six, and varied that number to as many as ten. The present number of nine has remained fixed since 1869, and is virtually certain not to change.

2. The Supreme Court has a limited but self-executing range of *original jurisdiction* embracing cases to which states or foreign diplomats are party. The Supreme Court rarely exercises its original jurisdiction, since it is not equipped to function as a trial court and must refer such cases for trial before a special master. Most such cases are within the concurrent jurisdiction of the federal district courts, where the Supreme Court prefers that they be tried. The only cases in which the Supreme Court will occasionally exercise its original jurisdiction are those brought by one state against another, usually involving a boundary or resource-allocation dispute.

3. The Supreme Court has *appellate jurisdiction* over the work of the lower federal courts and over final judgments of state courts that turn on issues of federal law.

    a. Congress has extensive procedural control over the appellate jurisdiction of the Supreme Court. Only in very rare circumstances is the Supreme Court required by statute to hear and decide an appeal.

    b. Under a reform that became effective in 1988, virtually all "appeals" heard by the Supreme Court are actually "writs of *certiorari*," a Latin phrase for a writ used to call up a record for purposes of review. The advantage of the certiorari procedure is that the party seeking Supreme Court review has no right to have her case heard by the high Court. The Supreme Court can pick and choose which cases to review according to their legal and national importance. The Supreme Court receives between four thousand and five thousand "cert" petitions every year, and usually chooses to review only about 150 of these cases.

III. THE FEDERAL QUESTION JURISDICTION OF THE DISTRICT COURTS

THE FEDERAL QUESTION JURIS-DICTION OF THE DISTRICT COURTS

A. *Summary of Current Law.* **The general federal question statute, 28 U.S.C. § 1331, confers on the district courts subject-matter jurisdiction over all substantial suits to enforce federally created rights to relief. In extremely rare circumstances the jurisdiction granted by § 1331 also extends to suits in which a well-pleaded complaint to enforce a state-created right to relief discloses a compelling need to resolve a substantial and disputed question of federal law. Practice under specialized forms of federal question jurisdiction generally conforms to these rules.**

B. **Background to the Narrow Scope of the General Federal Question Statute, 28 U.S.C. § 1331**

1. *Broad constitutional scope.* Article III of the Constitution gives Congress extremely broad authority to vest the lower federal courts with jurisdiction over cases "arising under" federal law. The Constitution does not require that an issue of federal law be crucial to a case or even contested by the parties. *Osborn v. Bank of the United States*, 22 U.S. 738 (1824). It is sufficient under the Constitution that some issue of federal law be the merest "ingredient" of an otherwise state-law cause of action, in order for the whole case to be tried in federal court, if Congress permits.

2. *Narrow statutory scope.* But Congress has exercised the full scope of its constitutional power to confer "arising under" jurisdiction on the district courts in only a few specialized contexts. With respect to the *general* grant of "arising under" jurisdiction, Congress has authorized the district courts to exercise jurisdiction in a much narrower range of cases than the Constitution permits. Congress demands far more than that a mere federal "ingredient" be perceptible somewhere in the litigation. Congress demands that there be a properly presented "federal question" in order for there to be federal trial court jurisdiction of a civil case under the general federal question jurisdictional statute, 28 U.S.C. § 1331.

3. *History of § 1331.* The first Congress decided in 1789 to implement diversity jurisdiction, but left the litigation of federal questions to the state courts, subject to Supreme Court review of state court rulings on matters of federal law. Not until 1875 was there enacted, in the aftermath of the Civil War, a comprehensive and enduring "general federal question" statute. The statute enacted in 1875 continues in effect to this day as 28 U.S.C. § 1331: "The district courts shall have original jurisdiction of all civil actions arising under the Constitution, laws, or treaties of the United States." The language of § 1331 is virtually identical to the "arising under" clause of Article III, and was originally construed just as broadly. The process by which Congress and the Supreme Court jointly narrowed the scope of § 1331 without changing its text is fascinating but beyond the scope of our discussion. It is now settled that the statutory and constitutional grants of jurisdiction serve different functions and (absent the clearest congressional command) should not be interpreted to like effect. "Although the language of § 1331 parallels that of the 'arising under' clause of Article III, … Article III arising under jurisdiction is broader than federal question jurisdiction under § 1331." *Verlinden B.V. v. Central Bank of Nigeria*, 461 U.S. 480 (1983).

C. **Doctrines Governing the Scope of General Federal Question Jurisdiction Under § 1331**

1. *The "well-pleaded complaint" rule.* The most important limiting doctrine adopted by the Supreme Court in its interpretation of § 1331 is a procedural doctrine directed to the manner in which the jurisdiction-conferring "federal question" is disclosed. The "well-pleaded complaint" rule requires as a condition of jurisdiction under § 1331 that the requisite "federal question" be ascertainable solely from the well-pleaded allegations of the complaint. This has the extremely important substantive consequence of prohibiting general federal question jurisdiction where the issue of federal law arises solely as a defense to the plaintiff's state-law cause of action.

    a. By requiring that the federal question be disclosed by the *complaint,* the well-pleaded complaint rule forecloses § 1331 jurisdiction based on the pleading in the answer of a federal defense.

    b. By requiring that the federal question be disclosed only by so much of the complaint as is *well-pleaded,* the well-pleaded complaint rule forecloses a plaintiff from "anticipating" a federal defense by including in the complaint unnecessary material alleging why the defendant is not doing voluntarily what the plaintiff is demanding in court. In determining whether the "well-pleaded" allegations of the complaint disclose the existence of a jurisdiction-conferring federal question, a court considers only those allegations of the complaint that are necessary to state a legally sufficient cause of action.

        Example: Mr. and Mrs. Mottley had settled a personal injury suit with a railroad in consideration of free transportation on the railroad for the rest of their lives. For 36 years, the railroad issued them free annual passes. In 1906, Congress enacted the Interstate Commerce Act, which sought to fight the unfair business practices of monopolies and trusts by prohibiting railroads from giving free transportation to anybody. In 1907, the railroad withheld the Mottleys' passes, claiming that their issuance would violate the new Act. Contending that the Act did not apply to them, and alternatively that it was an unconstitutional taking of their property, the Mottleys brought suit in federal court to compel specific performance of their contract with the railroad.

The trial court ruled in the Mottleys' favor, and the railroad appealed to the Supreme Court to settle the meaning of the Act. On its own motion the Supreme Court dismissed the case because *the only federal issue* was whether the Interstate Commerce Act provided the railroad with a valid federal *defense* to the Mottleys' state law contract action. The Mottleys were forced to begin again in state court. Three years later they lost the case for good when the Supreme Court concluded on appeal from a state court judgment in the Mottleys' favor that the railroad did, indeed, have a valid federal defense to the Mottleys' state-law action for breach of contract. *Louisville & Nashville R. Co. v. Mottley*, 211 U.S. 149 (1908); 219 U.S. 467 (1911).

2. *Special problems of the well-pleaded complaint rule as applied to declaratory judgments.* The Supreme Court modified the application of the well-pleaded complaint rule after Congress enacted the federal Declaratory Judgment Act in 1934. This Act threatened to permit modern-day Mottleys to litigate state-law claims in federal court by pleading them in conjunction with a request for a federal declaratory judgment on the validity of an anticipated federal defense to their state-law claims. Confronting this situation and the potential flood of federal cases that might result, the Supreme Court decided that nothing in the legislative history of the Declaratory Judgment Act indicated that Congress intended to sweep aside the well-pleaded complaint rule as a procedural constraint on the scope of general federal question jurisdiction.

a. In a declaratory judgment action the well-pleaded complaint rule is applied to the hypothetical *alternative or reciprocal coercive action* that one party or the other would file if declaratory judgments were not permitted. *Skelly Oil Co. v. Phillips Petroleum Co.*, 339 U.S. 667 (1950). If the declaratory judgment plaintiff could have brought a coercive federal question action as an *alternative* to a declaratory judgment action, § 1331's federal question jurisdiction exists over the declaratory judgment action. Similarly, if the declaratory judgment defendant has a *reciprocal* right to bring a coercive federal question suit against the declaratory judgment plaintiff, the plaintiff's "pre-emptive strike" (*i.e.*, filing an action for a federal declaratory judgment instead of waiting for the other party to file a federal coercive action) will be within § 1331's federal question jurisdiction. But if neither the declaratory judgment plaintiff's alternative action nor the declaratory judgment defendant's reciprocal action would have qualified for general federal question jurisdiction, then the plaintiff's action for a declaration of her rights against the defendant under federal law is not within § 1331's limited scope of jurisdiction.

Example: In a dispute between *A* and *B* over *A's* patent rights with respect to *B's* product, *A* could bring a coercive suit under the federal patent laws to seek damages or an injunction as relief from *B's* alleged infringement of *A's* patent. If *A* prefers to sue for a declaratory judgment instead of damages, the action is within the statutory federal question jurisdiction — declaratory relief is merely an *alternative* to a federal question suit for coercive relief.

Example: In the dispute between *A* and *B*, *A* might seek to deter *B* from producing an article that might infringe *A's* patent by simply threatening *B* and *B's* potential customers with a later suit for damages. *B* need not wait for *A* to file suit. *B* can file a declaratory judgment action to determine as a matter of federal law if *A's* patent is valid. Because this is the *reciprocal* to *A's* threatened coercive action for damages under the federal patent law, *B's* action for a declaratory judgment is within the statutory federal question jurisdiction.

Example: Politician *C* threatens to sue newspaper publisher *D* for libelling *C* in a critical article. *D* files a federal declaratory judgment action seeking to establish that the First Amendment prohibits any award of damages arising out of the publication of political opinion. *C* files a federal declaratory judgment action seeking to establish that *D* has no first amendment right to publish false charges against *C*. Under *Mottley* and *Skelly* neither declaratory judgment action is within the statutory federal question jurisdiction. Both actions seek to circumvent the well-pleaded complaint rule by asking a federal court to rule on whether *D* has a valid defense under federal law to *C's* threatened state-law suit for libel.

b. **No distinction between state and federal declaratory judgment actions.** The Supreme Court has extended *Skelly*'s modification of the well-pleaded complaint rule to state-court declaratory judgment actions. When a plaintiff files an action in state court asking for a declaration of rights under federal law, the state-court declaratory judgment defendant may remove the case to federal court only if the complaint, read in light of *Skelly*'s "alternative or reciprocal coercive relief rule," shows that the issue of federal law disputed by the parties is one that could have been raised by one party or the other in a coercive suit that would qualify for § 1331 jurisdiction. *Franchise Tax Board v. Construction Laborers Vacation Trust*, 463 U.S. 1 (1983).

3. *The Holmes "creation" test.* Just what a federal court should be looking for in the "well-pleaded" allegations of the complaint remains unsettled at the fringes but is reasonably well understood in the great majority of cases. The fail-safe test for determining affirmatively that a case does indeed present a jurisdiction-conferring "federal question" is the "creation" test of Justice Oliver Wendell Holmes: "A suit arises under the law that creates the cause of action." *American Well Works Co. v. Layne & Bowler Co.*, 241 U.S. 257 (1916). Restated in modern terms, the Holmes creation test tells you that there is *always* federal question jurisdiction when federal law has expressly created the remedy that is sought by the plaintiff.

Example: Congress enacts the National Widget Safety Act, which sets strict standards for the production and sale of widgets. Section 801 of the Act creates a private cause of action for damages on behalf of any person injured as a result of a violation of the Act. Jones sues Manufacturer in a federal district court, seeking money damages for injuries suffered in an automobile accident that was allegedly caused by a defective widget produced by Manufacturer in violation of its duties of care under the Act. Jones is suing for a remedy expressly authorized by federal law, *i.e.*, § 801 of the Act. Therefore, federal law has created Jones' cause of action, and it is indisputably within the general federal question jurisdiction of the district courts.

4. *Special problems of applying the Holmes "creation" test to cases based on judicially created federal remedies or duties*

a. *Remedy versus duty and the problem of implied private rights of action.* Sometimes federal law creates a duty without expressly creating a private remedy for harm caused by breach of the duty. This is frequently the case with regulatory statutes in which Congress has created some public enforcement agency, such as the Securities and Exchange Commission or the Food and Drug Administration. The Supreme Court has made clear in such cases that the existence of federal question jurisdiction under the Holmes "creation" test requires the party seeking to invoke jurisdiction to establish that there is, by implication, a private federal *remedy* as well as a federal *duty*.

(1) When a statute expressly creates a private remedy, as in the widget example, and a private lawsuit is filed seeking that express statutory remedy, it is easy to see that the suit is one to enforce a federally created right to relief and, hence, that the suit passes the Holmes "creation" test for federal question jurisdiction under § 1331.

(2) The most difficult applications of the Holmes "creation" test arise under federal statutes or provisions of the federal Constitution that clearly impose federal duties but do not expressly create private rights of action to redress harm caused by violation of those duties, and putative federal question suits are then filed by plaintiffs who argue that judicial implication of a private right of action is necessary to achieve the legislative purpose of the duty-imposing federal statute or constitutional provision. *See Merrell Dow Pharmaceuticals, Inc. v. Thompson*, 478 U.S. 804 (1986).

b. *Federal common law.* Federal question jurisdiction does not require that a case be rooted in the breach of a legislatively created federal duty. The Supreme Court has recognized that judicially created "federal common law" can in extraordinary situations be the basis for both the duty and the remedy components of a cause of action, and that suit on such a federal common law cause of action is within the general federal question jurisdiction of § 1331. *Illinois v. City of Milwaukee*, 406 U.S. 91 (1972) [federal common law cause of action to abate interstate water pollution].

c. *The "substantial federal question" requirement as applied to suits to enforce federal rights to relief.* Federal jurisdiction may be lacking over a case that appears formally to qualify for § 1331 jurisdiction under the Holmes "creation" test, if there is no plausible legal basis for the pleader's theory that the facts state a claim for relief under federal law. This is commonly called the "substantial federal question" requirement. The Supreme Court has used a variety of phrases to capture the degree of insubstantiality which is fatal to federal question jurisdiction even when the complaint purports to enforce a federally created right. A "'substantial' question [is] necessary to support jurisdiction … Over the years, the Court has repeatedly held that the federal courts are without power to entertain claims otherwise within their jurisdiction if they are 'so attenuated and unsubstantial as to be absolutely devoid of merit'; 'wholly insubstantial'; 'obviously frivolous'; 'plainly unsubstantial'; or 'no longer open to discussion.'" *Hagans v. Levine*, 415 U.S. 528 (1974).

5. *Rare instances of § 1331 jurisdiction over state-created causes of action.* On a very few occasions, the Supreme Court has squarely upheld the exercise of general federal question jurisdiction under § 1331, even though the Holmes "creation" test was not satisfied. The leading case, to which Holmes loudly dissented, is *Smith v. Kansas City Title & Trust Co.*, 255 U.S. 180 (1921). This presents the "'litigation-provoking problem'" of just when "the presence of a federal issue in a state-created cause of action" will suffice for federal question jurisdiction under the standards of *Smith* and the lower-court case law it has inspired. *Merrell Dow, supra*.

a. In order for § 1331 jurisdiction to exist in a suit to enforce a state-created right, it must appear from the well-pleaded allegations of the complaint that "some substantial, disputed question of federal law is a necessary element" of the state-created right to relief. *Merrell Dow, supra*.

(1) *"Necessary element"* means that it is not sufficient that the federal issue be a possible defense to the state-created right. It must be an element of the state-created right itself, as where state law grants a right to recover for negligence, state law declares that breach of any federal law regulating safety constitutes negligence per se, and the case turns on whether a federal safety law was indeed violated by the defendant.

(2) *"Disputed"* means that the case must actually turn on the proper construction of federal law. The issue of federal law must be crucial to the litigation, not just potentially relevant.

(3) *"Substantial"* is the most troublesome element of the formula. The requirement of substantiality in this context is much stricter than the "substantial federal

question" requirement applicable (along with the Holmes "creation" test) when the complaint is based on a federally created rather than a state-created cause of action.

(a) The Supreme Court has *suggested* that a federal issue arising in the litigation of a state-created cause of action cannot be substantial enough to qualify the case for § 1331 jurisdiction unless the importance of the federal issue transcends the facts of the case at hand and implicates federal policies of national significance. *Merrell Dow, supra.*

(b) The Supreme Court has *held* that such a federal issue can never be sufficiently substantial, in this special sense of jurisdiction-creating transcendent national importance, if the issue is simply the proper construction of a federal regulatory statute from which Congress chose to omit any express private federal remedies. *Merrell Dow, supra.*

b. The bottom line is that in an extraordinary case where a well-pleaded complaint reveals that a disputed issue of federal law is a necessary and crucial element of a state-created cause of action, the Supreme Court will uphold federal question jurisdiction when the federal issue is a matter of national importance the prompt resolution of which will serve public interests beyond those of the parties to the case, provided the exercise of jurisdiction on this basis would not be inconsistent with the intent of Congress as expressed in the legislation whose construction is in question. *Merrell Dow, supra; Smith, supra.*

D. Special Applications of Federal Question Jurisdiction

1. There are many statutes granting *specialized federal question jurisdiction* over actions that "arise under" particular substantive federal statutes, such as the patent laws, the antitrust laws, laws regulating commerce, laws protecting civil rights, and dozens of other laws.

a. Most of these specialized grants of federal question jurisdiction were enacted at a time when the general federal question statute, § 1331, was subject to a jurisdictional amount. That amount was set at $500 in 1875, was increased to $2,000 in 1887, was raised again to $3,000 in 1911, and reached its maximum of $10,000 in 1958. The proliferation of special federal question statutes that served as exemptions from § 1331's jurisdictional amount requirement, and the growing feeling that no financial barrier was appropriate when a dispute over federal rights otherwise qualified for the federal question jurisdiction, resulted in 1980 in the repeal of the jurisdictional amount requirement under § 1331. This has rendered redundant many special grants of federal question jurisdiction whose only function had been to waive the jurisdictional amount requirement. *See, e.g.,* 28 U.S.C. § 1337 (no jurisdictional amount required in actions arising under any act of Congress regulating commerce).

b. Some special grants of federal question jurisdiction remain important because they provide for *exclusive jurisdiction. See, e.g.,* 15 U.S.C. §§ 15, 26 (exclusive federal jurisdiction over certain actions arising under the antitrust acts); 15 U.S.C. § 78aa (exclusive federal jurisdiction over actions arising under the Securities Exchange Act); 28 U.S.C. § 1338 (exclusive federal jurisdiction over actions arising under any act of Congress relating to patents, plant variety protection, and copyrights). These provisions create express exceptions to the *general rule that federal jurisdiction is concurrent* with the jurisdiction of state courts.

c. In general, the well-pleaded complaint rule, the Holmes "creation" test, and the other rules for determining whether a case is within § 1331's federal question jurisdiction also apply under the various special federal question jurisdictional statutes. Congress can, and occasionally does, ease the normal restrictions on federal question jurisdiction with respect to cases arising under some specified statute. These highly specialized provisions are beyond the scope of our discussion.

2. Some cases that appear to involve only state-created rights are brought within federal question jurisdiction when Congress displaces state law and mandates that federal law govern exclusively.

    a. The result of such "displacement" is that all suits pertaining to the activity in question must necessarily arise under federal law — there is no other law that can constitutionally apply. Examples of this sort of federal question jurisdiction by displacement of state law are suits to enforce collective bargaining agreement governed by the Labor Management Relations Act, *Avco Corp. v. Machinists*, 390 U.S. 557 (1968), and suits to recover benefits under employee benefit plans governed by the Employee Retirement Income Security Act (ERISA), where state law is displaced by § 502(a)(1)(B) of ERISA, *Metropolitan Life Insurance Co. v. Taylor*, 481 U.S. 58 (1987).

    b. Sometimes, federal law does not entirely "displace" state law on a particular subject and merely qualifies the application of state law by selective "preemption" of certain of its provisions. If a plaintiff sues to enforce a state-created right that perhaps has been "preempted" by federal law, the plaintiff's suit *does not* qualify for federal question jurisdiction under § 1331. As first established in the *Mottley* case, the issue of possible federal "preemption" is regarded as a *defense* to a state-created cause of action, and the well-pleaded complaint rule precludes founding federal question jurisdiction on a federal defense whether or not the plaintiff seeks to anticipate it in the complaint and whether or not the legal merit of a possible federal defense is in fact the only matter in dispute between the parties. *Franchise Tax Board, supra.*

    c. Two special federal question statutes relating to foreign affairs are also based on the power of Congress to displace state law with federal law and, thus, to "federalize" what appears to be a state-created cause of action. 28 U.S.C. § 1330 was enacted as part of the Foreign Sovereign Immunities Act, discussed below with reference to diversity jurisdiction over suits involving aliens. It provides for federal question jurisdiction of suits against foreign governments or foreign corporations in which the parent country owns a majority interest. 28 U.S.C. § 1350 confers on the district courts "original jurisdiction of any civil action by an alien for a tort only, committed in violation of the law or nations or a treaty of the United States." Although this provision dates from 1789, it has recently figured in several prominent human rights cases. The courts of appeals are divided as to its scope. *See Tel Oren v. Libyan Arab Republic*, 726 F.2d 774 (D.C. Cir. 1984); *Filartiga v. Pena-Irala*, 630 F.2d 876 (2d Cir. 1980).

3. Two other areas of active federal litigation are suits under maritime law, referred to as "admiralty" cases, and suits to which the federal government is a party. Although federal jurisdiction in these cases is constitutionally authorized by Article III independently of its general provision concerning cases "arising under" federal law, maritime and federal government cases are close cousins of federal question jurisdiction. The substantive law governing maritime and federal government cases is always federal law.

IV. THE DIVERSITY JURISDICTION OF THE DISTRICT COURTS

THE DIVERSITY
JURISDICTION OF
THE DISTRICT COURTS

A. The constitutional purpose for diversity jurisdiction was to foster national political and economic unity by allowing Congress to protect out-of-staters from biased local courts. The inability of major national and international investors to rely on state courts to enforce debts was discouraging economic growth at the time the Constitution was drafted. While these concerns have waned, two forms of diversity jurisdiction remain statutorily authorized. Together, they account for about one-fifth of the cases filed in the federal district courts.

4

B. **The general diversity statute, 28 U.S.C. § 1332, requires complete diversity of citizenship and an amount in controversy that exceeds $50,000.**

1. The "general" diversity statute applies to all types of cases, without regard to the nature of the cause of action. In two important respects, Congress has always *narrowed* the scope of the general diversity jurisdiction. As a result, far fewer cases qualify for diversity jurisdiction than would be the case if § 1332 implemented the full scope of jurisdictional power authorized in "minimal diversity" cases by Article III of the Constitution.

   a. *The rule of "complete diversity."* The statutory provision for general diversity jurisdiction requires that there be *complete diversity* of citizenship between *all* opposing parties. This is known as the rule of *Strawbridge v. Curtiss*, 7 U.S. 267 (1806).

   b. *The jurisdictional amount requirement.* Article III makes no mention of a jurisdictional amount. Since 1789, however, Congress has required a minimum amount to be in controversy in order to qualify a case for the statutory grant of diversity jurisdiction. At present, that amount must exceed $50,000. We devote a separate section below to the rules for determining the amount in controversy.

2. There are *four configurations* of diversity that support federal jurisdiction under § 1332.

   a. Conventional *interstate diversity* jurisdiction where the suit is between "citizens of different States" [§ 1332(a)(1)].

   b. Conventional *alienage* jurisdiction where the suit is between "citizens of a State and citizens or subjects of a foreign State" [§ 1332(a)(2)].

      (1) Despite the pluralized references to "citizens" and "subjects," multiple parties are not required on either side of the litigation. This is true of all subsections of § 1332 that use plural terms.

      (2) A suit by one "citizen or subject of a foreign State" against another is not authorized under § 1332(a)(2), even if the aliens are each from a different foreign country. There is no federal alienage jurisdiction over a suit by a British citizen against a French citizen.

      (3) All parties on one side of the litigation must be exclusively citizens of states within the United States, and all parties on the other side must be aliens who are not citizens of a state.

         (a) As amended in 1988, a *permanent resident alien* is now considered a *citizen* of the state in which the permanent resident alien is *domiciled*, and is no longer considered a "citizen or subject of a foreign State."

         (b) Dual citizenship is not recognized under § 1332. A permanent resident alien who is a citizen of a state (of the United States) is no longer considered to be a "citizen or subject of a foreign State" for diversity or alienage jurisdiction purposes.

   c. *Combined* interstate diversity and alienage jurisdiction where the suit is between "citizens of different States and in which citizens or subjects of a foreign state are additional parties" [§ 1332(a)(3)].

      (1) In contrast to § 1332(a)(2), § 1332(a)(3) does allow an alien to sue another alien, but only when the aliens are additional parties to a suit filed between citizens of different states.

      (2) The aliens are allowed essentially to piggyback on litigation that in their absence would qualify anyway for diversity jurisdiction under § 1332(a)(1).

      (3) This is the only form of diversity jurisdiction under § 1332 in which the rule of "complete diversity" is relaxed. Complete diversity is required between the state citizens, but the effect of having aliens on both sides is disregarded.

d. *Special* foreign-state-as-plaintiff alienage jurisdiction where the suit is between "a foreign state, defined in section 1603(a) of this title, as plaintiff and citizens of a State or of different States" [§ 1332(a)(4)].

(1) The statutory definition of a foreign state includes any foreign corporation whose own government owns over half of its shares, provided its principal place of business is outside the United States. This includes many familiar foreign airlines, banks, manufacturers, and raw material producers.

(2) Subsection 1332(a)(4) diversity jurisdiction is available only when the foreign state is suing as a plaintiff. The importance of § 1332(a)(4) is that it preserves diversity jurisdiction, and, hence, the right to jury trial, in foreign-state-as-plaintiff cases.

(3) In order to avoid foreign relations problems posed by foreign-state-as-defendant suits, all suits (state or federal) *against* foreign governments (or their corporations) were made subject to federal sovereign immunity law by the Foreign Sovereign Immunities Act of 1976. In order to make sure that this federal law is carefully and properly applied, any *foreign-state-as-defendant* suit that is filed in federal court is within a special grant of *federal question jurisdiction*. 28 U.S.C. § 1330. Any suit filed against a foreign state in state court may be removed to federal court. 28 U.S.C. § 1441(d). All such cases, whether filed originally in federal court or brought there by removal, are *tried by a judge sitting without a jury*.

3. **Examples** of cases qualifying and not qualifying for general diversity jurisdiction. (In every case assume that the jurisdictional amount requirement, discussed below, has been satisfied.)

a. A Georgia citizen and a citizen of France sue a California citizen and a citizen of France. There is diversity jurisdiction under § 1332(a)(3).

b. A Georgia citizen and a citizen of France sue a citizen of Japan. There is no diversity jurisdiction. There is no suit here between citizens of different states, so § 1332(a)(3) is inapplicable. There is a suit between a citizen of a state and an alien, but the presence of an alien as a coparty of the citizen of a state destroys diversity of citizenship.

c. Two Texas citizens jointly sue Sabena World Airways, a Belgian corporation more than 50 percent owned by the Belgian government. There is no diversity jurisdiction. There is federal question jurisdiction under § 1330.

d. Sabena World Airways sues two Texas citizens. There is diversity jurisdiction under § 1332(a)(4).

e. An Indian citizen, admitted to the United States as a permanent resident alien and domiciled in New Jersey, sues a Dutch citizen. There is diversity jurisdiction under § 1332(a)(2).

f. A Colorado citizen sues an Illinois citizen and a citizen of Kenya. There is diversity jurisdiction; this is a proper combination of jurisdiction under § 1332(a)(1) as to the Illinois citizen and jurisdiction under § 1332(a)(2) as to the Kenyan citizen.

g. Coin collectors *A, B, C, D* and *E*, all citizens of the State of Illinois, joined as plaintiffs by colleague *F* from Florida and *G* from Georgia, have filed a federal district court suit against coin show promoters *X*, a citizen of the State of New York, *Y*, a citizen of the State of Nevada, and *Z*, a corporation of the State of Delaware with activities in many states and its headquarters in Atlanta, Georgia. The collectors' suit is based on state fraud law rather than any cause of action arising under federal law: there is no basis for invoking federal question jurisdiction. As we will discuss below in explicating the citizenship of corporations, Corporation *Z* will most likely be found to be a citizen of both Delaware (by incorporation) and Georgia (by virtue of having its principal place of business there). This "destroys" complete diversity, since one plaintiff (*G*) and one defendant (*Z*) are citizens of the same state (Georgia). If both *G* and *Z* remain parties, the suit will have to be dismissed from federal court.

C. There is one "special" diversity statute, 28 U.S.C. § 1335, which applies only to interpleader cases but in these cases authorizes a very broad scope of federal diversity jurisdiction. Under § 1335 only "minimal" diversity is required, and the required amount in controversy is only $500.

1. Section 1335 is part of the Federal Interpleader Act, which makes it as easy as possible to bring interpleader actions in federal court. Interpleader is a special type of joinder device that is discussed in detail in Chapter 6. In brief, someone who is subject to conflicting claims from others — classically an insurance company faced with conflicting claims to a policy of insurance — can "interplead" the rival claimants and thereby avoid the risk of multiple inconsistent liabilities when multiple claimants prosecute separate lawsuits.

2. To facilitate use of interpleader in federal court, Congress has authorized nationwide service of process [28 U.S.C. § 2361], liberal venue [28 U.S.C. § 1397], and federal subject-matter jurisdiction under 28 U.S.C. § 1335 whenever there is *any diversity at all* between any of the rival claimants.

   a. In upholding the constitutionality of § 1335, the Supreme Court emphasized that "minimal diversity" is all that Article III requires. Under the general diversity statute, § 1332, and its rule of "complete diversity," Congress has restricted the scope of jurisdiction much more narrowly than the Constitution requires. But in order to serve the policies of the Federal Interpleader Act, Congress has the power under Article III to authorize the district courts to adjudicate interpleader actions based on mere minimal diversity. *State Farm Fire & Casualty Co. v. Tashire*, 386 U.S. 523 (1967).

   b. The jurisdictional amount required by § 1335 is only $500, measured by the "stake" or fund to which the rival claimants are asserting conflicting claims. Even if no one claimant seeks the entire stake — *e.g.*, there are four people claiming to be the children of *X*, all actual children of *X* are entitled to share equally in the proceeds of a $1,000 insurance policy on the life of *X*, and it is conceded that *X* had only three children — the amount in controversy is the value of the stake, rather than the value of the largest disputed share of that stake.

D. The Citizenship of Natural Persons

1. *Overview.* The rules governing the diversity status of individuals are tricky. They use the familiar concepts of citizenship and residence, but these concepts are not given their usual meanings. The result is a high potential for mistake and confusion, and in one situation the existence of substantial doubt about the constitutionality of current law.

2. *Six classifications*

   a. An individual who is a citizen of the United States is for diversity purposes deemed a citizen of the state in which that person is domiciled.

   b. A United States citizen who is not domiciled in a state (*i.e.*, is domiciled in a foreign state) is for diversity purposes deemed a citizen of no state. Such a person is not considered a "citizen" for the "diversity of citizenship" species of diversity jurisdiction. Such a person is not considered an "alien" for purposes of the "alienage" species of diversity juridiction. The result is that such a person is deemed "U.S.-stateless." The federal courts can have no subject-matter jurisdiction based on diversity of citizenship or alienage over any case to which a U.S.-stateless person is party. (By "U.S.-stateless" we mean that the problem is a lack of affiliation with one of the states of the United States, not a lack of national citizenship, *i.e.*, "statelessness" as a matter of international law.)

c.   An individual who is not a citizen of the United States but who has been admitted to the United States for permanent residence (a "permanent resident alien") is for diversity purposes deemed a citizen of the state in which that person is domiciled. Such a person is thus considered a "citizen" for the "diversity of citizenship" species of diversity jurisdiction. Such a person is not considered an "alien" for purposes of the "alienage" species of diversity juridiction.

d.   A permanent resident alien who is not domiciled in a state but who is a citizen of a foreign state, is for diversity purposes deemed a citizen of that foreign state. Such a permanent resident alien is thus considered an "alien" for purposes of the "alienage" species of diversity juridiction.

e.   An individual who is neither a citizen of the United States nor a permanent resident alien, but who is a citizen of a foreign state, is for diversity purposes deemed a citizen of that foreign state regardless whether such a person is domiciled in a state. Such a person is thus considered an "alien" for purposes of the "alienage" species of diversity juridiction.

f.   An individual who is neither a citizen of the United States nor a permanent resident alien nor a citizen of a foreign country is for diversity purposes deemed a citizen of no state regardless whether such a person is domiciled in a state. Such a person is not considered a "citizen" for the "diversity of citizenship" species of diversity jurisdiction. Such a person is not considered an "alien" for purposes of the "alienage" species of diversity juridiction. The result is that such a person is deemed "stateless" in the international-law sense. The federal courts can have no subject-matter jurisdiction based on diversity of citizenship or alienage over any case to which a stateless person (other than a state-domiciled permanent resident alien) is party.

3.   *Analysis: diversity as a function of political status and domicile*

a.   For United States citizens, domicile in a state is essential to diversity jurisdiction. Domicile in the District of Columbia, Puerto Rico, or the federal territories of Guam, the Northern Mariana Islands and the Virgin Islands counts as domicile in a state for purposes of the general diversity statute. [§ 1332(d).] Domicile anywhere other than in the United States or its territories makes a United States citizen "U.S.-stateless" and outside the scope of any form of diversity jurisdiction.

b.   For citizens of foreign states who are permanent resident aliens, domicile in a state is important but not essential to diversity jurisdiction. Domicile in a state confers citizenship in that state for diversity purposes. Domicile anywhere other than the United States or its territories makes a citizen of a foreign state an alien within the scope of the alienage form of diversity jurisdiction.

c.   For citizens of foreign states who are not permanent resident aliens, domicile in a state is irrelevant to diversity jurisdiction. They are always within the alienage form of diversity jurisdiction regardless of where domiciled.

d.   Stateless persons who are not permanent resident aliens are always outside any form of diversity jurisdiction. However, a stateless person who is a permanent resident alien and is domiciled in a state is a citizen of that state.

4.   *Definition of domicile.* Domicile is a person's place of fixed residence. A person always has a domicile.

a.   From birth until adulthood, one's domicile follows the domicile of one's parents. If the parents are separated, domicile of the child is that of the custodial parent or, in cases of joint custody, of the parent with whom the child lives the greater part of the time.

4

b. Upon attaining the age of majority (in most places and for most purposes, one becomes an adult at the age of 18), one acquires the capacity to change one's own domicile. This requires a combination of both:

(1) presence in the new place of intended domicile; and

(2) the rather magical state of mind required to establish domicile, *i.e.*, the desire to make that place one's home for the indefinite future.

c. The subjective state of mind required to establish a new domicile is not a state of mind of which most people are ever conscious, even when they have in fact changed their domiciles. Moreover, the person whose state of mind is in issue will usually have a self-serving motive to report either the existence or absence of the requisite intent, depending on whether or not that person is seeking to invoke or resist federal diversity jurisdiction. Thus the establishment of a new domicile is generally proved in court on the basis of objective evidence of attachment to the new place of purported domicile.

(1) Among the probative evidence is the nature of the person's housing in the place of purported domicile (her own home? a rented apartment? a dormitory? a hotel room?), where she is registered to vote, where she is licensed to drive, where she claims to be resident for tax or governmental benefits purposes, where she works or studies and the long-term nature of that work or study, whether she has a domestic partner or family with continuing ties to the place of purported domicile, and so forth.

(2) Graduate students frequently present difficult problems of fact concerning their degree of attachment to a place of graduate study where they claim to be newly domiciled. Undergraduate students and military personnel are less likely than graduate students to succeed in proving that they have established their domicile at the place where they are resident during college and military duty, but this is by no means a general rule or even a presumption. Domicile is always subject to case-by-case adjudication.

(3) An intention to create diversity of citizenship by means of a change of domicile does not rule out a valid change of domicile, but such a goal may be probative of a lack of a genuine intention to remain in the new place of residence for the indefinite future.

5. *Constitutional doubt.* The extension of state citizenship to a permanent resident alien domiciled in a state was added to 28 U.S.C. § 1332(a) by amendment enacted November 19, 1988. It went into effect 180 days later, governing actions filed on or after May 18, 1989. The amendment is sure to generate constitutional litigation because it appears to authorize suit by a permanent resident alien who is domiciled in a state (and hence has state citizenship) against another alien — with one with foreign citizenship, or a permanent resident alien domiciled in a different state. As such the amendment conflicts with the rule of *Hodgson v. Bowerbank*, 9 U.S. 303 (1809), that Article III does not permit federal jurisdiction over a suit by one alien against another alien (except as additional parties under § 1332(a)(3)).

E. **The Citizenship of Unincorporated Associations**

1. An unincorporated association is any unincorporated group that has the legal capacity to sue and be sued as an entity. Partnerships, labor unions, and fraternal organizations are common examples.

2. Unincorporated associations have no diversity status independent of their members. For diversity purposes the associational form is *transparent*. A court must look through the associational form and determine the citizenship of each member of the association. An

unincorporated assocation is deemed to be a citizen of every state, domestic or foreign, of which any member of the association is a citizen.

a. A narrowly divided Supreme Court recently held that *all partnerships* are to be treated as transparent, and their diversity status must be determined by reference to the citizenships of *all partners*. It makes no difference that a partnership may include some "limited" partners who are mere investors without management prerogatives. Although limited partners may be organizationally analogous to corporate shareholders, a limited partnership may not be treated as if it were a corporation for diversity purposes until Congress so directs. *Carden v. Arkoma Associates*, 494 U.S. 185, 110 S.Ct. 1015 (1990).

b. It is possible under the laws of some states to organize an unincorporated group of managers and investors in a way that is distinct for diversity purposes from both corporations and partnerships. This organizational form is the "business trust," most commonly used to collect capital for investment in real estate. If the relevant state law gives the business trustees total management control of the trust assets for the benefit of the beneficiary-investors, the trust form will be respected for diversity purposes. In a diversity suit to which the trust is a party, only the states of citizenship of the trustees will be considered in determining whether complete diversity exists. The states of citizenship of the investors will be ignored. *Navarro Savings Association v. Lee*, 446 U.S. 458 (1980).

3. In a "direct action" against an unincorporated insurance company as insurer of the negligent party, the unincorporated insurer is deemed to be a citizen not only of every state in which a member of the association is a citizen, but also of the state in which its insured is a citizen. [28 U.S.C. § 1332(c)(1).]

a. A direct action is a suit by an injured party directly against the liability insurer of the tortfeasor.

b. Direct actions were unknown at common law but are a familiar feature of civil law systems. Within the United States they are presently permitted by the laws of a few states, such as Louisiana and Wisconsin, and by Puerto Rico.

F. The Citizenship of Corporations

1. *State(s) of incorporation.* A corporation "shall be deemed to be a citizen of any State by which it has been incorporated." [28 U.S.C. § 1332(c)(1).] "Any State" has been interpreted to mean "every State."

a. Most modern corporations are incorporated by just one state. Since virtually all modern commerce is at least partially interstate commerce, and since the government of a state cannot constitutionally impede "foreign" corporations (those created by sister states) from engaging in interstate commerce within the host state's borders, there is little reason for corporations to maintain more than one state of incorporation. For large corporations that one state will often be a state such as Delaware that has traditionally catered to corporate management with favorable business and tax laws.

b. A few corporations retain multi-state incorporation. Although the Supreme Court has not spoken directly to the issue, the dominant modern view is that a multi-state corporation should be deemed a citizen of *every* state by which it has been incorporated.

2. *State of principal place of business.* A corporation "shall be deemed to be a citizen of... the State where it has its principal place of business." [28 U.S.C. § 1332(c)(1).]

a. Everyone agrees that the statute limits a corporation's principal place of business (PPOB) to just one state. That may be the same state as the state of incorporation. But the popularity of incorporation in pro-management states such as Delaware and New Jersey means that many corporations do little or no business in their states of incorporation. Perplexing problems can arise in seeking to locate the PPOB of such corporations in just one of the many states in which they may do substantial business.

b. There is substantial agreement that one of the most important criteria for determining the PPOB should be the location of the corporation's operational activity. This test is generally referred to as the "place of activities" or "place of operations" test. We adopt *"place of operations"* as our preferred terminology because it better captures the distinction between the place where corporate operations occur — where the corporation does whatever it is that produces its revenue — and the place where corporate management is located.

(1) The location of operations rather than management is of primary importance in locating the PPOB, since Congress was attempting through the PPOB provision to cut down on corporate access to the diversity jurisdiction. The place where a corporation conducts most of its operations is the place where most lawsuits by or against the corporation are likely to arise. It is this essentially local litigation that Congress sought to foreclose from the federal courts by enacting the PPOB provision.

Example: A Delaware corporation is engaged exclusively in manufacturing furniture in North Carolina. It is sued in a North Carolina court by a local contractor for failure to pay for work done at its plant. Unless the corporation's PPOB is North Carolina, there is diversity of citizenship and the case can be removed to federal court on that basis (assuming there is a sufficient amount in controversy). Congress adopted the PPOB provision in order to rule out removal in this situation.

(2) There is also substantial agreement that when corporate operations are "far flung," the second major criterion for determining the PPOB should be the location of a corporation's administrative headquarters, where policy is made and operational activity is organized and directed. This is generally termed the *"nerve center"* test.

(3) There is no substantial agreement on the order of priority and the relationship between the "place of operations" and the "nerve center" tests. Some courts have argued that the two should be combined into a *"total activity"* test that sensibly considers the nature and dispersion of both operations and management — and the extent to which operational activity itself consists of management activity.

c. The best approach is to give priority to the "place of operations" test, to apply the "nerve center" test as the secondary criterion, and to resort to a "total activity" test only when the first two criteria yield no clear result.

(1) The "place of operations" should be conceived as looking for the place of maximum concentration of the corporation's *litigation-provoking* activity. This will give effect to the legislative intent to fence out as much essentially local litigation as possible by treating corporations as citizens of their PPOBs.

(2) If there is no single state in which there is a preponderant concentration of operational activity, but one state with substantial operational activity is also the site of the corporate "nerve center," then that state should be designated the PPOB.

(3) Where there is more than one state of significant managerial activity, the important state from a managerial perspective is where policy decisions are made — not just the "nerve center" but the "brain."

(4) When there is no overlap between the set of states that are plausible candidates for PPOB based on operational activity and the set of states to be considered based on managerial activity, only the "total activity" test can be applied. In applying this test, courts should assign as the PPOB that state in which a corporation is least likely to encounter local prejudice.

d. If a domestic American corporation has its PPOB outside the United States, it does not become a citizen of the foreign state where it has its PPOB, and is not treated as an alien corporation. It is a citizen solely of its state(s) of incorporation and has no other PPOB-based or alienage-based citizenship. *Cabalceta v. Standard Fruit Co.*, 883 F.2d 1553 (11th Cir. 1989).

e. **Examples** of how a corporation's principal place of business is determined.

  (1) *"Place of operations" test is determinative.* Benchmark Furniture Company is a Delaware corporation with its sole factory in Greensboro, North Carolina and a wholesale showroom in Patterson, New Jersey. Most of Benchmark's furniture is sold to distributors in New Jersey, who resell the furniture to retail outlets throughout the northeast. Furniture is not the sort of manufactured good that generates frequent products liability litigation arising from sale to, use by, and injury of the ultimate consumer. Most litigation to which Benchmark is party involves North Carolina employees and materials suppliers. Benchmark's day-to-day manufacturing activity is managed from its administrative office in Greensboro. Benchmark's senior executives work, and its board of directors meets, at its corporate offices in Richmond, Virginia. The place of litigation-provoking operational activity controls. North Carolina is Benchmark's PPOB.

  (2) *"Nerve center" test is determinative as between locations of operational activity.* Rent-A-Car Company is a State *X* corporation with 11 percent of its business in State *A*, 10 percent in State *B*, and 9 percent in State *C*. It does no more than 5 percent of its business in any other state. Headquarters is in State *D*, where the company does only 1 percent of its business. Legislative intent points to assigning PPOB to that state in which the corporation is most frequently sued. That may be either State *A* or State *D* depending on the nature of the business. Discovery might illuminate this issue. Courts are not agreed in giving great weight to litigation rates. The predominant solution in this situation is to apply the "nerve center" test. State *D* is the PPOB. In our minority view persuasive evidence that the corporation defends more lawsuits in one of the "far-flung" locations, such as State *A*, ought to result in assigning PPOB to that state.

  (3) *"Total activity" test is determinative where "place of operations" and "nerve center" tests point in inconsistent directions.* Innkeeper Corporation is a closely-held Delaware corporation that operates a chain of franchised bargain motels in 10 southern states. Each state has approximately the same value of Innkeeper assets and generates approximately the same volume of revenue. Innkeeper's franchisees manage the day-to-day activities of each motel. The solicitation, supervision and training of franchisees and market studies to select new locations are carried out at Innkeeper's administrative headquarters in Connecticut. Innkeeper's senior officers work at the Connecticut location. Innkeeper's major shareholders and most of its directors live in Palm Desert, California, where all meetings of the Board of Directors are held. Most customer complaints are handled informally with liberal rebates and free accomodation. Most litigation arises from disputes between Innkeeper and its franchisees concerning the division of costs and revenues at individual locations. These suits are generally filed against Innkeeper in the state in which the disgruntled franchisee is operating a motel. Innkeeper's activities and liabilities are basically managerial rather than operational. In light of its total activities Innkeeper's PPOB is Connecticut. Assigning the PPOB to one of the 10 states where retail lodging services are provided would reduce only slightly (by roughly 10 percent — the proportion of its retail operations in any one state) Innkeeper's access to federal court in suits arising from its retail operations. In most suits in these states Innkeeper will be perceived locally as an outsider.

4

Preserving Innkeeper's access to a federal forum in these states is consistent with the legislative intent of the PPOB provision.

3. *Miscellaneous principles of corporate citizenship*

a. *Direct actions.* In a "direct action" against an incorporated insurance company as insurer of the negligent party, the corporate insurer is deemed to be a citizen of the state in which its insured is a citizen, in addition to being deemed a citizen of its state(s) of incorporation and the state in which it has its principal place of business. [28 U.S.C. § 1332(c)(1).]

b. *Professional corporations.* Many partnerships of doctors, lawyers, and other professionals have been encouraged by the tax laws to reconstitute themselves as professional corporations. In some instances even sole practitioners may operate as single-shareholder professional corporations.

(1) Despite the dissimilarities between professional corporations and corporations organized for the traditional purpose of accumulating investment capital, the courts have thus far respected the corporate form of professional corporations and determine their corporate citizenship according to the conventional rules. *See Cote v. Wadel*, 796 F.2d 981 (7th Cir. 1986) (Posner, J.).

(2) A professional corporation's principal place of business is almost certain to be in the same state as its state of incorporation. The major effect of respecting the corporate form is to permit citizens of neighboring states to sue a law firm or medical practice without regard to whether members of the defendant firm are, as individuals, co-citizens of the complaining party.

c. *Municipal corporations.* Although the states themselves have no state citizenship for diversity purposes, and are in any event immune from being sued by individuals in federal court under the Eleventh Amendment, each state's incorporated local political subdivisions — cities, towns, counties and the like — are generally considered to be citizens of that state and are subject to the diversity jurisdiction.

d. *Federally chartered corporations.* National banks and various other types of national organizations are federally chartered corporations. A national bank is deemed a citizen of the state in which it is located. [28 U.S.C. § 1348.] Federally chartered farm credit institutions, whose activities are not generally confined to a single state, are deemed citizens citizenship in the state where they maintain their principal office. [12 U.S.C. § 2258.] Absent express statutory provision, the general view is that federally chartered corporations with activities confined to just one state are citizens of that state, but if their activities are not localized, such corporations lack any state citizenship. Diversity status is irrelevant to federal corporations in which more than half of the shares are owned by the federal goverement, since all suits to which such corporations are party are deemed to arise under federal law. *See* 28 U.S.C. § 1349.

e. *Alien corporations.* An alien corporation is one incorporated under the law of a foreign country. Alien corporations are citizens of the foreign states which have created them. An alien corporation will also be a citizen of a U.S.-state if it has its *world-wide* PPOB in the United States. As previously noted, special jurisdictional rules apply to alien corporations if their home governments own over half of their shares. Such corporations are treated as arms of their governments. They can invoke the alienage jurisdiction as plaintiffs [28 U.S.C. § 1332(a)(4)], but they can be sued as defendants only under a special grant of federal question jurisdiction [28 U.S.C. § 1330].

G. **Jurisdictional Amounts in Diversity Cases**

1. *Background.* The constitutional grant of federal judicial power in Article III makes no mention of a jurisdictional amount. From the very beginning of the federal court system, however, Congress has imposed amount-in-controversy requirements as one way (along

with the rule of "complete diversity") of cutting down on the number of cases qualifying for federal jurisdiction. Although jurisdictional amounts were also required in federal question cases for most of the history of the federal courts, the jurisdictional amount for all federal question cases (except in a few highly specialized instances) was repealed in 1980. For all practical purposes the requirement of a minimum amount in controversy remains significant only in diversity cases.

2. *The required amount*

    a.   For statutory interpleader cases under 28 U.S.C. § 1335, the amount in controversy need be only $500 (or more). (Interpleader actions are discussed in detail in Chapter 6.)

    b.   For general diversity cases, 28 U.S.C. § 1332(a) requires that the amount in controversy *exceed* $50,000, "exclusive of interest and costs."

        (1) *Former amount.* For cases filed prior to May 18, 1989, the amount must exceed $10,000.

        (2) *Excludable interest.* The interest excluded is interest that accrues *after* the cause of action has accrued, *i.e.*, after a promissory note has come due and the promise to pay it has been breached. The purpose of excluding such interest is to remove any incentive for a plaintiff to delay suit on a jurisdictionally insufficient claim for such time as sufficient interest accrues to raise the claim above the jurisdictional threshold.

        (3) *Excludable costs.* The costs excluded are the conventional taxable costs discussed below in Chapter 11. Attorneys' fees are not part of conventional taxable costs but may be provided for by statute or by contract. When so authorized, a claim for a reasonable amount of attorneys' fees will be treated as an element of damages for the underlying cause of action, and thus the amount of attorneys' fees claimed may be included in the amount in controversy.

        (4) *Amount must be exceeded.* The statute confers jurisdiction where damages *exceed* the stated amount. This creates a procedural trap for those who casually conclude (wrongly) that "the jurisdictional amount for federal diversity suits is $50,000." A complaint drafted to seek exactly $50,000 in damages will fail to qualify for federal jurisdiction by the margin of one cent.

3. The *value* of "the matter in controversy"

    a.   *Claims for monetary relief*

        (1) *The "good faith/legal certainty" standard.* When the plaintiff claims in *"good faith"* a specified amount of damages in the complaint, the amount prayed for by the plaintiff determines the amount in controversy in the litigation. Good faith is conclusively presumed, however, unless it is *legally certain* that the amount claimed (or so much of that amount as exceeds the jurisdictional amount) cannot be recovered. *St. Paul Mercury Indemnity Co. v. Red Cab Co.*, 303 U.S. 283 (1938). Although the "good faith/legal certainty" standard refers to the amount claimed in "good faith," this must be understood as referring to an *objective* rather than a *subjective* standard of good faith.

        (2) Since the law accepts at face value the plaintiff's own determination of the amount of damages to which she is entitled, the "good faith/legal certainty" standard makes it extremely easy for an intelligent plaintiff to meet the requisite amount in controversy in the great mass of ordinary suits for money damages. The "good faith/legal certainty" standard screens out claims that cannot meet the jurisdictional amount as a matter of law but seeks to avoid wasteful litigation of "a little more or a little less" arguments about the value of the plaintiff's claims. The Supreme Court

does not want to hold a mini-trial over the jurisdictional amount requirement in order to determine if there should be a full scale trial in federal court on the merits.

Example: A California wine broker brought a diversity action in South Carolina. The jurisdictional amount at the time was $2000. A shipment of wine and brandy sent by the plaintiff to South Carolina customers had been received by the defendants, who refused to turn the goods over to plaintiff's agent for delivery to the proper parties. The plaintiff sued for the $1,000 value of the goods withheld by the defendants, and for $10,000 in consequential damages to plaintiff's business relations with South Carolina customers. The South Carolina statute governing "claim and delivery" cases for wrongful detention of misdelivered goods did not allow recovery of consequential damages. Thus, there was a legal certainty that the jurisdictional amount could not be recovered, and the case was properly dismissed for lack of jurisdiction. *Vance v. W.A. Vandercook Co.*, 170 U.S. 468 (1898).

(3) The substantive law determining the measure of damages in a diversity case is state law, under the *Erie* doctrine discussed at the end of this chapter. When state law allows unlimited punitive damages to be claimed, a federal diversity plaintiff may properly rely on a claim of punitive damages, in whatever amount is needed, to bring the case within the jurisdictional amount. *Bell v. Preferred Life Assurance Society*, 320 U.S. 238 (1943). The same is true when state law permits unlimited claims for other forms of unliquidated damages, such as pain and suffering.

(4) Federal courts have generally been tolerant of highly optimistic claims for unliquidated or punitive damages in order to satisfy the jurisdictional amount. There is new reason for pleaders to be cautious, however.

(a) Since 1983, *Rule 11* has provided for mandatory sanctions when borderline-fictitious theories of fact or law are litigated in federal court. (*See* Chapter 5 for more on Rule 11.)

(b) In the much-cited case of *Burns v. Anderson*, 502 F.2d 970 (5th Cir. 1974), the Fifth Circuit reached the gag point regarding claims for unliquidated damages that have been palpably inflated in order to exceed the jurisdictional amount. The Fifth Circuit affirmed the district court's dismissal for lack of jurisdiction of a broken thumb case in which the plaintiff sought $1,026 in lost wages and medical expenses and $60,000 in pain and suffering. In a similar case today the plaintiff could expect to be hit with Rule 11 sanctions.

(c) One section of the general diversity statute, 28 U.S.C. § 1332(b), addresses the problem of inflated claims for damages but provides only the mild and ineffective sanction that if the plaintiff ultimately recovers a judgment worth less than the jurisdictional amount, the court may deny "costs" to the plaintiff and may force the plaintiff to pay the "costs" of the defendant. Section 1332(b) has proven to be toothless in practice, and its powers are rarely used by judges. Rule 11 is the major sanctioning device currently deterring far-fetched pleading of the jurisdictional amount.

(5) A federal court is not deprived of jurisdiction if the value of the judgment rendered after trial of the merits is for less than the jurisdictional amount. What matters is that the requisite amount was *in controversy*, in the sense that the parties were at risk to win or lose the jurisdictional amount. Even if there is a defense verdict and no damages are awarded at all, the claim is extinguished. It is the value of the claim when it was still subject to litigation that is at issue when the existence of a sufficient amount in controversy is challenged. Moreover, a claim for damages need not be contested by the defendant in order to count toward the amount in controversy. A plaintiff needs the court to exercise its jurisdiction in order to have a *judgment* that

will have force and value regardless whether the defendant's good intentions continue.

   b.   *Claims for injunctive relief*

      (1) The *"value of the object"* standard. In *Mississippi v. Missouri R.R. v. Ward*, 67 U.S. 485 (1862), the Supreme Court ruled that the amount in controversy in a suit for injunctive relief was the "value of the object."

         (a) The cost of the damage suffered to date by the party seeking the injunction is not controlling.

         (b) What matters is the value or cost to the parties if the plaintiff succeeds in winning the injunctive relief sought.

      (2) The *"either viewpoint"* standard. If the value of what plaintiff seeks to win in court is different for plaintiff and defendant — if plaintiff gains less from winning the injunction than the defendant loses, or vice versa, either party's viewpoint may be relied on to establish that the requisite amount is in controversy. *See McCarty v. Amoco Pipeline Co.*, 595 F.2d 389 (7th Cir. 1979).

4. *Aggregation of claims.* Federal law on aggregation of claims for purposes of the jurisdictional amount may not be well reasoned but is well settled and consistently applied.

   a.   All claims by any one plaintiff against any one defendant may be aggregated, even if the claims are unrelated to each other.

      Example: Suppose X owes A \$30,000 on an unpaid promissory note. A and X are citizens of different states, and A must go to X's home state in order to get personal jurisdiction over X. A would prefer to bring suit in federal court. The \$30,000 claim on the unpaid note is not a sufficient amount in controversy, however. The single plaintiff-single defendant aggregation rule allows A to join any other claim against X and add the value of the two claims together in order to meet the jurisdictional amount requirement. If A has a good faith claim against X for \$25,000 for X's fraudulent recommendation to A of a bad investment, A can join together the wholly unrelated contract and fraud claims in a single suit. The federal court will regard \$55,000 as the amount in controversy in this suit and will have subject-matter jurisdiction based on diversity of citizenship.

   b.   The single plaintiff-single defendant aggregation rule operates independently for each particular pairing of a plaintiff and a defendant in a multi-party action. The jurisdictional amount must be satisfied independently by each pair of plaintiff and defendant or the claims between that pair of parties will be dismissed for lack of subject-matter jurisdiction.

      Example: A and B might have jointly lent the \$30,000 to X, but B might have no interest in A's \$25,000 fraud claim against X. If A and B jointly file a two count complaint against X, with B joining only in the \$30,000 count, B's claims against X will be dismissed. But if B were to have her own independent claim against X, say a \$40,000 claim arising out of an automobile accident, B too could adjudicate the \$30,000 debt claim in federal court. A and B would simply file a three count complaint against X, joining in the assertion of the \$30,000 debt claim, with A (but not B) also asserting the \$25,000 fraud claim and B (but not A) also asserting the \$40,000 tort claim.

   c.   *No aggregation* is permitted of claims by multiple plaintiffs or against multiple defendants, even when the claims in question are related or even identical.

      (1) There is no exception for class actions. *Zahn v. International Paper Co.*, 414 U.S. 291 (1973). The claim of each class member must independently meet the jurisdictional amount. As previously noted, this forecloses federal diversity jurisdiction in virtually any conceivable class action.

(2) There is an exception to the rule against multi-party aggregation of claims when the interests of the multiple parties in the aggregated claims are "joint" rather than "several." The law is notoriously unclear in intermediate cases, but a clear illustration is afforded by joint versus several interests in real estate.

Example: Suppose *A* and *B* own a two room ski-resort cabin as tenants-in-common. *C* negligently causes the destruction of the cabin by fire. It will cost $90,000 to rebuild the cabin. Assuming complete diversity exists and there are no venue or personal jurisdiction problems, *A* and *B* can sue *C* in federal court. The amount in controversy will be deemed to be $90,000. But if the identical cabin had consisted in the eyes of the law as a two-unit condominium, with *A* and *B* each owning one unit, *A* and *B* could not jointly sue *C* in federal court. As condominimum owners *A* and *B* would each have suffered a $45,000 loss to their several interests.

H. Other Attributes of Diversity Jurisdiction

1. Diversity jurisdiction is non-exclusive. State courts have *concurrent jurisdiction* over cases eligible for federal trial on the basis of diversity jurisdiction.

2. Jurisdiction attaches if diversity exists *at the time the complaint is filed* in federal court. Changes in the citizenship of existing parties after the filing of the complaint do not divest the court of the jurisdiction previously acquired. This does not mean that new, non-diverse parties can be added later. Complete diversity must still exist at the time any new party is added, or that new party must be dropped.

3. The word "States" is defined by § 1332(d) to include the District of Columbia, Puerto Rico, and federal territories. Although unable to agree on the reasons why, the Supreme Court upheld the constitutionality of treating these localities as states for purposes of diversity jurisdiction. *National Mutual Ins. Co. v. Tidewater Transfer Co.*, 337 U.S. 582 (1949).

4. In a class action, the citizenship of absent class members is disregarded. *Supreme Tribe of Ben-Hur v. Cauble*, 255 U.S. 356 (1921). This judicially created exception to the rule of complete diversity has little practical impact, however, because virtually all class actions are disqualified from diversity jurisdiction by the jurisdictional amount requirement. Unlike the diversity of citizenship requirement (which applies only to the named class representatives), the jurisdictional amount requirement must be satisfied independently by every member of the class. It is a very rare class action in which there are so many class members that they cannot individually join together to sue in their own names, and yet each one of these many absent class members stands to win or lose more than $50,000.

5. Under § 1332(c)(2), adopted in 1988, the state of citizenship of a decedent (at the time of death), an infant, or an incompetent is attributed to the legal representative of the decedent's estate, the infant, or the incompetent. This attributed citizenship is the *only* citizenship used to determine the diversity status of a representative party in such actions.

Example: *A*, the executor of the estate of *B*, sues *C* for causing the wrongful death of *B*. *A* is a citizen of New York, *C* is a citizen of Maine, and *B* was also a citizen of Maine when she was killed. There is no diversity, because *B's* citizenship is attributed to *A*: in the contemplation of § 1332, one Maine citizen is suing another Maine citizen.

6. The party invoking diversity jurisdiction must plead and, if disputed, prove the factual basis for jurisdiction.

   a. This will be the plaintiff when the case has been filed originally in federal court. (Federal Rule 8(a)(1) requires the complaint to set forth a "short and plain statement of the grounds upon which the court's jurisdiction depends.")

   b. This will be the defendant when diversity jurisdiction is the basis for removal of a case from state court to federal court. (28 U.S.C. § 1446 requires the notice of removal to contain a "short and plain statement of the facts" supporting the right to remove.)

7. Parties may be realigned, defeating diversity, where nominally opposing parties have substantial common interests. This requires a judgment call by the district court in applying nebulous standards as to whether the interests that nominally opposing parties have in common are more substantial than their conflicting interests. *City of Indianapolis v. Chase National Bank*, 314 U.S. 63 (1941).

8. Although § 1332 confers jurisdiction on the district courts to adjudicate "all civil actions" where there is the requisite diversity and amount in controversy, by longstanding judicial practice the diversity jurisdiction does not extend to domestic relations and probate cases.

9. At the moment, general diversity jurisdiction is disfavored by judges and most commentators, who think it diverts the attention of the federal courts from the "federal question" cases with which they should primarily be concerned. General diversity jurisdiction remains very popular with lawyers, however, and is unlikely to be repealed in the near future.

V. REMOVAL JURISDICTION

REMOVAL JURISDICTION

4

A. **Overview. In some ways the removal jurisdiction of the federal courts resembles a third system of courts, featuring not only unique jurisdictional rules but also a special procedural system. Thus we might speak of state-court jurisdiction, federal jurisdiction, and removal jurisdiction under discrete headings. Complete mastery of all details of federal removal jurisdiction is beyond the scope of our discussion. We concentrate on the one fundamental rule of removabilty, its most important qualifications and extensions, and the basic time limits and procedures for invoking removal jurisdiction.**

B. *The Fundamental Rule of Removability.* **Any civil action within the original jurisdiction of the federal district courts that was filed instead in a state court may be removed by the defendant to the federal district court for the district in which the state court action is pending.**

1. The two great weapons that defendants in American civil litigation bring to the battle to control the choice of forum are the right to challenge the plaintiff's choice of the state in which to bring suit by attacking the territorial jurisdiction of the forum, and the right within the limits here explored to countermand the plaintiff's choice to proceed in a state rather than federal court. As a defendant in state court litigation you should begin planning your defense on the assumption that removal is possible. Thus alert to the standing possibility of removal, you should go on to examine whether you are barred from removal by a lack of original federal jurisdiction or by an exception to our fundamental rule. If you establish affirmatively that you do have the right to remove, you can then make an intelligent decision whether your interests are better served by removing the case to a federal forum or by acquiescing in the plaintiff's choice of a state forum.

2. There are two reasons to act quickly to evaluate removability. The right to remove generally expires within only *thirty days* of the date you were served with process. [28 U.S.C. § 1446(b).] Moreover, when removal jurisdiction exists from the very start, because at the time the plaintiff filed the case it qualified for the original jurisdiction of the federal district courts, you must also show at the time of removal that the case *still qualifies* for original federal jurisdiction. The longer you wait, the greater the chance that some change will occur that will render the case non-removable.

3. The fundamental rule looks to whether the complaint filed by the plaintiff would have qualified for federal question or diversity jurisdiction. A corollary is that defendant cannot remove on the basis of contentions pleaded in the answer. This rules out removal based on federal issues raised by the answer, whether by defense or by counterclaim. It also rules out removal of a diversity case where the jurisdictional amount requirement cannot

be satisfied without reference to a "compulsory counterclaim," although there are a few holdings to the contrary. (The compulsory counterclaim rule is discussed in Chapter 6.)

C. Qualifications of the Fundamental Rule

1. The right of removal is unlimited in the great mass of cases qualifying for *federal question jurisdiction*. In two categories of frequently litigated federal question cases, however, Congress has purposely barred removal in order to give plaintiffs the special advantage of an irreversible choice between state and federal forums.

   a. *FELA cases*. Actions against their employers by injured interstate railroad workers under the Federal Employers Liability Act (FELA), 45 U.S.C. §§51-60, are non-removable under 28 U.S.C. § 1445(a).

   b. *Jones Act cases*. The jurisdictional provisions of FELA suits are incorporated by reference into the Jones Act, 46 U.S.C. § 688, which provides "any seaman" or shipboard worker with a cause of action for work-related injury comparable to that provided for railroad workers under the FELA. Thus suits brought in state court under the Jones Act are non-removable by extension of 28 U.S.C. § 1445(a).

2. There are two limitations of the right to remove a case based on the existence of *diversity jurisdiction*.

   a. Citizenship of any defendant in the forum state. [28 U.S.C. § 1441(b).]

   b. *Workers' compensation cases*. Actions arising under state workers' compensation laws are non-removable pursuant to 28 U.S.C. § 1445(c).

3. There is a special rule for *admiralty actions*. A case arising under maritime law (which is exclusively federal law) may be filed in either state or federal court. [28 U.S.C. § 1333.] If the plaintiff elects to file an admiralty action in state court, removal is not permitted on the basis of federal question jurisdiction. Removal is permitted, however, if the case meets all the standard criteria for removal of a state court action based on diversity of citizenship.

D. Extensions of the Fundamental Rule

1. *Special grants of removal jurisdiction*. Consistent application of any shorthand rule of removal jurisdiction is complicated by a growing list of special removal provisions embedded in otherwise substantive statutes. *See, e.g., In re Resolution Trust Corp.*, 888 F.2d 57 (8th Cir. 1989). By and large these subject-matter-specific grants of removal jurisdiction are either redundant of the fundamental right to remove any case that is within the original jurisdiction of the district courts or expand that right by unlinking removal jurisdiction from the precondition of original jurisidiction.

2. *Extensions of general removal jurisdiction in special circumstances*. The fundamental rule describes the scope of the *general* removal jurisdiction of the federal district courts, that is, removal jurisdiction that is not specific to cases involving some given subject matter. Details at the margin of the general right of removal extend the scope of removal jurisdiction in circumstances that the fundamental rule cannot succinctly express.

   a. Removal is permitted under § 1441(a) even though original jurisdiction is barred by the naming in the complaint of fictitious "Doe" defendants. This 1988 amendment cured a long-standing problem in the law of the Ninth Circuit about the proper way to deal with California's unique procedural practice of permitting the joinder in the complaint of fictitiously named defendants of indeterminate citizenship.

   b. Removal may become possible in an originally non-removable case in light of some litigative development, such as a *change in the parties or the theory of the case*. This extension of the fundamental rule, so that a case not within the original jurisdiction of the federal courts when filed may become removable later on, is limited in diversity cases by an absolute one-year time limit for any removal. [28 U.S.C. § 1446(b).]

c.	Removal is in rare circumstances permitted under § 1441(c) even though original jurisdiction is barred by the joinder in the complaint of a removable claim and a *separate and independent claim* outside the scope of federal jurisdiction.

(1)	As amended on December 1, 1990, 1441(c) removal is limited to cases in which the removable claim qualifies for "federal question" jurisdiction under 28 U.S.C. 1331. If the only basis on which the removable claim would qualify on its own for federal jurisdiction is diversity of citizenship under 28 U.S.C. § 1332, removal under § 1441(c) is no longer permitted.

(2)	When a claim within the "federal question" jurisdiction of § 1331 is joined to another, non-federal claim between the same parties that arises out of the *same transaction or occurrence* as the "federal question" claim, removal is not permitted under § 1441(c) because, by definition, two claims arising out of the same transaction or occurrence cannot be "separate and independent" claims. *See American Fire & Casualty Co. v. Finn,* 341 U.S. 6 (1951). But removal is still authorized in such a case, because the joinder of a "federal question" claim to a non-federal but transactionally related claim between the same parties will qualify for removal anyway, under the fundamental rule that any case can be removed by the defendant if the plaintiff could have chosen to file the case in federal court to begin with. When a "federal question" claim is joined to a transactionally related claim under state law, the state law claim is within the "pendent jurisdiction" of the federal courts. (Pendent jurisdiction is a form of supplemental jurisdiction that is discussed below and in Chapter 6.) The plaintiff could have filed the case in federal court by invoking federal question jurisdiction combined with pendent jurisdiction. The defendant can do the same by invoking the ordinary right of removal.

E.	**Time Constraints on the Right of Removal**

1.	The notice of removal must be filed within *thirty days* of the defendants' receipt of notice that the case is or has become removable. [28 U.S.C. § 1446(b).]

2.	In suits brought against a *foreign state* (including state-owned corporations), a special form of original federal question jurisdiction exists under 28 U.S.C. § 1330. Operating in parallel with § 1330 is a special removal statute, 28 U.S.C. § 1441(d), which allows a foreign state sued in state court to seek removal at *any time* in the litigation. The district courts are given discretion "at any time for cause shown" to "enlarge" the time in which removal is allowed. This discretion to allow belated removal applies only to removal of cases by foreign-state defendants.

3.	There is an absolute time limit, applicable only in *diversity cases*, requiring that the notice of removal be filed within *one year* of the commencement of the action in state court. [28 U.S.C. § 1446(b).]

F.	**Procedures for Removal and Remand**

1.	The removal of a case is accomplished by filing a notice of removal with the federal district court to which it is removed, by filing a copy of the notice of removal with the state court from which it is removed and by giving written notice to all adverse parties. [28 U.S.C. §§ 1446(a), 1446(d).]

a.	All defendants must join in the notice of removal.

b.	The notice of removal must set forth a short and plain statement of the grounds for removal, prepared in accordance with Rule 11 standards of investigation, accuracy, and integrity, and should include copies of all pleadings and process served on the defendants. (Rule 11 is discussed in Chapter 5.)

2.	Procedures for remand of a removed case

4

a. Within thirty days of the filing of the notice of removal the plaintiff may move to remand the case because the removal was procedurally defective. [28 U.S.C. § 1447(c).]

b. This thirty-day time limit on motions to remand does not apply if at any time it appears that the district court lacks subject-matter jurisdiction. [28 U.S.C. § 1447(c).] In such a circumstance, the case must be remanded to the state court *from which it was removed*, even if it has been transferred by change of venue to a federal district court in another state since removal. *Bloom v. Barry*, 755 F.2d 356 (3d Cir. 1985).

c. Except where the terms or stated reasons of the order exceed the power of the district court, orders remanding removed cases are not subject to appellate review. [28 U.S.C. § 1447(d).] *See Thermtron Products, Inc. v. Hermansdorfer*, 423 U.S. 336 (1976).

d. 28 U.S.C. § 1447(e) provides: "If after removal the plaintiff seeks to join additional defendants whose joinder would destroy subject matter jurisdiction, the court may deny joinder, or permit joinder and remand the action to the State court."

   (1) This is designed to avoid prejudice to California plaintiffs who, but for removal, could take advantage of California state courts' unique procedural provisions for fictitious "Doe defendants." These provisions permit very liberal "relation back" of amended complaints, even when new defendants are added to the action, thereby functioning as extensions of the California statutes of limitation.

   (2) Because the denial of joinder in these circumstances is appealable but the permission of joinder and ensuing remand of the case is non-appealable (as are all remand orders), it can be expected that district courts will rarely deny joinder when it will expose plaintiffs to significant prejudice that they would not have faced but for the exercise of removal jurisdiction.

G. Miscellaneous Provisions

1. Removal is permitted under § 1441(a) even though the plaintiff had no right to file in federal court for *lack of proper venue*. All that is required by 28 U.S.C. § 1441(a), the general removal statute, is that the federal court have had "original jurisdiction," *e.g.*, that the action filed in state court was within the subject-matter jurisdiction of the federal district courts under some variant of the diversity or federal question jurisdictions previously discussed in this chapter. There is no requirement that the district court to which the defendant has the right of removal — the district court geographically embracing the place where the state suit is pending — be a district court with proper venue of the action had plaintiff chosen to file suit in federal court in the first place.

2. Removal jurisdiction exists even if the action is within the *exclusive original jurisdiction* of the federal courts and was improperly filed by plaintiff in state court. [28 U.S.C. § 1441(e).]

SUPPLEMENTAL JURISDICTION

VI. SUPPLEMENTAL JURISDICTION

A. The jurisdiction that a federal court acquires over a "case or controversy" based on a federal question or the diversity of the parties extends, as a matter of the constitutional power of the federal courts under Article III, to all disputes that arise out of the same transaction or occurrence. An alternative formulation for this "same transaction or occurrence" relationship is "a common nucleus of operative fact."

1. When a lawsuit qualifies for federal jurisdiction based on the central dispute disclosed by the pleadings, federal courts acquire discretion to also decide additional disputes that would not independently qualify for federal jurisdiction, but share a common nucleus of operative fact with the central, jurisdiction-conferring dispute.

2. The jurisdiction-conferring dispute is called the "anchor" claim, and the related matters are called "pendent" or "ancillary" claims.

B. **"Pendent jurisdiction" and "ancillary jurisdiction" are supplemental doctrines of jurisdiction that use the broad Article III dimensions of a "case" or "controversy" to justify the exercise of federal judicial power over all related matters that ought sensibly to be adjudicated at the same time. Because the need to exercise pendent and ancillary jurisdiction arises as a byproduct of the liberal joinder of claims and parties permitted in the federal courts, we reserve further discussion of supplemental doctrines of federal subject-matter jurisdiction for Chapter 6. As discussed in Chapter 6, a new federal statute, 28 U.S.C. § 1367, significantly expands the supplemental jurisdiction of the federal courts in civil actions filed on or after December 1, 1990.**

4

VII. FEDERAL VENUE

A. **The basic federal venue rules vary according to the type of jurisdiction being invoked.**

1. *Diversity jurisdiction.* When jurisdiction is based exclusively on diversity of citizenship, and there are no alternate grounds for jurisdiction, venue is proper (1) in a district where any defendant resides, provided all defendants reside in the same state; (2) in any district in which "a substantial part of the events or omissions giving rise to the claim occurred, or a substantial part of property that is the subject of the action is situated"; or (3) in any judicial district in which "the defendants" (presumably this means "*all* of the defendants") are subject to personal jurisdiction at the time the action is commenced. [28 U.S.C. § 1391(a), as amended Dec. 1, 1990.]

All
×
Any one.

2. *Federal question jurisdiction.* Whenever diversity is not the sole ground for jurisdiction, *i.e.,* federal question jurisdiction is an alternate or the only ground for jurisdiction, venue is proper (1) in a district where any defendant resides, provided all defendants reside in the same state [same rule as for diversity actions]; (2) in any district in which "a substantial part of the events or omissions giving rise to the claim occurred, or a substantial part of property that is the subject of the action is situated" [same rule as for diversity actions]; or (3) a "judicial district in which any defendant may be found, if there is no district in which the action may otherwise be brought." [28 U.S.C. § 1391(b), as amended Dec. 1, 1990.]

Narrower

   a. Note that in federal question actions the third alternative venue rule is applicable only as a "fallback" rule if no venue is possible under the rules basing venue on the residence of the defendant(s) or where a "substantial part" of the claim arose. Given the breadth of the transactionally-based venue option — wherever there occurred a "substantial part" of the events or omissions giving rise to the claim — this means that "fallback" venue will come into play only in cases in which the complained-of transaction or occurrence took place almost entirely outside of the United States.

   b. Where "fallback" venue is needed for a federal question case, the test is extremely liberal: the presence of only one defendant in a judicial district is required to make that district a proper venue for the action, regardless of how many other defendants there might be. Moreover, there is no requirement that the defendant be "found" in that district at the time of the commencement of the action. If no other venue is available, the presence of a defendant in the United States after the filing of the action will apparently suffice to make the place of that defendant's presence a proper venue for the previously filed action.

3. *Removal jurisdiction.* The normal rules of venue do not apply. The only proper venue is the district that embraces the state court in which the action is pending at the time of removal. [28 U.S.C. § 1441(a).]

4. *Former law.* Prior to December 1, 1990, 28 U.S.C. § 1391(a) provided that in diversity cases venue was proper based on *plaintiffs' residence.* Diversity had to be the only grounds for federal jurisdiction, and all plaintiffs had to reside in the same district. The special rules recited below for determining where corporations and unincorporated associations *as plaintiffs* "reside" for federal venue purposes remain in effect for federal diversity suits filed by such plaintiffs before December 1, 1990.

B. **Venue Rules for Corporations**

1. A *corporate defendant* is deemed a resident of "any judicial district in which it is subject to personal jurisdiction at the time the action is commenced." [28 U.S.C. § 1391(c).] Once a corporate defendant is found subject to personal jurisdiction at the state-wide level of analysis, each district within a state should be analyzed as if it were a separate state. The corporate defendant is a resident for venue purposes of any of the districts "within which its contacts would be sufficient to subject it to personal jurisdiction if that district were a separate State." When a corporate defendant has minimum contacts with a state as a whole but there is no single district within the state with which the corporation's contacts amount to "minimum contacts" independently of its contacts with the other districts in the state, "the corporation shall be deemed to reside in the district within which it has the most significant contacts."

2. A *corporate plaintiff* is deemed a resident for federal venue purposes only in the state(s) of its incorporation. There is unsettled law on the proper district of residence when the state of incorporation has multiple judicial districts and the corporation has no office in any of them. The soundest choice is the judicial district where the seat of state government is located, on the theory that this is the center of corporate activity in that state.

C. **Venue Rules for Unincorporated Associations**

1. *Unincorporated defendants.* In *Denver & Rio Grande Western Railroad v. Brotherhood of Railroad Trainmen,* 387 U.S. 556 (1967), the Supreme Court held that in the absence of Congressional action, unincorporated associations should be analogized to corporations. Under the law then in effect, that meant that an unincorporated association could be sued in federal court with proper venue wherever it was "doing business." Under current law, the *Denver & Rio Grande* analogy between corporate defendants and unincorporated defendants presumably requires analysis of a defendant unincorporated association's jurisdictional contacts at both the state-wide and district-wide level.

2. *Unincorporated plaintiffs.* There is no clear rule for this relatively infrequent situation. There are scattered holdings that the unincorporated association can sue wherever it does business, but this is inconsistent with the *Denver & Rio Grande* analogy of unincorporated associations to corporations for venue purposes.

    a. Another possible rule would be to treat the unincorporated association's principal place of business as the proper analogy to the state (and district) of incorporation test for the residence of a corporate plaintiff. The issue will arise only in diversity cases, since only in diversity suits is there proper venue in the district in which the plaintiff resides. The "capacity to sue" of the plaintiff unincorporated association in a diversity suit must be established by state law — the special "entity status" or "capacity to sue" conferred on unincorporated associations by Rule 17(b) of the Federal Rules of Civil Procedure applies only in federal question suits.

    b. Thus, the best-reasoned rule is to determine the *residence* of an unincorporated plaintiff in the same way as the *citizenship* of an unincorporated plaintiff. That means treating the unincorporated association simply as the aggregation of its members, and imputing to it the residence of all of its members. Since venue is proper only in the district in which *all* plaintiffs reside, an unincorporated associational plaintiff can base venue on plaintiffs' residence only if all of its members live in the same district.

D. Venue Rules for Individuals

1. Some courts have credited individuals with multiple places of residence for purposes of the venue rules. These courts deem an individual to reside both in the state (and district) in which an individual is domiciled for purposes of determining diversity of citizenship, and in any other district in which the individual may be resident but not domiciled.

2. The better view is to equate residence with the domicile that determines state citizenship. When there are multiple districts in a state, the district of residence is that one in which the individual's domicile is located.

E. Venue Based on Where the Claim Arose

1. *Former law.* For actions filed prior to December 1, 1990, venue in both diversity and federal question actions was proper under 28 U.S.C. §§ 1391(a) and 1391(b) in the district "in which the claim arose." The Supreme Court assumed that Congress meant to restrict this venue option to just one district for any given claim, laying down guidelines for picking that unique district in cases in which common sense did not point to a single obvious location. The Court ruled that a district court should weigh the relative availability of witnesses, accessibility of evidence, and convenience to the defendant in deciding whether to grant a defendant's motion objecting to venue. Because venue limitations are not designed to protect the convenience interests of the plaintiff, district courts were directed to give the plaintiff's interests no weight at all in determining whether a particular district qualified as the district in which the claim arose. *Leroy v. Great Western United Corp.*, 443 U.S. 173 (1979).

2. *New law effective December 1, 1990.* 28 U.S.C. §§ 1391(a) and 1391(b) now specify a much more liberal test for venue based on the location of the transactions or occurrences giving rise to the litigation. Under the new law it is clear that Congress contemplates that transactionally-based venue may be proper in several different districts at once. All that is required is that a "substantial part" of the relevant "events or omissions" or of the disputed property be situated in a particular district.

F. Miscellaneous Venue Rules

1. In addition to the basic federal venue rules reviewed above, Congress has provided special venue options under a wide variety of substantive statutes dealing with such matters as antitrust, securities, and patents.

2. There are also special, party-specific venue rules for suits against the United States, federal officers, national banks, foreign states, and aliens. The special rule for aliens is of particular interest. 28 U.S.C. § 1391(d) provides simply: "An alien may be sued in any district." This provision was not changed when Congress provided in 1988 for permanent resident aliens to be deemed citizens of their state of domicile. [28 U.S.C. § 1332(a).] It is probable, however, that § 1391(d) will be held inapplicable to permanent resident aliens who have state citizenship for diversity purposes.

3. Where all defendants reside in different districts of the same state, any of such districts may be treated as the residence of all the defendants. [28 U.S.C. § 1392(a).] There is no similar provision for multiple plaintiffs resident in the same state but different districts.

4. Statutory interpleader actions under 28 U.S.C. § 1335 are specially governed by an especially liberal venue rule.

    a. A statutory interpleader action may be brought in any judicial district in which any of the claimants resides. [28 U.S.C. § 1397.] Thus, the residence of any defendant, rather than of all defendants, is sufficient to create proper venue.

    b. This special venue rule for "statutory interpleader" actions does not apply to "rule interpleader" actions brought under Federal Rule of Civil Procedure 22 and the general diversity statute, 28 U.S.C. § 1332. Rule interpleader actions are governed by the basic diversity venue rules. (The different types of interpleader actions are discussed in Chapter 6.)

5.   Local actions must be brought in the district where the property is located, or in one of the districts if the property is located in more than one district of the same state. [28 U.S.C. § 1392(b).] We discuss the criteria for local actions in Chapter 2.

G.   Change of Venue Doctrines

1.   28 U.S.C. § 1404 permits discretionary transfer "(f)or the convenience of parties and witnesses, in the interests of justice," from a district of proper venue to another district where the action "might have been brought." The transferee district must be one in which the plaintiff might have unilaterally prosecuted the suit without any waiver of jurisdictional or venue objections by the defendant.

2.   28 U.S.C. § 1406, as construed, mandates transfer of an action filed in a district of improper venue if there is another district in the federal system in which the action "could have been brought." This is interpreted to the same effect as § 1404's "might have been brought." As with § 1404 transfers, the transferee district must be one that was open to the plaintiff without any cooperation from the defendant.

3.   28 U.S.C. § 1407 provides for transfer of a case by the Judicial Panel on Multidistrict Litigation when the case is part of a complex bundle of litigation being litigated simultaneously in multiple districts. Section 1407 is a conservative transfer provision for complex litigation, because the transfer is effective only for consolidated pre-trial proceedings. After the pre-trial phase has ended, the case must be retransferred to the plaintiff's original choice of forum if trial is still necessary or if both parties fail to agree to keep the case at the transferee court. More far-reaching proposals for irreversible transfer and permanent consolidation of complex litigation cases involving mass torts and products liability (*e.g.*, aviation and environmental disasters) are gaining wide currency, and could represent a major innovation in the future of federal jurisdiction.

4.   The common law doctrine of forum non conveniens is an additional forum-shifting mechanism in the federal court system. Although the enactment of the § 1404 transfer mechanism in 1948 superseded development and application of forum non conveniens as an inter-district transfer device, the common law doctrine remains available in federal court to defendants who would prefer to litigate the case in the courts of a foreign country (where substantive duties and compensation rules might be more favorable). *See Piper Aircraft Co. v. Reyno*, 454 U.S. 235 (1981).

H.   Objection to Venue

1.   Venue is a waivable defect. It must be objected to in the defendant's first appearance, by Rule 12 motion or inclusion in the answer. [Rule 12(h)(1).]

2.   When the defendant makes a timely objection, the plaintiff bears the burden of proving the facts needed to establish that the plaintiff's choice of venue was proper.

3.   If a venue objection is sustained, dismissal is inappropriate unless there exists no district to which the case can be transferred pursuant to § 1406, discussed above.

   a.   Since venue and personal jurisdiction objections are both waivable if not made at the first opportunity, they are frequently made and granted simultaneously. If venue is lacking, transfer is appropriate even if personal jurisdiction did not exist in the district of improper venue. *Goldlawr, Inc. v. Heiman*, 369 U.S. 463 (1962).

   b.   If a federal district court rules that venue is proper but that it lacks personal jurisdiction, all federal courts agree that the case may be transferred to a district that offers both good venue and good personal jurisdiction. The courts are split, however, on whether the authority to transfer a case from a district of "good venue/bad personal jurisdiction" to a district of "good venue/good personal jurisdiction" transfer derives from § 1404 or § 1406.

4. It is inappropriate (although not unheard of) for a district court to transfer a case on its own motion when venue is improper. This confuses the nature of venue as a personal privilege of the defendant — which is waived if not promptly asserted — with the sytematic concerns for compartmentalized and decentralized government that inspire the much stricter control of subject-matter jurisdiction.

VIII. THE *ERIE* DOCTRINE

A. What *Erie* Held

1. *Expressly:* Federal courts must follow state law in deciding the rights and liabilities of the parties in diversity cases.

2. *Implicitly:* Even in diversity cases, federal courts may follow their own procedures for conducting the litigation.

B. Why *Erie* Matters

1. *Erie* is a classic choice-of-forum and choice-of-law case. It illustrates how these choices can fundamentally affect the outcome of a case, and how difficult it is to foreclose structuring litigation in order to benefit from these choices.

2. *Erie* fundamentally influences every intelligent lawyer who is considering litigating a cause of action that is within the concurrent jurisdiction of state and federal courts. The bottom line of the *Erie* doctrine, broadly conceived, is that the choice between a federal and a state forum must be made on the ground of their relative procedural advantages and disadvantages. The substantive law applied will be the same in either court.

C. *Erie* Explained

1. The case of *Erie Railroad Co. v. Tompkins*, 304 U.S. 64, was decided by the Supreme Court on April 25, 1938. The case at first attracted little attention even within the legal profession. It was a classic "sleeper," a case decided on a ground not argued by the parties.

2. *The facts and the law behind Tompkins' choice of forum.* The plaintiff in *Erie*, Harry Tompkins, had been injured while walking along the railroad's right of way in Pennsylvania. An object projecting from a passing train struck and caused serious injury to Tompkins. Tompkins retained a lawyer, who did everything a plaintiff's lawyer should do. He evaluated Tompkin's choices of forum and choices of law.

   a. The railroad had an agent for service of process in Pennsylvania but, as a New York corporation, could also be sued in New York.

   b. If Tompkins sued in Pennsylvania, there was no doubt whatsoever that a Pennsylvania court would apply Pennsylvania law to decide whether the out-of-state railroad was liable to a Pennsylvania citizen for an accident that occurred in Pennsylvania. But Pennsylvania law was unfavorable to Tompkins.

      (1) Had he been walking along a common pathway *across* the railroad's right-of-way, he would have been on safer ground (in all respects). The pathway he was using when he was injured ran *along* rather than across the railroad's right of way. This was critically important under Pennsylvania's substantive law governing the duties of landowners to unauthorized persons injured on their lands.

         (a) Pennsylvania law gave a person a limited right to enter a railroad's property if the railroad formed an obstacle to a common pathway. Someone walking from *A* to *B* could permissibly walk *across* a railroad lying between *A* and *B*.

Such a person was a permissive user or "licensee" under Pennsylvania law to whom the railroad owed a duty of ordinary care.

    (b) But Pennsylvania law did not give a person the privilege of walking *along* the railroad's right of way, *i.e.,* of using that right of way as his pathway from *A* to *B*. Such a person walking along rather across the railroad's right of way was treated under Pennsylvania law as a mere trespasser to whom the railroad did not owe a duty of ordinary care.

    (2) Because he would be classified as a trespasser under Pennsylvania law, Tompkins would have to establish that his injury resulted from wanton or willful conduct by the railroad in order to recover damages from the railroad under Pennsylvania law.

c. Tompkins had a reasonable chance of convincing a jury that a lack of ordinary care by the railroad led to his being struck and injured by some unknown but unreasonably protruding object. A jury would be entitled to infer that such an accident could only occur as a result of negligence by the railroad. But Tompkins had no factual basis to contend that the hazardous condition that injured him had resulted from wanton or willful conduct by the railroad. Under Pennsylvania law, Tompkins was destined to lose his lawsuit.

d. Under New York law, a person using a common pathway was entitled to a duty of ordinary care from a railroad regardless whether they were walking along or across the railroad's right of way. But Tompkins was not in a position to benefit from New York's regulation of the substantive rights and obligations of users and owners of land. This was an era in which choice-of-law doctrine was unambiguous and well-understood. A lawsuit filed in New York would be governed by New York procedural rules — mode of pleading, statute of limitations, rules of evidence, and the like — but New York would apply Pennsylvania law under the inflexible choice of law doctrine called *lex loci delicti,* meaning "the law of the place where the wrong occurred."

e. Tompkins' attorney was too good a lawyer to stop at this point in the analysis of Tompkins' legal rights. There was a third jurisdiction whose choice of law might differ from the law that a Pennsylvania or a New York court would apply to Tompkins' case.

    (1) In the federal courts, choice-of-law questions were addressed by § 34 of the Judiciary Act of 1789, a section which had come to be known on its own as the Rules of Decision Act.

        (a) As construed in *Swift v. Tyson*, 41 U.S. 1 (1842), the Rules of Decision Act required federal courts to apply any federal substantive law legislated by the Constitution or Acts of Congress. In the absence of federal legislation, the Rules of Decision Act required a federal court to apply the substantive law of the state in which the federal court was located, *but only if* these substantive rules of state law had been formally legislated by enactment in the constitution or statutes of a state, or were of strictly "local" application.

            i) Federal courts were under no obligation to apply the unlegislated, "common law" rules of substantive law followed by state courts, except regarding "local" matters.

            ii) The scope of "local law" — where state common law rules of substantive law had to be followed by federal courts under the Rules of Decision Act — was vaguely and narrowly defined. It was said to consist of "rights and titles to things having a permanent locality, such as the rights and titles to real estate, and other matters immovable and intraterritorial in their nature and character."

        (b) Outside of the limited domain of "local" law, federal courts were free to apply their own best interpretation of the rights and liabilities of the parties under the federal general common law in cases where no federal legislation provided the governing substantive law.

(2) Because Tompkins was a citizen of Pennsylvania and the railroad was a citizen of New York, Tompkins could invoke the diversity jurisdiction of the federal courts. There was no applicable federal statute. The Pennsylvania rule that treated as a trespasser someone walking along rather than across a railroad was not a statute. It was also not the view of the common law followed by most other states. As a general matter, federal law and federal courts held railroads to a fairly rigorous standard of care. It was likely that if a federal court regarded Tompkin's case as one subject to the federal general common law, Tompkin's jury would be instructed to return a verdict for Tompkins if it found that his injuries had resulted from a lack of ordinary care in the operation of the railroad.

(3) Tompkin's best choice of forum was clearly a federal court. But one further choice remained to be made. Should Tompkins bring suit in federal court in Pennsylvania or New York? There was good federal venue in both states. Several factors favored suit in the Southern District of New York, the highly urban district located in Manhattan.

    (a) Jury awards are generally higher in urban districts because of the higher incomes of the jurors.

    (b) Much more important was the fact that Tompkins was still very vulnerable to an adverse decision by a federal judge on the issue of whether the Rules of Decision Act required application of Pennsylvania's "local" common law to the case instead of the federal general common law. Tompkins would want to have a judge steeped in a common law tradition other than Pennsylvania's when it came time to decide whether Pennsylvania law or the federal general common law applied to Tompkins' case.

3. *What happened in the lower courts.* Things went just as Tompkins' clever lawyer had hoped they would. The federal judge in New York instructed the jury on the railroad's duty of ordinary care under the general federal common law, and they returned a generous mid-Depression verdict of $30,000 in favor of Tompkins. On appeal the Second Circuit affirmed the judgment in Tompkins' favor.

4. *What happened in the Supreme Court.* The briefs and the argument all focused on the "local law" question. The railroad did not challenge the continuing validity of the construction of the Rules of Decision Act adopted in *Swift v. Tyson.* The railroad argued only that *Swift* had been misapplied, and that the case did indeed turn on an issue of Pennsylvania's local law about which the jury had not properly been instructed. But the Supreme Court decided that the problem lay deeper, and that *Swift* should be overruled. The case was sent back to the lower courts with instructions to determine what law a Pennsylvania court would apply to this case, and to instruct the jury accordingly. Tompkins' case was retried before a jury instructed that willful or wanton conduct was required for liability. Not surprisingly, Tompkins lost. He faded from sight. But the Supreme Court's reasoning in his case forms the core of the "*Erie* doctrine" of today.

5. *The Supreme Court's reasoning*

    a. As a matter of statutory construction, *Swift v. Tyson* had been wrongly decided. Recent academic research had established that the First Congress had almost certainly intended state rules of common law to govern the federal courts under the Rules of Decision Act.

    b. As a matter of legal policy, *Swift v. Tyson* had turned out badly. Uniformity in the application of federal general common law by federal courts came at the expense of uniformity in the application of state common law. State courts had not rallied behind the federal vision of the common law. Diversity jurisdiction, intended to protect outsiders against discrimination, had been perverted into a cause of far-reaching discrimination in its own right. Lawsuits were being decided in different ways depending on the citizenship of the parties, and it was possible to manipulate citizenship solely in order to create the forum-shopping opportunity of suit in federal court and thus to change the law to be applied to litigation one wanted to bring.

c. As a matter of jurisprudence *Swift v. Tyson* was incoherent. The common law does not exist independently of the laws of whatever government enforces it. A body of federal general common law capable of displacing state common law in the decisions of the federal courts must, if legitimate, be supported by the power of federal government to make law for such cases.

d. The mistake of the Supreme Court in *Swift v. Tyson* was thus more drastic than a mere mistake as to what Congress had intended in the Rules of Decision Act. Even Congress lacks the power to enforce federal rules of common law in every case that happens to come to federal court because of the diversity of citizenship of the parties. It is one thing to sue in federal court to enforce a federal right that Congress has created in the valid exercise of its lawmaking powers. It is another thing to sue to enforce a federal "common law" right, as Tompkins did. The power of Congress is, by definition, limited. Except where the federal government is granted power by the Constitution, state governmental power remains supreme. To allow the federal government to impose its will whenever diversity jurisdiction exists would be to extend the power of the federal courts beyond even the powers given to Congress.

D. Subsequent Development of the *Erie* Doctrine

1. *Substance versus procedure.* In an influential concurring opinion, Justice Reed argued in *Erie* that the misinterpretation of the intent of Congress was reason enough to overrule *Swift v. Tyson*'s construction of the Rules of Decision Act. Justice Reed criticized the Court for going further and holding that, in a diversity action, "Congress is without power to declare what rules of substantive law shall govern the federal courts." Clearly Congress did have power to declare rules of procedural law, and "[t]he line between procedural and substantive law is hazy." Justice Reed thus raised the important question of how the Court was going to distinguish between procedural and substantive law in deciding the future scope of the *Erie* doctrine.

a. Federal procedure was a hot topic in April of 1938. The Federal Rules of Civil Procedure had already been adopted and were soon to go into effect, on September 16, 1938, ending a century and a half of federal conformity to local state civil procedure. There was no question what Justice Reed had in mind when he declared in *Erie* that "no one doubts federal power over procedure."

b. In the first wave of follow-up cases, the *Erie* doctrine was conceived as requiring careful attention to whether a particular state rule was procedural or substantive. Issues of burdens of proof and choice of law arising in diversity cases were declared to be substantive, and state law was followed. In the one case featuring a direct conflict between a Federal Rule of Civil Procedure and state practice, involving the right to pre-trial "discovery" of relevant evidence (discussed below in Chapter 7), the issue was deemed procedural, and state law was disregarded. *Sibbach v. Wilson & Co.*, 312 U.S. 1 (1941).

2. *Impact on outcome.* The *Erie* doctrine was reconceptualized in *Guaranty Trust v. York*, 326 U.S. 99 (1945). The issue concerned application of a statute of limitations. There was much legal precedent treating limitations issues as procedural. In *York,* the Supreme Court rejected the distinction between substantive and procedural law as formless and result-oriented, and adopted a new test that required the application of state law whenever disregard of state law would cause a difference in outcome in a federal diversity suit vis-a-vis the state court outcome that would have occurred absent the availability of diversity

jurisdiction. In a diversity action, the Supreme Court declared, a federal district court is "in effect, only another court of the State." Where state and federal law diverge in a way that would "significantly affect the result" of a diversity case, state law must be followed.

3. *Balancing state and federal interests.* The *York* reformulation of the *Erie* doctrine was itself reformulated in *Byrd v. Blue Ridge Rural Electric Cooperative*, 356 U.S. 525 (1958).

   a. Unqualified deference to state laws regulating the practice of courts is required only when state practice is one that has been *"bound up"* with the definition of a state-created right, in the sense that the state is willing to extend the right only if it is enjoyed or enforced under the conditions imposed by the accompanying state practice.

      Example: A state civil rights law grants a right to sue for damages for racial discrimination on condition that the plaintiff first receive a "right to sue" letter after complaint to a state civil rights commission. The receipt of the "right to sue" letter would be "bound up" with the right to sue, and it would be improper for a federal court to allow a suit for damages to proceed without compliance with this condition of the state-created right to sue for damages.

   b. If there is some practice under state law inconsistent with federal practice but not bound up with the definition of the state substantive right upon which the plaintiff relies, the federal court is not bound to defer to state practice just because it may have some impact on the outcome of the case. In *Byrd* the practice in question was requiring a judge to decide, in what was otherwise a trial to a jury, whether a special statutory defense was factually supported.

      (1) The Court decided that this practice might well have an impact on outcome, although the magnitude of its probable impact was difficult to measure. The significance of *Byrd* was the Court's decision that the potential impact on outcome of the state practice, whereby the judge alone ruled on the special statutory defense, did not *automatically* require that the federal court follow the state practice. This was a significant retreat from *York*.

      (2) The policies of *Erie* mandate due deference to state procedure so as to mitigate disparities in outcome created by the availability of federal diversity jurisdiction. But "affirmative countervailing considerations" of the independence of the federal court system, combined with the "influence — if not the command — of the Seventh Amendment" and its right to jury trial in federal court, carried the day in *Byrd*. Balancing these competing state and federal concerns, the *Byrd* Court concluded that the special statutory defense should be left to the jury's determination in a federal diversity trial, notwithstanding the contrary practice in state court.

4. *The supremacy of the Federal Rules.* The last of the major doctrinal steps in the *Erie* line of cases was taken in *Hanna v. Plumer*, 380 U.S. 460 (1965). The *Hanna* Court confronted a direct, outcome-determinative conflict between state practice and the dictates of the Federal Rules of Civil Procedure.

   a. The issue was the proper manner for effective service of process. The defendant had been served under Federal Rule 4(d)(1)'s provision for substituted service on an individual defendant by service at the defendant's residence on a person of suitable age and discretion then living there with the defendant, to wit, the wife of the defendant. Under state law substituted service was not authorized. By the time the trial court's attention was focused on this conflict between state and federal law, it was too late to effect proper service under state law within the time specified by the applicable statute of limitations. If the plaintiff's service under Rule 4 were held ineffective, her action would have to be dismissed.

   b. All four of the lower court judges who had passed on the case — the trial judge and a unanimous panel of the First Circuit Court of Appeals — treated the case as a statute of limitations problem. State law required that the defendant receive personal "delivery in hand" of process within the period of limitations. That had not occurred, and therefore the plaintiff had not complied with the state's conditions for enforcing a state-created right. The Supreme Court reached a contrary conclusion. The error of the courts below lay in conceiving of the issue as one of the statute of limitations, when in fact it was the means for serving effective process. The state was entitled to condition its state-created substantive right on effective service of process, but it did not have the right to demand that federal courts depart from their own established procedures in order to comply with an idiosyncratic state definition of "effective service of process."

    c. The *Hanna* majority first addressed the issue as if the established federal procedures for service of process were simply a matter of traditional federal practice, without taking account of the fact that the plaintiff had relied on an express, codified Federal Rule of Civil Procedure. (This part of the opinion was dicta, but it has had great influence on the lower courts.)

        (1) Concern for "outcome-determination" alone missed the point of *Erie*. What matters are "the twin aims of the *Erie* rule: discouragement of forum-shopping and avoidance of inequitable administration of the laws."

        (2) Failure to comply with state practice will frequently be "outcome-determinative" when, as in *Hanna*, the problem arises after it is too late to start the litigation over. But there was no basis to think that the plaintiff picked a federal forum in which to assert her rights just to get the tactical advantage of substituted service. Nor was the impact on the plaintiff — learning of the suit well within the time required by state law, but from his wife rather than directly from the process server — an abridgment of the sort of substantial state-created right that would raise concerns about the inequitable administration of the law.

    d. The *Hanna* Court did not ground its decision, however, on the lack of conflict between the federal mode of service and the twin aims of *Erie*. The case was really governed not by the principles of *Erie* but by a federal statute, the Rules Enabling Act, 28 U.S.C. § 2072.

        (1) The Federal Rules of Civil Procedure are promulgated by the Supreme Court under the authority granted to the Court by the Enabling Act. Federal Rule 4(d)(1) was within the scope of the legislative power delegated to the Supreme Court by Congress by the Enabling Act, and if the Enabling Act is within the scope of the legislative power granted to Congress by the Constitution, that is the end of the matter under the Supremacy Clause of the Constitution. When state law conflicts with a constitutionally valid federal law, state law must yield.

        (2) The test for the constitutionality of a Federal Rule of Civil Procedure gives very great latitude to Congress and the Supreme Court to regulate any matter that is even *arguably procedural*. The "constitutional provision for a federal court system ... carries with it congressional power to make rules governing the practice and pleading in those courts, which in turn includes a power to regulate matters which, though falling within the uncertain area between substance and procedure, are rationally capable of classification as either."

        (3) Since the Supreme Court is the very body that will be deciding whether it is irrational to classify one of its own Federal Rules as a regulation of procedure rather than substance, it is unlikely that state practice will ever be held to govern when in conflict with an express Federal Rule.

5. *The expanding role of the Federal Rules in federal practice.* The quarter-century since *Hanna* has witnessed refinements but no major changes in the *Erie* doctrine. Significant doctrinal development has occurred with respect to interstate transfer, discussed below;

three cases have applied the principles of *Hanna* to various supposed conflicts between state and federal law at the margins of procedure and substance; and the fields of federal procedure regulated by formal Federal Rules have increased in number.

a. In *Walker v. Armco Steel Corp.*, 446 U.S. 740 (1980), the Court rejected a claim that Federal Rule 3 ("A civil action is commenced by filing a complaint with the court.") was meant to control over contrary definitions of the date of commencement incorporated in state statutes of limitations. The Court indicated that a federal court should not be hasty to interpret the Federal Rules in a way that would lead to a disparity in state and federal practice of the sort that *Erie* sought to avoid. In *Burlington Northern Railroad Co. v. Woods*, 480 U.S. 1 (1987), the Court found an unavoidable conflict between the Federal Rules of Appellate Procedure and state law requiring a 10 percent "affirmance penalty" when a money judgment was upheld on appeal after having been stayed pending appeal. The Court ruled under *Hanna* that Rule 38 was within the scope of both the Rules Enabling Act and congressional power over federal procedure. In *Stewart Organization, Inc. v. Ricoh Corp.*, 487 U.S. 22 (1988), the Court ruled that state law disfavoring enforcement of a contractual forum-selection clause should be ignored by a district court in ruling on a motion to transfer a case to a more convenient venue under 28 U.S.C. § 1404(a). In deciding that § 1404(a) was a valid exercise of congressional power over federal procedure, the Court expressly reaffirmed the generous *Hanna* standard of congressional power to regulate any subject that was "rationally capable of classification" as procedural.

b. *Burlington Northern* expressly established that all Federal Rules promulgated under the authority of the Rules Enabling Act are subject to the *Hanna/Walker* standards for analysis of their scope, effect, and constitutionality. The Rules Enabling Act, as amended, 28 U.S.C. § 2072, now provides express authority for the Federal Rules of Evidence, the Federal Rules of Civil Procedure, and the Federal Rules of Appellate Procedure, and implied authority for the Supreme Court's special body of Copyright Rules. The Federal Rules of Civil Procedure include the Supplemental Rules for Certain Admiralty and Maritime Claims (pursuant to F.R.C.P. 9(h)) and the Appendix of Forms (pursuant to F.R.C.P. 84). Presumably the *Hanna/Walker* standards apply as well to formal Federal Rules authorized by other statutes, such as the Bankruptcy Rules promulgated by the Supreme Court under 28 U.S.C. § 2075, the Rules for Multidistrict Litigation promulgated by the Judicial Panel on Multidistrict Litigation under 28 U.S.C. § 1407(f), the Rules for Multidistrict Petitions for Review promulgated by the Judicial Panel on Multidistrict Litigation under 28 U.S.C. § 2112(a)(3), and the local rules of particular federal courts, all of which draw their authority from 28 U.S.C. § 2071(a).

6. *Interstate Erie.* In its early years, the *Erie* doctrine assumed that the plaintiff's alternative forum, absent diversity jurisdiction, would be in the courts of the state in which the federal court was located. Thus federal judges were instructed to model their substantive legal reasoning in diversity cases on local state law. A decade after *Erie* was decided, two procedural innovations were introduced into the federal system that complicated the question of which state's law should furnish the rule of decision in an *Erie* case. In 1948, Congress enacted 28 U.S.C. § 1404(a), permitting interdistrict transfer within the federal system for reasons of convenience, and 28 U.S.C. § 1406, permitting interdistrict transfer within the federal system as an alternative to dismissal for improper venue. In most instances transfers under these statutes result in interstate as well as interdistrict transfers, posing the question of which state's law should control the substantive issues in a diversity case: the state of the *"transferor"* court in which plaintiff originally filed suit, or the state of the *"tranferee"* court to which the case is transferred?

a. After a *§ 1404* transfer, the law of the state of the *transferor* court governs for *Erie* purposes, provided the action could have been litigated to judgment in the courts of that state. *Van Dusen v. Barrack*, 376 U.S. 612 (1964). It makes no difference if the plaintiff is the party who has initiated the transfer from the district of the plaintiff's own choosing. *Ferens v. John Deere Co.*, 494 U.S. 516, 110 S. Ct. 1274 (1990).

b. After a *§ 1406* transfer, the law of the state of the *transferee* court governs for *Erie* purposes. The Supreme Court has not addressed the *Erie* issues posed by interstate transfers under § 1406. The lower courts have had no doubt, however, that a plaintiff who had no right to proceed to judgment in her chosen forum, because it lacked either proper venue or personal jurisdiction over the defendant, has no right to claim that the state law of that ineffective forum controls the transferred case. *See Ellis v. Great Southwestern Corp.*, 646 F.2d 1099 (5th Cir. 1981).

7. *Running the Erie Railroad in reverse: when Congress requires state courts to follow federal procedure*

a. You may encounter references to the "reverse *Erie*" doctrine of cases like *Dice v. Akron, Canton & Youngstown Railroad Co.*, 342 U.S. 359 (1952). This terminology is confusing, since such cases have little to do with the *Erie* doctrine.

b. "Reverse *Erie*" cases involve suits on federally created rights by plaintiffs who have chosen to sue in state court. The governing substantive law is federal, and that binds state courts no less than federal courts. The focus of the "reverse *Erie*" doctrine, however, is not substantive law. Sometimes the federal statute that creates a federal substantive right also specifies some procedure to be followed in suits to enforce that right, such as the right to jury trial of all issues in an FELA action at issue in the *Dice* case. "Reverse *Erie*" cases hold that state courts must follow federal procedures that are "bound up" with federally created substantive rights. Where Congress has the power to make law, it can specify the procedures it wants followed, and it can compel state courts to follow those procedures.

c. The vice of calling this the "reverse *Erie*" doctrine is to confuse (1) the very muddy issues of the scope of state power posed when some arguably substantive, arguably procedural state rule conflicts with contrary federal practice that has not been codified in a formal Federal Rule, with (2) the well-established, repeatedly upheld federal power to force procedural rules on state courts in service of federal substantive policy.

E. **Does federal or state law apply? A step-by-step guide to analysis of "*Erie* problems."**

A true "*Erie* problem" can arise only when a civil action is being litigated in federal court solely because there is federal diversity jurisdiction, *i.e.,* federal subject-matter jurisdiction is based solely on the diversity of citizenship of the parties. To determine if federal diversity litigation presents an *Erie* problem, imagine that the same action were being litigated in the court system of the state in which the federal court sits. Keep this hypothetical state court action in mind when tracking the litigation of the actual lawsuit in federal court. An *Erie* problem arises when, with respect to some disputed issue in the federal diversity litigation, "state law" [*i.e.,* the legal rule that would govern the issue in the hypothetical state court litigation] is different from "federal law" [*i.e.,* the legal rule that the federal court would follow in a non-diversity case]. Such a conflict between federal and state law presents an "*Erie* problem." It must be resolved as follows:

Step 1: Is the issue clearly one of substantive law?

a. If so, state law must control under the constitutional principles of *Erie*. [Analysis ends.]

b. If not, go to **Step 2.**

Step 2: If the answer to **Step 1**'s question is negative — the issue is *not* clearly one of substantive law — the next question is whether the federal rule is mandated by federal legislation or merely by the decisional law of the federal courts. In other words, are federal courts required to follow the federal rule by some express act of federal legislation — such as a provision of the Constitution, an Act of Congress, or a formally enacted Federal Rule

— or is the rule followed by the federal courts simply as a matter of their own customs and precedent?

a. If the federal rule is legislatively imposed, *Hanna* requires the federal court to follow it. It has already been established at **Step 1** that the federal rule that is not "clearly substantive." Any rule that is not clearly substantive must, by definition, be arguably procedural. *Hanna* established that any legislatively ordained, arguably procedural rule of practice in the federal courts is within the constitutional scope of federal legislative power to regulate the federal court system. [Analysis ends.]

b. If the federal rule is merely a customary or "common law" rule of federal judicial practice, go to **Step 3**.

Step 3: If the answer to **Step 2**'s question is that the arguably procedural federal rule is established only by the decisional law of the federal courts, the next question is whether the conflicting state rule is "bound up" with the definition of rights and liabilities under the state law that governs the indisputably substantive issues in the case.

a. If so — if the state rule is "bound up" with state substantive law — *Byrd* indicates that the state rule must control in the federal diversity case. [Analysis ends.]

b. If not, go to **Step 4**.

Step 4: If the answer to **Step 3**'s question is negative — if the conflicting state rule is not "bound up" with state substantive law — the next question (under *Hanna*'s reformulation (in dicta) of *Byrd*'s reformulation of *York*'s reformulation of *Erie*) is whether the conflict between the federal and state rules is one which might *foreseeably influence* litigants' choice of a federal forum instead of a state forum, so that application of the federal instead of the state rule might jeopardize the "twin aims of *Erie*": avoidance of forum shopping and avoidance of the inequitable administration of the law.

a. **Step 4**'s "foreseeably influence?" question requires a *prospective* assessment of the outcome-determinative impact of application of the federal rule instead of the state rule.

(1) If the hypothetical state litigation went forward in compliance with the state rule (such as the service of process rule in *Hanna*) and the federal litigation goes forward in compliance with the disparate federal rule, so that any impact on outcome would occur despite compliance with each rule, without any default because the wrong rule was relied upon by the parties, is it likely that the results of the federal litigation and the hypothetical state litigation would vary?

(2) Is any such foreseeable variance in the outcome of the litigation because of the difference between federal and state law of sufficient significance that it would be likely to induce a litigant to select a federal forum just for that reason?

b. If the answer to **Step 4**'s "foreseeably influence?" question is negative — if the conflict between state and federal law is unlikely to affect the choice of a federal instead of a state forum — *Hanna*'s dicta requires that a federal court follow federal law. [Analysis ends.]

c. If the answer to **Step 4**'s question is affirmative — if there is some likelihood that litigants would choose a federal forum simply to have the benefit of federal law as to the disputed issue — go to **Step 5**.

Step 5: *Byrd* requires that the degree to which the difference in outcome under the federal rule might foreseeably influence litigants' choice of a federal forum be *balanced* against "affirmative countervailing considerations" of "federal policy."

a. *Erie*'s policy of "uniformity of outcome" (per *Byrd*) is always offset to some degree by "the goal of uniformity of federal procedure" (per *Hanna*). Therefore even if there is no other countervailing federal interest, the federal court should not defer to state law unless the foreseeable influence of federal law on choice of forum is substantial.

b. Even if federal law's foreseeable influence on choice of forum is sufficiently substantial to outweigh the federal interest in uniformity of procedure, there may still be other countervailing federal interests, such as the "federal policy of favoring jury decisions of disputed fact questions" (per *Byrd*), that may on balance outweigh "the twin aims of *Erie*" and thus require adherence to the federal rule despite its foreseeable and substantial influence on the litigants' choice of forum.

F. Summary of *Erie* Analysis

1. **[Step 1]** Is the issue clearly substantive, *i.e.,* not even arguably procedural?

    a. If your answer is yes, **state law controls.**

    b. If your answer is no, the next question **[Step 2]** is whether federal law is specified by federal legislation or an express Federal Rule.

    (1) If your answer is yes, **federal law controls.**

    (2) If your answer is no, the next question **[Step 3]** is whether the state has conditioned the enjoyment of the state-created right in issue on enforcement of it according to state law.

      (a) If your answer is yes, **state law controls.**

      (b) If your answer is no, the next question **[Step 4]** is whether the *foreseeable* impact on outcome of conforming to state law is likely to jeopardize the "twin aims of *Erie*" by encouraging forum shopping and the inequitable administration of the laws.

        i) If your answer is no, **federal law controls.**

        ii) If your answer is yes, the last question **[Step 5]** is whether there are "affirmative countervailing considerations" of "federal policy" that outweigh *Erie*'s policy of applying state law in diversity cases so that the choice of a federal forum will not substantially affect the outcome of the case.

          a) If your answer is yes, **federal law controls.**

          b) If your answer is no, **state law controls.**

PLEADING

▶ **CHAPTER SUMMARY**

PLEADING

INTRODUCTION: Modern pleading systems developed as a reaction to common law pleading. Common law pleading, and the writ system that accompanied it, developed detailed and arcane rules tied to the substantive law that governed the pleading. Equity pleading developed separately and made more extensive use of detailed fact-based pleading. Two reforms of common law pleading have had the strongest influence on modern pleading practice: (1) the "Field Code" of 1848 and (2) the Federal Rules of Civil Procedure adopted in 1938. Both reforms were guided by the desire to simplify pleading rules and eliminate decisions based on technical defects. The Field Code grew out of the work of New York's Commission on Practice and Pleading and takes its name from David Dudley Field, one of the commissioners. The Field Code abolished the writ/forms of action system and unified law and equity practice. It adopted a pleading system that purported to require simple, non-technical facts that set out the elements of a given cause of action. Today, successors to the Field Code are referred to as "code pleading" or "fact pleading." Code pleading is the basis for the pleading systems of New York and California, and remains an influential competitor to federal rules pleading systems.

BACKGROUND AND OVERVIEW

I. **BACKGROUND AND OVERVIEW**

A. **The modern alternative to code pleading is the Federal Rules of Civil Procedure model. At the time of their initial adoption in 1938, the Federal Rules of Civil Procedure were themselves a reaction to the stylized system that code pleading had become. The Federal Rules also merged law and equity. As their model, they avoided using the terms "facts" and "cause of action" in favor of what has come to be called "notice pleading." Rule 8(a) of the Federal Rules requires only "a short and plain statement of the claim."**

B. **In order to better understand the difference between code pleading and federal notice pleading, it helps to understand what purposes the pleadings have served or could serve in civil litigation. Comparing these purposes with the requirements of any pleading system helps us understand just what the pleading system values. The following functions may be served by the pleadings:**

1. to demonstrate that the court has jurisdiction of the subject matter of the action (*see* Federal Rule 8(a)(1));

2. to give notice of the nature of the party's claim to adversaries;

3. to identify and separate the legal issues in the action;

4. to identify and separate the factual issues in the action;

5. to present evidence;

6. to narrow the issues for trial;

7. to provide a guide for discovery and trial;

8. to expose insubstantial claims; and

9. to provide a record for the scope of judgment for use in application of preclusion doctrines.

C. **A major issue underlying all pleading questions is whether the pleader, especially the plaintiff, should be required to be so specific in pleading that the court can clearly evaluate the merit of the claim, or whether the pleader should be allowed to state the claim so generally that the court is assured that the pleader with a truly meritorious claim can get the claim to a jury. This debate over the role of pleadings is guided in turn by a debate about litigation itself or an attitude toward litigation.**

1. If you believe that most claims are meritorious, or, to the contrary, that many claims are frivolous, this, in turn, leads to differing approaches to pleadings, especially to the complaint.

5

2. If you believe that most claims are meritorious, then pleading should be generous or liberal in allowing claims that are imprecisely stated to go forward.

3. If you believe that most claims are frivolous, then pleaders should be required to state their claims in greater detail because the need for more factual detail will expose the non-meritorious claims. It may be possible to put this in a negative fashion, that is, is the greater danger that meritorious claims will be lost because of technical or burdensome pleading requirements, for example, through detailed factual pleading; or is the greater danger that frivolous suits will be brought exposing defendants to damaging publicity and the costs of discovery in order to expose the worthless allegations which, in turn, may lead to nuisance settlements?

D. **Typical Pleadings**

1. The pleadings allowed in federal court are: complaints, answers, replies (to counterclaims), answers to cross-claims, third-party complaints, and third-party answers. *See* Federal Rules 7(a) & 7(c).

   a. The complaint is the initial pleading filed in any civil action and contains the basic allegations that describe the plaintiff's reason to complain of the defendant and the relief or response the plaintiff seeks. Each pleading system has its own specific rules adding details to the form of the complaint. A number of these will be discussed in sections II and III of this chapter.

   b. Answers contain the defending party's responses to the material in the pleadings and can add additional material constituting defenses of various sorts. In federal practice, the answer may also contain a counterclaim that presents allegations a defendant makes against a plaintiff and a cross-claim in which the defending party would make allegations concerning her codefendant. When the answer contains a true counterclaim and it is labeled as such, the Federal Rules require a reply by the plaintiff to these allegations. Likewise, under federal practice, answers to cross-claims respond to the allegations a co-party makes.

   c. Finally, third-party complaints and their accompanying third-party answers are allegations made by a defending party against additional persons who are not yet parties to the controversy and the responses of those parties. In the federal system, a third-party complaint must assert at least one claim that the third party must indemnify or reimburse defending parties in case of a judgment against them.

2. Pleadings in a typical code-pleading state (for example, California) are: complaints, answers, demurrers, and cross-complaints. Complaints and answers serve the same functions in general as their counterparts in federal practice.

   a. California uses the cross-complaint in place of the counterclaims, cross-claims, and third-party complaints used in federal practice. That is, one type of document, the cross-complaint, may be used for all three purposes. Responses to cross-complaints are in the form of answers.

   b. Finally, the demurrer is a device unique to code pleading. Although nominally it is a pleading, in effect it serves as a challenge to a previous pleading and raises the question of the legal sufficiency of that pleading, whether it is a complaint, an answer, or a cross-complaint.

II. **CODE-PLEADING REQUIREMENTS — THE COMPLAINT**

A. **Modern versions of the Field Code, including California's, require two basic elements in pleadings. Focusing on plaintiff's pleadings, the pleadings must be in the form of statements of "facts," and those facts must be such that they constitute a "cause of action." These** two elements correspond to a formal pleading requirement, *i.e.*, that the form of allegation must be ultimate facts, not conclusions or evidentiary facts; and a substantive pleading requirement, *i.e.*, the facts must constitute a cause of action.

1. The requirement that the pleading be in the form of ultimate facts has given rise to an inordinate amount of litigation.

    a. By "ultimate facts," the drafters in a code-pleading system mean a level of generality that is neither so specific as to be evidence nor so general as to be in the form of a legal conclusion.

    b. Ultimate facts are really degrees of specificity and vary among causes of action and elements of causes of action. Precise definitions are difficult. As a guide, the pleading must describe in a general way the particular conduct or events that are the essential elements of the claim for relief. It is not ordinarily enough to say that "Defendant negligently caused injury to the plaintiff," but rather that "Defendant, driving an automobile, injured plaintiff by colliding with an automobile in which plaintiff was riding."

2. Guidelines are available with regard to when more or less detail is required. Greater detail is necessary for the most crucial or central allegations. Less detail is required where the allegation is a matter of common experience or the expected course of events. More detail is required for disfavored claims or allegations, and less detail is necessary where the defendant has equal or greater access to the facts.

    Example: In the case of *Gillespie v. Goodyear Service Stores,* 128 S.E.2d 762 (N.C. 1963), plaintiff stated that the defendants without just cause or just excuse, "maliciously came upon and trespassed upon the premises occupied by the plaintiff as a residence." The court found that use of the allegation that defendant "trespassed" was a legal conclusion. Plaintiff should have detailed in a general manner the actions of the defendants which constituted the trespass and included elements such as ownership or her right to possess the property.

    At the other extreme, pleading in great detail, even evidentiary detail, is also disfavored and formally insufficient under code pleading.

3. The formal statement of facts must together constitute a "cause of action." This second substantive requirement requires the pleader to state the essential elements of the claim in the form of ultimate facts. These ultimate facts must demonstrate that the particular factual instance of which plaintiff complains falls within those classes of instances that the substantive law recognizes as entitling the pleader to relief.

    a. In general, rules of substantive law come in the form of a syllogism: if plaintiff shows that defendant owed her a duty, that defendant breached that duty, that the breach caused actual injury to her and that there is a sufficient causal relation between the breach of duty and the injury, plaintiff is entitled to recover.

    b. Proper statement of a cause of action would consist of statements of ultimate facts to show the duty, the breach of the duty, the actual injury and the requisite causal relationship.

    c. Causes of action fall within the traditional areas of torts, contracts, property, and the like and are the elements that you learn in these courses.

4. In addition to the formal and substantive aspects, some code-pleading systems historically insisted upon a "theory of the pleadings" doctrine. This doctrine meant that a plaintiff's pleading had to be based on only one substantive theory of why, as a matter of law, the defendant was liable to the plaintiff. At trial, you were not allowed to show a different or distinctive cause of action. Thus, if at trial you offered evidence showing defendant damaged you by breaching a contract, but your pleading had alleged fraud by defendant, you could not recover for the mere breach of contract; you had to show the elements of

fraud consistent with your single theory of the pleadings. Most code-pleading systems today, including California, have abandoned the theory of the pleadings doctrine. It is enough that one or more recognized theories appear in the pleadings. Liberalized amendment and variance doctrines now allow you to prove facts at trial different from those alleged in the complaint.

III. **NOTICE PLEADING REQUIREMENTS — THE COMPLAINT. Federal or notice pleading also has distinctive formal and substantive elements, both different from those found in code pleadings. Under Federal Rule 8, the elements of a federal pleading are simple. A federal pleading stating a claim for relief must contain (1) a jurisdictional statement showing the court it has jurisdiction of the subject matter; (2) a short and a plain statement of the claim showing that the pleader is entitled to relief; and (3) a demand for judgment.**

A. **Formally, under federal or notice pleading, ultimate facts are not required. Only a short and plain statement of the claim is necessary.**

   Example: In the leading case of *Conley v. Gibson*, 355 U.S. 41 (1957), the Supreme Court held that the short and plain statement of the claim requires only that plaintiff give the defendant "fair notice" of what the plaintiff's claim is and the grounds upon which it rests. The Court indicated that facts or ultimate facts were not required and were not the test under the Federal Rules.

B. **Federal rules pleadings also have a substantive aspect. It is still necessary for the pleader to give grounds or show that she is entitled to relief. The test here, which also comes from** *Conley v. Gibson, supra,* **is that a complaint should not be dismissed for failure to state an adequate claim "unless it appears beyond doubt that the plaintiff can prove no set of facts in support of the claim which would entitle him to relief." Thus, there can be no dismissal under the Federal Rules for insufficiency of the complaint except in the unusual case where the pleader's allegations on the face of the complaint show that no relief is possible under the facts stated. This extraordinarily generous stand appears to have been made less lenient as reinterpreted in recent statements by the Supreme Court.**

   Example: In *Hishon v. King & Spaulding*, 467 U.S. 69 (1984), the Court indicated that a complaint could be dismissed if "it is clear that no relief could be granted under any set of facts that could be proved consistent with the allegations." This standard does not require a court to imagine any set of facts under any set of allegations in order to dismiss the complaint for failure to state a claim. It is the premise of the Federal Rules that cases should ordinarily not be dismissed on the basis of the pleadings. Rather, plaintiff is ordinarily entitled to undertake discovery in order to unearth facts that could be used to support claims, and the pleader is given greater leeway in amending or modifying the pleadings in order to show a right to relief even when one may not have been apparent at the outset of the litigation. Modern federal courts tend to require that the plaintiff in a pleading show at least some set of circumstances, however sketchy, that indicate that plaintiff has reason to believe are true and that if true would entitle her to some relief.

IV. **SPECIAL PLEADING REQUIREMENTS. Under state systems in general and under the Federal Rules in particular, there is a category of claims, properly categorized as disfavored claims, that must be pleaded with greater than usual factual specificity. These claims are identified in Federal Rules 9(b) and 9(g).**

A. **Rule 9(b) requires that in making allegations of fraud or mistake, the pleader must state the circumstances constituting fraud or mistake with particularity. Federal Rule 9(g) also provides that special damage claims must be specifically stated. Both sections have a similar basis and similar requirements. For these disfavored allegations, the federal pleader must add factual information similar to that required of a code pleader. More detail is required with regard to the elements of special damage and the circumstances of fraud or mistake.**

Example: In *Sweeny Co. v. Engineers-Constructors, Inc.*, 109 F.R.D. 358 (E.D. Va. 1986), the pleader alleging fraud was required to allege the time, place, and content of false representations, the facts misrepresented, and what was gained or given up as a consequence of the fraud in order to state a sufficient fraud claim in what was otherwise a standard breach of contract case. The purpose here is very simply to pose a greater burden on the pleader to specify the allegations in the claim with a view to exposing insubstantial or inadequate allegations.

B. **However, pleaders should be cautioned that the general requirements of notice pleading otherwise apply and indeed have to be taken into account in the claim for fraud. See, for example, Form 13 appended to the Federal Rules with regard to its allegations of fraudulent conveyance. Only the facts of the particular allegation must be stated specifically.**

C. **The similar requirement in special damage claims is necessary for those unusual damages that do not ordinarily occur as a result of the standard claims.**

   1. In torts, these would be unusual or unforeseeable damages or injuries, including suicide or epilepsy, for example, from an auto crash.

   2. In contracts, it would be damages not within the contemplation of the parties.

   3. Finally, there are separate categories of cases where special damages are an integral part of the substantive claim. These include claims of defamation, trade libel, disparagement of property, and malicious prosecution. In each instance, a federal pleader must state with particularity, the elements of the special damage.

D. **Although the Federal Rules officially recognize only the additional pleading requirements in Rules 9(b) and 9(g), federal judges have judicially created special pleading rules requiring greater specificity or factual detail in a variety of settings. These include big cases, that is, cases that are very complex or alleging major patterns of, for example, antitrust behavior, such as shareholder's derivative suits and allegations under the Racketeer-Influenced Corrupt Organizations Act (RICO); in *pro se* pleadings; and in certain civil rights cases. The propriety of judicially-created extraordinary pleading requirements is subject to considerable debate, and the Supreme Court has, on the whole, rejected arguments that special pleading requirements apply beyond those settled in the Federal Rules.** *See Baldwin County Welcome Center v. Brown*, **466 U.S. 147 (1984).**

E. **Alternate and Inconsistent Allegations**

   1. The Federal Rules, and modern code-pleading rules, tolerate the pleading of alternate and inconsistent allegations. Thus, the pleader within the same complaint may first allege that it was free of any contributory negligence and deserves damages as a result of another party's negligence, and in a separate claim allege that it is entitled to damages under other theories in which it may have acted negligently.

   2. As long as the pleader is not pleading inconsistent facts under circumstances which it must have had knowledge of the true facts, this is tolerable under Federal Rule 8(e)(2), which allows statements to be made "alternatively or hypothetically."

F. **Form of Pleadings**

   1. Rule 10 of the Federal Rules governs other matters of form. It requires that every pleading contain a caption setting forth the name of the court, the title of the action, file number and the designation of the pleading. It also requires that all allegations be made in separately numbered paragraphs and allows incorporation by reference of exhibits.

   2. Lawyers also need to consult local rules with regard to the formalities of pleading.

V. **ANSWERS.** In federal court, the answer contains three distinct elements. First, it contains admissions and denials of the allegations in the complaint, ordinarily on a paragraph-by-paragraph basis. *See* **Federal Rule 8(b).** Second, the answer will contain new matter, that is, affirmative defenses available to the party. Third, the answer may contain other defenses often of a preliminary nature, especially those provided for in Rule 12(b). A fourth element in federal practice only, is that the answer may contain a counterclaim or cross-claim making affirmative allegations of liability owed to the answering party.

A. **Admissions and Denials.** Under Rule 8(b), defendant's answer must admit or deny the allegations of the complaint. If the defendant is without knowledge or information sufficient to form a belief as to the truth of one of the allegations of the complaint, defendant can cite this lack of information or belief as the basis of a denial.

1. *General denial.* Federal practice discourages use of a general denial. A general denial is an all-inclusive denial of all the matters within the complaint.

Example: In California, the general denial form contains the statement that defendant "generally denies each and every allegation of plaintiff's complaint." In federal practice, a general denial is only allowed when in fact and in good faith defendant seeks to deny every allegation, including allegations of jurisdiction, found in the complaint. General denials are disfavored because they fail to advance resolution of the case in the pleadings and, in fact, may obscure the actual basis upon which defendant seeks to deny liability. Federal pleaders will often plead with great detail in their answers in order to obtain admissions from the plaintiff or to demonstrate the sincerity of their defense.

B. **Affirmative Defenses.** Affirmative defenses are provided for in Federal Rule 8(c). It requires that in responding to a pleading, a defending party should affirmatively set forth a laundry list of defenses. Affirmative defenses are matters which are not principally a denial or rebuttal of any of the elements of plaintiff's claim but, rather, avoid that claim. Thus, an affirmative defense will provide a full defense to the plaintiff's complaint even if everything that plaintiff claims is true.

[handwritten: AFFIRMATIVE DEFENSES - IN ANSWER BEFORE EVIDENCE IS INTRODUCED.]

1. In federal practice, defenses that constitute an affirmative defense are determined on a case-by-case basis, and, likewise, case-by-case determination generally governs listings of affirmative defenses in code-pleading states. But the policy behind affirmative defenses remains the same. If the plaintiff would be taken by surprise to find the basis of the claim that defendant makes avoiding its allegations, then ordinarily that defense should have been raised as an affirmative defense.

2. In practice, it is often difficult to determine what defenses constitute an affirmative defense.

Example: A complaint for trespass ordinarily must include allegations of plaintiff's ownership of the property that the defendant entered without permission. Some courts will hold that a defense that the plaintiff no longer owned the property because the defendant had obtained title under adverse possession is not an affirmative defense. The adverse possession claim negates one of the elements of plaintiff's complaint. However, it seems obvious that the plaintiff ordinarily would be taken by surprise to find defendant challenging ownership not on the basis of some defects in record title but by setting up an independent claim to the title. Conversely, another court has found that where the defendant seeks to defend on the ground that she entered the property because of an easement, an easement defense is an affirmative defense and must be pleaded before evidence can be introduced to establish it. *See Layman v. Southwestern Bell Telephone Co.,* 554 S.W.2d 477 (Mo. App. 1977). The easement does not show lack of ownership in the plaintiff but merely an excuse for the entry.

a. Because of differences from state to state, and even court to court, on what constitutes an affirmative defense, it is ordinarily in defendant's interest to raise doubtful materials as a specific affirmative defense. In this way, the defendant will certainly be entitled to introduce evidence at trial and obtain it by discovery in support of the defense.

b. The only potential risk of this strategy is that the defendant may be saddled with the burden of proof with regard to a defense which she raises as an affirmative defense.

C. **Rule 12 provides that the defenses listed there may be made by motion or in the answer. Thus, one of the elements of an answer can be any of the Rule 12 defenses, sometimes called preliminary or dilatory defenses, that have not been raised previously by a motion or waived by failure to include them in a pre-answer motion. These defenses may be stated in a very conclusory fashion.**

Example: Federal Rules Form 20 provides as a first defense: "The complaint fails to state a claim against defendant on which relief can be granted."

5

Cross Claims & Counter Claims in Answer.
3rd Party Claim Requires a Separate (3rd Party) Complaint

D. **In federal practice a defending party may respond to the plaintiff by asserting her own claim against the plaintiff in the form of a counterclaim that is part of the answer, and she may make cross-claims against her co-defendant by stating a cross-claim in the answer. If the defendant wishes to bring in new parties and state a third-party claim for indemnity against them under Rule 14, she must, however, file a third-party complaint.**

TRUTHFULNESS IN PLEADING

VI. **TRUTHFULNESS IN PLEADING. Federal notice pleading permits the statement of a claim in vague terms. There is no requirement that the pleader disclose, or even possess, knowledge of concrete facts to back up a claim of liability. It was clear in the early days of federal practice under the Federal Rules that they tolerated just this kind of approach, in which claims would be made initially in the hope that discovery would substantiate them. Today things have changed dramatically, and courts' skepticism toward plaintiffs' claims has led to an increased emphasis on the mechanisms available for ensuring that plaintiffs, and all parties, are being candid and proceeding in good faith in their pleadings. Traditionally, two means are available for ensuring truthfulness and candor in pleading. The first, and older, method is to have the party verify the pleading. The newer method is the one used by Federal Rule 11, which requires a lawyer's certification that the pleading meets certain standards or that the lawyer has completed certain activities before filing.**

A. **Verification. Although seldom used under the Federal Rules, verification of pleadings is still required in some state systems. This means that the party who files the pleading must do so under oath, signing his/her name that the matters stated in the pleading are true (to that person's best information and belief).**

1. Verification changes the pleading into a form of affidavit or declaration, and allows it to be used as evidence, for example, in support of a request for a temporary restraining order or preliminary injunction. However, verifying pleadings does not require that the lawyer certify in any way that the facts and law used in support of the pleading have been checked or researched.

2. In federal practice, the only verification requirement is found in Rule 23.1, requiring verification of pleadings in shareholder's derivative suits. This longstanding requirement is apparently an effort to discourage the use of such actions as mere strike suits, that is, attempts to obtain a settlement despite the merits of the claim. However, there is no indication that the verification rule of federal practice has been particularly effective.

More Recent Revisions - See FRCP.

B. **Rule 11 and Lawyers' Certifications. In 1983, Federal Rule 11 was amended to impose stricter standards on lawyers and parties who file papers in federal court. The new Rule 11 has generated a torrent of litigation over its meaning and application. Only now are its requirements beginning to take shape in a coherent manner.**

5

1. The new Rule requires an individual lawyer (or unrepresented party) to sign "[e]very pleading, motion, and other paper" filed in federal court. This signature becomes a certificate (1) that the signer has read the paper; (2) "that to the best of the signer's knowledge, information and belief formed after reasonable inquiry, it is well-grounded in fact and is warranted by existing law or a good-faith argument for the extension, modification, or reversal of existing law;" and (3) "that it is not interposed for any improper purpose, such as to harass or to cause unnecessary delay or needless increase in the cost of litigation."

2. The new Rule imposes an objective standard on the signing party. That person's inquiry into the facts and law must be "reasonable," and it is insufficient to have "a noble heart and an empty head." *See Eastway Construction Corp. v. City of New York*, 762 F.2d 243 (2nd Cir. 1985).

3. Thus, the new Rule requires a reasonable factual inquiry before filing the pleading or paper, taking into account the time and information available to the lawyer or party making the inquiry. The Rule, in practice, has required that lawyers (1) make some factual investigation, including at least a complete interview with the client and any readily available key witnesses, and (2) check on elements of the client's story, at least those which put the lawyer on notice that further inquiry is warranted.

4. Rule 11 also requires reasonable inquiry into the legal basis for the pleading or other paper. Presumably this requirement is similar to the malpractice requirement that lawyers must do a reasonable amount of research including consultation with the usual sources of the law and, where necessary, with specialists in the law. A secondary issue has arisen here which is whether lawyers must identify arguments that they make in connection with a pleading or other paper as to whether those arguments are supported by existing law or require modification or reversal of existing law.

   Example: General Electric filed an action for fraud, negligence, and breach of contract against Burroughs in a Minnesota state court. General Electric's claim was that Burroughs had sold it an allegedly defective computer system, causing it injury. Burroughs, through its counsel, removed the case to federal court and then transferred it under § 1404(a) to the Northern District of California where Burroughs moved for summary judgment. The summary judgment motion involved complex arguments under the *Erie* doctrine. Burroughs argued that California's statute of limitations should be applied to the action and that its application would bar all of General Electric's claims. Burroughs also argued that California law did not allow recovery for economic loss due to negligent manufacture. The parties filed the usual and somewhat lengthy papers in connection with the motion for summary judgment. Burroughs, represented by the law firm of Kirkland & Ellis, filed a Memorandum of Legal Points and Authorities along with its factual material; General Electric filed a response; Burroughs replied; and General Electric replied, in turn, to the reply. After a hearing, Judge Schwarzer of the Northern District of California denied summary judgment and directed Burroughs' attorneys to submit a memorandum explaining for the first time why Rule 11 sanctions should not be imposed against them. After further memoranda from both sides on the question of sanctions, Judge Schwarzer held that Burroughs' memorandum in support of summary judgment violated Rule 11 and imposed sanctions against Kirkland & Ellis for attorneys' fees in the amount of $3,155.50. Although Judge Schwarzer found that the motion itself had merit, that is, that it was legitimate to argue for a summary judgment, he imposed sanctions because of Kirkland & Ellis' "misleading argument" in the support motion. On appeal, the Court of Appeals reversed, holding that it is sufficient under Rule 11 that the paper or the overall argument is supported by law. *Golden Eagle Dist. Corp. v. Burroughs Corp.*, 801 F.2d 1531 (9th Cir. 1986).

5. Even though a paper or pleading is appropriately supported by reasonable factual and legal inquiry when made, subsequent discoveries may undercut the basis for the paper.

a. Courts are divided over whether Rule 11 imposes a continuing duty on lawyers to modify or amend their filings to disclose such adverse information. The better approach seems to be that a paper ought to be judged on the basis of information available at the time it was filed.

b. In most cases, there will be subsequent filings and subsequent motions that also must be signed, and the lawyer who fails to take into account changed circumstances will, if that lawyer continues to insist upon the initial formulation, at a later time be found in violation of Rule 11 in connection with subsequent filings. Thus, the distinction may not, in the end, be much of a difference.

6. Courts are in agreement that if a violation of Rule 11 occurs, the trial court "shall," *i.e.,* is required to, impose a sanction upon the attorney or party, either upon timely motion or upon its own initiative.

a. The requirement of mandatory sanctions leaves open the question of what the sanction will be.

(1) The most popular sanction has been a requirement that the party in violation of Rule 11 pay the reasonable expenses, including attorney's fees, of the party injured by being required to respond to or contest the improper pleading or other paper.

(2) However, monetary sanctions are not the only form of sanction recognized by the Rule, or even the most appropriate when the goal is to deter improper conduct. Courts have issued reprimands to lawyers, fined them, and required publication of the order identifying the offending conduct.

b. A secondary issue that has arisen here is to what extent notice and opportunity to contest are required to be given lawyers faced with Rule 11 sanctions. Gradually emerging is a sliding due process requirement based upon the severity of the potential sanction which does require some form of prior notice to the allegedly offending party and may require early notification that the court or other party considers a violation of Rule 11 to have occurred, coupled with an opportunity to present evidence at least by affidavit or other writings and to be heard on the question of and the amount of sanctions.

7. Evolving case law on Rule 11 and the scope of appellate review

a. In *Cooter & Gell v. Hartmarx Corp.,* ___U.S. ___, 110 S.Ct. 2447 (1990), the Supreme Court held that the decision to impose sanctions and the initial finding of a Rule 11 violation as well as any district court factfinding should all be evaluated on appeal according to a single abuse-of-discretion standard. That is, the trial court will not be second-guessed on either the issue of whether there was a violation of Rule 11 or the form of sanction to be ordered. In *Cooter & Gell,* the Supreme Court also held that plaintiff's voluntary dismissal of its action does not deprive the district court of jurisdiction over a Rule 11 motion and that the Rule does not authorize the district court to award, as an additional sanction, expenses incurred on appeal of a sanctions award, as well as settling the standard of review for appeal of Rule 11 sanction determinations in district court.

b. In *Pavelic & Le Flore v. Marvel Entertainment Group*, 493 U.S. 120, 110 S.Ct. 456 (1989), the Supreme Court held that sanctions may be imposed only on the individual lawyer (or party) signing the offending paper, and not on the law firm with which the lawyer was associated at the time. The Court's decision reflects a narrow and technical reading of the Rule and close attention to its language. A strong dissent argued that the deterrent and compensatory functions of the Rule would have been better served by allowing sanctions to be imposed against the entire law firm.

c. It will take further empirical-based studies in order to evaluate the larger issues under Rule 11. These include whether Rule 11 has been applied to unfairly burden plaintiffs, particularly civil rights plaintiffs, and other lawyers engaged in creative extensions of the law; whether the expense involved in litigating the question of Rule 11 sanctions outweighs the benefits gained as a result of the deterrent effect of the Rule in practice; and whether Rule 11 should be interpreted primarily as a fee-shifting device, or whether its sanctioning aspect should be central to the Rule's understanding and application.

(1) Initial returns suggest that creative lawyering is indeed at greater risk, which is almost inevitable given the language of Rule 11, requiring a reasonable basis in law or fact for any filing period. Otherwise, however, initial findings suggest that the Rule's benefits may be outweighing at least the burdens of the satellite litigation that arises from Rule 11.

(2) Nevertheless, serious dangers remain, including the possibility that judges will use hindsight in evaluating the conduct of a lawyer as reflected in the judge's rulings on the lawyer's product, and the risk that judges will use the Rule to impose their own versions of what is appropriate professional conduct by the bar.

VII. AMENDMENTS TO PLEADINGS

A. Overview. Rule 15 of the Federal Rules of Civil Procedure covers the question of amendments to pleadings, including complaints, answers, and replies under federal practice. Under either the federal pleading system or a code pleading system, there are three basic issues in regard to amending pleadings: First, will the party seeking to amend be permitted to amend her pleading at all; second, if the statute of limitations on a particular claim or defense has expired before the time at which amendment is sought, will the proposed amendment relate back to the date the original pleading was filed and thus avoid the problem of the statute of limitations; and third, if a new party is being added to the pleading, what additional requirements must be satisfied in order to hold a new party potentially liable under the allegations of the original pleading? Each of these three issues will be taken up below and explored in further detail. The discussion that follows refers to the practice under Federal Rule 15.

B. Will the plaintiff, defendant or third party be permitted to amend its pleading at all?

1. *Before trial.* There are three ways of amending a pleading before trial.

a. Amendments can be made as a matter of course (that is, without seeking permission from the court or opposing party) *once* at any time before a responsive pleading is served, or, if the pleading is one to which no responsive pleading is permitted and the action has not been placed on the trial calendar, the party may amend that pleading as a matter of course within 20 days after it was served on the opposing party or parties. *See* Rule 15(a).

(1) The Rule is framed in the alternative because only a few pleadings in federal practice require or allow responsive pleadings. The most obvious is the complaint. Thus, a plaintiff may amend her complaint at any time before an answer is served on her. Since a motion to dismiss under Rule 12(b) is not a responsive pleading, the party seeking relief may amend the complaint after receiving a Rule 12(b) motion to dismiss for failure to state a claim in order to cure the defects identified in such a motion. And, the court is usually required to provide leave to amend a pleading against which a motion to dismiss has been granted, because again, no responsive pleading has been served.

(2) In the case of most answers and replies, to which there are no responsive pleadings, one amendment is permitted as of right within 20 days after they have been served, as long as the action has not been placed on the court's trial calendar (a highly unlikely situation early in the pretrial stage).

b. Pleadings may be amended at any time before trial, and even after trial, if the party seeking an amendment obtains in writing the consent of all adverse parties.

c. Before trial, parties may amend any pleading not falling within the first two categories only by leave of court. Usually this leave is sought through a noticed motion to amend the pleading.

(1) Rule 15(a) requires that leave of court "shall be freely given when justice so requires." By case law this phrase has been interpreted to mean that there is a presumption in favor of allowing any amendments sought before trial, and that the burden is on the opponent to the amendment to show reasons why the amendment should be rejected.

Example: In *Beeck v. The Aquaslide 'n' Dive Corp.*, 562 F.2d 537 (8th Cir. 1977), defendant sought and obtained leave to amend its answer to deny manufacture of a product alleged to have caused the plaintiff injury, despite having previously admitted that it had manufactured the product. The effect of this amendment was to place in issue the question of whether the product was in fact defendant's product, a fact which was critical to plaintiff's chances for success. The court ruled that even though allowing the amendment substantially reduced plaintiff's likelihood of winning a judgment against defendant, leave should not be denied unless plaintiff could show that the amendment would prejudice the conduct rather than the outcome of the litigation, or that the defendant was guilty of bad faith or undue delay. Otherwise, any time an amendment to a pleading is seriously contested (presumably because it would alter the chances of success of the objecting party), the amendment would have to be denied. The court found negligence on both sides in failing to discover earlier that the product was not in fact manufactured by defendant and allowed the amendment, which ultimately resulted in a decision in favor of the defendant.

(2) By seeking to amend in the very early course of the proceedings, a party stands a much better chance of success under Rule 15(a). The earlier amendment is much less likely to impose serious prejudice, cost, or other injury on the opposing party, and thus it is more appropriate to allow the amendment. And, early amendments mean less difficulty for the court in rearranging the case and less likelihood the amendment is the product of negligence or bad faith or an attempt to obtain special advantage by one party. Correspondingly, as trial approaches and after trial, obtaining an amendment becomes more difficult, as we will see below.

2. *During or after trial.* Rule 15(b) specifically allows amendments even at or following trial under two circumstances.

a. First circumstance: When issues that had not been raised by the pleadings are in fact tried by the express or implied consent of the parties, the court is directed to treat the pleadings as if they had been amended to include the new issues, and the court is directed to allow an amendment of the pleadings to cause them to conform to the evidence, if this is appropriate. However, the express amendment is not necessary because the amendment is supplied by the trial of the issues themselves.

b. Second circumstance: In addition, the court is directed to allow an amendment to the pleadings even when amendment is sought for the first time at trial after evidence is proffered by one party and the party objecting to the evidence does so on the ground that it is pertinent to issues not present in the pleadings. In these circumstances the court is allowed to amend the pleadings on appropriate motion, and is directed to "do so freely when the presentation of the merits of the action will be subserved thereby and the objecting party fails to satisfy the court that the admission of such evidence would prejudice the party in maintaining the party's action or defense on the merits." The

Rule also allows the court to grant a continuance to the party opposing the amendment in order to allow that party to meet the evidence so presented.

c. Rule 15(b), allowing amendments freely even at trial, often places a party who wants to resist amendment or object to evidence in a difficult dilemma. If that party allows the evidence to come in even though not relevant to the pleadings, the court is likely to treat the party as having acquiesced in, or impliedly consented to, amendment of the pleadings by allowing trial of the issues. On the other hand, if the party objects to the evidence, the court is directed to allow amendment of the pleading to conform to the evidence that the opponent seeks to admit. Thus, standing idly by is likely to result in the amendment being granted, and very likely objecting will also result in the pleadings being amended to allow the new evidence to come in, with a trial continuance the objecting party's only benefit.

(1) The dilemma is even more severe when the proponent seeks to introduce evidence that might be relevant both to issues already raised by the pleadings and potential additional issues outside of the pleadings. Here, however, the dilemma is more easily resolved. Courts generally hold that failure to object to such evidence does not give implied consent to the trial of the new issues, and thus the party faced with this dilemma is probably better off not objecting and therefore not educating her opponent on the possible additional claims that the new evidence might raise.

(2) An example of this situation is one in which plaintiff seeks to proceed entirely on a negligence theory in a product liability case, but where there is the possibility of proceeding under a strict liability theory as well. If evidence comes in that tends to show that the product has been defectively designed or manufactured, it may be difficult to determine whether the evidence goes to the question of negligence properly raised by the pleading, or to the unpleaded questions of design defect or manufacturing defect under doctrines of strict liability. Failure to object to the admission of such evidence should not expose the defending party to a claim that it has impliedly allowed an amendment of the pleadings to assert the additional strict liability claim. However, objecting to the evidence and thereby pointing out the possibility of a strict liability claim will educate the opponent, who may then seek to add a strict liability claim to the complaint.

C. **Will the proposed amendment relate back to the date the original pleading was filed? The second issue concerning amendments is what happens if the party can amend but the statute of limitations has expired on the claim which the party seeks to add. The issue here becomes whether the amendment should or is able to relate back to the date upon which the pleading was originally filed, thus avoiding the bar of the statute of limitations.**

1. First, the party must establish that amendment of the pleading is procedurally permissible without regard to statute of limitations problems. Thus, the party must meet the criteria for amendment set forth above as Part VII.B. of this chapter.

2. Second, even if the party can amend, the party must then satisfy the Rule 15(c) "transaction or occurrence" test. An amendment to a pleading will relate back to the time of the original pleading, according to the language of Rule 15(c), "[w]henever the claim or defense asserted in the amended pleading arose out of the conduct, transaction or occurrence set forth or attempted to be set forth in the original pleading." This transaction or occurrence test is similar to the kinds of tests used regarding joinder of parties and compulsory counterclaims, as discussed in Chapter 6.

a. Usually it is necessary only that the new contention and the original pleading raise issues that each relate back to a common factual source. Thus usually this will involve additional claims that plaintiff simply forgot to add or defenses that the defendant forgot to raise initially.

See test @ 13 a. Plant v. Blazer.

5

b. When very distinct, and <u>especially disfavored</u>, causes of action or claims are sought to be added by an amendment after the statute of limitations has run, courts may interpret Rule 15(c) strictly, claiming that the new claim or cause of action has no relation to the claim(s) or cause(s) of action in the original pleading. This is a strange interpretation of the rule, but is sometimes used when, for example, a party seeking breach of contract relief for discharge from employment seeks to add additional claims of slander or defamation based upon statements made at or near the time of discharge. Because the defamation claims are usually treated as a disfavored cause of action, a conservative court may deny leave to amend even though they arise from the same basic set of facts as the breach of contract or wrongful discharge claims, because of their distinct legal character.

D. **What additional requirements must be satisfied when the amendment adds a new party?** **The most difficult amendment issues arise when a party seeks to amend her original pleading to add an additional party, usually an additional defendant, and seeks to have this amendment relate back to the time of the filing of the original pleading. In this instance, where the statute of limitations has run, the plaintiff seeks to bring what is, in effect, a new and original claim because a new party is involved, even though that claim could not be asserted in a separate action brought initially against the new party because of the statute of limitations bar. For this reason the requirements for adding a new party are particularly onerous. Moreover, Rule 15(c) as it relates to this issue has been very strictly interpreted by the U.S. Supreme Court. Under current law, even a fairly obvious mistake in the name of a party cannot be corrected after the running of the statute of limitations unless the misnamed party had already received actual notice of the action more promptly than would have been required had the misnamed party been correctly identified.**

1. First, under Rule 15(c), in order to amend a pleading changing the name of a party against whom a claim is made and to have that claim relate back, all of the elements discussed above in Part VII.B., regarding amendments generally, must be satisfied. Second, the transaction or occurrence test discussed above in Part VII.C. must be satisfied. And, third, the "new" party must have received notice within the time required by the rule.

2. In sum, Rule 15(c) as it relates to parties requires: (1) the claim against the new defendant or other new party must have arisen out of the conduct, transaction or occurrence set forth or attempted to be set forth in the original pleading; (2) the "new" party must have received notice so as not to be prejudiced in conducting its defense; (3) the "new" party must or should have known that but for a mistake by the opponent, the action would have been brought against him; and, most important, (4) both types of notice per (2) and (3) must have occurred within the prescribed limitations period.

3. The Supreme Court has interpreted the required limitations period for notice (the language of Rule 15(c) is "within the period provided by law for commencing the action against the party to be brought in by amendment") as meaning the limitations period is strictly interpreted. Thus, a new party or even an incorrectly named party must receive notice of the action within the limitations period. However, correctly named parties in jurisdictions that allow the limitations period to be tolled or satisfied by the filing of the complaint as long as service is made within a reasonable time will often receive for the first time notice that they have been sued after the statutory limitations period has run. This happens when the complaint is filed within the time limit, but notice is received outside of the time limit. However, for new parties brought in by amendment under Rule 15(c), the complaint must have been filed *and* notice actually received within that limitations period. Thus, new or even misnamed parties must receive notice more promptly than properly named parties.

4. The Supreme Court adopted this strict interpretation in the case of *Schiavone v. Fortune*, 477 U.S. 21 (1986). Alleging that they had been libeled by Fortune Magazine in a cover story, the *Schiavone* plaintiffs had sued "Fortune" within the appropriate statute of limitations period. Their complaints were then mailed to the registered New Jersey agent of Time, Inc. (Fortune's publisher), but they were received by that agent after the running of the statutory period. Time, Inc., refused service on the ground that Time, Inc., was not named as a defendant. At this point, plaintiffs apparently realized their mistake — they had sued a tradename and not the proper defendant. They drafted amended complaints naming "Fortune, also known as Time, Inc.," as defendant, filed those complaints, and served Time, Inc., in a proper manner. Time, Inc., moved to dismiss the complaints as barred by the applicable statute of limitations and the Supreme Court affirmed the trial court's dismissal of the action. Had the plaintiffs correctly identified Time, Inc., rather than Fortune, in their original complaint, Time, Inc., would have received exactly the same notice at the same time that it did. However, because the Supreme Court treated the amendment as one changing the name of a party under Rule 15(c), the Court held that Time, Inc., had not been notified in the manner required for relation back. Time, Inc., first received the incorrectly identified complaints after the running of the statutory limitations period. It made no difference to the Supreme Court that, had Time, Inc., been correctly named initially, it still would have received its first notice of the action after the expiration of the statutory period of limitations, and yet could not have raised a statute of limitations defense.

5. The *Schiavone* case has led to a proposal to amend Rule 15(c) to avoid this seeming injustice and to allow amendments to relate back when the "new" party has received notice of the action within such reasonable time after the timely filing of the original complaint as is permitted by the relevant statute of limitations for the notification of the original parties.

E. **Fictitious ("Doe") Defendants. Alternative use of fictitious ("Doe") defendants is used to avoid some of the problems of amending when the statute of limitations has run under the California code pleading system, and to a lesser extent, in other code pleading states, especially in the western United States. Under California practice, whenever a party files her initial pleading, she may include a number of wholly fictitious or "Doe" defendants within the charging allegations of the complaint. If the statute of limitations runs, and plaintiff then realizes that there were additional defending parties whom she had not named in the complaint, she may simply amend the complaint by substituting the actual named party for one of the "Does."**

1. Limitations on this right require that at the time of designating the party fictitiously as a "Doe," plaintiff must not have known the true identity of the particular party. Thus, it is not available in order to correct misnamed or misidentified parties, but rather to add truly new parties following the statute of limitations. The theory is that the Doe party was always a party to the suit, having been named in the complaint as "Doe 1" or "Doe 2," etc.

2. Other California limitations include a requirement that service be made on all parties named in a complaint, including "Doe" defendants, within three years after the filing of the complaint [Cal. Code Civ. Proc. § 583. 210], and that each "Doe" have been named properly as a defendant in the original complaint with respect to a properly alleged cause of action. However, even with these restrictions, California law greatly simplifies amendments adding new parties after the statutory period of limitations has expired.

F. **Supplemental Pleadings. Rule 15(d) allows parties to file a supplemental pleading that alleges events, transactions, and damages that have occurred since the filing of the original pleading. Unlike an amended pleading, a supplemental pleading cannot be used to cure defects in a prior pleading. The purpose of a supplemental pleading is not to change the contentions of the original pleading, but rather to add new elements, especially damages, that may have accrued following the date of the pleading. The party must obtain court permission by noticed motion to file a supplemental pleading.**

VIII. PROCEDURES FOR ATTACKING THE PLEADINGS

5

A. Preliminary Objections. These objections may be raised either by motion or in the responsive pleading. They include matters that do not have to do with the merits of the action but raise objections to the manner in which the action was initiated, such as lack of jurisdiction over the subject matter, lack of jurisdiction over the person, improper venue, insufficiency of process, insufficiency of service of process, and failure to join an indispensable party. *See* **Rule 12(b).**

B. Formal Pleading Objections. These objections highlight procedural errors in the pleadings of a formal nature. They do not attack preliminary matters, nor do they dispute the facts alleged or attack the substantive legal theory on which the pleader relies.

1. The motion for a more definite statement [Rule 12(e)] is used to attack a pleading which does not even meet federal notice pleading standards. If granted, it requires the pleading party to particularize his or her pleading to enable the party making the objection to respond to the pleading. It is not intended to add evidentiary matter to the pleading or as a substitute for discovery.

2. The Rule 12(f) motion to strike also has a formal use when it is used in order to strike out of any pleading any extraneous matter including redundant, immaterial, impertinent or scandalous allegations.

3. In code-pleading jurisdictions, there may be a number of miscellaneous grounds for a formal pleading objection, such as, in a contract action, that the pleading fails to allege whether the contract was written, oral, or implied by conduct [Cal. Code Civ. Proc. § 430.10(g)], or, in certain malpractice actions, that the pleading has not been substantiated by the filing of a certificate of merit [Cal. Code Civ. Proc. § 411. 35(g)].

C. Substantive Pleading Objections. These objections attack the legal theory implicit in the pleader's claim. Since most legal theories take the form of "If x and y and z are shown, then defendant is liable," substantive pleading allegations ordinarily attack the pleading on the ground that it fails to indicate that elements x, y or z are present and therefore fails substantively.

1. The primary method for making a substantive pleading objection is the motion to dismiss for failure to state a claim upon which relief can be granted [Rule 12(b)(6)]. This motion is successful if the pleader had obviously left out or negated a critical element necessary for relief or if, on the face of the pleading, a defense is shown. In the latter category is the statute of limitations objection, applicable where plaintiff shows that the injury or the claim arose more than one year (or whatever the appropriate statutory period is) before the complaint was filed. These motions have less chance of success in federal court than in state courts because the federal standard from *Conley v. Gibson, supra,* requires the court to deny such a motion unless it is clear that under no set of facts plaintiff would be able to prove under the complaint would there be any basis for relief.

2. Motion to strike [Rule 12(f)]. The motion to strike in federal practice is most frequently directed at a legally insufficient defense asserted in an answer or reply. Many courts also allow the motion to strike to be used substantively to attack substantive failures that are not sufficient to throw out the entire complaint. Such a motion to strike seeks to eliminate portions of claims, or some element of relief which is legally inadequate. The motion to strike used in this way is helpful to eliminate, for example, an allegation of punitive damages or other special damages when it is apparent under the law that such damages are not recoverable under the claim the plaintiff alleges.

3. Although not a pre-answer pleading motion, the motion for judgment on the pleadings, allowed by Rule 12(c), permits substantive objections to be raised after the close of all the pleadings. For such a motion, both matters alleged in the answer and matters alleged in

the complaint are taken into account. For example, the complaint may allege facts establishing on the face of the complaint that one or more of the claims asserted in the complaint is barred by the statute of limitations. After asserting in her answer the affirmative defense of the statute of limitations, as required by Rule 8(c), the defendant could properly move for judgment on the pleadings as to such a limitations-barred claim. Conversely, if the complaint states a legally sufficient claim and the answer admits the relevant facts, relying solely on a legally insufficient affirmative defense, the plaintiff could properly move for judgment on the pleadings as to that claim. In order to grant the motion for judgment on the pleadings a court must find that all the relevant facts appear on the face of the pleadings, as construed in the light most favorable to the party opposing the motion, and that in light of these facts a final judgment may be entered completely disposing of the merits of the claim addressed by the motion. If there are several alternative statements of a claim, or several alternative defenses asserted in answering a single claim, a motion for summary judgment or (with respect to an answer) a motion to strike are the proper methods for attacking the legal sufficiency of just one of the alternative defenses or statements of claim. Similarly, if the movant depends on contentions of fact beyond the face of the pleadings the proper motion to make is for summary judgment rather than for judgment on the pleadings. *See* Chapter 8 for more on the motion for summary judgment.

D. Federal Pleading Objections

1. Pleadings may be attacked by responsive pleadings (generally an answer or reply) or by motion. In federal court, any defense listed in Rule 12(b) may be made by a pre-responsive-pleading motion or in the pleading filed in response to a claim. Other pre-responsive-pleading motions are listed in Rules 12(c), 12(e), and 12(f).

2. Usually only one pre-responsive-pleading motion is allowed. If a party makes a Rule 12 pre-responsive-pleading motion raising any of the listed defenses, the party must join all other such defenses that the party has at the same time or face losing them by waiver. The rules for joining motion defenses and their waiver are found in Rules 12(g) and 12(h). Making a pre-responsive-pleading motion suspends the time in which the party must respond to the opposing pleading until 10 days after the motion is denied or deferred until trial.

3. There are three categories of defenses and objections found in Rule 12.

    a. One group — lack of jurisdiction over the person, improper venue, insufficiency of process and insufficiency of service of process — are waived unless joined in any pre-responsive-pleading motion, or unless asserted in the first responsive pleading or an amendment allowed as a matter of course to such a pleading if no pre-responsive-pleading motion was made.

    b. The second group — failure to state a claim upon which relief can be granted, failure to join a party indispensable under Rule 19, and the objection that a previous responsive pleading has failed to state a legal defense — can be raised by pre-responsive-pleading motion, or, if omitted, by any allowable pleading, or by motion for judgment on the pleadings or at trial. Thus, if ignored, these defenses and objections remain viable through trial.

    c. The third type of defense — lack of jurisdiction over the subject matter — can be raised by any party or the court at any time, including for the first time on appeal even when not previously asserted at the trial court.

4. Motions to strike [Rule 12(f)] and motions for a more definite statement [Rule 12(e)] must also be made before responding to the challenged pleading. The motion to strike is the Rule 12 means for attacking the legal sufficiency of a defense.

5. Defenses on the merits in the form of factual denials of a claim must be pleaded in an answer or response. Factual disputes will be resolved at trial, or, if there is no genuine factual dispute, on motion for summary judgment as discussed in Chapter 8.

5

E. **Code Pleading Objections**

1. Under most code pleading systems, many of the same motions are allowed although they may go by different names. In particular, code pleading uses the demurrer. Under California practice, for example, the demurrer is technically a pleading. However it raises only legal issues, only attacks defects found on the face of the pleading, and does not allow the use of any evidentiary material except that available through judicial notice. The demurrer, although filed as a pleading, must be accompanied by a request for hearing and legal memorandum in support of the demurrer. In this respect, the demurrer looks exactly like a motion to dismiss under federal practice. When a demurrer is filed in response to an answer, on the ground that the answer alleges a legally insufficient defense, the demurrer functions like a motion to strike under Federal Rule 12(f).

2. In California practice, the demurrer can be used to raise the defenses of lack of jurisdiction over the subject matter, failure to join an indispensable party, another action pending, lack of capacity to sue, pleading too vague or ambiguous, failure to specify whether a pleading involving a contract is based upon a written, oral or implied in fact contract, and lack of special initial procedural requirements such as a certification of the merits. California also allows motions to strike as in federal practice, but under separate statutory authority, and allows a motion for a judgment on the pleadings, established under California practice by case law rather than specific statute. California practice also allows use of a bill of particulars in limited circumstances to allege accounts and require a more particularized pleading. Under federal practice, the bill of particulars has been replaced by the Rule 12(e) motion for a more definite statement.

F. **Effect of Granting Motions to Dismiss and the Like. Motions brought under Rule 12 are seldom successful. Statistics indicate that such motions are made in fewer than 5 percent of all cases and are successful in fewer than 2 percent of all cases. Even the most drastic of these motions, the motion to dismiss for failure to state a claim upon which relief can be granted [Rule 12(b)(6)], if successful, may not result in the dismissal of the claim or complaint. Most courts will allow leave to amend to attempt to meet the objections raised by the motion, and thus the matter may not be disposed of at all.**

JOINDER OF CLAIMS AND PARTIES

JOINDER OF CLAIMS AND PARTIES

INTRODUCTION: Joinder doctrines govern how and how many *claims* and *parties* may be *joined together* in a single lawsuit. Modern American civil procedure encourages "liberal joinder" of both claims and parties in order to dispose efficiently and consistently, at just one trial, of all claims with common issues or between common parties. Historically, the common law severely limited opportunities for joinder. Some joinder devices, such as class actions and interpleader, were available only from courts exercising equitable jurisdiction. The liberalization of American joinder policy began with "code pleading" modeled on the "Field Code" that New York adopted in 1848 as its Code of Civil Procedure. From their inception in 1938, the Federal Rules of Civil Procedure have gone much farther, permitting joinder in almost any circumstance in which a rational party would seek joinder. The 1966 amendments to the Federal Rules marked the zenith of liberal joinder, making class actions [Rule 23] and intervention [Rule 24] easier to sustain in federal courts, and adopting a more expansive set of criteria for those parties to a particular lawsuit who are deemed "necessary parties" [Rule 19] who must be joined if feasible. As litigation has become increasingly expensive, however, there has been some reevaluation of the benefits of unitary adjudication of a multi-faceted dispute through complex constellations of parties, claims, and defenses. There has been a slackening of enthusiasm for ultra-liberal joinder, especially as to class actions. But a policy of generally liberal joinder is still one hallmark of practice under the Federal Rules and has been facilitated by the expansion of federal subject-matter jurisdiction through the doctrines of pendent and ancillary jurisdiction. Although our discussion focuses on the practice of the federal courts, similar policies of liberal joinder are generally followed even in states which otherwise do not conform closely to the federal model of civil procedure.

JOINDER OF CLAIMS

I. JOINDER OF CLAIMS IS GENERALLY PERMISSIVE AND IS UNRESTRICTED BY ANY REQUIREMENT OF COMMONALITY AMONG CLAIMS. Even inconsistent or unrelated claims may be joined in a single action. The joinder of claims arising from a common transaction or occurrence is virtually compulsory because of principles of res judicata.

A. The basic Federal Rule regarding joinder of claims is Rule 18(a). It permits, but does not require, *unlimited* joinder of claims: "A party asserting a claim to relief as an original claim, counterclaim, cross-claim or third-party claim, may join, either as independent or alternate claims, as many claims, legal, equitable, or maritime, as the party has against an opposing party."

1. *The breadth of Rule 18(a) is easily overlooked.* Usually rules set limits. There really is *no limit* to the number or subject matter of additional claims that a claiming party may "tack on" to a properly pleaded claim against a defending party. Joinder of claims is permissible even when one claim must be reduced to judgment in order for the claiming party to have a legal right or standing to assert the joined claim. [Rule 18(b).]

2. *Rule 18(a)'s permission for unlimited joinder of claims operates only as to claims between one specific claimant and a specific defending party.* Separate issues arise about the proper joinder of additional *parties* as opposed to *claims*. Joinder of parties is not unlimited. But where there has been a proper joinder of parties, the fact that there are multiple defendants or multiple plaintiffs does not alter the operation of unlimited joinder of claims as between any given pair of one claiming party and one defending party.

3. *Joinder of claims is often required by the rules of res judicata.* Except for the compulsory counterclaim rule of Federal Rule 13(a), discussed below, all rules relating to joinder of claims are in form "permissive" rather than "compulsory." That is, the rules regarding joinder of claims *permit* you, the pleader, to *choose* to join additional claims against an existing party if you wish to do so. The fact that you are permitted to join additional claims imposes *no obligation* to do so. As a practical matter, however, the rules of res judicata and other preclusion doctrines (discussed in Chapter 12) force you to join all claims that arise out of the same transaction or occurrence once you have chosen to litigate any

one of these related claims. The rules of res judicata thus operate as *indirect rules of compulsory joinder.*

4. *Joinder of defenses is also unrestricted and, in effect, compulsory.* Although there is no specific Federal Rule comparable to Rule 18(a) addressed expressly to the joinder of claims, provisions in a number of Federal Rules establish that the joinder of defenses is just as unrestricted as the joinder of claims. [Rules 8(c), 8(e)(2), 12(b), 14(a).] As a practical matter, joinder of defenses is compulsory because the failure to plead an available defense results in its waiver unless delayed assertion of the defense is allowed by an amended pleading authorized under Rule 15. [Rules 12(b), 12(g), 12(h).]

5. *Liberal joinder provisions addressed to parties are accompanied by broad judicial powers to expand or contract the scope of litigation.* Liberal joinder policies contemplate a dynamic process of "cut" as well as "paste." The Federal Rules contain numerous provisions that provide an antidote to excessive joinder by vesting virtually unlimited discretion in the trial court, on motion of the parties or sua sponte, to order separate trial of particular claims and issues. [Rule 13(i); Rule 14(a)(sentence 8); Rule 20(b); Rule 21.] In addition, Rule 42 confers on the trial court blanket authority both to consolidate related actions that could have been joined by the pleaders and to sever joined claims or separately try particular issues when necessary for sound and efficient adjudication.

B. **The law of joinder and the law of pleading are closely related. Pleadings are the procedural devices for asserting claims and, hence, for joining claims. An understanding of joinder of claims requires an understanding of what a claim is, and how the type of claim varies with the type of pleading.**

1. *Definition of a "claim for relief."* The Federal Rules refer to the basic unit of civil litigation as a "claim for relief," generally abbreviated simply as a "claim." A "claim for relief" is the allegation in a pleading of a set of facts that, if true, entitles the claimant as a matter of law to some form of redress from the defending party. The code pleading equivalent of a claim for relief is a "cause of action." Unless the situation calls for special attention to form, most lawyers and judges use the terms interchangeably regardless of the court involved.

   a. *Unrestricted joinder of factually unrelated claims for relief.* The Federal Rules (and most state procedural systems) allow a claimant to join in a pleading any entirely separate and distinct claims for relief — arising from different transactions or occurrences — that the claimant may have against some particular defending party. [Rules 10(b), 18(a).] This is the strong sense of "unrestricted joinder of claims." You might expect some requirement that the joined claims be factually related, but there is none.

   b. *Unrestricted joinder of different statements of factually related claims.* Sometimes the facts complained of are in doubt, as when the claimant indisputably suffered injury but is not entirely sure what the defending party did to cause the injury. Sometimes, whether or not there is also doubt about the facts, there may be doubt about the legal consequences of the possible factual scenarios under a variety of possibly applicable legal theories. The Federal Rules (and virtually all state procedural systems) allow a claimant to join in a pleading different "statements of a claim" even though these different "statements" arise out of the same transaction or occurrence and differ only in the particular version of the facts they present or in the particular vision of the law upon which they are premised. [Rules 8(e)(2), 18(a).] This is a weaker, less surprising sense of "unrestricted joinder of claims." This sort of joinder of claims is a practical necessity, in order for the rules of claim preclusion and res judicata to work fairly. Obviously, if the pleading of any one statement of a claim is preclusive of all other possible claims or statements of claims arising from the same transaction of occurrence, there should be permission to join together all of the related claims in one pleading.

6

Until the advent of liberal joinder, however, claimants were often required to elect between available remedies or inconsistent contentions of fact.

2. *Definition of a "count."* All pleadings should be subdivided into numbered paragraphs. [Rule 10(b).] The next higher level of organization of a pleading is to group together into a particular numbered "count" those paragraphs that constitute a particular claim or statement of a claim. The Federal Rules strongly encourage use of separate counts when a pleading joins claims arising from different transactions or occurrences. [Rule 10(b).] Wise pleaders go further and use separate counts for *all* statements of claim, even those arising from a common transaction or occurrence. [Rule 8(e)(2).] This assists courts in reviewing a pleading and allows opposing parties to identify by number the particular counts to which they object.

3. *Types of claims and pleadings.* All types of pleadings may serve as the vehicle for the assertion and joinder of claims. The type of claim varies with the type of pleading, however, and this may impose additional restrictions on joinder of claims.

    a. Rule 7(a) authorizes two basic types of pleadings: complaints and answers. The other pleadings allowed under Rule 7(a) — third-party complaints, third-party answers, answers to cross-claims and replies to counterclaims — are simply specialized versions of these basic pleadings.

    b. Rule 18(a) specifies four different types of claims to which additional claims may be joined. Except for original claims, each type of claim is accompanied by special restrictions.

        (1) *Original claims* are asserted in the complaint. Original claims are subject only to the general rules of pleading set forth in Rules 8 and 9. (*See* Chapter 5.)

        (2) *Counterclaims* are asserted against the claiming party in the responsive pleading of a defending party. This responsive pleading may be an answer to a complaint, a reply to an answer asserting a counterclaim, or a third-party answer to a third-party complaint. As discussed below, the pleading of counterclaims is governed by Rules 13(a)-(f) in addition to Rules 8 and 9.

        (3) *Cross-claims* are asserted against a co-defending party in the responsive pleading of a defending party — an answer, reply, or third-party answer. As discussed below, the pleading of cross-claims is governed by Rule 13(g), in addition to Rules 8 and 9.

        (4) *Third-party claims* are asserted against a new party brought into the action for purposes of indemnification. The pleading of third-party claims is governed by Rule 14 in addition to Rules 8 and 9. Because Rule 14 involves joinder of parties as well as joinder of claims, we discuss it in our section on joinder of parties. We also defer to that section our discussion of the joinder of additional parties to counterclaims and cross-claims under Rule 13(h).

C. Joinder of Counterclaims

1. A counterclaim is asserted by including it in the appropriate responsive pleading. [Rules 13(a), 13(b).] Most counterclaims are asserted in the defendant's answer to the complaint, but they may also be asserted in the plaintiff's reply to the defendant's answer, if that answer asserted a counterclaim, or in a defendant's answer to the cross-claim of a co-defendant.

2. There is a vitally important procedural distinction between counterclaims that are *related* and counterclaims that are *unrelated* to the transaction or occurrence giving rise to the claim against which the counterclaiming party is responding.

    a. *Compulsory counterclaims.* Counterclaims that arise out of the same transaction or occurrence as the claim to which the counterclaiming party must respond are compulsory counterclaims. [Rule 13(a).] If a compulsory counterclaim is omitted from an action in violation of Rule 13(a) or its state law equivalents (*see, e.g.*, Calif. Code of Civ. Pro. § 426.30), it is waived. Thus the compulsory counterclaim rule is in essence a *mandatory joinder* rule, since "you use it or loose it" — if you have a claim against an opposing party that falls within the compulsory counterclaim rule and you fail to assert it as the rule requires, you are precluded from suing on the claim in any other lawsuit.

(1) The only exceptions to the *federal* compulsory counterclaim rule are when the counterclaim requires the presence of third parties whose joinder is not jurisdictionally possible [Rule 13(a)], when the counterclaim has not yet matured at the time the responsive pleading is filed [Rule 13(a)(1)], or when the claim against the potential counterclaimant is founded on in rem rather than in personam jurisdiction [Rule 13(a)(2)].

(2) Other exceptions may be recognized under state law. For instance, the compulsory counterclaim rule can lead to injustice in automobile accident cases. The problem is that both drivers may have serious injuries and both may have plausible claims against the other. Only happenstance determines which driver sues first. When the first driver sues, the second driver will ordinarily turn his defense over to a liability insurer. That insurer will focus on settling the claim as cheaply as possible and has no incentive to complicate settlement by asserting counterclaims for affirmative relief on behalf of its insured, the second driver. Injustice can result if a cheap settlement of the first driver's claim bars the second driver's more serious claim by operation of the compulsory counterclaim rule. Some states have altered their compulsory counterclaim rules to avoid this result. *See, e.g.*, Alabama Civil Rule 13(a)(3); Maine Rule of Civil Procedure 13(a).

b. *Permissive counterclaims.* Counterclaims that do not arise out of the same transaction or occurrence as the claim to which the counterclaiming party must respond are permissive counterclaims. [Rule 13(b).] These counterclaims may be asserted at the option of the pleader. They are not precluded if the pleader chooses to litigate them in a separate action.

3. *Joinder of additional parties named in a counterclaim.* Under Rule 13(h) a counterclaim against an opposing party can also name as an additional claiming or responsive party someone not presently a party to the action. We discuss this special use of the counterclaim in our discussion below of joinder of parties.

D. Joinder of Cross-claims

1. Cross-claims are asserted between *co-parties* in response to a claim for relief filed jointly against them. [Rule 13(g).]

2. A cross-claim is asserted in the pleading that answers the claim against the co-parties. Thus, a cross-claim may be asserted in the same manner and in the same pleading as a counterclaim. But whereas the counterclaim strikes back at the party who has filed the claim requiring a responsive pleading, the cross-claim is directed to a co-party who, along with the cross-claiming party, has been put in a defending position by the claim to which the cross-claiming party must respond.

3. Unlike counterclaims, which may be joined permissively even when unrelated to any other claim in the action, *cross-claims* must be *related* to existing claims. Three types of relationships will suffice under Rule 13(g).

a. The cross-claim may arise out of the same transaction or occurrence as was the basis for one of the claims in the original complaint.

b. The cross-claim may arise out of the same transaction or occurrence as a counterclaim.

c. The cross-claim may relate to any property at issue under the claims asserted in the original complaint.

4. A common type of cross-claim seeks *indemnification* from a co-party. In the typical situation, some claim in the action, whether an original claim or a counterclaim, is asserted against two or more defending co-parties. One of these co-parties may cross-claim for indemnification from the others on the ground that the others are primarily at fault. Cross-claims are not limited to indemnification, however. Cross-claims for independent relief are also common.

5. As with a counterclaim, a cross-claim can be used under Rule 13(h) as a device for the joinder of new parties. We discuss Rule 13(h) below in our section on joinder of parties.

E. Examples of Joinder of Claims

Example 1: Scalia is drafting a complaint against Kennedy to recover for damages suffered in an automobile accident. Scalia contends that Kennedy caused the accident by driving carelessly. Scalia also contends that after the accident Kennedy promised to make good any damage caused, and that Scalia relied to his detriment on Kennedy's broken promise. Scalia has an additional grievance against Kennedy, arising from damage to Scalia's property caused several months ago by one of Kennedy's children. Scalia has a good faith basis for believing that Kennedy is legally responsible for his child's action. Assuming that Scalia is a skillful pleader, his complaint against Kennedy will probably be divided into three counts.

Count 1: Here Scalia would plead the facts giving rise to a right to recover damages from the car crash because it was caused by Kennedy's negligence. It might be that there are several concurrent acts of negligence that Scalia alleges, each of which would be sufficient if proved to establish Kennedy's negligence. Scalia might allege that Kennedy was traveling at an excessive speed, had failed adequately to maintain his brakes, and was operating his car with unsafe tires. Typically, these allegations of different negligent acts leading up to the car crash would be set forth in separate paragraphs of a single count to recover damages arising from the negligently-caused car crash.

Count 2: Here Scalia would plead the facts giving rise to a contractual right to recover the same damages for the same car crash. This is the joinder of an alternative statement of claim under Rule 8(e)(2), but is not the joinder of claims in the strong sense of the joinder of completely unrelated claims. Scalia can recover only once for the damages caused by the accident, whether or not recovery is premised on tort law, contract law, or both. Moreover, the contract and tort claims are so closely related that Scalia is wise to avoid any chance of claim preclusion by joining both claims in a single suit. The use of a separate count for the contract as opposed to the tort claim makes clear, however, that despite the many facts in common to both claims, their legal theories differ.

Count 3: Here Scalia would plead the facts giving rise to a right to recover from Kennedy compensation for the property damage caused by Kennedy's child. This is joinder of claims in the strong sense. The claims are unrelated, and suit on one would not be preclusive (under "res judicata" principles) of later suit on the other. Joinder here is not in any sense compelled; it is simply convenient to allow Scalia at his option to assert any other outstanding grievance he may have against Kennedy. Because these are transactionally distinct claims, the use of separately numbered counts is virtually mandatory under Rule 10(b).

Further comment with respect to Count 1. Rule 8(e)(2) permits the use of separate counts instead of separate paragraphs for the pleading of alternative or compound contentions of fact. Scalia might elect to use separate counts if he felt it important to alert the trial judge that he need prove only one of the factual predicates for negligence in order to recover. Suppose, for instance, that Scalia does plead separate negligence counts based on excessive speed, unsafe brakes, and unsafe tires, and Scalia's strongest evidence relates to the objectively unsafe condition of Kennedy's tires as inspected by the police after the accident. Even if Kennedy succeeds in winning a motion for summary judgment based on Scalia's lack of evidence of excessive speed and unsafe brakes, the pleading of the unsafe tire theory of negligence in a separate count will make clear to the judge that the unsafe tire count should go forward for trial notwithstanding the granting of summary judgment as to the other counts.

Further comment with respect to Counts 2 and 3. Reciprocal latitude in joinder of claims is afforded to Kennedy by the counterclaim rules. If Scalia had promised after the accident to pay Kennedy, Kennedy would need to assert Scalia's contractual obligation to pay Kennedy by pleading it as a compulsory counterclaim under Rule 13(a). If Scalia's child had caused damage to some property of Kennedy's, Kennedy could elect to assert a permissive counterclaim for that damage under Rule 13(b).

Example 2: In another car crash case, Bush was the driver and Quayle is the owner of the car with which Ferraro's car collided while it was being driven by Mondale. Bush and Quayle jointly file a complaint naming Mondale and Ferraro as defendants in an action seeking damages arising out of the car crash, which they allege was caused by the negligence of Mondale. Under the applicable substantive law, Ferraro is vicariously liable for the negligence of Mondale. Ferraro does not concede that Mondale was at fault, however. In her answer, she denies liability and properly asserts a Rule 13(a) compulsory counterclaim against the negligent Bush and the vicariously liable Quayle for the property damage suffered by Ferraro's car at the time of the collision. She also properly asserts in her answer a Rule 13(g) cross-claim against Mondale to recover her property damage from Mondale in the event that the jury determines that he rather than Bush was the negligent driver. In cross-claiming against Mondale, Ferraro also properly joins two additional cross-claims. One is for indemnification in the event that Ferraro is held liable to Bush and Quayle for any damage caused by Mondale's negligent driving of Ferraro's car. Cross-claims for indemnification are expressly approved by Rule 13(g). The second is an entirely unrelated claim against Mondale for breach of a promise to paint Ferraro's house. While this unrelated cross-claim could not properly be joined to the action as Ferraro's *only* cross-claim, since Rule 13(g) limits cross-claims to those arising out of the same transaction or occurrence as the underlying action, once Ferraro has properly asserted some other cross-claim that meets the relatedness criterion on Rule 13(g), Rule 18(a) lets Ferraro "tack on" as many additional claims against Mondale as she wishes to assert.

II. JOINDER OF PARTIES IS MORE CLOSELY REGULATED THAN JOINDER OF CLAIMS.

JOINDER OF PARTIES

Permissive joinder of parties requires some relatedness among the claims by or against the joint parties. The law of compulsory joinder of parties seeks to protect against inconsistent adjudication and prejudice to non-parties.

A. The basic Federal Rule regarding permissive joinder of parties is Rule 20(a). It allows joinder of parties whenever at least one claim by or against all the joint parties arises from a common transaction or occurrence and presents a common question of fact or law.

1. Federal Rule 20(a) provides that all persons may join as plaintiffs in one action, or be joined as defendants in one action, if they assert or if there is asserted against them "any right to relief jointly, severally, or in the alternative in respect of or arising out of the same transaction, occurrence or series of transactions or occurrences, and if any question of law or fact common to all these persons will arise in the action." Any given joint plaintiff or joint defendant need not have a stake in all the claims being asserted in the action. There does not have to be a single judgment common to all parties; judgments are to be entered for or against the various plaintiffs and defendants according to their unique rights as individually established by the litigation.

2. Rule 20(a)'s joinder provisions are *permissive*. They merely *allow* joinder when there exists the requisite bare minimum of a logical relationship between the claims or defenses asserted by or against the joined parties. Rule 20(a) does not require joinder in these circumstances — the decision is left to the party (or parties) drafting the complaint.

B. Compulsory joinder of parties is an important and challenging feature of the Federal Rules.

1. The basic Federal Rule regarding *compulsory* joinder of *parties* is Rule 19. This rule has historically proved to be one of the more difficult for students to understand. Careful attention to the principles of Rule 19 will reveal the rule to work quite simply once the relevant terminology is understood.

2. Violation of the compulsory joinder of parties rule may result in dismissal of the action. Although such a violation may be raised by an opposing party in the responsive pleading and at any time thereafter until the end of trial on the merits [Rules 12(b)(7); 12(h)(2)], the violation is also one that the trial court is free to raise on its own motion, and one that can be raised for the first time on appeal. *See Provident Tradesmens Bank & Trust Co. v. Patterson*, 390 U.S. 102 (1968).

3. *Necessary parties.* Rule 19(a) specifies the standards for parties whose joinder is required if feasible. Such parties are conventionally called "necessary parties." There are *three reasons* why a party may be a necessary party.

   a. The joinder of a party may be necessary in order for the court to grant complete relief among those already parties. [Rule 19(a)(1).]

      Example: *The Case of the Misidentified Masterpiece (Version I).* Art collector A sold a painting to gallery owners B and C, based on their representations that it was the work of Student rather than Master. B and C have now announced to the world their discovery that A's former painting is in fact the work of Master and are offering the masterpiece for sale at a price vastly in excess of what they paid to A. A sues B for fraud, seeking to rescind his sale of the painting and to gain restitution of the painting. If the painting is in the possession of C rather than B, C's presence is required in order to grant complete relief. C is therefore a necessary party under Rule 19(a)(1), who must be joined as a co-defendant if her joinder is feasible.

   b. The joinder of a party may be necessary in order to protect the interests of that party. [Rule 19(a)(2)(i).]

      Example: *The Case of the Misidentified Masterpiece (Version II).* Suppose that A has sued C, seeking restitution of the painting on grounds of fraud but has not joined B as a party. As C's partner, B claims an interest in the painting (and in the huge profit that B and C will jointly realize if B and C are indeed legally free to sell the painting as their own property). The entry of a judgment against C requiring C to return the painting to A may not bind B as a matter of res judicata doctrine (unless the relationship between B and C is so close that they are deemed to be "in privity," as discussed in Chapter 12), and so as a technical matter B would be free to go to court on his own to establish as against A that B and C are legally entitled to ownership of the painting. But, as a practical matter, the judicial transfer of possession of the painting from C to A might well prejudice B's ability to protect his interest in the painting. Before B could recover possession by prosecution of a separate lawsuit, A might do something with the painting that would put it beyond the control of either A or the court. B is therefore a necessary party under Rule 19(a)(2)(i), whom A must join as a co-defendant if B's joinder is feasible.

   c. The joinder of a party may be necessary in order to protect the interests of other parties already before the court. [Rule 19(a)(2)(ii).]

      Example: *The Case of the Misidentified Masterpiece (Version III).* Now suppose that prior to A's suit the painting is accidentally destroyed. A, although heartbroken at the aesthetic loss, is still anxious to be treated by the law as the true owner of the painting. This is especially significant in light of the fact that the loss occurred at a museum to which C had lent the painting. The museum had insured the painting for several millions of dollars, payable directly to its owners. No longer interested in suing B and C, A has sued the insurance company, *D*, to recover the insurance proceeds. There is no need to join *B* and *C* under Rule 19(a)(1) — *B* and *C* now have nothing *A* needs to obtain complete relief. Nor is there any need to join *B* and *C* under Rule 19(a)(2)(i) — *D* is an insurance company with plenty of money available to pay claims, and *B* and *C* will suffer no practical impairment of their claim against *D* for the insurance proceeds simply because *A* has already recovered the same sum of money from *D*. But the joinder of *B* and *C* is required in order to protect *D* from the unfairness of having to pay twice on the same policy of insurance. *B* and *C* are therefore necessary parties under Rule 19(a)(2)(ii), whom *A* should join if feasible.

4. *Non-feasible joinder.* There are three reasons why the joinder of a necessary party may not be feasible.

   a. Lack of subject-matter jurisdiction. This is a serious problem in federal court but will rarely be a problem in state court actions. Most states have a trial court of general jurisdiction competent to try any civil action in which more than the minimum jurisdictional amount is in controversy. The subject matter jurisdiction of the federal courts is far more strictly limited. (*See* Chapter 4.) A lack of subject-matter jurisdiction cannot be cured by waiver or consent, and "ancillary jurisdiction" (discussed later in this chapter) does not apply to make possible the compulsory joinder of a necessary party. A "necessary" party whose joinder is not feasible may, however, invoke ancillary jurisdiction in order to intervene as of right in an action that the trial court has allowed to proceed in the absence of that party. *See* the discussion at the end of this chapter of ancillary jurisdiction under Rule 24(a).

   b. Lack of personal jurisdiction. This is only a problem where the absentee objects to joinder. Because objection to personal jurisdiction is waivable, the absentee can permit her joinder should she care to do so.

   c. Lack of venue. As with personal jurisdiction, this is a waivable objection to joinder of a necessary party. It will defeat joinder of a necessary party only when that party chooses to object to venue.

5. *Indispensable parties.* Rule 19(b) specifies the standards to be considered by the trial court in deciding whether the absence of necessary parties whose joinder is not feasible requires the dismissal of the action. If the presence of the necessary parties is so important that the action must be dismissed in their absence, these parties are regarded as "indispensable parties."

   a. The overall standard is whether, "in equity and good conscience," the action should be allowed to continue despite the absence of the persons who should be joined if feasible. There are four illustrative, non-exhaustive factors set forth in Rule 19(b), to be considered by the trial court as part of its determination whether "equity and good conscience" require that the action continue on or be dismissed.

      (1) The extent of the prejudice to the absentee or existing parties if the action continues.

      (2) The extent to which such prejudice can be lessened or avoided by protective provisions in the judgment.

      (3) Whether a judgment rendered without joinder of the absentee will be adequate.

      (4) Whether the plaintiff will have an adequate remedy in another forum if the present action is dismissed.

   b. *Rule 19(a)(1) necessary parties.* The Rule 19(b) calculation is no great problem where the necessary party is one in whose absence the judgment will be inadequate. If there is another forum open to the plaintiff in which more adequate relief can be obtained, obviously the action should be dismissed. If no alternative forum is available, the

6

plaintiff should be allowed to proceed with the present suit unless the relief would be so completely inadequate as to waste the court's time.

c. *Rule 19(a)(2)(i) necessary parties*. There is also no great problem when the necessary party is the one exposed to prejudice and there is another forum in which the plaintiff can bring suit and obtain adequate relief. If the plaintiff can do as well or better suing elsewhere, and by suing elsewhere prejudice to others can be avoided, obviously the action should be dismissed. Dismissal is never warranted, however, if the only choice that must be made by the trial court is between proceeding with the action (risking prejudice to the absentee) and dismissing the action (risking prejudice to a plaintiff who has no other available forum in which adequate relief may be obtained). Any prejudice to the absentee can be avoided by the absentee's own self-protective action. If the problem is venue or personal jurisdiction, the absentee can waive the objection. If the joinder of the absentee is not feasible because of a lack of federal subject-matter jurisdiction, the absentee can intervene to protect itself. (Although there is no ancillary jurisdiction to facilitate compulsory joinder under Rule 19(a) of a party who would otherwise be regarded as indispensable under Rule 19(b), there is ancillary jurisdiction over a merely necessary (but not indispensable) party who seeks on her own initiative to intervene as of right under Rule 24(a). *See* our discussion of ancillary jurisdiction under Rule 24(a) at the conclusion of this chapter.)

d. *Rule 19(a)(2)(ii) necessary parties*. The only really hard choice presented to a trial court under Rule 19(b) thus arises when two conditions exist.

(1) First, there is *no adequate alternative forum* in which the plaintiff may seek relief.

(2) Second, continuing with the suit in the present forum, where the absentee cannot feasibly be joined, risks *prejudice to an existing party rather than the absentee*. The absentee has no interest in effectuating its own joinder in order to avoid prejudice to others. Therefore a genuine choice "in equity and good conscience" must be made by the trial court between the prejudice faced by the plaintiff if the action is dismissed, and the prejudice faced by some other party to the lawsuit if it is not dismissed.

JOINDER OF ADDITIONAL PARTIES

III. **JOINDER OF ADDITIONAL PARTIES IS PERMITTED IN REACTION TO THE COMPLAINT FOR PURPOSES OF INDEMNIFICATION OR IN CONNECTION WITH A COUNTERCLAIM OR CROSS-CLAIM.**

A. **Joinder of Claims for Indemnity Against Impleaded Third Parties**

1. "Impleader" is the joinder of an additional party who may be liable to indemnify an existing party against whom a claim has been asserted. Federal Rule 14 sets forth a comprehensive set of procedures for impleading new parties. Rule 14 is limited to impleader — joinder of a new party is allowed under Rule 14 only if there is a claim for indemnification by that party — but once a party is properly impleaded by a claim for indemnification, Rule 18(a) allows the joinder of additional claims against the impleaded party. The duty of the impleaded party to indemnify the impleading party does not have to be complete or undisputed. It is sufficient if the impleaded party "is or may be liable" to the impleading party.

2. Rule 14(a) contains a series of significant sentences, each of which functions as a separate joinder rule. Unfortunately these individual sentences of Rule 14(a) lack separate numbers within the Rule itself. For clarity and convenience, we will refer to the individual sentences of Rule 14(a) by bracketed number as if each sentence were numbered from 1 to 10 in the order in which it appears in Rule 14(a). Thus, when we cite to "Rule 14(a)[7]," we refer to the seventh sentence of Rule 14(a).

a. At any time in the litigation of an action, a "defending party" may implead a new party "who is or may be liable" to the impleading party "for all or part" of a claim against the impleading party. [Rule 14(a)[1].] Impleader requires leave of court, however, if delayed more than 10 days after the impleading party answers the claim for which indemnification is sought from the impleaded party. [Rules 14(a)[2], 14(a)[3].] The impleader is accomplished by asserting the claim for indemnification in a "third-party complaint" that, together with a summons, is served on the impleaded party according to the standard rules for service of process. (*See* Chapter 2.) The impleading party is called the "third-party plaintiff," and the impleaded party is called the "third-party defendant." [Rule 14(a)[4].]

b. Rule 14(a)[4] makes the provisions of Rules 12 and 13 applicable to a third-party defendant. Thus, the third-party defendant must respond to the third-party complaint by Rule 12(b) motion or by answer. The answer must assert any compulsory counterclaims [Rule 13(a)] the third-party defendant may have against the third-party plaintiff and may, in addition, assert any permissive counterclaims [Rule 13(b)] or any cross-claims [Rule 13(g)] the third-party defendant may have against other third-party defendants named as co-parties in the third-party complaint. Rule 14(a)[5] permits the third-party defendant vicariously to assert on behalf of the third-party plaintiff any defenses the third-party plaintiff may have against the claim for which indemnification is sought by the third-party plaintiff.

c. Rule 14(a)[6] permits (but does not require) the third-party defendant to assert against the original plaintiff any claim that the third-party defendant may have against the original plaintiff that arises out of the same transaction or occurrence as the original plaintiff's claim against the third-party plaintiff. Rule 14(a)[7] is the reverse of Rule 14(a)[6]. It authorizes the original plaintiff to join to the action a claim directly against the impleaded third-party defendant, provided that this claim arises from the same transaction or occurrence as the original plaintiff's claim against the original defendant who has become the third-party plaintiff. This is ordinarily done by amendment of the complaint. *See Owen Equipment & Erection Co. v. Kroger*, 437 U.S. 365 (1978). However, if there has first occurred the assertion of a claim against the original plaintiff under Rule 14(a)[6], any transactionally related claim the original plaintiff may have against the third-party defendant is now a compulsory counterclaim under Rule 13(a). As such, it *must* be included in the plaintiff's answer to the claim of the third-party defendant.

d. Rule 14(a)[8] permits any party to move to strike, sever, or separately try a third-party claim. This allows parties to keep the litigation of the main issues in a lawsuit from becoming unduly complicated by simultaneous litigation of indemnification issues. The degree of complication created by joinder of third parties can reach potentially epic proportions, since Rule 14(a)[9] and Rule 14(b) allow any defending party to implead additional defendants for purposes of indemnification. Thus, there may be a "daisy-chain" of third-party defendants impleaded to indemnify other third-party defendants. (For convenience, most courts refer to a third-party defendant's complaint under Rule 14 as a "fourth-party complaint." The fourth-party defendant might in turn become a "fifth-party plaintiff," and so forth.) There may also be a daisy-chain on the other side of the litigation if the assertion of a counterclaim makes the original plaintiff a defending party.

B. Joinder of Additional Parties to Counterclaims and Cross-claims

1. By their terms, Rule 19 (compulsory joinder of parties) and Rule 20 (permissive joinder of parties) speak only of joinder in the pleading of the complaint. But by express incorporation in Rule 13(h), the terms of Rules 19 and 20 also govern joinder of parties in the pleading of counterclaims and cross-claims.

6

2. The joinder of additional parties under Rule 13(h) differs in several respects from impleader under Rule 14. Although Rule 13(h) can be used to implead additional defending parties for purposes of indemnification, a counterclaim or cross-claim joining additional parties under Rule 13(h) need not be for indemnification. Moreover, Rule 13(h) additional parties may be joined as additional claimants rather than as additional defending parties.

Example 1: *Rule 13(h) functioning as a form of impleader parallel in function to Rule 14(a).* Pedestrian sues Driver and Owner for injuries suffered when struck by Owner's runaway truck. Defendant Owner may cross-claim for indemnification against co-defendant Driver and may invoke Rule 13(h) to join Mechanic as an additional party to that cross-claim. This assures that Owner will receive indemnification from either Driver or Mechanic, depending on who is found at fault.

Example 2: *Rule 13(h) used to join an additional party as a co-claimant seeking independent relief.* Builders *A* and *B* are preparing jointly to sue contractor *C* for damages each incurred because of defective concrete work performed by *C* on various projects of *A* and *B*. Before *A* and *B* file suit against *C*, *C* serves *A* with a complaint for non-payment of *C*'s bills for the concrete work in question. *A* must now assert her damages claim against *C* as a compulsory counterclaim under Rule 13(a). Under Rule 13(h) and its incorporation of Rule 20, however, *B* can join as an additional party to *A*'s counterclaim against *C*.

3. Rule 19's compulsory joinder provisions apply with full force to counterclaims and cross-claims. In answering a counterclaim or cross-claim, the defending party may insist on the joinder of parties necessary under the terms of Rule 19(a), and may move for dismissal if the joinder of such parties is not feasible.

ADDITIONAL PROCEDURAL DEVICES

IV. ADDITIONAL PROCEDURAL DEVICES FOR JOINDER OF PARTIES: INTERPLEADER, CLASS ACTIONS, INTERVENTION, AND SUBSTITUTION

A. Interpleader

1. Interpleader is a form of joinder used by someone whose property is subject to multiple conflicting claims. Interpleader forces all the rival claimants to defend their claims *inter se* (among themselves) in a single court proceeding. The person holding the disputed property is called the "stakeholder." The stakeholder brings the interpleader action as the plaintiff. The complaint "interpleads" the rival claimants as defendants. Under modern interpleader procedure, the stakeholder need not surrender its own claim to the disputed property (the "stake"). If the court acquires jurisdiction over all of the rival claimants, it will generally issue an injunction to keep them from proceeding with any individual actions that might expose the stakeholder to duplicative or otherwise inconsistent liabilities.

2. *Statutory interpleader.* In federal court, two types of interpleader actions are possible. The most common type is "statutory interpleader" under the Federal Interpleader Act, which has been codified as 28 U.S.C. §§ 1335, 1397, and 2361.

   a. Section 1335 sets forth the basic procedures for statutory interpleader and provides for federal subject-matter jurisdiction wherever there is mere "minimal" diversity between any two rival claimants, regardless of the citizenship of the stakeholder and all other claimants. *See* Chapter 4 and *State Farm Fire & Casualty Co. v. Tashire*, 386 U.S. 523 (1967). The especially generous grant of federal subject-matter jurisdiction under 28 U.S.C. § 1335 requires a jurisdictional amount of only $500, measured by the amount of the stake itself rather than the amount of any particular claimant's share of that stake.

   b. Section 1397 sets forth an especially generous venue provision, allowing a statutory interpleader suit to be brought in any district in which any claimant resides.

   c. Section 2361 complements the generous subject-matter jurisdiction and venue provisions of the Federal Interpleader Act by providing nationwide service of process in statutory interpleader actions. Far-flung rival claimants are within the personal jurisdiction of any federal district in which good venue exists (*i.e.*, in which any claimant resides, per § 1397).

3. *Rule interpleader.* The less common type of federal interpleader action is called "rule interpleader." This is used when there is a total lack of diversity among the interpleaded claimants. If there is no diversity at all — the stakeholder and all claimants are co-citizens — the suit must proceed in state court. But if the interpleaded claimants are all co-citizens (thus ruling out § 1335 statutory interpleader jurisdiction), and the stakeholder is a citizen of some other state, there is "complete diversity" between the plaintiff/stakeholder and all defendants/claimants. Provided that the value of the stake exceeds $50,000, the stakeholder can therefore invoke the "general" diversity jurisdiction of 28 U.S.C. § 1332. When suing under § 1332, the procedural authority for bringing an interpleader action jointly against all claimants is provided by Federal Rule 22 — hence, the term "rule interpleader." In terms of pleading and joinder, rule interpleader and statutory interpleader suits are virtually identical. If given a choice, however, a stakeholder will always prefer to bring a statutory rather than a rule interpleader action in order to take advantage of the liberal venue and jurisdiction rules for statutory interpleader.

B. **Class Actions**

1. *In general.* Class actions are authorized in federal court by Rules 23, 23.1 (shareholder derivative actions), and 23.2 (class actions relating to unincorporated associations). As liberalized in 1966, Rule 23 encouraged the filing of class actions in federal courts. Since that time, however, the Supreme Court has shown little enthusiasm for federal class actions except where the relief sought is injunctive rather than money damages.

   a. Damages class actions based on diversity of citizenship are virtually impossible to maintain in the federal courts. Under *Snyder v. Harris*, 394 U.S. 332 (1969), and *Zahn v. International Paper Co.*, 414 U.S. 291 (1973), each member of a plaintiff class must individually present a claim valued in excess of the jurisdictional amount of $50,000. Although the long-established rules for determining the diversity status of a class action are quite liberal — only the citizenship of the named class representatives is considered in determining whether the requisite "complete diversity" exists under 28 U.S.C. § 1332 — the refusal of the Supreme Court to permit any aggregation of the amount in controversy in damages class actions has turned the diversity class action into a procedural dinosaur.

   b. Damages class actions are still jurisdictionally possible in federal court when the class is suing on a claim created by federal law, such as the private rights of action created by the federal securities, antitrust, and civil rights laws. Federal claims are not generally subject to any "amount-in-controversy" requirement for federal jurisdiction. But even on such claims, the litigation of federal class actions for money damages has been discouraged by the Supreme Court's uncompromising construction of the notice requirement of Federal Rule 23(c)(2). *See Eisen v. Carlisle & Jacqueline*, 417 U.S. 156 (1974).

   c. Class actions for money damages remain alive and well in state courts, which generally follow the procedures of Federal Rule 23, but interpret those procedures more liberally. Many states allow aggregation of amount for purposes of satisfying the amount-in-controversy requirements of their trial courts of general jurisdiction. *See, e.g., Daar v. Yellow Cab Co.*, 67 Cal.2d 695 (1967). It has been recognized on the state level that the notice requirements of Rule 23(c)(2) are merely a matter of federal judicial policy and are not a constitutional requirement obligatory on the state courts. *Cartt v. Superior Court*, 50 Cal. App. 3d 960 (1975). The Supreme Court has encouraged state class actions to the limited extent of holding that a state court has jurisdictional power, provided there is proper notice and a suitable class representative, to render a binding

6

judgment on the claims of absent class members who lack "minimum contacts" with the forum state. *Phillips Petroleum Co. v. Shutts*, 472 U.S. 797 (1985).

d. The vast majority of class actions are brought as plaintiff class actions against individual defendants. A defendant class action is possible, but rare. *See, e.g., In re Gap Stores Securities Litigation*, 79 F.R.D. 283 (N.D. Cal. 1978) [plaintiff class versus defendant class]. We confine our discussion to plaintiff class actions.

2. *Requirements applicable to every class action.* Rule 23(a) sets four *conjunctive* criteria which must *all* be satisfied in order for a putative class action to receive certification as a proper class action. These are the requirements of *numerosity, common questions, typicality of claims,* and *adequate representation*.

a. Rule 23(a)(1)'s *numerosity* requirement demands that the number of class members be too great to practically be joined individually under the liberal joinder of parties provisions of Federal Rule 20. All courts agree that a class of fewer than 40 members is too small to warrant a class action, and that more than 100 class members is too many for individual joinder under Rule 20. The zone of litigation over numerosity involves proposed class actions with between 40 and 100 putative class members. Determination of the numerosity requirement in such cases will turn on the enthusiasm for class actions of the particular trial judge.

b. Rule 23(a)(2)'s *common questions* requirement is generally unimportant. No class action could rationally be proposed that did not involve some "questions of law or fact common to the class." Far more important is a different provision, sometimes confused with the Rule 23(a)(2) common question requirement — the requirement of Rule 23(b)(3) that consideration be given to the *predominance* of common questions over individual questions. We discuss the predominance requirement below. What is important to your understanding of Rule 23(a) is that the "predominance" requirement applies *only* to 23(b)(3) class actions and is not part of the "common questions" requirement that applies to *all* class actions under Rule 23(a)(2).

c. Rule 23(a)(3)'s *typicality of claims* requirement focuses on the suitability of the named class representatives. A class action is brought by one or more named individuals who are suing on behalf of a large group (or "class") of similarly situated but unnamed individuals. The typicality requirement demands that the claims of the named representatives be sufficiently characteristic of the claims of the class as a whole for it to be likely that, in litigating their claims, the named representatives will adequately protect the interests of the absent class members.

d. Rule 23(a)(4)'s *adequate representation* requirement is sometimes confused with the typicality of claims requirement. Whether the named class representatives are themselves suitable or "adequate" class representatives is the gravamen of Rule 23(a)(3). The focus under Rule 23(a)(4) should shift from the characteristics of the named class representatives (who generally have little to do with the conduct of the litigation) to the adequacy of class counsel (whose performance will have a major bearing on the success of the class action). Inquiry under Rule 23(a)(4) properly extends to the skill, experience, and resources of the attorneys who seek to represent the class.

3. *Types of class action.* Rule 23(b) sets three *disjunctive* criteria, just one of which need be satisfied in order for a putative class action to receive certification as a proper class action. These criteria result in three overlapping but generally distinct types of class action.

a. A Rule 23(b)(1) class action seeks to avoid the risk that individual adjudication of their claims by class members would, as a practical matter, resolve the matter for the class as a whole. There are two sub-types of Rule 23(b)(1) class action.

(1) A Rule 23(b)(1)(A) class action is justified by the risk that individual adjudication of their claims by class members would establish incompatible standards of conduct

for the party opposing the class. This justification for proceeding with the litigation on a class-wide basis focuses on the effect of the litigation on the class opponent.

Example: *A*, *B*, and *C* are citizens and taxpayers of municipality *X*. They challenge the validity of a new school bond issue enacted by *X*, and of the resulting taxes levied on them to pay off the school bonds. The bonds and taxes are of citywide application and cannot be valid as to some taxpayers but not as to others. If *A*, *B*, and *C* litigate their action as individuals and establish that the bond issue is invalid, the result will not be simply to excuse *A, B,* and *C* from paying the tax. The bonds will not be issued and the school will not be built. Therefore, it is desirable that their litigation of this issue of general applicability be brought under the protections and supervision of Rule 23.

(2) A Rule 23(b)(1)(B) class action is justified by the risk that adjudication of the present lawsuit on an individual rather than class basis would be dispositive or prejudicial, as a practical matter, of the parallel claims of those class members not presently represented in court. This justification for proceeding with the litigation on a class-wide basis focuses on the effect of the litigation on other members of the class, rather than on the class opponent, if the present lawsuit were to proceed as an individual action rather than as a class action.

Example: *E*, *F*, and *G* are investors in a business venture that has gone sour. The have brought an action to recover compensatory and punitive damages from the promoters of the venture. The venture and its promoter have limited assets to satisfy such claims. If *E*, *F*, and *G* obtain full recovery, there will be no assets left to satisfy the similar claims of several hundred similarly situated investors. Therefore, it is desirable that the litigation of their widely shared claims be brought under the protections and supervision of Rule 23, so that the class as a whole can share on a proportional basis in such compensation as may be available.

b. A Rule 23(b)(2) class action is justified by the fact that the injunctive or declaratory relief sought must necessarily operate on a class-wide basis. If individual awards of money damages are a substantial part of the relief sought, class certification under Rule 23(b)(2) is inappropriate and the standards of Rule 23(b)(3) must be met.

Example: *H*, *I*, and *J* are female employees of a trucking firm. They allege in a federal civil rights action that they have been confined to lower-paying jobs because of sex discrimination by the management of the defendant firm. If they seek injunctive relief requiring future hiring and promotions by the firm to be conducted on a gender-neutral basis, it would be appropriate for *H*, *I*, and *J* to seek class certification under Rule 23(b)(2). They may maintain their class action for injunctive relief under Rule 23(b)(2) even if they seek incidental damages relief in the form of back pay owed to them as individuals for the higher paying jobs they were qualified to perform and would have held but for the sex discrimination. (The trial court would have to make sure that the terms of the decree did not foreclose other class members from seeking back pay as well.) If *H*, *I*, and *J* seek class-wide damages as well as injunctive relief, so that other class members will recover back pay only through this lawsuit or not at all, the damages component of the relief sought will probably be so substantial that certification under Rule 23(b)(2) would be improper, and class action status would be proper only if the class action meets the criteria of Rule 23(b)(3).

c. A Rule 23(b)(3) class action is the "loosest" form of class action in terms of the inherent community of interest among the class members. The relief sought is generally damages. The incentive for seeking class action status under Rule 23(b)(3) is that the compounding effect of the amount of damages sought per individual, times the number of individuals in the putative class, produces a potential amount of damages to be recovered (if all goes well for the class plaintiffs) that both makes it economically

6

practicable to litigate the claims of the plaintiff class members and makes it economically reasonable for the defendants to consider settlement of those claims.

(1) Certification of a Rule 23(b)(3) class action requires only that the action meet the four criteria of Rule 23(a) and that the trial court make two further findings.

    (a) The questions of law or fact common to the class members must *predominate* over individual questions affecting only particular class members.

    (b) A class action must be *superior* to other available methods for the fair and efficient adjudication of the class-wide controversy.

(2) The trial court is given a non-exhaustive list of four criteria to consider in determining whether common questions predominate and whether class adjudication is superior to alternative methods of adjudication.

    (a) The degree of *individual interest* of class members in controlling the litigation. [Rule 23(b)(3)(A).] This disqualifies most mass tort cases — such as airplane crashes — from Rule 23(b)(3) certification. These torts support large individual recoveries, in which individual claimants have large financial and emotional stakes. Individual litigation of these claims is preferable unless the inability of the defendant to satisfy all likely judgments makes Rule 23(b)(1)(B) certification appropriate.

    (b) The extent and nature of *other litigation* already commenced by or against members of the putative class. [Rule 23(b)(3)(B).]

    (c) The desirability or undesirability of the *concentration* of the litigation of claims of all class members in just one particular forum by proceeding with litigation on a class-wide rather than individual basis. [Rule 23(b)(3)(C).]

    (d) The difficulties the trial court and class counsel will encounter in the *management* of the action as a class action. [Rule 23(b)(3)(D).]

4. *Powers of the trial court.* Once joinder of the absent class members is conditionally permitted, Rule 23 provides the trial court with extraordinary powers to manage the litigation of the class action.

    a. The order certifying that an action may be maintained as a class action remains open to reconsideration. This makes sure that the class representatives and their counsel remain on their best behavior. [Rule 23(c)(1).]

    b. The class certification order may limit litigation on behalf of the class to particular issues (such as liability), leaving other issues (such as damages) to be litigated on an individual basis by individual class members. [Rule 23(c)(4)(A).] In addition, the district court's certification of an action as a class action gives the court virtually unlimited power to control the structure and conduct of the litigation. [Rule 23(d).]

    c. The trial court may subdivide the class into subclasses represented by different named plaintiffs. [Rule 23(c)(4)(B).] This is often done to overcome conflicts of interest within the class. A named party with claims typical of a particular group within the class as a whole is certified as the representative of that particular "subclass."

Example: Named plaintiffs *A* and *B* bring a class action to redress sex discrimination by employer *X*. *A* and *B* are both existing female employees of *X*. The trial court might decide that, although the claims asserted by *A* and *B* might generally benefit all victims of *X*'s allegedly discriminatory policies of hiring and promoting women, there could be different relief available to, and a potential conflict of interest between, those women *denied* jobs with *X* because of sex discrimination as opposed to those women *hired* by *X* but denied equal opportunities for benefits and advancement. The trial court might withhold certification of the class action until *A* and *B* amend their complaint to assert the class claims jointly with newly added plaintiff *C*, who is among the class of women discriminatorily denied jobs by *X*. If the amended complaint properly asserts class-wide claims and additional subclass-specific claims on behalf of *A* and *B* (representing female employees of *X*) and on behalf of *C* (representing women denied employment by *X*), the action may now qualify for class certification.

    d.   With respect *only* to class actions certified under *Rule 23(b)(3)*, members of the class must be given *notice* of their right to *"opt out"* of the class action. [Rule 23(c)(2).]

        (1)   The notice must be "the best notice practicable under the circumstances, including individual notice to all members who can be identified by reasonable effort." The Supreme Court has held that this standard was intended to assure the binding effect of the class judgment by providing absent class members with notice that would be upheld as adequate under the due process clause of the fourteenth amendment. *Eisen v. Carlisle & Jacqueline*, 417 U.S. 156 (1974) [reading into Rule 23(c)(2) the due process standard for adequate notice set forth in *Mullane v. Central Hanover Bank & Trust Co.*, 339 U.S. 306 (1950)].

        (2)   The notice must also inform class members that they will be bound by the judgment, whether favorable or not, if they fail to opt out within the specified time, and that if they do not opt out they may still enter an appearance through counsel in order to make sure that their interests are fully protected.

    e.   Settlement of a class action requires court approval under Rule 23(e). This prevents abuse of the class action device as a way of extorting an *overvalued* but quick settlement from a frightened defendant. Similar reasoning has led some courts to hold that the mere filing of a class action complaint subjects the action to Rule 23(e)'s judicial control of the settlement process, even though no class action was certified prior to settlement. Rule 23(e) review also limits the risk that a class action will be concluded by an *undervalued* settlement negotiated by class counsel in collusion with defense counsel.

5.   Rule 23.1 provides specially for derivative actions brought by shareholders of a corporation or the members of an unincorporated association who challenge the organization's management by suing as a class.

    a.   There is no "numerosity" requirement under Rule 23.1. It suffices that the named plaintiff is suing derivatively in the name of *all* the shareholders or members, whatever their number.

    b.   The complaint alleging a derivative cause of action must be verified. (This is an exception to the general policy of Rule 11 that pleadings need not be verified.)

    c.   The complaint must allege with particularity (*i.e.*, with more detail than the normal "notice" pleading permitted by Rule 8) the efforts of the derivative plaintiff to have the right in issue enforced directly by the management of the entity and the reasons for management's failure to do so.

6.   Rule 23.2 provides for class litigation of claims by or against unincorporated associations. For the most part, unincorporated associations lack the capacity to sue and be sued as entities independent of their membership. Litigation under Rule 23.2 solves the problem of the lack of legal capacity of an unincorporated association to sue or be sued by permitting suits by or against unincorporated associations to proceed as class actions. A Rule 23.2 class action is litigation *directly* for or against the association as such. This is different from litigation brought under Rule 23.1, which is maintained *on behalf of* the association and is brought *derivatively* by a dissident member when management has failed to act in the best interests of the association.

C. Intervention

1. Intervention occurs when an outsider initiates her joinder to an action already being litigated by other parties. In limited circumstances, the Federal Rules permit the absentee to intervene as of right; otherwise, the absentee may intervene only after obtaining the permission of the trial court.

2. *Intervention as of right.* Rule 24(a)(1) merely affirms that certain substantive federal statutes confer an unconditional right to intervene on specified parties who may be affected by litigation under these statutes. Far more important is Rule 24(a)(2), which as a matter of fair procedure also confers in certain circumstances an unconditional right to intervene. There are basically three criteria for intervention as of right under Rule 24(a)(2): a risk of *practical impairment* of a relevant interest, *timely application*, and *lack of adequate representation.*

   a. The requirement of a risk of *practical impairment* parallels the terms of Rule 19(a)(2)(i), relating to necessary parties, and of Rule 23(b)(1)(B), relating to class actions. All three rules recognize that judgments not technically binding on non-parties may nonetheless cause them serious prejudice. The interest at risk of impairment must be directly related to the property or transaction at issue in the litigation.

   b. The intervenor must seek leave to intervene by *timely application*. This requirement has been very leniently construed by the federal courts. Although the determination of timeliness is within the sound discretion of the trial court, in many cases intervention as of right has been permitted even when the application was not filed until after a final judgment was entered, where intervention at this late date is necessary to protect the intervenor's interests by permitting the intervenor to file an appeal. *See United Airlines, Inc. v. McDonald*, 432 U.S. 385 (1977).

   c. The interests of the intervenor must be *inadequately represented* by existing parties. This requirement has also been leniently construed. Under the revised language of Rule 24(a), as amended in 1966, it is generally assumed that existing parties' representation of the interests of an intervenor as of right is *not* adequate and intervention should be allowed unless the trial court is persuaded to the contrary.

   Example: *Background facts.* A and B are rival developers who each seek to erect commercial structures on the same coral reefs off the coast of Florida. It is controversial whether the reefs are within the jurisdiction of the United States. Neither developer wants to invest substantial sums of money in a project that will have to be torn down if the United States wins a court battle over title to the property. The sovereign immunity of the United States prevents either developer from initiating a suit for declaratory relief against the United States. When the United States finally sues to establish its property rights, it names *B* as the only defendant despite *A*'s request that it be joined as a co-defendant in any litigation against *B*.

   Procedure for intervention. Soon after the complaint is served on *B* by the United States, *A* files a motion for leave to intervene as of right, accompanied by a proposed answer as an intervenor in which *A* asserts defenses against the claims of the United States and asserts a cross-claim to establish priority of title as against *B*.

   Analysis. Intervention as of right should be granted under Rule 24(a)(2). The application is timely. The applicant claims an interest in the same "property or transaction which is the subject of the action," *i.e.*, the reefs both *A* and *B* seek to develop. The interest of the applicant may be impaired as a practical matter because of the stare decisis effect of a determination as to *B* that the reefs are subject to the jurisdiction of the United States. Although not technically binding on non-parties who have not yet had the opportunity to litigate the facts and the law, as a practical matter the adverse resolution of the issue as to *B* will create highly unfavorable caselaw prejudicial to *A*, especially if the action against *B* results on appeal in a decision upholding the power of the United States to control the development of the reefs in question. Although *A* and *B* have common interests in resisting the assertion of jurisdiction by the United States, their adverse interests inter se rule out *B* as an adequate representative of *A*'s interests. *See Atlantis Development Corp. v. United States*, 379 F.2d 818 (5th Cir. 1967).

3. *Permissive intervention.* There are two alternative grounds for permissive intervention. Under Rule 24(b)(1), the intervenor may rely on a conditional right to intervene under a federal statute. Under Rule 24(b)(2), the trial court may allow anyone else to intervene provided only that the "applicant's claim or defense and the main action have a question of law or fact in common." This test is so liberal that it extends the class of potential permissive intervenors to the outer limits of rationality. The only real limit to permissive intervention is the discretion of the trial court. One of the most frequently cited reasons for denial of permissive intervention is a disinclination to risk delay of the underlying litigation. The "timely application" constraint of Rule 24(b) is much more rigorously applied than the similar requirement of Rule 24(a). Trial courts almost always deny leave to intervene permissively if the application was not filed very early in the course of the litigation.

4. Rule 24(c) governs the procedure to be followed in seeking leave to intervene. The applicant files a motion to intervene which is served (like any other motion) on all parties by mail through counsel unless a party is appearing *pro se* ("for oneself," *i.e.*, without benefit of counsel). The motion states the grounds for intervention and is accompanied by a proposed pleading, which sets forth the claims or defenses of the applicant in the form of a complaint or answer. (An official example of a motion to intervene and a proposed intervenor's answer is given as Form 23 in the Appendix of Forms accompanying Federal Rule 84.)

D. Substitution

1. Upon the death [Rule 25(a)], incompetency [Rule 25(b)], or transfer of interest of a party [Rule 25(c)], abatement or dismissal of the action is not automatic. The trial court upon motion may order the joinder of an appropriate substitute party, if any. If the substitution involves the joinder of a new party, service of process must be accomplished as provided by Rule 4. When a party dies, dismissal of the action as to that party is automatic if no motion for substitution has been made within 90 days of service on all parties of a statement of the fact of the death.

2. Suits by or against public officers may be maintained either in the name of the office or in the name of the officer. [Rule 25(d)(2).] Regardless whether the public officer is identified by official title or by the officer's name, the suit continues unabated when the officer leaves office by death, resignation, or for any other reason. The officer's successor is automatically substituted as a party. [Rule 25(d)(1).]

V. SUPPLEMENTAL JURISDICTION IN AID OF LIBERAL JOINDER IN THE FEDERAL COURTS: NON-STATUTORY DOCTRINES APPLICABLE TO ACTIONS COMMENCED PRIOR TO DECEMBER 1, 1990

SUPPLEMENTAL JURISDICTION

A. **The non-statutory doctrines of *pendent* and *ancillary* jurisdiction allow the federal court system to enjoy the benefits of liberal joinder by *supplementing* the subject-matter jurisdiction of the federal courts.**

1. Because federal courts are courts of limited subject-matter jurisdiction, provision for liberal joinder of claims and parties would be of little practical import if each and every joined claim and party had to qualify in its own right as within the subject-matter jurisdiction of the federal court. The many benefits of efficiency and fairness conferred by liberal joinder

6

rules could not be enjoyed by the federal courts without the twin doctrines of non-statutory federal supplemental jurisdiction: pendent and ancillary jurisdiction.

2. The constitutional basis for the doctrines of pendent and ancillary jurisdiction is the broad scope of a single "case or controversy" that is within federal judicial power under Article III of the Constitution. A single transaction or occurrence may give rise to a complex cluster of claims based on many different theories of law and possibly involving many sets of parties. If any one of these claims is within the federal question or diversity jurisdiction of the federal courts, then the entire "case or controversy" of which that claim is a part, including all other claims involving the same or different parties which arise out of "a common nucleus of operative fact," may constitutionally be adjudicated by the federal courts. *See United Mine Workers of America v. Gibbs*, 383 U.S. 715 (1966).

3. The non-statutory doctrines of supplemental jurisdiction determine when, as a matter of sound judicial discretion, it is proper for a federal court to exercise this potentially vast jurisdictional power in cases commenced before December 1, 1990. For actions commenced on or after December 1, 1990, the federal district courts have statutory supplemental jurisdiction under 28 U.S.C., § 1367, discussed below in Part VI. The non-statutory doctrines discussed here in Part V continue to govern all cases commenced prior to December 1, 1990, even if the occasion to invoke ancillary or pendent jurisdiction does not arise until after December 1, 1990.

B. **Pendent jurisdiction deals with the joinder of claims and parties *in the complaint*. There are two types of pendent jurisdiction. *Pendent claim* jurisdiction is liberally exercised in the federal courts on an everyday basis. *Pendent party* jurisdiction, although constitutionally permissible, is disfavored absent express congressional authorization.**

1. *Pendent claim jurisdiction* involves an action in which all parties are concededly subject to federal jurisdiction to adjudicate at least one claim arising under federal law. In addition to this *"anchor claim"* that is within the federal question jurisdiction of the federal courts, the plaintiff has joined in the complaint one or more *state law* claims arising from the same out-of-court transaction or occurrence. The "pendent" state law claims may be against some or all of the same parties as are defending the federal "anchor" claim, but *no new parties* may be brought into federal court by the joinder of the pendent claim.

   a. Pendent claim jurisdiction is widely exercised because it offers significant economies. Duplicative litigation and inconsistent results are avoided.

   b. Pendent claim jurisdiction never exists as of right, however. Its exercise is a matter for the sound discretion of the trial court. If the federal anchor claim is dismissed prior to trial, the pendent state law claim should ordinarily be dismissed as well without prejudice to adjudication of the claim in state court.

2. *Pendent party jurisdiction* is disfavored without express congressional authorization. Pendent party jurisdiction was occasionally exercised by the lower federal courts until the United States Supreme Court disapproved these cases in 1989.

   a. Pendent party jurisdiction involves the assertion of a federal "anchor" claim against one party and the assertion of a "transactionally related" state law claim against a different party not already subject to federal jurisdiction with respect to the anchor claim. "Transactionally related" means that the federal anchor claim against defendant *A* and the state law claim against defendant *B* arise from a "common nucleus of operative fact."

   b. Despite strong practical reasons for permitting pendent party jurisdiction, a sharply divided Supreme Court ruled against such jurisdiction in *Finley v. United States*, 490 U.S. 545 (1989).

   Finley's facts: *P* sued for the wrongful death of her husband and two children, who died in an airplane accident that she contended was caused by some combination of the negligence of the Federal Aviation Authority, a municipal airport, and the power company with whose power lines the airplane collided. *P*'s suit against the United States for the negligence of the FAA had to be brought exclusively in federal court. Congress does not permit the United States to be sued in state court. The federal statute that makes the United States liable for conduct that is tortious under state law does not, however, create any federal liability on the part of other parties who may have been joint tortfeasors with the United States. There was no diversity of citizenship to support adjudication by a federal court of *P*'s state law tort claims against the other parties, *i.e.*, the city and the power company.

Finley's holding: The Supreme Court held that *P* could not invoke pendent party jurisdiction as the basis for federal jurisdiction over the claims against the other parties, even though these claims arose from the same occurrence as the claim against the United States. While willing to assume that there was constitutional power under Article III for federal courts to adjudicate the other, non-federal claims in federal court, since they were part of the same "case or controversy" as the claim against the United States, the majority held that it would be a violation of the separation of powers principles of the Constitution for the federal courts to exercise pendent party jurisdiction unless congressionally authorized to do so.

c. Although most instances of pendent claim jurisdiction have not been authorized by Congress, the Supreme Court took pains in *Finley* to reaffirm the propriety of pendent claim jurisdiction. The key distinction between pendent party jurisdiction (for which congressional authorization is required) and pendent claim jurisdiction (for which congressional authorization is not required) appears to be that pendent claim jurisdiction expands the *scope* of federal litigation but does not bring into federal courts any new parties.

C. *Ancillary jurisdiction* **deals with joinder of claims and parties in** *reaction* **to the way the litigation has been framed by the complaint and subsequent pleadings. The ambition of ancillary jurisdiction is to achieve a fair and comprehensive settlement of all related disputes between the parties by opening the federal courts to the myriad possibilities of liberal joinder.**

1. Not every joinder of additional claims or parties permitted by the joinder rules previously discussed is supported by ancillary jurisdiction. The general theme, however, is that ancillary jurisdiction supports the litigation of most "transactionally related" claims, even if the joinder of additional parties is required.

2. *Finley* raised doubts about the propriety of ancillary jurisdiction to permit the joinder of new parties. Ancillary jurisdiction is distinguishable from both pendent claim and pendent party jurisdiction, however, on the ground that ancillary jurisdiction is a *reactive* rather than an *initiative* form of supplemental jurisdiction. Parties who invoke ancillary jurisdiction are simply reacting to claims filed against them in federal court. This lessens the chance that ancillary jurisdiction will be manipulated so as to evade congressional limits on federal jurisdiction. In light of this distinction, *Finley* is unlikely to lead to constriction of ancillary jurisdiction in cases filed before December 1, 1990, especially since Congress has expressly authorized ancillary jurisdiction to be exercised over new parties in all subsequent cases. *See* 28 U.S.C. § 1367, discussed below in Part VI.

3. *Summary checklist of rules of ancillary jurisdiction.* There is ancillary jurisdiction over the joinder to a federal civil action of:

a. all compulsory counterclaims under Rule 13(a);

b. permissive counterclaims under Rule 13(b), but only to the extent of a set-off;

c. cross-claims under Rule 13(g), if for indemnity (and in some circuits, if for independent relief);

    d.   additional parties under Rule 13(h) who are necessary parties to counterclaims or cross-claims that would qualify for ancillary jurisdiction were joinder of the additional parties not necessary;

    e.   all claims arising from third-party practice under Rule 14(a), except for original claims by the original plaintiff against an impleaded third-party defendant; and

    f.   intervenors as of right under Rule 24(a), provided that they are not indispensable parties under Rule 19(b).

3. *Explication of ancillary jurisdiction checklist*

    a.   *Rule 13(a). Compulsory counterclaims* are *always* within ancillary jurisdiction.

    b.   *Rule 13(b). Permissive counterclaims* are within ancillary jurisdiction *only as a set-off.* A set-off reduces the amount of money otherwise recovered by an opposing party. A set-off can provide no affirmative recovery to the party who litigates a claim as a set-off.

        Example: *A* sues *B* for damages caused by *B*'s breach of a federally regulated contract. There is federal question jurisdiction over *A*'s claim against *B*. *B* counterclaims for damages caused by an unrelated business tort committed by *A*. There is no independent basis for federal jurisdiction over *B*'s permissive counterclaim. Both claims go to the jury.

        (1) If the jury finds that *B* is liable to *A* for $500,000 in damages on the original claim and that *A* is liable to *B* for $100,000 in damages on the unrelated counterclaim, the federal court will have jurisdiction to enter a judgment in the amount of $400,000. In this fashion, the court will have adjudicated the permissive counterclaim as a set-off against the amount of liability awarded against the counterclaimant on the original claim.

        (2) If the jury finds that *B* is liable to *A* for only $75,000 in damages on the original claim and that *A* is liable to *B* for $100,000 in damages on the unrelated counterclaim, the federal court has jurisdiction only to enter a judgment that neither party recovers any amount. The ancillary jurisdiction of the federal court over the permissive counterclaim extends only up to the amount that sets off any damages otherwise owed by the counterclaimant to the party defending against the counterclaim.

    c.   *Rule 13(g). Cross-claims* are *always* within ancillary jurisdiction when seeking *indemnification* for the liability of the cross-claimant to the party who has claimed against the cross-claimant. *Some circuits*, but not all, also allow ancillary jurisdiction to be exercised over a cross-claim for *independent relief*. This is the better rule, since any cross-claim, whether for indemnification or independent relief, must be transactionally related to the claims asserted in the underlying action.

        Example: *X* sues *Y* and *Z* for injuries suffered in the collapse of a building designed by *Y* and constructed by *Z*. *Z* includes in her answer a two-count cross-claim against *Y*. In Count I of the cross-claim, *Z* contends that *Y*'s plans for the building were defective and caused the collapse. *Z* accordingly seeks indemnification from *Y* in the event *Z* is held liable to *X*. In Count II of the cross-claim, *Z* contends that *Z*'s reputation has been harmed as a result of *Z*'s reliance on *Y*'s plans in building to *Y*'s exact specifications a structure that has collapsed because of defective design. *Z* accordingly seeks substantial damages from *Y* regardless whether *Z* is found liable to *X*.

        (1) In all circuits there will be ancillary jurisdiction to support the adjudication of Count I of *Z*'s cross-claim.

        (2) In only some circuits will there be ancillary jurisdiction to adjudicate Count II of the cross-claim as well, since it seeks independent relief for *Z* rather than merely indemnification.

d. *Rule 13(h):* claims against *additional parties to counterclaims* and cross-claims are within ancillary jurisdiction only if *two requirements* are met. The counterclaim or cross-claim to which the additional parties are joined must itself be within ancillary jurisdiction. The additional parties must not be merely parties whose joinder is permitted under the loose terms of Rule 20(a) — they must be *necessary parties* whose joinder is *required* by Rule 19(a).

e. *Rule 14(a):* all claims authorized by rules of *third-party practice* are within ancillary jurisdiction *except* for an original claim by the plaintiff against an impleaded third-party defendant under Rule 14(a)[7]. *See Owen Equipment & Erection Co. v. Kroger, supra.* If the third-party defendant has first asserted a claim against the original plaintiff under Rule 14(a)[6], however, then a responsive claim by the plaintiff must be analyzed as a counterclaim. Ancillary jurisdiction over counterclaims and cross-claims asserted by or against impleaded third-parties should be analyzed according to the normal rules for ancillary jurisdiction over counterclaims and cross-claims.

f. *Rule 24(a):* intervenors as of right can always invoke ancillary jurisdiction, with the single exception of intervenors who are "indispensable parties" under Rule 19(b), *i.e.,* that are so crucial to the action that in their absence the action would have to be dismissed. The purpose of this exception is to rule out evasion of the requirement of complete diversity in litigation in which an obviously essential but non-diverse party is wilfully omitted from the complaint on the assumption that the omitted party will promptly intervene as of right. *See Chance v. County School Board,* 332 F.2d 971 (7th Cir. 1964). Virtually by definition, an intervenor as of right under Rule 24(a)(2) will be a necessary party under Rule 19(a)(2)(i), since both rules are articulated in terms of protecting the party from practical impairment of an interest directly affected by the litigation. If the proposed intervenor is not so crucial to the action that it must be dismissed in its absence, then the intervenor is merely "necessary" under Rule 19(a) but not "indispensable" under Rule 19(b), and can freely invoke ancillary jurisdiction.

4. *Ancillary venue and personal jurisdiction.*

a. Where ancillary jurisdiction exists, ancillary federal venue exists.

b. There is no *general* doctrine of ancillary personal jurisdiction as to newly impleaded parties. Ancillary personal jurisdiction is authorized within a 100-mile radius of the court by Rule 4(f).

(1) If a party is already subject to the federal court's personal jurisdiction with respect to a claim against that party independently within the federal court's personal jurisdiction, then the assertion of an additional claim against that party dependent on ancillary jurisdiction needs no independent basis for personal jurisdiction — no new service of process under Rule 4 is required.

(2) To implead a party not already subject to the personal jurisdiction of the federal court, proper service of process must be accomplished under Rule 4. In addition to the provisions of Rule 4(e), service of process on parties impleaded under Rule 13(h) or Rule 14 may be accomplished under the "100-mile bulge" provision of Rule 4(f). Because Rule 4(f) requires that there be on-going litigation into which new parties are impleaded in order for the special "100-mile bulge" provision to become effective, it is functionally a specialized and highly limited form of ancillary personal jurisdiction.

VI. **STATUTORY SUPPLEMENTAL JURISDICTION UNDER 28 U.S.C. § 1367, APPLICABLE TO ACTIONS COMMENCED ON OR AFTER DECEMBER 1, 1990**

6

A. **The Judicial Improvements Act of 1990, Public Law 101-650, 104 Stat. 5089, became law on December 1, 1990. Section 301 of the Act adds new § 1367 to Title 28 of the United States Code. Section 1367, which is effective only as to civil actions commenced on or after December 1, 1990, is a broadly phrased, express Congressional authorization of "supplemental" jurisdiction that encompasses not only the familiar applications of "pendent claim" and "ancillary" jurisdiction, but also repudiates *Finley v. United States, supra,* by authorizing "pendent party" jurisdiction.**

1. The grant of supplemental jurisdiction in new 28 U.S.C. § 1367 is phrased in mandatory language that extends the jurisdiction to the limits of Article III, subject to the two exceptions discussed below. The net effect of § 1367 is to create a strong presumption in favor of the exercise of supplemental jurisdiction.

a. Supplemental jurisdiction under new § 1367 is subject to district court discretion to decline to exercise jurisdiction according to relatively strict standards for identifying where state law issues will predominate or whether there are both "exceptional circumstances" and "compelling reasons" for declining jurisdiction.

b. Congress also limited supplemental jurisdiction under new § 1367 by prohibiting its exercise over persons made parties or seeking to become parties under Federal Rules 14, 19, 20 or 24 "when exercising jurisdiction over such claims would be inconsistent with the jurisdictional requirements of section 1332." While this limitation seems intended only to preserve the rule of complete diversity under 28 U.S.C. § 1332 as applied in *Owen Equip. & Erect. Co. v. Kroger, supra* [forbidding ancillary jurisdiction over a claim asserted by the original plaintiff against an impleaded third-party defendant under the sixth sentence of Rule 14 (a)], it is so broadly worded as possibly to call into question the continuing power of federal district courts to exercise supplemental jurisdiction over nondiverse parties who are necessary parties under Rule 19(a) but are not indispensable parties under Rule 19(b), and who seek to intervene as of right under Rule 24(a).

2. Section 1367 also enacts a tolling provision to preserve litigants' rights to effective relief in state court in the event a federal court finds it lacks or declines to exercise supplemental jurisdiction.

B. **The full text of new § 1367 is as follows:**

"28 U.S.C. § 1367. Supplemental jurisdiction

"(a) Except as provided in subsections (b) and (c) or as expressly provided otherwise by Federal statute, in any civil action of which the district courts have original jurisdiction, the district courts shall have supplemental jurisdiction over all other claims that are so related to claims in the action within such original jurisdiction that they form part of the same case or controversy under Article III of the United States Constitution. Such supplemental jurisdiction shall include claims that involve the joinder or intervention of additional parties.

"(b) In any civil action of which the district courts have original jurisdiction founded solely on section 1332 of this title, the district courts shall not have supplemental jurisdiction under subsection (a) over claims by plaintiffs against persons made parties under Rule 14, 19, 20 or 24 of the Federal Rules of Civil Procedure, or over claims by persons proposed to be joined as plaintiffs under Rule 19 of such rules, or seeking to intervene a plaintiffs under Rule 24 of such rules, when exercising supplemental jurisdiction over such claims would be inconsistent with the jurisdictional requirements of section 1332.

"(c) The district courts may decline to exercise supplemental jurisdiction over a claim under subsection (a) if—

"(1) the claim raises a novel or complex issue of State law,

"(2) the claim substantially predominates over the claim or claims over which the district court has original jurisdiction,

"(3) the district court has dismissed all claims over which it has original jurisdiction, or

"(4) in exceptional circumstances, there are other compelling reasons for declining jurisdiction.

"(d) The period of limitations for any claim asserted under subsection (a), and for any other claim in the same action that is voluntarily dismissed at the same time as or after the dismissal of the claim under subsection (a), shall be tolled while the claim is pending and for a period of 30 days after it is dismissed unless State law provides for a longer tolling period.

"(e) As used in this section, the term 'State' includes the District of Columbia, the Commonwealth of Puerto Rico, and any territory or possession of the United States."

6

DISCOVERY

▶ **CHAPTER SUMMARY**

DISCOVERY

INTRODUCTION: Discovery is the formal process by which parties obtain information from their adversaries and other witnesses relating to the litigation. Discovery developed in modern litigation from the "bill of discovery" known to equity practice, but common law pleading also allowed limited inquiry into evidentiary matters. Modern discovery practice dates from the reforms included in the Federal Rules of Civil Procedure in 1938. By liberalizing pleading and deemphasizing its role in narrowing legal and factual issues for trial, the drafters of the Federal Rules transferred these functions to the discovery phase of litigation. The Federal Rules' model proved so attractive that it has been adopted in large part in a majority of states, including those that continue to use code pleading as their model. This latter group includes the State of California. However, extensive formal discovery also has its drawbacks. In most modern litigation, discovery — not trial — dominates the process. More time, money, and effort go into discovery than into any other phase of civil litigation. And discovery is the object of intense criticism for its alleged overuse and abuse by overly zealous adversaries. Discovery is unusual in litigation practice because, although judicially sanctioned, the rules contemplate that the parties and their lawyers will conduct the discovery process without direct, immediate judicial supervision. The failure of this self-monitoring has led to recent amendments to the Federal Rules and elsewhere: (1) to limit the frequency and use of the available discovery devices and (2) to give judges more responsibility for controlling discovery and greater authority to impose sanctions on the parties for abusive discovery and unjustified resistance to discovery.

PURPOSES OF DISCOVERY

I. PURPOSES OF DISCOVERY. There are both legitimate and improper purposes served by modern discovery. Most commentators agree upon the following purposes:

A. Discovery enables the parties to find out about the lawsuit by learning information necessary to prepare for trial. Under this process, plaintiff learns the facts needed to fill out her complaint; the defendant learns of plaintiff's case and its own defenses by investigating the factual basis for the claims and defenses in the civil action.

B. Discovery may narrow issues for trial by eliminating from the litigation uncontested issues, by being available in support of motions for summary judgment as background upon which to base a dismissal, and as the basis for possible settlement of the litigation. This narrowing of the factual issues was a purpose formerly served by pleadings systems but now must depend upon discovery under federal practice.

C. A third purpose is to freeze the opponent's evidence and basis for her case. The discovery process produces a record of evidence and makes it more difficult for parties to shift the evidentiary ground upon which they base their claims and defenses.

D. Discovery may be used in order to obtain and preserve evidence that will be used directly at trial. Real evidence — the automobile involved in the collision, the knife used in the assault — documentary evidence, and the testimony of witnesses who may be unavailable at trial can all be obtained and preserved through the discovery process. This is, in fact, how most real evidence and documentary evidence is obtained, and where witnesses are likely to be out of the jurisdiction or possibly are at risk of dying or becoming seriously ill, it is best to take a deposition which can be used at trial in lieu of the witness' appearance.

E. Among the many improper purposes discovery serves are its use by one party to obtain advantages over other parties through harassment of the other parties, through delay in drawing out the trial process and attrition or the wearing down of an opponent attempting to go forward with discovery of its case.

II. **REVIEW OF THE BASIC DISCOVERY DEVICES.** Under federal practice, and under most state practices, there are five major formal discovery devices. These are the oral deposition (and a variant of the oral deposition, the deposition on written questions); interrogatories directed to the parties; requests to produce documents and things and orders for the inspection of relevant material; physical and mental examinations of a party; and requests to admit the genuineness of documents or truthfulness of facts. Each of these discovery tools has its particular virtues and limitations.

A. The oral deposition provided for by Federal Rules 27-32, (especially Rule 30) and Rule 45 regarding subpoenas, is considered the standard discovery device. The oral deposition is a self-executing discovery device. It usually needs no court order and becomes compulsory for a party simply upon sending a notice that the deposition has been scheduled. Depositions may be taken of parties and non-parties, and thus this discovery device is particularly useful in obtaining information from those who are not formal parties to the litigation. The usual rules regarding scope of discovery found under Rule 26(b) apply to the oral deposition. Variants of the oral deposition include a deposition on written questions and special rules for use of the deposition before filing a formal action or after completion of an action but pending appeal.

B. The second major discovery device is written interrogatories which are sent to parties pursuant to Rule 33 of the Federal Rules of Civil Procedure. Interrogatories are best used for obtaining background facts and information regarding the claims and defenses of a party, including the existence of documents and witnesses. Interrogatories are just that, a series of written questions directed to parties only — this device is not available for witnesses — to be answered under oath and with at least some minimal requirement of investigation before answering. Like depositions, interrogatories are intended to be self-executing and use the usual scope of discovery rules found under Rule 26(b).

C. The third discovery device is a Rule 34 request for production (or inspection) of documents, things and land. The request for production of documents and things is a request made to inspect (and perhaps copy) writings and to inspect and take photographs of other items, including land of another party. This device applies to parties only, and not to witnesses. In order to obtain documents and other things from non-parties, the proponent must use the deposition and subpoena *duces tecum* in order to require the non-party to produce documents in connection with that party's deposition. A request to produce is also intended to be self-executing and uses the usual scope of discovery under Rule 26(b). Although a good-cause requirement was once a part of the production of documents and things, that requirement was eliminated in 1970.

D. The fourth discovery device is the physical and mental examination of persons under Rule 35. This device differs significantly from all of the others because it imposes additional scope requirements beyond those found in Rule 26(b). In order to obtain court approval for a physical or mental examination of a party or other person, a proponent must show that the physical or mental condition of the party or a person under control of that party is "in controversy" and that there is "good cause shown" for the examination. The requirement of a motion indicates that the device is not self-executing but requires court approval prior to any use other than that agreed to among the parties. The device is also limited to parties to the action, although it includes allowance for examination of persons in the custody or under the legal control of the party, thus allowing for the examination of minors in actions that are formally brought by the guardian or parent.

E. The fifth discovery device is a Rule 36 request for admission. This device is sometimes treated as a form of pretrial practice rather than pure discovery because a request for admission served on a party requests that that party admit the truth of matters specified or the genuineness of documents described in the request. Thus it is not aimed purely at discovering or obtaining new information but also at clarifying the parties' positions and narrowing either the scope of issues for trial or the scope of potential contests with regard to documentary evidence. However, as in the case of most of the other discovery devices, the request for admission is self-executing, it does not require a court order, and it is used in connection with parties only, and thus is not available for non-party witnesses. Finally, the usual Rule 26(b) scope applies to the request for admission. Unlike the other discovery provisions, however, the effect of an admission is a binding admission of the truth of the facts for purposes of trial in that particular matter. Deposition answers, interrogatory requests, and even documents produced all may be challenged at trial as being not authentic or incorrect, even by the party who gave the answers or responses. Requests for admission terminate any controversy with regard to the correctness or authenticity of matters admitted.

OUTLINE OF THE SCOPE OF DIS- COVERY UNDER THE FEDERAL RULES

III. **OUTLINE OF THE SCOPE OF DISCOVERY UNDER THE FEDERAL RULES. The scope** of discovery is provided primarily through Rule 26, although other rules come into play. The basic scope rule is an inclusive one to begin with but is limited by a series of exclusions or exceptions to the basic scope. We begin with the basic scope rule and detail the exceptions.

A. Inclusive Scope. Under Rule 26(b)(1), discovery is available for "any matter . . . which is *relevant to the subject matter* **involved in the pending action" and which "appears reasonably calculated to lead to the discovery of admissible evidence."**

1. The matter of which discovery is sought need not itself be admissible. as long as it has some connection to potentially admissible evidence. This is an extremely broad scope. The phrase "relevant to the subject matter" is intended to be broader than other suggested alternatives such as "relevant to the issues," or "relevant to a claim or defense," or "relevant evidence" in the matter. Professors Wright and Miller declare that the relevance standard used in Rule 26 applies "if there is any possibility that the information sought may be relevant to the subject matter of the action." In *Oppenheimer Fund, Inc. v. Sanders*, 437 U.S. 340 (1978), the Court stated that "the key phrase in this definition — 'relevant to the subject matter involved in the pending action' — has been construed broadly to encompass any matter that bears on, or that reasonably could lead to other matter that could bear on, any issue that is or may be in the case . . . . Consistent with the notice-pleading system established by the Rules, discovery is not limited to issues raised by the pleadings, for discovery itself is designed to help define and clarify the issues …. Nor is discovery limited to the merits of a case, for a variety of fact-oriented issues may arise during litigation that are not related to the merits." As a result, the current rule may allow inquiry into the practices of an entire business or industry on the ground that the business or industry is the "subject matter" of the action, even though only specified industry practices raise "issues" in the case.

   Example: In *Blank v. Sullivan & Cromwell*, 16 Fair Empl. Prac. Cas. (BNA) 87 (S.D.N.Y. 1976), women lawyers who had not been hired in 1970 by Sullivan & Cromwell sued the law firm for alleged sex discrimination in hiring. Plaintiffs sought information from the law firm through interrogatories about Sullivan & Cromwell associates who became partners before 1970, in an effort to show a possible pattern of discrimination that extended from the hiring decision to the partnership decision. The court eventually allowed this discovery although at the time it was not at all clear that Title VII prohibitions against discrimination in the terms, conditions or privileges of employment applied in any way to the decision to make individuals a partner.

2. This relevance standard also allows inquiry into matters that cannot be admitted in evidence, such as subsequent remedial measures taken by a party accused of some form of product liability or negligence on the ground that this might lead to the discovery of evidence showing that a better system or a better device was available at the time of the injury.

3. In addition to this broad relevance standard, Rule 26(b)(2) allows discovery of the existence and contents of any insurance agreement that may be available to the party in order to pay some or all of the judgment that may be entered against that party. This permits discovery of material that almost certainly could not be admitted in most trials and that is not ordinarily relevant to the issues or subject matter in the case but is only relevant in that it facilitates settlement and determination of a proper demand by the complaining party. Thus, this additional insurance agreement provision also broadens the scope of available discovery.

B. There are *numerous exceptions* to these broad standards. The most important are the exceptions for "privileged matter" found within the basic relevance rule, the exception for trial preparation materials in general and specifically for experts, and the availability of protective orders under Rule 26(c). Each of these provisions limits the otherwise broad potential scope of discovery.

1. The basic relevance standard exempts from its coverage "privileged" matter. *See* Rule 26(b)(1). Privileged matter is treated very narrowly. It does not include confidential or sensitive matter, or even matter in which the parties may have been advised that what they do or say is "confidential" as in the case of meetings regarding tenure of potential university professors or disciplinary and other hearings that are defined as confidential by the relevant authority. *See University of Pennsylvania v. Equal Employment Opportunity Comm'n*, 493 U.S. 182, 110 S. Ct. 577 (1990). It is limited to the recognized evidentiary privileges, such as the attorney/client privilege, the self-incrimination privilege, the spousal privileges against testifying, physician/patient privileges, and the like. The question of the existence of these privileges in federal court depends upon the basis of the claim or defense.

    a. Federal law-based claims and defenses look to Federal Rule of Evidence 501, which declares that privilege of witnesses is governed by "the principles of the common law as they may be interpreted by the courts of the United States in the light of reason and experience." Thus the federal evidence privileges are case-law developed privileges.

    b. Where the claim or defense rests upon state law, the appropriate state law privileges are applied. Some states, such as California, have extensive statutorily provided privileges that are not universally applicable, such as the psychotherapist/patient privilege, the clergyman/penitent privilege, sexual-assault victim/counselor privilege, a domestic-violence victim/counselor privilege, political-vote privilege, trade-secret privilege, and official-information and identity-of-informer privileges. Federal privilege rules are more limited.

2. In addition to purely privileged matter, since the case of *Hickman v. Taylor*, 329 U.S. 495 (1947), the federal courts have recognized an attorney's work product privilege or, as it is now codified in Rule 26(b)(3), a trial-preparation privilege affording limited immunity from discovery. The scope of the *Hickman v. Taylor* rules and Rule 26(b)(3) differ in part, however, and each is worth a brief look.

    a. The *Hickman* case. In 1943, shortly after the adoption of the Federal Rules, the tugboat J. M. Taylor sank near Philadelphia while pulling a railroad car float across the Delaware River. Five of the nine crew members drowned. Shortly afterwards, the owners of the tug hired one Fortenbaugh, a lawyer, to defend against possible suits on behalf of the drowned crew members and to sue the B & O Railroad. Within a month of the accident, the U.S. Steamboat Inspectors held a public hearing at which all four survivors testified. Their testimony was recorded and was available to all parties. About this time, Fortenbaugh interviewed each of the survivors privately and obtained statements from them that were signed by the crew members. Fortenbaugh also interviewed others having information about the accident and made memoranda of some of the information. Eventually the representatives of the five drowned crew members sought compensation; four representatives settled their claims, and the fifth (Hickman) sued the owners of the tug and the railroad under the Jones Act. In the course of that litigation, Hickman sought

7

discovery from the tugboat owners of any oral or written memoranda or statements concerning the sinking, including any statements by crew members. The tug owners, through Fortenbaugh, declined to answer. They admitted that statements had been taken from crew members but claimed the discovery request called for "privileged matter obtained in preparation for litigation" and was an "attempt to obtain indirectly counsel's private files" that might even mean turning over "the thoughts of counsel." The trial court held that the requested matters were not privileged and ordered the owners and Fortenbaugh to produce the witnesses' statements and state the substance of any factual memoranda and, further, to produce Fortenbaugh's memoranda or submit those memoranda to the court. The owners and Fortenbaugh refused; Fortenbaugh was held in contempt and imprisoned. The Third Circuit reversed, holding that the information was "the work product of the lawyer" and privileged. Ultimately, the case was taken to the Supreme Court.

The Supreme Court rejected the attorney/client privilege as applying to the requested matters. Because these were not confidential communications from a client to his attorney, they could not be shielded under the standard privilege exception. However, the Court for the first time recognized that certain trial preparation materials constituting "the work product of the lawyer" were largely exempt from discovery. The Court recognized that it was necessary to protect the lawyer's work product because otherwise a party would be able to invade the files and the mental impressions of the attorney. Justice Jackson, in an important concurrence, wrote that requiring the lawyer to produce written notes of witnesses' statements, or to reconstruct from memory witnesses' unrecorded oral statements, would culminate in setting the lawyer against his own client wherever there was any inconsistency in the evidence of what the lawyer had learned investigating the case. This was an intolerable result even with the advent of the Federal Rules and their intent to end litigation by surprise.

The Court did, however, limit its holding. It addressed at least four different categories of material. First, the Court noted that its protections from discovery did not apply to facts learned by parties or their attorney while investigating a potential lawsuit. These facts could be obtained by appropriate discovery device, although the materials in which the facts were embedded were not available. Second, the Court looked at the signed written statements of the witnesses obtained by Fortenbaugh. These witnesses' statements, although they fall within the broader policy against invasion of the lawyer's files, are not entirely immune from discovery. However, the party seeking disclosure of statements must show special circumstances in order to obtain them, and, when the substantial equivalent of that material is available elsewhere, as was true in this case, an inadequate showing was made to require their production. A lawyer's personal written notes of unsigned oral statements, however, are the lawyer's own memoranda describing the status of the case and possibly evaluating it. These are not discoverable, nor are oral statements that must be retrieved from the lawyer's own unrecorded recollection. These cannot be disclosed because they are an integral part of the attorney's preparation and necessary for an effective functioning of the adversary system. The Court was buttressed here by the fact that the plaintiff apparently had all this information already and had candidly admitted that he was seeking only to protect against the possibility that he might have overlooked something. Thus he had made no attempt to show any special need for the materials that would require producing the documents in Fortenbaugh's possession. The Court suggested such a showing might be possible if a witness were hostile or otherwise unavailable and had been contacted earlier by the opponent's attorney. With regard to memoranda that detail theories of the case or incorporate an attorney's impressions and non-documentary recollections of oral interviews of witnesses, they could not be disclosed whatever showing the proponent might make. These matters are inseparable from the attorney's thought processes and are entirely exempt from disclosure under the *Hickman* decision.

b. *Rule 26(b)(3)*. In 1970, Rule 26 was amended to add Rule 26(b)(3), entitled "Trial Preparation: Materials," thus codifying the 23 years of accumulated case law under *Hickman* dealing with protection of an attorney's trial preparation material.

    (1) Rule 26(b)(3) is different in several respects from the *Hickman* decision. It is broader in that it applies not just to an attorney's work product but to any materials "prepared in anticipation of litigation or for trial by or for another party or by or for that other party's representative *(including the other party's attorney, consultant, surety, indemnitor, insurer, or agent)*." [Emphasis added.]

    (2) On the other hand, aspects of *Hickman* were narrowed. Although absolute protection is required against disclosure of the "the mental impressions, conclusions, opinions or legal theories of an attorney or other representative," the three- or four-part analysis used by the Court in *Hickman* was abandoned for more generalized treatment of trial preparation materials that are subject to disclosure.

    (3) Under Rule 26(b)(3), trial preparation immunity applies to "documents and tangible things." The documents and tangible things must come within the basic scope rules of 26(b), that is, they must be "otherwise discoverable under subdivision (b)(1) of this Rule." Finally, to be subject to immunity, the materials must be prepared "in anticipation of litigation or for trial" by the appropriate representative.

    (4) In order to discover these materials, the party seeking discovery must first show "substantial need" for the materials in the preparation of that party's case and, second, that the party is unable to obtain the "substantial equivalent" of the materials by any other means "without undue hardship." The Rule further provides for the absolute protection from disclosure of the mental impressions, etc., of the attorney or representative and makes special provision for a relaxed standard allowing parties and other persons to obtain their own statements.

    (5) Each of the requirements of Rule 26(b)(3) has generated litigation of its own. With regard to the requirement that materials must have been prepared in anticipation of litigation, one of the main controversies has been whether routine investigative or other reports prepared, for example, by a bus company whenever there is any kind of accident or collision, are prepared with an eye to litigation. Obviously, litigation remains one of the possibilities that gives rise to the preparation of such reports, but since they are prepared in the regular course of business, the general rule is that such reports do not receive the special protection of Rule 26(b)(3), but are freely discoverable under the general scope requirements of 26(b)(1). Likewise, there is an exception when the investigation is itself a subject of the claim, for example, when an allegation is made that there was a negligent investigation itself causing injury or a wrongful denial of a claim. Documents that are produced or prepared because they are required by law, even though prepared for litigation, are not subject to the special rules under 26(b)(3). The Rule does not permit discovery of the ideas or mere sense impressions of an attorney or representative who has not reduced them to a written record of discoverable facts.

    (6) Slightly different rules apply in connection with a party's or non-party witness's own statement. When a lawyer investigating a case obtains the statement of a party or other person, the party or other person, upon request and without a special showing of need, can obtain the statement from the lawyer or other investigator. Controversy has arisen under this section regarding what constitutes a statement. The Rule permits discovery of more than standard verbatim or transcribed statements, but issues regularly arise when a lawyer has recorded the substance of an individual's remarks along with other materials and commentary by the attorney. Decisions here are very fact-specific and likely to turn in part on the need and urgency for the request as well as the percentage of a statement which is verbatim

or near verbatim and the proportion that constitutes the attorney's opinions. Even if a statement of such a mixed character is produced, the court is required to delete the portions that constitute mental impressions, conclusions, and opinions of the attorney.

(7) Most litigation under Rule 26(b)(3) concerns whether the party seeking production has made the special showing of need for the materials in the preparation of the case and that the equivalent is unobtainable without undue hardship.

(a) One easy set of cases involves situations where statements and information have been obtained from eyewitnesses or others by only one party very near the time of the event, and the other party had no ability to obtain similar statements either because an attorney had not been retained or the party refused to speak except to the one side. Under these circumstances, courts have been sympathetic to the claim that an excluded party needs this material for the preparation of the case. Similar situations arise when witnesses, especially eyewitnesses, have suffered substantial loss of memory, have died, or are beyond the reach of the subpoena power even in connection with a deposition.

(b) More difficult are situations where one party could obtain the equivalent, but only with considerable expenditure of time and money. Most courts have been unsympathetic to the claim that it would be unduly expensive for one party to obtain the same information as another, and disparities in relative wealth of the parties have been disregarded. Ordinarily something more must be shown than that it would be more difficult or more expensive to obtain the same information without Rule 26(b)(3) discovery.

(c) Finally, issues have arisen as to whether one party can obtain information held by the other party that may impeach the discovering party's witnesses or otherwise attack the nature of its case. Consider whether a plaintiff may seek to obtain from the defendant any videotaped observations or movies made by defendant that show the allegedly disabled plaintiff walking or gardening or the like. Obviously such a movie or observation may serve to impeach the degree of disability claimed by the plaintiff. It is understandable that a defendant does not want to give up this information which would enable the plaintiff to reconstruct her case to meet the impeaching evidence and eliminate the element of surprise. Courts have often required the production of such materials in order to obtain and understand the impeachment of another side but have delayed the discovery until shortly before trial begins.

3. The third area in which the general relevance rules are limited is with regard to experts consulted in anticipation of litigation. Discovery from experts could also be seen as a subcategory of the general trial preparation provisions. But the special problem of the *expense* of expert preparation led to a separate treatment in Rule 26(b)(4). Discovery of expert preparation of one side by the other is a microcosm of the discovery world generally. On one side of the balance is the need to determine what the other side's evidence and information will be in order to prepare fully and adequately for trial so that the result at trial will be based on the merits of the case and not on one side's ability to hoard essential information requiring experts. On the other side of the balance is the danger that one party may use the discovery rules, including the expert witness rule, to freeload on the efforts of the other side without making a similar investment of time, money, or thought. Rule 26(b)(4) attempts to balance these concerns by distinguishing among at least three categories of experts. A closer look at the Rule reveals that there are probably five, and maybe more, categories of experts used in preparation for, or at, trial. The extent to which information can be discovered from these experts depends first on their classification.

a. Rule 26(b)(4) expressly recognizes two types of experts to whom the special immunity or limited discovery rules apply.

    (1) The first type of expert, and the one most subject to discovery, is the expert whose factual information and opinions were required or developed in anticipation of litigation or for trial, and whom the party from whom discovery was sought expects to call as an expert witness at trial. Discovery may be obtained from this type of expert initially through interrogatories that require the expert to (i) state the substance of the facts and opinions on which the expert is expected to testify and (ii) a summary of the grounds for each opinion. Rule 26(b)(4)(A)(ii) allows a party seeking discovery to make further inquiry by applying to the court for an order to allow, for example, a deposition of the testifying expert.

    (2) The second type of expert explicitly recognized in Rule 26(b)(4) is the expert who has been "retained or specially employed" by another party in anticipation of litigation or preparation for trial, but who is not expected to be a witness at trial. Discovery may be sought from these experts only upon "a showing of exceptional circumstances under which it is impracticable for the party seeking discovery to obtain facts or opinions on the same subject by other means." The extent that discovery may be permitted of this kind of expert remains subject to conflicting interpretations in the lower federal courts.

        (a) Most courts have required the exceptional showing in order to obtain even the *identity* of experts who have been retained formally but who will not testify at trial. These courts point out that once an expert of this sort is identified, the expert can be contacted by the opponent. Damaging information might be revealed. The expert could now be called by the adverse party as a witness and asked, for example, what it was about that expert's opinion that caused the other party not to put her on the witness stand. As a result, these courts note that ready identification of this second category of experts would reduce the number of candid opinions to be given by experts in controversial cases.

        (b) Nevertheless, the Rule contemplates that in certain circumstances this kind of expert may be identified and information obtained from the expert. Potential circumstances include where an expert has conducted experiments that may have destroyed or altered evidence to be used at trial, or where there are few or perhaps only one expert in an area, and that expert has been retained by the other side but will not testify. Under these circumstances, the identities of the experts and some limited discovery from those experts is possible under the Rule.

b. Left outside the scope of Rule 26(b)(4) are experts who are eyewitnesses — as actors or viewers — to the events in question. A doctor who happens to witness an automobile accident is not protected from discovery by virtue of the fact that she is a doctor. It is only when her special expertise is used by one of the parties in preparation for litigation that the protections of the Rule apply. Thus, for actor and viewer experts, their information is freely discoverable subject to the usual scope rules of 26(b).

c. In addition to the categories of experts recognized by the Rule, and eyewitness experts who fall outside of the Rule, lower courts have had to deal with two other categories of experts that are not directly addressed in the Rule.

    (1) Some experts may be *informally or casually* consulted by one of the parties, rather than "retained or specially employed." Whether a party has been formally or informally consulted depends upon resolution of factual matters including whether the party was paid, the extent of any consultation, the circumstances of the consultation, and the like. If a party, for example, happened to speak to a doctor

friend while golfing together and talked very informally about the case, it is likely a court would treat such an expert as informally consulted.

Example: In *Ager v. Jane C. Stormont Hospital & Training School*, 622 F.2d 496 (10th Cir. 1980), the court indicated that these factors and the type of information provided to the experts should be used by the court in making a determination as to how to characterize the witness. The court further found that this kind of determination must be made *in camera* by the court in order to avoid revealing the witness's identity. The court rejected as overbroad a rule that would place into the category of "informally consulted" any witness whom the party rejected as of no assistance in preparation of the trial. If, however, an expert is found to fall in the informally consulted category, not even the name of that expert may be revealed, much less any opinions, facts, or information from the expert.

(2) The final expert category that has given the courts some trouble is the employee expert. Most courts have found employee experts to fall outside the scope of Rule 26(b)(4), which gives protection to information and opinions of experts only when acquired or developed in anticipation of litigation or for trial. Where reports and documents are routinely prepared, they are not subject to qualified immunity under the general trial preparation material provisions of Rule 26(b)(3). Likewise, where experts work for a party as employees, most courts have found their facts and opinions are not protected from discovery by Rule 26(b)(4). Their reports and findings are discoverable to the extent that any party's employee's information may be discovered. Some courts have attempted to distinguish between the employee's generalized information and special consultation that occurs in connection with litigation, but making the distinction has proved more difficult than it is worth. Also falling within this group may be experts whose opinions are fully prepared and developed outside of litigation, but who are retained to testify about how their opinions relate to particular litigation. This would include, for example, academic experts who have independently studied the problem and who are not specially retained by a party to give it advice but are merely called as witnesses. Their information should also be freely discoverable within the general scope of the Rules and not protected under Rule 26(b)(4).

d. *Fee allowances.* In order to prevent the problem of freeloading with regard to expenses, Rule 26(b)(4)(C) provides that the court "shall require that the party seeking discovery pay the expert a reasonable fee for the time spent in responding to discovery" where that party is a witness testifying in trial, and must engage in further discovery, including a deposition, or where discovery is had of a party not testifying in trial but formally consulted. Second, where discovery has been obtained from the expert under either circumstance, the court is to require the party seeking discovery to pay the other party a fair portion of the fees and expenses that had been incurred by the adversary in obtaining the facts and opinions from the expert. Thus when expert discovery is successfully obtained, the party obtaining the expert discovery and the party that originally retained the expert share the expenses of that discovery. In effect, the party seeking discovery becomes a co-retainer of the expert.

e. Other jurisdictions, including California, make at least depositions of experts who will testify at trial available as a matter of course. This seems more desirable than the cumbersome two-stage process in federal court regarding testifying experts, especially since the courts have been unable to develop any real criteria to distinguish situations when deposition discovery is allowed and in which it is denied. The consequence of failing to identify experts who may testify at trial is either to bar their testimony at trial or to allow a continuance to enable the opposing party to take the deposition or obtain the required discovery from the other party's expert before resuming the trial.

4. Protective orders are available to parties to guard against specific instances of discovery overreaching or overintrusiveness.

    a. Under Rule 26(c), a further exception to discovery is available when a party opposing discovery, upon motion and for good cause shown, obtains a protective order. The court is allowed to make any order which "justice requires to protect a party or person from annoyance, embarrassment, oppression, or undue burden or expense." Rule 26(c) specifies a range of protective orders including that the discovery not be made; that discovery be limited to certain specified terms and conditions including time or place; that an alternative method of discovery be used; that the scope of discovery or the matters inquired into be limited; that the persons present for discovery be limited; that a deposition be sealed; that trade secrets and other confidential research development and commercial information be protected; and that documents be filed simultaneously under seal as directed by the court. Most litigation under this section has concerned the protective order available for trade secrets or other confidential business information.

    b. The burden is on the party who seeks protection under Rule 26(c) to demonstrate the existence of a need for protection, for example, that there is a trade secret involved, and that disclosure will be harmful to that party. Then, depending upon the protective order sought, the other party will have the burden of showing that no protection is required or that full discovery should be available. Finally, the court has balanced the need for secrecy and protection and the degree of injury from disclosure against the need for the information and the degree of injury from lack of disclosure, taking account of the availability of safeguards that may lessen the need for a broad or intrusive protective order.

    c. A modern problem has arisen in connection with "umbrella" confidentiality agreements or protective orders that shield all discovery or virtually all discovery in a particular case from disclosure in any public manner or release to any other party. The public and other parties have asserted that there may be a first amendment right to obtain discovery information. This claim has met with a mixed reaction in the courts. Although court proceedings are generally open to the public, this has not been the usual case with regard to discovery, which is intended as an informal, not court-mandated, function undertaken by the parties "inter se" (between themselves).

    Example: In the case of *Seattle Times Co. v. Rhinehart,* 467 U.S. 20 (1984), the Supreme Court rejected a newspaper's challenge to a protective order restricting access to discovered information regarding religious groups' membership and donor lists. At the same time, the Court acknowledged that there may be some first amendment rights pertaining to discovery material, at least when the materials are used in conduct of the litigation.

5. Amendments to the Federal Rules in the past decade have given judges significant managerial power and control over the discovery process and recently imposed on the parties a certification requirement, paralleling that in Rule 11, that requires them to attest to the need for discovery. Both of these devices act as restraints upon the scope of available discovery.

    a. *Discretionary judicial limits on discovery.* Before 1983, Rule 26(a) provided that unless there was a special court order, "the frequency of use of these [discovery] devices is not limited." In 1983, Rules 26(a) and (b) were amended to add the language now found in the second paragraph of 26(b)(1), providing that the court should intervene to limit the scope of discovery if it determines that the discovery sought is unreasonably cumulative or duplicative or obtainable from another more convenient, less burdensome source, that the party seeking discovery has had an ample discovery opportunity to obtain the information sought, or that on balance the discovery sought is unduly burdensome and expensive, taking into account the scope of the controversy, the amount in controversy, limitations on the party's resources, and the needs of the case. The court may impose these limits on discovery on motion for a protective order or on its own initiative after reasonable notice. Thus, the new discretionary judicial limits include a proportionality control, allowing the court to restrict the scope and extent of discovery when it is disproportionate to the needs and scope of the litigation.

(1) In exercising this limitation, the court can make use of the discovery conference. First provided in the 1980 amendments to Rule 26, the discovery conference is, in part, merely a supplement to the Rule 16 general pretrial conference. It allows the court at any time after the action has begun, at the request of an attorney for any party or on its own initiative, to require the parties to appear before it for a discovery conference. The parties must provide necessary information, including a discovery plan and schedule and any limitations needed on discovery to enable the court to enter an order identifying issues for discovery purposes, establishing a plan and schedule, of discovery, setting limitations on discovery, if any, and allocating expenses of discovery. The rule specifically provides that the conference may be combined with a pretrial conference under Rule 16.

(2) These processes are highly discretionary with the court and are utilized to a different degree by judges in different parts of the country and within different courts depending upon the troubles that those particular courts or judges have encountered with discovery disputes, including overly intrusive discovery or excessive resistance to discovery.

6. Finally, the discovery device of physical and mental examination of a party, Rule 35 (covered in detail below), has a special scope rule more limited than the general scope of discovery. In order to engage in discovery concerning the mental or physical condition of a party or person under the custody or control of the party, the physical or mental condition must be "in controversy," and then the court must "for good cause shown" consider whether it is appropriate to order the person/party to submit to a physical or mental examination by an appropriate medical expert.

a. Physical or mental conditions of a party are in controversy when the party places them directly in controversy, for example, when a plaintiff alleges she suffered physical or mental injuries as a result of a defendant's negligence. The party seeking discovery may also be able to place the condition of another party in controversy. This requires making an appropriate factually-based showing that the other party's physical or mental condition in some way was involved in or contributed to the events relevant to the lawsuit and the determination of liability or damages.

b. Before the amendments to Rule 34 regarding production of documents and tangible things, that Rule also had a good-cause requirement, but it has since been dropped. This leaves Rule 35 alone as imposing a special limitation on the scope of discovery.

SPECIFIC DISCOVERY DEVICES

IV. SPECIFIC DISCOVERY DEVICES

A. Depositions: Federal Rule 30

1. Depositions are distinct from the other major discovery devices because they are available not just for parties but for "any person" under Rule 30(a). Thus the deposition can be used to obtain information from bystanders and other persons who are not formal parties to the action.

a. Parties must attend a deposition and be examined upon proper notice under Rule 30(b)(1). Although no time is specified, the courts usually insist upon a minimum of five- or ten-days' notice. But no formal subpoena or other process is necessary to compel the attendance of a party witness.

b. On the other hand, non-party witnesses can only be compelled to attend by use of a subpoena. Rules 30(a) and 45(d) outline the procedure and the geographical limits of the court's subpoena power.

c. Under Rule 30(b)(6), a corporation served with a deposition notice may designate the officer or other party within the corporation who is the appropriate person having information on the subjects referred to in the deposition notice. This allows the examining party to send a notice addressed only to the corporation, specifying "with reasonable particularity the matters on which examination is requested," and the corporation is required to exercise good faith in designating an appropriate and knowledgeable person.

2. Where can depositions be held?

a. Under federal practice, there is no geographical limit on the place where a deposition may be held.

(1) However, plaintiffs must ordinarily submit to depositions at the place where they bring suit regardless of its convenience or inconvenience to the plaintiff.

(2) In order to change the location of any deposition, the opponent must obtain a protective order under Rule 26(c) and make a sufficient showing that it would be inconvenient, burdensome, or exceedingly expensive to have the deposition occur at the designated place. This limit helps insure that depositions cannot be used merely to harass parties by scheduling them in out-of-the-way places or at exceptionally inconvenient times.

b. Non-party witnesses who must be subpoenaed under Rule 45 can be deposed only where the witness (i) resides; (ii) is employed; (iii) transacts business; (iv) where the non-party witness was served; (v) within 100 miles of the place where the non-party witness was served; or (vi) "at such other convenient place as is fixed by an order of the court." [Rule 45(d)(2).]

c. Corporations can be deposed where they reside, that is, where they do business. However, protective orders are available to restrict the place at which the corporation, through its officers, may have its deposition taken. For example, the protective order may limit the deposition of the corporation to the corporation's principal place of business.

3. When can depositions be taken?

a. The general rule is that depositions can be taken any time "[a]fter commencement of the action." This rule applies on its face to either party. [Rule 30(a).]

b. However, the plaintiff must seek leave of court in order to take a deposition within 30 days after service of summons and a complaint unless the defending party has already served a deposition notice or otherwise sought discovery. This lag time gives the defendant an opportunity to proceed with its discovery first, or, at least, prevents plaintiff from initiating litigation and immediately initiating discovery without giving the defendants time to consider their response.

c. "Reasonable notice" in writing is required of any deposition. [Rule 30(b)(1).]

4. Federal practice compared to California's practice

a. Under California practice, depositions may be taken "any time after the service of the summons ... or after the appearance of the defendant." However, the plaintiff must seek leave of court if notice of the taking of the deposition is to be served within 20 days after a service of the summons and complaint. Thus, the differences are 20-day notice versus the 30-day presumption under federal practice; dating from the service of the notice rather than the taking of the deposition itself as under federal practice.

      b.   California requires 10 days' notice for the taking of depositions. Cal. Code Civ. Pro. § 2019(a)(1).

B.   Interrogatories: Federal Rule 33

    1.   Interrogatories are available only from parties on behalf of parties. Thus, interrogatories cannot be directed to a witness or a bystander but only to a party. Interrogatories are a series of formal written questions directed to another party that the other party must respond to in writing and under oath.

    2.   Tactically, interrogatories have proved helpful in making initial inquiry into the basis of the claims, contentions, and pleadings of other parties; for identifying witnesses and other persons with relevant information about the claim or defense or the litigation generally; and for identifying relevant documents in preparation for later document requests.

    3.   On the other hand, interrogatories are often considered the most abused of the discovery devices. If boilerplate or standardized interrogatories are used by parties in case after case, without much thought or preparation, they can impose an enormous burden on the responding party which must review its records in making inquiry of knowledgeable persons and perhaps respond in enormous detail to a few standard questions. As a result, many courts now by local rule limit the number of interrogatories that a party may employ in connection with any other party and require court approval when that number is exceeded. A frequent number is 30 or 35 interrogatories, including all subparts.

        a.   Aside from local rules limiting numbers of interrogatories, courts have been reluctant to excuse parties from responding to interrogatories because they are burdensome or seek a large quantity of material or require a large scope of investigation. Most courts recognize that there is a burden involved in responding to interrogatories, but it is one that each party must bear in the course of litigation. Moreover, it is clear that it is not an appropriate objection simply to claim that an interrogatory or set of interrogatories is burdensome; the burdened party must make an appropriate motion for a protective order to limit the scope of response required or investigation or the time period covered by the request in the interrogatory.

        b.   The parties and the court may also take advantage of Rule 33(c) in responding to burdensome or wide-ranging interrogatories. This subsection allows a responding party to specify records from which the answers to the interrogatories may be obtained and allow the propounding party to inspect and review those records.

    4.   Earlier there was considerable litigation over "contention interrogatories" inquiring broadly about the opinions and contentions of the parties. It is now settled that it is proper to inquire into the contentions of the parties and the factual basis for those contentions, even when that requires the responding party to express an opinion as to the legal basis for the claims and thus entails some degree of legal analysis. [Rule 33(b).]

C.   Requests to Produce Documents and Other Tangible Things and for Entry into Real Property: Federal Rule 34

    1.   This discovery device, like interrogatories, applies only to parties.

    2.   In order to obtain documents or other tangible things from non-parties, a party must either notice the deposition of the non-party and in the accompanying subpoena request that the non-party bring with her to the deposition the records, documents or tangible things sought (this is called "subpoena duces tecum"), *see* Rules 45(b) and 45(d)(1); or the party must bring an independent action, the purpose of which is the discovery of material or information or a request to enter upon the property of a non-party. The independent action is a cumbersome and expensive device, and is seldom used. However, it is available as a last resort when there is no other convenient way to obtain information from non-parties.

3. California, by contrast, has provided what is in effect a distinctive discovery device allowing deposition notices to be sent to non-parties to produce records. The parties need not attend in person at the deposition if they return the records with a requisite affidavit citing their authenticity and reciting the requirements of the statute. Thus, this device functions as a request to produce documents from third parties utilizing the deposition subpoena and notice as a mere formality.

4. Controversies have arisen over requests for document production that require the availability of continuing access by one party to another party's documents or other records. Today, most courts are willing to grant continuing access — not just a one-time-only right to inspect — especially when it is available reciprocally and when notice is required in order to take advantage of this access. That is, access is usually granted only on five- or ten-days' advance notice.

5. The second area of dispute arises when one party requests production and copying by the other party of large numbers of documents or other business records. Rule 34(b) gives the responding party the option of identifying the location of the relevant records and allowing the party seeking discovery to come in and make the search for the documents themselves. Protections in Rule 34(b) guard against parties burying or shuffling the records. They must be produced as they are kept in the ordinary course of business or according to the categories specified in the request.

D. Physical and Mental Examinations: Federal Rule 35

1. This discovery device has proved among the most controversial because of its intrusiveness and potential for abuse, and because of the special rights persons have under privacy-related doctrines to the security of their physical body and mental state.

2. As we noted above, the request for physical and mental examination contains special scope rules.

    a. The physical or mental condition of a party must be "in controversy."

    b. Even if the condition is in controversy and involves a party, a court order is required in order to obtain discovery by this device, and "good cause" must be shown in order to obtain this court order.

3. The well-known Supreme Court case of *Schlagenhauf v. Holder*, 379 U.S. 104 (1964), considered some preliminary challenges to the Rule and provided guidance in determining when a condition is in controversy and what kind of a showing will amount to good cause.

    a. *Schlagenhauf* arose out of a collision between a bus and a tractor-trailer. Following the collision, bus passengers sued Greyhound Corporation, the bus owner; Robert L. Schlagenhauf, the bus driver; Contract Carriers, Inc., owner of the tractor; Joseph L. McCorkhill, the tractor driver; and National Lead Company, the trailer owner. Greyhound then filed a cross-claim against Contract Carriers and National Lead for damage to its bus based on the alleged negligent operation of the tractor-trailer. Contract Carriers responded by denying negligence and alleging affirmatively that the bus driver (Schlagenhauf) had been negligent in causing Greyhound's damages. This response included a letter alleging that Schlagenhauf was not "mentally or physically capable of bus driving at the time of the bus accident." At this point, Contract Carriers and National Lead petitioned the court for an order directing Schlagenhauf to submit to examinations by a team of specialists in internal medicine, ophthalmology, neurology, and psychiatry. Contract Carriers, in connection with the petition, alleged Schlagenhauf's condition was "in controversy" as a result of their answer to the cross-claim and the affidavit of their attorney who had been present at Schlagenhauf's deposition that (i) Schlagenhauf had testified that he had seen red lights for some 10-15 seconds before the accident, (ii) that another witness had seen red lights for some three-quarters to one-half mile before the accident, and (iii) Schlagenhauf had previously been involved in a similar bus accident. Before the court's ruling on the petition, National Lead filed its answer to the Greyhound cross-claim and itself cross-claimed against Greyhound and Schlagenhauf for damages to its trailer. The district court judge (Holder) ordered Schlagenhauf to submit to nine different examinations, although only four had been requested, by each of the doctors suggested by Contract Carriers and National Lead, all without any hearing. The court of appeals then denied the writ of mandamus sought by Schlagenhauf and brought against the judge.

b. The Supreme Court decided first that Rule 35's physical and mental examinations are available and apply to both defendants and plaintiffs because both are parties, thus rejecting Schlagenhauf's claim that applying the rule to a defendant was an invasion of privacy. The Court rejected objections claiming that this was a modification of substantive rights under the Rules Enabling Act, and that only plaintiffs could be examined on the basis of a waiver theory.

c. Second, the Court ruled that a person is a "party" under Rule 35 if he is a party to any claim in the entire case even if that person is not a party to the particular claim as to which discovery is sought. This was necessary because at the time the physical examinations were sought of Schlagenhauf, he was not a party to any claim by Contract Carriers or National Lead, although he was a party in the action having been named a defendant by the bus passenger plaintiffs.

d. Third, the Court found the "in controversy" and "good cause" requirements could not be satisfied merely by an assertion on behalf of the party seeking the exams that these conditions were relevant. Instead, the moving party must make an affirmative showing on both counts. The pleadings alone may suffice for this showing. For example, in a personal injury action when an exam is sought of the plaintiff or complaining party, the party has put her physical or mental condition in issue by seeking damages on the basis of personal injury. In this case, however, other defending parties placed Schlagenhauf's condition in issue; he did not initially raise the issue. Consequently, specific support of a factual nature and first-hand information (not hearsay affidavits) were necessary to satisfy the good cause requirement. Under the record, the Court found support only for an eye examination but remanded the case for further trial court consideration of all of the examinations.

4. Rule 35 makes specific provisions for and actively encourages the parties to make agreements by stipulation with one another to provide for these examinations and thus avoid the need for a coercive motion and court order. When such an examination does occur, the courts have shown great willingness to impose protective requirements such as limiting the doctors who can make the examinations, providing for examination at the time and place of the examined party's choosing, and at times permitting an attorney or other representative to be present because of the danger that admissions or other statements may be made in the course of the examination or that the examination may be unduly intrusive and painful. When an examination is conducted and a report made and that report is provided to the other parties, it is a waiver of any privilege regarding that report. Providing such a report requires production of similar reports in the hands of the parties receiving the report.

E. **Requests for Admission: Federal Rule 36**

1. Requests for admission cover two general areas: requests to admit the truthfulness of facts, which include statements of opinions of fact and the application of law to fact; and requests to admit the genuineness of any documents. Requests to admit the genuineness of documents have not proved controversial. They are helpful in establishing a sufficient foundation for admitting documents at trial. Much more controversial has been the use of the request to preclude litigation over truthfulness of certain issues.

2. Rule 36 admissions are fully binding at trial, unless they are set aside, and are, in effect, stipulations for that trial. They may not be used outside of the pending trial. In contrast, interrogatory answers are not binding at trial. They may be disputed and may not even be admissible at trial.

3. When a party properly serves requests for admission on an opposing party and there is no response, after 30 days the requests are deemed admitted just as if the answers had been in the affirmative. However, caution requires ordinarily that when there has been no response, the party seeking the admissions proceed to obtain a court order stipulating that the non-responses amount to and will be considered an admission.

4. Rule 36(a) provides a device for seeking relief from the court from improper or negligent admissions. The party seeking relief must show that the presentation on the merits will be served by granting relief from the admissions, and the opposing party must fail to show that the granting of relief would prejudice its case.

5. It is not grounds for refusing to answer a request for admission that it seeks resolution of central issues or disputed facts within the case. Instead, the party must deny the requested admission and briefly state the reasons for the denial.

6. When a party improperly denies a request for admission, and the opponent succeeds in proving the matter at trial, Rule 37(c) gives the court authority to allow the party that has proved the truth of the matter its "reasonable expenses," including attorney's fees incurred in making the proof.

F. **Discovery Available Through Non-discovery Methods. Attorneys have other sources of information apart from the formal and official federal discovery rules. Lawyers make frequent use of federal and state freedom-of-information laws that were enacted to make governmental information generally available to the public, when the information concerns matters of particular value in the specific litigation. Federal agencies must make their records available for inspection and copying on request unless those records are subject to exception, including ones for trade secrets or commercial information that is privileged or confidential and "inter-agency or intra-agency memorandum or letters which would not be available by law to a party … in litigation with the agency."**

G. **Discovery in International Litigation. The United States and some 16 other countries are parties to the Hague Evidence Convention which prescribes the procedures by which a judicial authority in one of the Contracting States (country) may request evidence located in another of the Contracting States.**

1. In *Societe Nationale Industrielle Aerospatiale v. United States District Court*, 482 U.S. 522 (1987), the United States Supreme Court limited the impact that this Convention will have on litigation conducted in the United States. In the *Societe Nationale* case, plaintiff had been injured when one defendant's airplane crashed in Iowa. Suit was brought in federal court in Iowa, and the plaintiff sought discovery under the usual provisions of the Federal Rules from defendants, which included corporations owned by the Republic of France. These defendants in turn requested a protective order and argued that as French corporations the Hague Convention provided the exclusive procedures for obtaining discovery from them in France. The district court declined to issue the protective order, holding instead that once the district court has jurisdiction over anybody, including a foreign litigant, the Hague Convention does not apply, even though the information sought is physically located outside the United States in the territory of one of the Contracting States. The Supreme Court upheld the district court's ruling. It rejected defendants' contention that the Convention "provides the exclusive and mandatory procedures for obtaining documents in each nation located within the territory of a foreign signatory." The Court held that the text and history of the Convention and its ratification by the United States supported the conclusion it was intended to establish merely optional procedures to facilitate reception of evidence outside the United States. Therefore, the alternative mechanism of discovery

under the Convention does not oust the district court of its usual discovery authority even though the evidence is located outside the United States in the territory of one of the signatories to the Convention. Finally, the Court rejected defendants' contention that international comity required American litigants to resort first to the Convention's procedures before initiating discovery within the Federal Rules.

2. After the *Societe Nationale* case, the order in which the Convention might be used is a matter of discretion with the district court and not subject to any mandatory rule. The procedures of the Convention are often more cumbersome than the self-executing rules of the federal discovery rules. The Convention usually requires the use of an intermediary official authority in each of the Contracting States and proceeds more along the lines familiar to the world of diplomacy than the world of pretrial litigation. Thus, it appears that American lawyers will be able to avoid the Convention whenever they otherwise have jurisdiction over a party in the United States. The Convention will still have to be used when seeking evidence from a third party not subject to the jurisdiction of the U.S. courts.

V. **THE DUTY TO SUPPLEMENT RESPONSES: FEDERAL RULE 26(e)**

A. **General Rules. Absent specific contrary language or authority, parties who have given accurate answers in response to discovery requests at the time the information was sought are under no duty to supplement or amend a response to include later-required information nor even to correct the response except as so provided.**

B. **Exceptions. Under Rule 26(e), there are three instances in which a party who has responded to discovery is under a duty to supplement, amend or correct an earlier response.**

1. A party is under a duty to supplement the response with regard to questions that sought the identity and locations of witnesses (both ordinary lay witnesses and expert witnesses) by disclosing newly discovered or newly identified witnesses.

2. Parties must amend their responses if they obtain information that leads them to conclude that the response was incorrect when it was made, or, although a response was correct when made, when failure to correct the response now would be the equivalent of knowing concealment of information.

3. Responses must be supplemented whenever the court or parties by agreement require supplementation of responses. Additional requirements may also arise through the Rules of Professional Responsibility and other ethical rules that are beyond the scope of this outline.

VI. **DISCOVERY ABUSE AND SANCTIONS: FEDERAL RULES 26(f)-(g) AND 37**

A. **In general, discovery abuses break down into two major categories: (a) unreasonable or excessive use of discovery requests or abuse of the process ("pushing") and (b) unreasonable, hypertechnical compliance or refusal to engage in discovery ("tripping").**

B. **In order to deal with unreasonably burdensome or excessive discovery (including the use of canned or boiler-plate interrogatories), the rules drafters have recently added three amendments designed to encourage federal court judicial supervision of the discovery process. They include: (1) judicial authority to limit the frequency and extent of use of specific discovery devices [Rule 26(b) (second paragraph) (1983)]; (2) authority for the court to convene discovery pretrial conferences [Rule 26(f) (1980)]; and (3) requiring** attorneys to certify their discovery requests, responses, and objections [Rule 26(g) (1983)]. The first two amendments have been covered previously.

1.   The certification required by Rule 26(g) includes three elements: first, that the discovery request, response or objection [RRO] is consistent with the rules and warranted by existing law or reasonable extension or modification of that law; second, that the RRO is not interposed for any improper purpose such as to harass or unnecessarily delay or increase the expense of litigation; and third, that the RRO is not unreasonable or unduly burdensome or expensive "given the needs of the case, the discovery already had in the case, the amount in controversy, and the importance of the issues at stake in the litigation." This certification is the substantial equivalent of the Federal Rule 11 certification for pleadings and other papers.

2.   In addition, courts have always had authority under the federal discovery rules to impose protective orders at the request of the party from whom discovery is sought that will limit the scope or burden of a particular discovery request or series of requests. *See* Rule 26(c).

C.   **To deal with the refusal to cooperate with discovery requests, Rule 37 provides for the imposition of sanctions through what is usually a two-step process. The two steps are: (1) a motion by the party seeking discovery for an order to compel the discovery, which may include an expense order and minimal or monetary sanction; (2) followed, if necessary, by more severe sanctions, including the so-called "doomsday" sanctions found in 37(b), if the party from whom discovery is sought continues to refuse to comply with the discovery order. As an alternative, when a party completely fails to appear for its deposition, to serve answers to interrogatories, or to serve a written response to a request for inspection, the party seeking discovery may immediately seek the most severe level of sanctions available under Rule 37(b) without the need for an initial court order. [Rule 37(d).]**

1.   The usual route is to use a Rule 37(a) motion for an order compelling discovery. The requisites for a Rule 37(a) motion are unexceptional. The party has to give reasonable notice to all other parties and persons affected thereby and can then apply for an order to compel discovery. The order can be sought either in the court in which the action is pending or, in the case of depositions, the district where the deposition is being taken. Orders that seek to compel answers by a deponent not a party must be made in the court where the deposition is being taken.

     a.   Rule 37(a) motions apply specifically to failure to answer questions in a deposition, written or oral, failure of a corporate party to make a designation of an appropriate person to be deposed under Rules 30(b)(6) or 31(a), failure to answer an interrogatory, and failure to respond to a request for inspection or to allow inspection. Rule 37(a) also applies when the answers given are evasive or incomplete.

     b.   Rule 37(a) requires the court after hearing to award the expenses of the motion, including attorney's fees, to the prevailing party "unless the court finds that the opposition to the motion was substantially justified or that other circumstances make an award of expenses unjust." A similar provision applies where the motion is denied. Thus, the assumption is that the court should award the expenses, including attorney's fees, of making the motion, although court practice here is not uniform or dependable.

2.   If a Rule 37(a) court order to compel discovery has been granted, and the party from whom discovery is sought continues to refuse to answer or respond, then under Rule 37(b), the court in the district in which the deposition is being taken may declare the continued failure to be a contempt of court, and the court in which the action is pending may impose one of five types of orders in addition to an award of expenses. The five orders include (1) an order that the matters regarding which the order was made or other designated facts should be taken as established for the purpose of the action; (2) an order refusing to allow the disobeying party to introduce evidence in support of the claims or defenses involved in the action; (3) an order striking out pleadings or parts of the pleadings or staying the action

until the order is obeyed or dismissing the action or proceeding in any part including rendering judgment by default against the disobedient party; (4) to treat the failure to comply as a contempt of court (except regarding orders to submit to physical and mental examinations); and (5) to impose one of the first three orders on a party who has failed to produce another party for examination under the physical or mental examination rules unless the party shows that it is unable to obtain compliance by the party to be examined. These five types of sanctions fall into three major categories.

    a.   First, there are preclusion-based sanctions. These are imposed in order to prevent the non-complying party from benefiting from its non-compliance, and include the orders refusing to allow the introduction of evidence or declaring matters over which discovery is sought as established against the non-complying party.

    b.   Second, there are specific deterrent actions taken to encourage or compel compliance by this party in this case. These include staying the action, or refusing to allow evidence to be admitted in support of either claims or defenses, and contempt of court.

    c.   Finally, there are general deterrent sanctions that have the purpose of deterring not just the party in this particular case but presumably others who learn of the court's actions. These include the doomsday-type sanctions of dismissing the action in whole or in part, rendering judgment by default, and some of the restrictions on the introduction of evidence which may amount in effect to dismissal.

3.   Lower courts have struggled with the requirement of fault on the part of the disobedient party that may be necessary in order to impose the most drastic of the Rule 37(b) sanctions, especially general deterrents.

    a.   In a well-known case from the Second Circuit, *Cine Forty-Second Street Theatre Corp. v. Allied Artists Picture Corp.* 602 F.2d 1062 (2nd Cir. 1979), the appellate court held that gross negligence, not amounting to conscious disregard of court orders or reckless or intentional or knowing conduct, is sufficient to support the most drastic sanctions. In that case, the sanction was refusal to allow any evidence to be introduced on the issue of damages, thus effectively dismissing the damage claims. The *Cine Forty-Second Street Theatre* case, however, showed a pattern of misconduct by counsel and involvement by the party that is more easily characterized as intentional or at least reckless, although the lower court did not characterize it as such. As the *Cine* court recognized, however, a critical problem arises when misdeeds potentially attributable to the client include those that may be entirely the lawyer's responsibility.

    b.   Although the Supreme Court has stated that clients are responsible for the persons they retain as lawyers, there is still some reluctance in the lower courts to impose the most severe sanctions without full due process procedures — notice, hearing, opportunity to be heard — and when the client will suffer in a situation in which it may not have been on notice as to the fault of its attorneys. For this reason, the federal courts have carved out an exception that sanctions will not be imposed, at least not the most extreme sanctions, when compliance with the court's orders is impossible. Most often this has arisen where conduct is required in a foreign country and that conduct is prohibited by the laws of that country. *See, e.g., Societe Internationale pour Particpations Industrielles et Commerciales v. Rogers*, 357 U.S. 197 (1958) (compliance would violate Swiss banking non-disclosure laws).

D. Miscellaneous Sanction Issues

1.   A special section of Rule 37 deals with the failure of a party to admit the truthfulness of acts or the genuineness of documents under Rule 36. If the party requesting the admissions later proves those facts or the genuineness of documents, that party may request that the court award it reasonable expenses in making the proof, including attorneys' fees. The court is required to make such an order unless it finds that the request was objectionable or the admission sought was of no importance, or the party that had failed to admit had a reasonable ground to believe it would prevail on the issue, or other good reason. [Rule 37(c).]

2. There is a separate sanction for failure to participate in good faith in framing a discovery plan that requires the non-complying party to pay the other party's reasonable expenses, including attorneys' fees. [Rule 37(g).]

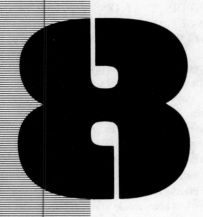

PRE-TRIAL PROCEDURE AND DISPOSITIONS

▶ ## CHAPTER SUMMARY

PRE-TRIAL PROCEDURE AND DISPOSITIONS: ALTERNATIVES TO TRIAL, PRE-TRIAL CONFERENCES, DISMISSAL, DEFAULT JUDGMENT, AND SUMMARY JUDGMENT

INTRODUCTION: Although most civil procedure is pre-trial procedure, this chapter deals with the more immediate pre-trial stage of litigation. The assumption here is that the pleadings have been filed and amendments made, discovery is well under way or completed, and all parties have been served and joined. At this point, the trial court has managerial powers granted under Rule 16 of the Federal Rules of Civil Procedure. The court may encourage the parties to resolve their dispute by resort to one of the many alternatives to litigation. For a variety of reasons, the party initiating litigation may seek to dismiss the action voluntarily under Rule 41(a). Parties who have failed to comply with the court's orders or to prosecute the case effectively are subject to involuntary dismissal under Rule 41(b). The major pre-trial disposition device is summary judgment under Federal Rule 56. Summary judgment allows actions to be terminated short of trial when a sufficient showing has been made that there are no factual issues necessary for the trier of fact (judge or jury) to resolve. Finally, under Rule 55, a party's failure to respond to the pleadings or other court orders may result in a default judgment against that party without a full-blown trial on the merits. Although these pre-trial subjects are related, each forms a distinctive body of law and procedure that will be addressed separately.

ALTERNATIVES TO TRIAL

I. **ALTERNATIVES TO TRIAL**

A. **In connection with the pre-trial conference, Rule 16 of the Federal Rules of Civil Procedure directs the trial court to consider expediting the disposition of the action and facilitating settlement of the case. The subjects to be discussed at pre-trial conferences under Rule 16 include "the possibility of settlement or the use of extra-judicial procedures to resolve the dispute," as well as "such other matters as may aid in the disposition of the action." These provisions empower the federal trial judge at a pre-trial conference to encourage, and perhaps even require, the parties to participate in alternatives to standard full-scale litigation as a means of resolving the dispute before the court. These procedures commonly go under the name of "alternative dispute resolution" or "ADR." The following are the most common types of alternatives to standard civil litigation.**

1. *Arbitration* is a contractual proceeding by which the parties submit their dispute to a third party decisionmaker, often one with special expertise in the subject matter of the dispute, whom they have selected.

   a. Arbitration may vary in its formality from very informal discussion or presentation of the issues orally by the parties, to formalized procedures approaching those found in a full-scale trial.

   b. Arbitration usually is binding by contractual agreement, although an alternative often used by California courts, and now being experimented with by federal courts, is known as "judicially-annexed arbitration." In this form, cases are diverted by court rule to arbitration and the arbitrator's award may be rejected by either party in favor of trial de novo. Often this process comes with a series of penalties and rewards to encourage abiding by the arbitrator's decision. If a party who rejected the award does not do better at trial than that party did in arbitration, the party may be required to pay the costs, including the arbitrator's fees, litigation costs, even attorneys' fees, incurred following rejection of the arbitrator's award.

2. *Mediation* also involves a third-party who acts as a facilitator or go-between rather than an arbitrator, judge, or decisionmaker in an effort to bring the parties together to reach a voluntary resolution of their dispute. Usually the mediator is not empowered to resolve any issues and will not be successful unless the parties themselves eventually agree to and adopt a compromise.

3. *"Mini-trial"* is a scaled-down version of litigation, sometimes used in an effort to resolve large scale business disputes. In a mini-trial, the parties present summary versions of their cases to a referee — either an individual or a group of persons intended to emulate a jury — in order to inform their settlement negotiations. As a result of mini-trial, the referee issues a judgment and the parties use this judgment as the basis for settlement negotiations. The time available for a mini-trial is limited, and the aspects of the trial presented are limited usually by contractual agreement between the parties.

4. *"Summary jury trials"* are a variant on mini-trials in which the advisory jury is used as a fact-finder and in which the jury typically renders a "verdict" and is available for interview by the parties regarding the strengths, weaknesses, and status of their cases. Parties often use a unilateral version of summary jury trial in order to prepare their cases for full-scale litigation before an actual jury, but in this cooperative context it functions as a settlement device.

5. *Private judging* is an alternative to litigation that very much resembles litigation in the scope of the evidence considered and the method of its presentation, but is analytically a form of binding private arbitration because the parties agree to submit to the decision of a judge whom they jointly select. Sometimes disparagingly referred to as "rent-a-judge" proceedings, parties privately hire a judge (often a retired judge; in some instances a sitting judge who is able to serve privately) who then hears and decides their dispute after hearing appropriate evidence in the traditional manner.

   a. However, the trial is a private affair. No public record is made of the trial proceedings or any judgment, and thus the parties are able to maintain full confidentiality in addition to flexibility in arranging for the trial, its location, and the identity of the judge.

   b. A problem with this form of dispute resolution is that it is expensive and arranged by the parties and thus available usually only to parties with substantial resources who are in this way able to keep their dispute out of public view.

   c. Today, around the country, retired judges have joined together to form affiliations or actual companies doing private judging.

B. **The most traditional and effective alternative is simply settlement of the dispute through private negotiation by the parties. In most cases, negotiations commence before any civil action is filed and continue up through the time of judgment and appeal. Many times more disputes are resolved by settlement before any litigation begins than are subsequently settled or litigated to judgment.**

   1. As an alternative to litigation, almost all court systems today have a regular process of settlement conferences, often scheduled at the time of or in connection with pre-trial conferences, in which the parties must make formal presentations, document their positions and demands, outline their evidence, and usually present their positions to a judge of the court system in which they are litigating — either the actual judge who will try their case or, more commonly, an additional judge selected because of that judge's ability as a settlement judge or by rotation among available judges. The settlement judge quizzes each of the parties with regard to their positions and attempts to find a basis for settlement. Settlement conferences of this sort are ordinarily not voluntary. The parties must appear, and usually the clients or someone with settlement authority must appear in person. Judges are often relatively heavy-handed in attempting to push the parties to some kind of settlement that will avoid a trial.

C. **Benefits of Alternative Dispute Resolution**

   1. *Cost savings*. These alternatives to litigation are promoted as cost-saving devices. There is no doubt that avoiding the cost of attorneys and their attendant fees is the single biggest barrier to use of the courts by all parties, rich and poor. To private parties with substantial resources — in some instances virtually unlimited resources — that may be devoted to

8

destructive litigation, alternative dispute resolution is indeed an inexpensive alternative. For parties with relatively small-scale disputes, however, the courts themselves often provide a fairly low-cost means of resolving the controversy, especially when small claims procedures are used.

2. *Avoiding delay.* Another virtue of alternative dispute resolution is the ability to reach quicker, easier resolution of the issues and the possibility of creative resolution of the issues. Courts today are backlogged, especially on the civil side with the influx of criminal litigation, and thus result in justice delayed more often than not.

3. *Avoiding undue harm to the parties' long-term relationships.* Many potential litigants — spouses, neighbors, or businesses that depend upon one another — risk harming beneficial long-term relationships through the intensely adversarial litigation process. When litigation may be counterproductive, alternatives are a better solution. This helps account for the popularity of mediation in divorce litigation.

4. *Privacy.* Most litigation alternatives allow the parties to conduct their proceedings in private. This gives better protection to trade secrets and other proprietary information than would public judicial proceedings. On the other hand, much private dispute resolution removes from the public arena disputes in which the public may have a significant interest, especially in an era of litigation over environmental and toxic torts, unsafe products, and the like. It also avoids or prevents a public pronouncement resolving the issues. Thus, matters of public controversy are not resolved definitively or openly in court. There is no case or precedent that results from private litigation and alternative dispute resolution.

D. **Recent court decisions have somewhat reined-in overly-zealous judges who have attempted to force the parties to participate in mini-trials or summary jury trials or to compel jurors from the court's standard jury list to serve as jurors in a summary jury trial. Court-enforced alternatives to litigation have been restricted to annexed arbitration procedures which are not final and binding and to the regular use of settlement conferences with a settlement conference judge. Both of these procedures allow the parties to avoid or reject the private resolution and to insist upon taking the case to trial, although substantial burdens may accompany this process.**

PRE-TRIAL CON-FERENCES AND PRE-TRIAL ORDERS

II. **PRE-TRIAL CONFERENCES AND PRE-TRIAL ORDERS. The movement in the past decade to give judges greater tools and encouragement to manage all aspects of litigation is particularly prominent with regard to pre-trial procedure.**

A. **Both Rule 16 regarding pre-trial conferences and its companion Rule 26(f), providing for a discovery conference, allow the parties or the judge supervising the litigation to bring together all parties either at regular intervals or a specific time before trial to resolve pending matters of discovery and procedure; to consider settlement or other early disposition of the case; and to simplify the legal and factual issues for trial.**

1. The outcome of pre-trial conferences is a pre-trial order or orders.

2. The outcome of a discovery conference is a discovery plan and schedule.

3. The final pre-trial conference produces a final pre-trial order that supersedes the pleadings and controls the subsequent course of the litigation.

B. **Rule 16 was amended in 1983 to expand its terms to conform with the practice that had evolved under the narrower terms of old Rule 16.**

1. New Rule 16 specifies as its purposes (1) expediting litigation; (2) establishing control of the case; (3) discouraging wasteful pre-trial activities; (4) encouraging preparation for trial; and (5) encouraging settlement.

2. In order to facilitate these purposes, the Rule lists possible subjects for discussion. These include: (1) simplification of the issues and elimination of frivolous claims or defenses; (2) amendments to the pleadings; (3) possible admissions of fact and of documents to avoid proof at trial; (4) avoiding duplicative and unnecessary proof; (5) identifying witnesses and documents and the filing of pre-trial briefs before trial; (6) references to a master or magistrate; (7) possibility of alternative dispute resolution in settling the matters; (8) the pre-trial order; (9) disposition of pending motions; (10) need for any special procedures for managing complex issues or cases; and (11) any other matters that aid in disposing of the action.

3. Unless a case is exempt from pre-trial scheduling and planning, the district court is required to schedule conferences and arrange a pre-trial schedule that limits the time in which pleadings can be amended and other parties joined, motions can be filed, and discovery completed. Further scheduling, including other conferences, is encouraged. This order is to be issued no later than 120 days after the complaint has been filed.

4. The ultimate goal of the pre-trial process under Rule 16 is the final pre-trial conference, held close to the time of trial. *See* Rule 16(d).

    a. This conference and any other pre-trial conferences must be attended by at least one attorney for each party who is to have authority to enter into stipulations and make admissions.

    b. The final pre-trial conference must be attended by at least one of the attorneys for each of the parties and by any unrepresented parties on their own.

5. Following the final pre-trial conference and any other conferences held under the Rule, the court is to enter an order reciting the action taken.

    a. This order then controls the subsequent course of the action unless modified by a later order.

    b. Rule 16(e) provides that the order issued after a final pre-trial conference "shall be modified only to prevent manifest injustice."

        (1) This standard should be contrasted with the standard for amending complaints and other pleadings under Rule 15, which encourages leave to amend pleadings to be given "freely" when justice so requires. Even amending pleadings at trial is to be done freely when the presentation of the merits of the action will be served thereby and there is no prejudice.

        (2) The standard under Rule 16(e) is obviously more stringent, and pre-trial orders are less susceptible to amendment than the pleadings. Thus parties need to take more care in reaching agreements and in preparing for and conducting pre-trial conferences since the resulting order will be more difficult to change than had the pleadings alone continued to govern the action.

6. Finally, the pre-trial conference rule provides for sanctions. If a party or a party's attorney fails to obey a scheduling order, fails to make an appearance, is habitually unprepared at such conferences, or in other ways fails to participate in good faith, the judge on motion or sua sponte may make any of the orders as are just.

    a. These orders may include any of the discovery sanction orders under Rule 37(b)(2)(B), (C), or (D).

    b. In addition, the judge is to require any of the parties in non-compliance with Rule 16 to pay the reasonable expenses incurred because of that party's non-compliance, including attorney's fees, unless the judge finds non-compliance was substantially justified or that such an award would be unjust.

7. The use of pre-trial conferences remains subject to some dispute, however.

a. Empirical studies have been unable to demonstrate that pre-trial conferences result in a greater disposition of cases before trial, although there is evidence that they shorten trial.

b. On the other hand, they impose a substantial additional burden on the parties. Their lawyers must attend the pre-trial conference or conferences, and by local rule must ordinarily prepare pre-trial statements that specify the issues and list all witnesses and exhibits. Usually, co-operation among the adversaries is necessary to success in preparing these statements. Finally, parties are often required to prepare the initial form of the post-trial order. Thus, the court is able to transfer pre-trial preparation and disposition directly on the parties and their attorneys.

8. In addition to the specific pre-trial conference schedules and orders authorized by Rule 16, most federal courts and many state courts have adopted local rules giving even greater pre-trial control to the court and in many instances imposing stricter or more absolute timing requirements on all parties.

a. For example, it is common for federal courts to monitor their dockets and, when one of the cases on file shows no activity for a period as short as 90 or 120 days, to require the plaintiff (and possibly all parties) to appear before the court to show cause why the action should not be dismissed for lack of prosecution. These rules are not without cost, however. Lawyers must move the case along according to the court's rules rather than at a schedule that might suit them, and they must take on the additional burdens of appearing and preparing for conferences, at least when they have had a lack of docket activity within the required period.

b. On the other hand, some kind of judicial pre-trial management is necessary, in the federal system, where the pleadings no longer serve the narrowing of issues and factual resolution purposes of the older code pleading and common law pleading systems. Rule 16's management provisions can work well when combined with the discovery conference provisions that allow courts to supervise discovery, to insure that neither the discovery process nor discovery disputes gets out of hand, and to limit discovery as appropriate for the particular issues present in that case. *See* Chapter 7, *supra*.

RULE 41 VOLUNTARY AND INVOLUNTARY DISMISSALS

III. **RULE 41 VOLUNTARY AND INVOLUNTARY DISMISSALS**

A. **Voluntary Dismissal. Under Rule 41(a), plaintiffs may, for a variety of reasons, seek to dismiss actions at a pre-trial stage before any decision on the merits.**

1. Plaintiff may dismiss an action on her own behalf by filing a notice of dismissal if the other party or parties have not served an answer or motion for summary judgment. Plaintiff may also dismiss if she obtains the consent of all parties who have appeared in the action and files a stipulation to that effect.

2. Plaintiff must obtain an order of approval by the court if she seeks to dismiss the action after service of the appropriate response by an adversary and where she cannot obtain all adversaries' agreement to dismiss.

a. In this instance, the court is entitled to impose such terms and conditions as it deems proper.

b. In particular, plaintiff may not dismiss an action in which a counterclaim has been filed unless the counterclaim can be adjudicated independently of plaintiff's initial claim, that is, unless there is sufficient subject matter jurisdiction for that counterclaim in the absence of plaintiff's initial claim.

3. A variety of circumstances may impel a plaintiff to seek dismissal of her own action. For example, the plaintiff may have had her case removed to federal court from state court, where she would rather litigate. Plaintiff may seek to dismiss a case that is going badly because of weak evidence or adverse procedural rulings. It may be advantageous to plead the case anew, with different claims and parties, or in a different court.

4. If plaintiff can dismiss the action, why would the defendants or other parties seek to resist dismissal, that is, why limit the plaintiff's right to dismiss? At common law, plaintiff was allowed to dismiss the action at any time before judgment. However, an opponent may have invested substantial time and effort in defending the action or have obtained important procedural or substantive advantages in the action, all of which might be lost in a dismissal. Therefore, Rule 41(a) permits voluntary dismissal of right only when there is little chance of prejudice to the defendant or other parties, and otherwise conditions voluntary dismissal on approval by the trial court.

5. What is the effect of a voluntary dismissal by plaintiff, whether done as of right or according to court order?

   a. Under Rule 41(a), the presumption is that voluntary dismissals are without prejudice. Thus, the plaintiff is free to reinstate the action at another time or place, if the statute of limitations allows.

   b. However, where a court order is necessary in order to dismiss, the order may specify that the dismissal is with prejudice; and under Rule 41(a)(1), if this is the plaintiff's second voluntary dismissal, the dismissal is a dismissal with prejudice unless the court or the parties in a stipulation specify to the contrary.

   Example: In *McCants v. Ford Motor Co.*, 781 F.2d 855 (11th Cir. 1986), plaintiff had filed an action in Alabama federal court, before learning that there was a significant risk that her claim would be subject to dismissal under the applicable statute of limitations. Plaintiff sought to dismiss the action, forthrightly acknowledging that she would refile in a state with a longer limitation period. Defendant sought to block a dismissal without prejudice or to condition dismissal upon plaintiff's payment of its pre-trial expenses and plaintiff's continued adherence to a sanction order that had been entered against plaintiff precluding plaintiff from using certain expert witnesses. The district court granted plaintiff's motion without any conditions and without prejudice. The defendant appealed. The court of appeals held there was no abuse of discretion by the trial court in dismissing the action without prejudice. In looking at defendant's interests, the court concluded it had suffered no prejudice beyond the threat of a second suit and the loss of its statute of limitations defense, and this was insufficient to prevent dismissal. There was no evidence of bad faith or delay on the part of the plaintiff. However, the appellate court remanded to the trial court for consideration of whether monetary and non-monetary sanctions should be imposed on the plaintiff because of the favorable discovery orders the defendant obtained.

B. **Involuntary Dismissal. Under Rule 41(b) there are two types of involuntary dismissal.**

   1. In the usual case, where an action is yet to be tried or will be tried by a jury, Rule 41(b) allows dismissal for plaintiff's failure to prosecute the action in an effective or procedurally proper manner.

      a. Most such dismissals are for want of prosecution, that is, lack of diligence in moving the case to trial.

      Example: In *Link v. Wabash R.R.*, 370 U.S. 626 (1962), plaintiff's action was dismissed for failure of plaintiff's counsel to attend pre-trial conferences without sufficient excuse. The Supreme Court held that dismissal is appropriate when there is both (1) a clear record of delay or bad conduct by or attributable to the plaintiff and (2) a finding that lesser sanctions would not serve the best interests of justice.

   b.   Dismissal is also available for other failures to comply with the Federal Rules, including the discovery rules. *See also* Rule 37(b).

   c.   Dismissal is also available for failures to comply with specific court orders.

2. In cases tried to the court, Rule 41(b) dismissals may also operate in the manner of a non-suit.

   a.   After the close of plaintiff's case-in-chief, the court as trier of fact may weigh the evidence to determine whether plaintiff has shown a sufficient right to relief. If the court finds that plaintiff has not adequately proven her case, the court may dismiss the action, or may decline to rule until the close of all the evidence.

   b.   This dismissal is distinguished from the directed verdict in a jury trial, discussed *infra*, because the court actually weighs the evidence and makes a determination based on credibility of the witnesses and weight of the evidence. If the court finds the plaintiff should not prevail, the court dismisses the case and enters judgment accordingly, making the findings of fact required by Rule 52(a).

3. Involuntary dismissal under Rule 41(b) is presumptively with prejudice, that is, it constitutes an adjudication in favor of the defendant on the merits of the plaintiff's claim. Unless the court in its dismissal order specifically states to the contrary, an involuntary dismissal bars the plaintiff from bringing the action again under the rules of preclusion or "res judicata" discussed in Chapter 12.

4. All involuntary dismissals authorized elsewhere in the Federal Rules are also presumptively with prejudice, except for dismissals for lack of jurisdiction, for improper venue, or for failure to join a party under Rule 19. In these exempted cases, all that has been decided is that the court lacks jurisdiction or proper venue or proper parties, not that the plaintiff is unable to prove a case and prevail on the merits.

SUMMARY JUDGMENTS

IV. SUMMARY JUDGMENTS

A. Purposes of Summary Judgment

1. Under the Federal Rules, the pleadings are relatively free of detailed factual allegations. Obtaining facts to narrow issues for trial is largely the work of the discovery process. This system requires some device to detect and dismiss claims or defenses that are immune from attack and dismissal at the pleading stage (because of the generous notice pleading standards) but are revealed by the discovery process to be unsupported by facts provable in court. This device is the motion for summary judgment under Rule 56.

2. The deceptively simple language of Rule 56 requires that judgment be rendered at the request of a party "if the pleadings, depositions, answers to interrogatories, and admissions on file, together with the affidavits, if any, show that there is no genuine issue as to any material fact and that the moving party is entitled to a judgment as a matter of law."

   a.   Thus, the motion for a summary judgment is decided upon the papers submitted. The court does not hear testimony. In support or opposition, the parties offer the fruits of the discovery process plus affidavits — statements of witnesses and interested parties made under oath — that the court is to read in order to determine whether or not there is a factual dispute requiring resolution by a trier of fact.

   b.   Whenever such material is introduced in connection with a Rule 12(b)(6) motion to dismiss for failure to state a claim or a Rule 12(c) motion for judgment on the pleadings, that motion is automatically converted into one for summary judgment.

B. Standard for Granting the Motion

8

1. Rule 56's standard for summary judgment is that there must be an absence of a "genuine issue as to any material fact." For most of its history, this standard was interpreted to mean that as long as the party responding to a summary judgment motion could show any possibility that the factual contentions of the moving party could be resolved by the trier-of-fact in favor of the non-moving party, summary judgment should be denied.

2. In *Anderson v. Liberty Lobby, Inc.*, 477 U.S. 242 (1986), the Supreme Court clarified this standard by declaring that a showing merely of the *possibility* of a factual dispute at trial is insufficient to prevent summary judgment. Instead, a motion for summary judgment should be seen as a pre-trial version of a directed verdict motion.

    a. The standard now applied in federal court is similar to the one used in California that requires the motion to be granted in the absence of any "triable issue as to any material fact." If, at trial, based on the evidence presented in support of and opposition to the motion for summary judgment, the trial judge would have to grant a directed verdict in favor of the moving party, then the trial court should likewise grant the motion for summary judgment. To resist the motion, the party with the burden of proof must show evidence at the summary judgment stage that would be sufficient at the directed verdict stage to justify the court in leaving the question to the jury.

    b. In effect, this mandates that a more generous standard be applied to summary judgment motions, and more such motions should be granted where the response shows the mere possibility of factual dispute, but not a genuine or triable dispute.

    c. It may also mean that where exceptional burdens of proof are required by one party, that party must make a sufficient showing that it is able to meet the exceptional burden of proof.

        Example: In the *Liberty Lobby* case, *supra*, plaintiff had to show by clear and convincing evidence actual malice by the defendant in a defamation case. The Supreme Court held that the summary judgment motion must be decided in light of plaintiff's burden under this more demanding standard.

C. **Under current practice, the summary judgment motion is almost always a motion made by the party without the burden of proof, generally the defending party. It is much harder to establish a fact if it is your burden to establish that fact to the satisfaction of a jury or judge than it is to find a gap or hole in the proof of every fact necessary to establish a claim for relief. Defending parties have two avenues they can use in seeking summary judgment.**

    1. *The moving party establishes the non-existence of a critical fact.* Usually the moving party submits affidavits and discovery material by which it seeks to negate one of the critical elements of the plaintiff's, or party-with-the-burden-of-proof's, case. Thus, for example, plaintiff in a typical personal injury claim must establish that a duty was owed to the plaintiff, that the defendant breached that duty, that the breach of duty was the cause-in-fact of injury to plaintiff, and that the breach of duty was also the proximate cause of plaintiff's injuries. If defendant produces undisputed evidence of a fact that negates any one of these elements, the defendant is entitled to summary judgment. Thus the defendant may attack plaintiff's claim by showing undisputed facts establishing a lack of cause or duty, or, less frequently, undisputed facts establishing a lack of a breach of that duty or of damages suffered by the plaintiff.

        a. The moving party will have to establish the absence of one of the elements conclusively by its papers and supporting evidence, which should be in the form of admissible evidence. In response to this initial showing, the non-moving party must then demonstrate that with respect to the challenged element of its case there remains an issue of fact — a genuine dispute of fact — that precludes summary judgment.

b. The plaintiff or responding party need not show that its version is correct or more likely than not true; it must only show that there is a triable dispute as to which version is correct to avoid granting of summary judgment.

c. The trial court is not to weigh the evidence presented in support of and opposition to the motion nor make determinations about the credibility of witnesses who may testify. It is these restrictions that have resulted in relatively modest success for summary judgment motions until recently.

2. *The moving party establishes that the non-moving party lacks evidence sufficient to prove a critical fact.* The Supreme Court recently recognized in the case of *Celotex Corp. v. Catrett*, 477 U.S. 317 (1986), a defending party may alternatively show that on the basis of the record as it exists after sufficient time for discovery, the plaintiff lacks the ability to prove one of the critical elements of its case. This second method differs from the first in that the moving party need not affirmatively show that one of the elements does not exist; it is enough to show that plaintiff appears to be without the ability to prove one of the critical elements. In response, the party with the burden of proof (almost always the plaintiff) must make a showing that it has or can obtain admissible evidence which would tend to establish the challenged element in the case.

Example: In the *Celotex* case, defendant's motion was aimed at plaintiff's lack of evidence of causation. Plaintiff sought to recover for the asbestos-related death of her husband and had to show that her former husband had been exposed to a Celotex product. Celotex argued that after more than a year of discovery there was no evidence that plaintiff's husband had had any contact with any Celotex product. The trial court denied defendant's motion for summary judgment on the ground that this form of a showing made by defendant — roughly analogous to a statement of "prove it" — was insufficient to carry the initial burden of a movant for summary judgment. The Supreme Court reversed, holding that defendant had adequately made an initial showing that plaintiff would be unable to prove this critical element. The Court returned the case to the trial court to decide whether plaintiff had responded to the motion for summary judgment with an adequate showing that it had or could obtain evidence that would indicate exposure to a Celotex product.

D. **Mechanics of the Summary Judgment Motion**

1. Plaintiff is able to move for summary judgment at any time after 20 days following commencement of the action. [Rule 56(a).] A defending party may move immediately for summary judgment. [Rule 56(b).] In either case, the moving party may support its motion with or without affidavits or other discovery material. The motion must be served at least 10 days before the time fixed for a hearing date. [Rule 56(c).]

2. Since the *Celotex* case, it is clear that supporting affidavits are not necessary to make an adequate initial showing on a motion for summary judgment. However, the more substantial the evidentiary showing made in support of the motion, the greater the likelihood of success for the motion.

E. **Evidence Pertaining to a Motion for Summary Judgment. Rule 56 contemplates that the products of discovery may be used in support of or opposition to the motion for summary judgment and that in most instances there should be supporting and opposing affidavits or statements under oath.**

1. These affidavits must show that they are made upon personal knowledge, setting forth facts admissible in evidence and demonstrating the competency of the witness to testify. That is, they must be the equivalent of evidence that could be introduced at trial if the witness was present testifying in person.

2. There is an opportunity for the responding party, where it has not had sufficient time to obtain affidavits, to make that showing to the court and seek additional time in which to

respond to the motion for summary judgment. This decision is discretionary with the court under Rule 56(f).

F. **Disposition of the Motion. Rule 56(d) allows the court to render a partial summary judgment on any contested issue of fact or law. A common example is the grant of partial summary judgment establishing defendant's liability, reserving the question of damages for fuller trial. This could happen where liability is established through the application of the preclusion doctrine of collateral estoppel.**

   1. Rule 56(d) indicates it is proper for the court to make an order specifying the facts established by partial summary judgment, thus using the summary judgment device as a form of pre-trial order narrowing the issues prior to trial.

   2. Unless the court's ruling on a summary judgment motion disposes of all aspects of the case and entitles one party or the other to judgment in its favor, it is an interlocutory order that is not ordinarily appealable until the rest of the case has been concluded. Thus, the grant of "summary judgment" is often a misnomer. Absent a special order to enter judgment under Rule 54(b), a decision of part of a case does not result in a final judgment. *See* Chapters 10 and 11.

G. **Significant recurring summary judgment issues include how to deal with questions of credibility and state of mind.**

   1. A party seeking to avoid summary judgment may often argue that the affidavits and other materials presented in support of the motion should not be taken at face value because there has been no opportunity to cross-examine the affiant and determine her credibility.

   2. A similar problem occurs when the evidence, particularly affidavits, is offered to show the state of mind or absence of state of mind of a party that cannot easily be tested by objective or verifiable means.

   3. When the issue of state of mind or intent is a central one to the case or where the affidavits are offered by highly interested and therefore potentially biased parties, the court should and does have discretion to deny a motion for summary judgment unless there is an adequate opportunity to cross-examine and challenge the credibility of the witnesses or offer alternative explanations of the state of mind.

      a. California law expressly grants judges this power. Rule 56 is silent on the issue, but federal courts have in general followed the California approach.

      b. An alternative approach is to require the party challenging credibility or state of mind to offer sufficient facts to show that there are reasons to doubt the credibility of a witness, or to present facts supporting a viable alternative theory of state of mind.

      c. When a party presents information from a non-self-interested witness that conclusively establishes or negates an element in the case, the court should not hesitate to grant summary judgment simply on one party's claim that it ought to be allowed to cross-examine the witness in court. This approach is necessary to the effectiveness of the summary judgment process when it depends on the testimony of neutral witnesses.

   4. The Supreme Court recently resolved a third issue: whether summary judgment is available in highly complex cases. In *Matsushita Electric Industrial Co. v. Zenith Radio Corp.*, 475 U.S. 574 (1986), the Supreme Court held that the complexity of a case is not alone sufficient reason to deny summary judgment. As a practical matter, trial courts may be especially disposed to grant partial summary judgments in order to narrow the issues in complex litigation.

8

V.   DEFAULT JUDGMENTS

A. **Default judgments occur through a procedure that differs from the usual trial process because they are based upon something less than a fully contested adversary proceeding. One party, the party in default, is either not present or seriously handicapped in its presentation of the merits.**

B. **The actual procedure for obtaining default judgments is very much like the procedure for seeking and obtaining summary judgments. Most of the evidence is usually presented by affidavit or other documents, rather than through oral testimony of witnesses. Obtaining a default judgment is usually a two-step process, as exemplified by Federal Rule 55.**

1. First comes entry of the party's default.

a.   This occurs when a party against whom affirmative relief is sought fails to plead or defend in response to a claim for relief, whether asserted in a complaint, counterclaim, cross-claim, or third-party claim. Default is obtained simply by filing an affidavit with the clerk who then makes an entry in the record that the appropriate party is in default. [Rule 55(a).]

b.   The most common form of default is failure to file a responsive pleading. Failure to perform other essential and mandatory procedural acts can also constitute a default, however. A Rule 55 default judgment may thus be the counterpart sanction — directed at a defending party instead of a claimant — to a Rule 41(b) involuntary dismissal of a claim for failure to prosecute.

2. The second step is to obtain the default judgment.

a.   In a minority of cases, the clerk is able to enter the default judgment when the amount of the judgment may be calculated from the complaint or is a sum certain. [Rule 55(b)(1).]

b.   In all other cases, the court must enter default judgment. [Rule 55(b)(2).]

(1) Parties who have never appeared are not given any notice.

(2) Parties who have appeared must be given three days' written notice that the moving party is applying for judgment. Thus, parties who have answered or filed a 12(b)(6) motion or made "some presentation or submission to the court" going to the merits of the action are entitled to notice before the default judgment may be entered against them, although they still may not be entitled to introduce contrary evidence or to contest the proceedings unless their default is set aside under Rule 55(c).

(3) When damages or other ancillary issues must be determined as a matter of fact, the court must hold a hearing, including a jury trial where required by statute. [Rule 55(b)(2).] The court is limited in the amount and type of the default judgment by the prayer in the complaint. [Rule 54(c).]

3. Defaults and default judgments may be set aside by motion to the trial court. Prior to the entry of judgment, a default may be set aside merely upon a showing of "good cause." [Rule 55(c).] Once judgment by default has been entered, it too can be set aside, but only according to the far less forgiving standards of Rule 60(b), as discussed in Chapter 9.

TRIAL AND POST-TRIAL MOTIONS

▶ **CHAPTER SUMMARY**

TRIAL AND POST-TRIAL MOTIONS

INTRODUCTION: Much of what happens in the actual trial of civil cases is beyond the scope of the typical civil procedure course. This is more the province of evidence and trial practice courses. However, it is helpful to have a basic overview of the steps in the typical civil jury trial, both to understand the purposes for which lawyers do the pre-trial work that they do, and to focus on those areas that traditionally form a part of the civil procedure course.

OVERVIEW OF THE TRIAL PROCESS

I. OVERVIEW OF THE TRIAL PROCESS

A. **Stages of the Trial Process**

1. *Pre-trial conference.* The beginning of the jury trial proper is ordinarily preceded by a final trial-setting and pre-trial conference that is held just a few weeks or days in advance of trial. At this conference, the judge may require the parties to produce all of the evidence that they will offer as documents and other real evidence, and have it pre-labeled and pre-prepared and indicate to the court any problems they anticipate with regard to admission of evidence, jury instructions, and the like.

2. *Motions in limine.* On the very eve of trial, the lawyers for each side are likely to make one or more motions *in limine.* These are motions literally at the threshold of the case in which the parties seek procedural protections and attempt to obtain advance rulings on certain evidence. For example, they may move to have individual *voir dire* of jurors, to exclude all witnesses from the trial other than the parties and the witness testifying at the time, and to exclude certain evidence that one or the other party believes will be highly prejudicial. These motions are made to the trial judge outside of the presence of the jury.

3. *Voir dire.* The trial proper begins with a *voir dire* examination of potential jurors. Jurors have already been selected randomly from the population in large groups and are called to the courthouse on a particular day or days. Jurors for the specific trial are then assembled in the courtroom and perhaps examined en masse in groups of up to 50 at first, or, more typically, the group of 12, 8, or 6 jurors that may sit as the actual trial jurors are called to the jury box by name and examined by the judge or the lawyers. Federal practice tends toward judicial examination of jurors and the exclusion of lawyer questioning of the jurors except in unusual circumstances or briefly at the conclusion of the judge's examination. Many state systems, including the states of New York, Texas, and California, employ extensive lawyer *voir dire* examination of individual jurors to the virtual exclusion of the trial judge. In either case, this examination is to determine if there is a basis for disqualification of the jurors. They may be disqualified for cause because of bias, because the juror knows one of the parties or witnesses, because the juror has been involved in the incident in question, or because the juror may suffer extreme hardship in the case of lengthy jury proceedings. Alternatively, each side ordinarily has a limited opportunity to exercise peremptory challenges or challenges for which no reason need be given but in which the lawyer believes that the juror is an inappropriate one because of biases that do not rise to the level of cause, or, perhaps, because of hunches or suggestions from the client. Once a sufficient number of jurors have been accepted and each side has passed on making further challenges, the jury is seated and the case is ready to proceed with the plaintiff's opening statement.

4. *Opening statement.* The plaintiff or party with the burden of proof generally makes the first opening statement and at the end of trial makes the last closing argument. Plaintiff's opening statement is a preview of the evidence in the case. It is not intended to be argument but is an opportunity for the plaintiff to set out an outline of the events and circumstances and highlight the testimony in the case. Defendant usually follows by making an opening statement in which the defense presents its view of the evidence and its witnesses and gives its outline of its theory of the case.

5. *Plaintiff's case-in-chief.* At the conclusion of the opening statements, the plaintiff typically puts on its case-in-chief. This consists of the testimony of witnesses called by the plaintiff and the presentation of real and documentary evidence which the plaintiff believes supports its case and tends to show the existence of each of the elements that the plaintiff must prove in order to obtain a verdict and judgment. During the presentation of plaintiff's case-in-chief, the defendant and any other parties have an opportunity to cross-examine witnesses presented by the plaintiff, to develop their own evidence or to challenge plaintiff's evidence, and to object to the introduction of real and documentary evidence as well as testimony offered by the plaintiff.

6. *Motion for a directed verdict.* At the conclusion of the plaintiff's presentation of its case-in-chief or direct evidence, the defense typically will make a motion for a directed verdict, arguing that the evidence plaintiff has presented is not sufficient to enable the jury, acting rationally, to find in favor of the plaintiff on each of the elements which the plaintiff is required to prove. A directed verdict motion can come as early as the conclusion of the opening statement, but such early directed verdict motions are granted only in the unusual case where the plaintiff's opening statement definitively reveals the absence of one of the critical elements of its case. If the trial judge believes the plaintiff has produced sufficient evidence on each of its elements to make out a prima facie case which the jury could possibly decide in its favor, the judge will deny a directed verdict motion and proceed to presentation of defendant's case.

7. *Defendant's case-in-chief.* Next the defendant and other parties present their case-in-chief, putting on witnesses that they choose to call and presenting real and documentary evidence or, in some cases, excerpts from depositions of unavailable parties, in order to demonstrate the non-existence of the essential elements of the plaintiff's claim or to establish affirmative defenses which would entitle the defendant to judgment. At the conclusion of the defendant's presentation of its case, the plaintiff might make a motion for a directed verdict. Such motions are more difficult because the party with the burden of proof must establish that there is no way a rational jury could disbelieve the plaintiff's evidence or accept a version of the facts other than the plaintiff's version. During the presentation of defendant's evidence, the plaintiff is able to make challenges similar to the defense challenges mentioned earlier. Plaintiff can cross-examine the defense witnesses, object to the defendant's evidence, and seek to exclude portions of it.

8. *Rebuttal evidence.* Next plaintiffs, followed by defendants and other parties, may introduce rebuttal evidence tending either to meet evidence presented by the other party or to bolster their case where holes my have been knocked in it.

9. *Motions for directed verdict.* At the conclusion of all the rebuttals, plaintiff or defendant may make motions for a directed verdict. This is a critical moment in federal practice, because the failure to make or renew a motion for directed verdict at the conclusion of all the evidence precludes such party from making a subsequent motion for judgment notwithstanding the jury's verdict. Again, motions by the defense are much more common than motions by the plaintiff or party with the burden of proof. The trial judge may grant a directed verdict motion if she is convinced that the evidence was insufficient upon reflection for the jury to have any role in the case, or the judge may withhold ruling on the motion until after the jury has rendered its verdict on the basis of the evidence.

10. *Closing arguments and summation.* Plaintiff then makes its closing argument or summation to the jury, in which the plaintiff reviews the evidence presented and argues to the jury why the plaintiff should prevail on the basis of the evidence presented. Defendant responds to the plaintiff's summation, and the plaintiff gets to make a final summation to the jury. If the case were tried without a jury, *i.e.,* "to the court," at this point the judge would take the case under submission and weigh the evidence herself and proceed to make findings of fact and conclusions of law that would resolve the case. But in the case of a jury trial,

9

9

it is for the jury to decide questions of fact, and the next stages in the trial process are instruction of the jury and jury deliberation.

11. *Jury instructions.* After the lawyers have finished, it is the trial judge's turn. At this point, the judge reads jury instructions to the jury. These instructions may be quite extensive and take considerable time to read. A half day is not uncommon, and instructions can go for more than a day. The parties will have prepared jury instructions in advance. Some judges require that they be prepared in advance of the trial, but, in any case, they will have been prepared in advance of the arguments that the lawyers make, which must take into account the instructions the judge will give. Under Rule 51, federal judges are now allowed to instruct the jury throughout the trial, for example, giving instructions on how to evaluate the credibility of witnesses at the time witnesses are testifying. But most instructions are confined to the conclusion of the trial. They are often the basis for the assertion of error on appeal. Parties objecting to any instructions must do so at the time they are given, but outside of the presence of the jury.

12. *Jury deliberation.* At this point, the jurors retire typically to a room with privacy where they choose a foreperson and proceed to apply the instructions to the facts and return a verdict. The jurors will have been instructed either to return a general verdict finding in favor of the plaintiff and awarding damages of a particular sum or finding in favor of the defendant; or to respond to a series of questions narrower in scope that have significance the jurors may not know. In the latter case, the special verdicts or interrogatories are submitted to the judge, and it is the judge who eventually determines whether they are sufficient to enter judgment. In any case, at the conclusion of their deliberations, if they are able to reach a verdict, the jurors typically sign a verdict form, and this verdict is then read in open court. At this point, the jurors may be polled to see if that is indeed their verdict, and then excused.

13. *Entry of judgment.* It is important to realize that the jurors' verdict is not the conclusion of the case. The judge must still enter judgment on the verdict, or grant a motion that may be made for judgment notwithstanding the jurors' verdict. And it is this final step—the entry of judgment accompanied by a formal docket entry—that effectively concludes the trial and starts the time running for post-trial motions and appeal. *See* Rules 54, 58 and 79(c), discussed below in Chapter 11.

B. **For purposes of an introductory course in civil procedure, trial issues are generally restricted to the circumstances in which a party is entitled to trial by jury; the motion for a directed verdict; jury instructions and verdicts; post-trial motions for judgment notwithstanding the verdict or for new trial; and motions for extraordinary relief from judgments. The next sections examine these issues.**

THE RIGHT TO JURY TRIAL IN FEDERAL COURT

II. **THE RIGHT TO JURY TRIAL IN FEDERAL COURT**

A. **The seventh amendment to the Constitution provides that "in suits at common law, where the value in controversy shall exceed twenty dollars, the right of trial by jury shall be preserved . . . ." This portion of the seventh amendment, known as the preservation clause, requires federal courts to respect the right to trial by jury in cases where that right would have existed at the time of the adoption of the seventh amendment in 1791.**

1. In 1791, there was little difficulty in determining whether a matter should be tried by a jury or to a judge. At that time, there were distinct courts of equity and courts of law, and you could find out whether you were entitled to a jury trial by finding out in which of the two systems the action had been filed. Jury trials were provided in the law courts but not in the courts of equity. To this day, the historical basis for an action is one of the critical factors in determining the right to a jury trial.

2. When law and equity were merged, as happened in many states in this century (and happened in the federal courts by virtue of the adoption of the Federal Rules of Civil Procedure in 1938), the equity-law distinction had to be applied to a system of civil litigation where law and equity were no longer separate, and the question of whether the seventh amendment required a jury became much more complicated.

3. The right to jury trial in federal courts has since evolved in a series of Supreme Court decisions. The Court initially favored a very broad interpretation of the jury trial right, later seemed to withdraw somewhat, and recently has resumed vigorous protection of the right to jury trial.

4. The basic problem with the jury trial right is that the central historical test is both accidental and based on antiquated policy considerations (for example, questions of the power of the King versus Parliament in England) that are unrelated to the modern issue of suitability of the jury as a decisionmaker in modern litigation. A functional jury trial test would focus instead on questions of whether the parties preferred a collective decisionmaker versus a single person, *i.e.*, the trial judge; whether lay judgments or legal professional judgments should be applied to the concepts of relevance and justice in an action; class distinctions because jurors' socioeconomic backgrounds often differ significantly from those that characterize the federal bench; and differences of sympathy and skepticism in the resolution of certain types of conflicts. While these factors may motivate one party or another to seek a jury trial, they have no direct relevance to the question of whether any party is *entitled* to a jury trial.

5. Currently, the right to jury trial turns upon:

    a. the nature of the proceeding and the relief sought;

    b. the historical derivation of the particular civil action and the relief available in it; and

    c. the degree to which part of the relief is subordinate or incidental to other relief sought.

6. Even when the right to jury trial exists by virtue of the seventh amendment, a party must make a timely demand for a jury trial and not waive that demand prior to the beginning of the trial. [Rule 38(d).]

7. Because jury trial is based on the seventh amendment, and the seventh amendment has not been applied to the states as one of the fundamental rights protected by the due process clause of the fourteenth amendment, these issues are principally issues for the federal court. In the various states, the right to jury trial is protected, if at all, by state constitutional or statutory guarantees.

8. Jury trial issues have troubled the federal courts in two major areas: first, the situation in which legal and equitable elements or claims are both contained in a single civil action so that the jury trial right is in part applicable and in part not applicable; second, the applicability of the jury trial right in new statutory actions unheard of in 1791.

B. **The Jury Trial Right in Cases Involving Mixed Elements of Law and Equity**

1. Following the merger of law and equity in the Federal Rules, there were at least three possible effects this might have on the right to jury trial in cases with both legal and equitable issues. It could be that the legal elements would be tried to a jury and the equitable elements decided by the judge; or it could lead to subordination of the right to jury trial by prior trial to the court of all but the most clearly "legal" issues, or it could lead to a subordination of equitable procedure by a preference for jury trial of disputed factual issues. The third of these approaches is currently dominant in the federal courts.

2. The first major Supreme Court decision of the modern era concerning the scope of the jury trial right remains the leading case: *Beacon Theatres, Inc. v. Westover*, 359 U.S. 500 (1959).

9

a. Fox, the operator of movie theatres in San Bernardino, California, sought declaratory and injunctive relief in federal court against Beacon, the operator of a drive-in theatre that had been threatening anti-trust action against Fox to invalidate Fox's exclusive first-run contracts and clearance provisions with movie distributors. Beacon responded to Fox's complaint by answering and filing an anti-trust counterclaim that sought treble damages from Fox based upon the anti-trust allegations. When Beacon demanded a jury trial of the factual issues, the district court held that the issues in the case were essentially equitable and ordered that the issues be resolved by the court with regard to the injunctive and declaratory relief although the resolution of those issues would be binding in the later anti-trust counterclaim brought by Beacon. The result would be a court trial of all of the significant factual issues in the case.

b. The Supreme Court granted mandamus relief against the district judge (Westover), establishing the basic law on jury trial rights in federal court. The Court first determined that there were indeed equitable issues in Fox's initial complaint, and that the non-jury trial of these claims to the court would resolve factual issues also presented by the concededly "legal" anti-trust claim. The Court held that the merger of law and equity in the Federal Rules necessarily reduced the scope of equity because it broadened the class of cases in which legal remedies would be adequate. Although the Court suggested that the trial judge retain discretion with regard to the order of trial of the issues, it also severely restricted that discretion. Justice Black's opinion noted that the right to jury trial is a constitutional one, and without any similar requirement protecting trials by the court, the judge's discretion will be limited. In his famous language, he stated that "only under the most imperative circumstances, circumstances which in view of the flexible procedures of the Federal Rules we can not now anticipate, can the right to a jury trial of legal issues be lost through prior determination of equitable claims." The dissenters pointed out that this was a significant departure from the kind of discretion typically available to the federal court judge, and that the Court was undermining the basic historical distinctions that had always characterized the right of jury trial.

3. The *Beacon Theatres* mandate of extreme deference to the right to jury trial in mixed law and equity cases was reaffirmed and extended in *Dairy Queen, Inc. v. Wood,* 369 U.S. 469 (1962), and *Ross v. Bernhard,* 396 U.S. 531 (1970).

a. *Dairy Queen* was an action that appeared to be almost entirely equitable in nature. Dairy Queen sought an injunction and accounting on its claims of trademark infringement — all elements that were equitable or developed in equity. Nevertheless, the Supreme Court held that, in essence, money damages were being sought, although by way of an accounting, and that this claim to essentially "legal" relief must be tried to a jury whether the trial court considered it "incidental" or not.

b. In *Ross,* the Court required a jury trial in a shareholder's derivative action, a form of action previously considered entirely equitable. The Court held the action could be split into legal and equitable elements, finding that the right to bring the action by the shareholders was an equitable issue, but the nature of the relief sought against the corporation and its officers (money damages) was legal. The seventh amendment required jury trial of the legal issues.

c. Following the *Ross* decision, it appeared that all litigation with mixed issues would be dominated by the right to jury trial. Whenever a case could be separated, however artificially, into equitable and legal elements, the Court was ready to protect the right to jury trial of the legal elements.

4. Although *Beacon, Dairy Queen,* and *Ross* suggest an absolute preference for jury trial of issues that can be characterized in any way as legal, the Court was simultaneously carving out exceptions to this right in two other major decisions.

9

a.   In *Katchen v. Landy,* 382 U.S. 323 (1966), the Court held that a claimant in a bankruptcy proceeding, who is later sued by the trustee in bankruptcy to recover payments allegedly made by the debtor to the petitioner as preferences, was not entitled to a jury trial on the question of whether payments were in fact preferences, although the claimant would concededly have been entitled to a jury trial on this question outside of the bankruptcy proceedings. The Court concluded that bankruptcy courts have summary jurisdiction to adjudicate controversies relating to matters over which they have actual or constructive possession. These proceedings are inherently equitable and there is no seventh amendment right to a jury trial for objections to bankruptcy claims. Significantly, the Court noted that the delay inherent in the use of jury trials would be inconsistent with the equitable purposes of the Bankruptcy Act.

b.   In *Parklane Hosiery Co. v. Shore,* 439 U.S. 322 (1979), the Court held that prior determination of issues regarding a proxy statement in an injunction proceeding brought by the SEC and tried by a court without a jury could preclude the losing party — in this case, the Parklane Hosiery Company — from relitigating the same issues in a subsequent, separate legal action brought by shareholders to recover damages. Parklane's argument was that collateral estoppel could not have been used in this way in 1791 and that the relaxed standards for asserting collateral estoppel should not prevent jury trial of legal claims, citing *Beacon Theatres.* The Supreme Court denied the jury trial right, however, noting that collateral estoppel and other procedures available have evolved since 1791 and that such procedural evolution should not be absolutely checked by an inflexible interpretation of the jury trial right. Significantly, Justice (now Chief Justice) Rehnquist wrote a vigorous dissent to *Parklane's* weak view of the right to jury trial.

c.   *Katchen* and *Parklane Hosiery* suggest that there are limits to the extent all procedure must be shaped to accommodate the jury trial right. Instead, *Beacon Theatres, Dairy Queen,* and *Ross,* as limited by *Katchen* and *Parklane Hosiery*, stand for:

   (1) a principle emanating from the seventh amendment that jury trial is the preferred method of fact-finding in judicial proceedings; and

   (2) when it is a relatively easy matter to allow jury trial without seriously disturbing established procedures, the right must prevail. The balance rested there for almost 10 years, until the Court again took up the jury trial issue in 1989.

5.   Recently, the Supreme Court has been extremely active in taking up the jury trial issue and, in a trio of decisions in the past two years, has retreated somewhat from the jury trial limitations in both *Katchen v. Landy* and *Parklane Hosiery v. Shore.*

a.   First, in *Granfinanciera, S.A. v. Nordberg,* 492 U.S. 33, 109 S. Ct. 2782 (1989), the Supreme Court held that a party who has not submitted a claim against the bankruptcy estate is entitled to a jury trial when sued by the bankruptcy trustee to recover an allegedly fraudulent monetary transfer. The Court found that the trustee's efforts to recover a fraudulent transfer was a private, not a public, right equivalent to a state law contract claim and limited *Katchen v. Landy* to its own facts, in particular the fact that the *Katchen* creditor had submitted a claim against the estate. The fraudulent conveyance dispute in *Nordberg* was not a part of the claims allowance process as it had been in *Katchen.* Justice White, author of the *Katchen* decision, dissented, believing that the Court's opinion could not be reconciled with the *Katchen* holding.

b.   Second, in *Lytle v. Household Manufacturing, Inc.,* 494 U.S. 545, 110 S. Ct. 1331 (1990), the Supreme Court limited the scope of *Parklane Hosiery.* Lytle, an African-American, had brought an action under both Title VII of the Civil Rights Act of 1964 and 42 U.S.C. § 1981 for alleged employment discrimination. The district court erroneously concluded that Title VII provided Lytle's exclusive remedy, dismissing the § 1981 claims and holding a court trial of the Title VII claims. The Supreme Court held that the erroneous dismissal of the § 1981 remedies, which would have entitled Lytle to a jury trial, required that the findings against Lytle on the Title VII claims could not collaterally estop and prevent relitigation of the same issues by a jury in the § 1981 proceeding. The Court noted that had the § 1981 claims not been erroneously dismissed, *Beacon Theatres* and its progeny would have required that a jury consider all of the claims common to both the legal § 1981 action and the equitable Title VII action. Although the cases are distinct on their facts, *Lytle,* a unanimous Supreme Court decision, effectively restricts *Parklane Hosiery* to its particular factual circumstances and indicates a reemergence of the dominance of the jury trial right established in *Beacon Theatres, Dairy Queen*, and *Ross*.

c. Third, in *Chauffeurs, Teamsters and Helpers, Local No. 391 v. Terry,* 494 U.S. 558, 110 S. Ct. 1339 (1990), a divided Court upheld the jury trial right in an action brought by employees of a trucking company who charged that their union had violated its duty of fair representation in processing grievances against the employer when those grievances also involved a breach of the collective bargaining agreement. The Court ended up separating the two elements of the claim as in *Ross*. In order to succeed in a duty of fair representation claim against a union alleging breach of a collective bargaining agreement, the union members must prove two elements: first, that the employer's action violated the terms of the collective bargaining agreement; and, second, that the union breached its duty of fair representation. The Court concluded that the fair representation issues were essentially equitable, but that the issues pertaining to violation of the collective bargaining agreement were clearly legal. The Court then turned to the question (which it characterized as more important) of the remedy available. In this case, the remedy was compensatory damages, backpay, and benefits. Although concluding that not all requests for monetary relief are necessarily legal, the Court found that a backpay award in this case was more appropriately characterized as a form of damages. Accordingly, the majority opinion concluded that jury trial is required. In an interesting concurrence, Justice Brennan suggested rejecting entirely the effort to search for an appropriate eighteenth century analog to the particular statutory form of action under consideration. He urged the Court to focus entirely on the question of whether the remedy sought is legal or equitable in nature, and if legal in nature, require a jury trial regardless of the historical analogy. Justice Stevens, in a concurrence, also emphasized that the search for an exact analogy was misguided, and he seemed to suggest that unless there was some important functional reason for denying the jury trial right, it ought to be available whenever there was an appropriate analogy to a legal claim. Justices Kennedy, O'Connor, and Scalia, in dissent, argued that the case should have been resolved by finding no right of jury trial because the most appropriate historical analogy was one of trust, and a breach of trust historically carried with it no right of trial by jury.

C. **New statutory causes of action that did not exist in 1791 present recurrent issues of the right to jury trial. In the easiest cases, the statute itself specifies that the matter should be tried by a jury, as in the case of the anti-trust laws. Where Congress has not mandated jury trial of a statutory cause of action, the court must turn to the question of whether the statute is a codification or elaboration of a common law action that either did or did not have a jury trial right in 1791; examine the kind of relief that is available and whether it should be characterized as legal or equitable; and, finally, consider whether the new cause of action or claim is part of a pattern of regulation that includes other enforcement mechanisms and in which insistence on a jury trial might substantially interfere with the statutory enforcement program.**

1. The leading decision in this area is *Curtis v. Loether,* 415 U.S. 189 (1974). In *Curtis,* plaintiff, an African-American woman, brought an action under the Civil Rights Act of 1968 against white defendants, claiming the defendants had refused to rent her an apartment because of her race in violation of Title VIII of the 1968 Act. She sought injunctive relief

and actual and punitive damages. Eventually trial was held on the actual and punitive damages claims only. Defendants demanded a jury trial. The demand was refused by the district court, and the plaintiff was awarded $250 in punitive damages. The court of appeals and ultimately the Supreme Court reversed on the ground that defendant was entitled to a jury trial. The Court found little legislative history available from Congress to determine whether it had actually intended jury trials to accompany damage actions under Title VIII. Accordingly, the Court turned directly to the seventh amendment.

a. First, the Court held that the seventh amendment is fully applicable to new causes of action passed by Congress since 1791 and found in statutes of the United States. The Court concluded, "Whatever doubt may have existed should now be dispelled. The seventh amendment does apply to actions enforcing statutory rights, and requires a jury trial upon demand, if the statute creates legal rights and remedies, enforceable in an action for damages in the ordinary courts of law."

b. The Court noted that there are a few exceptions to this rule. For the most part, these exceptions occur in the context of congressional action creating specialized rights or remedies that are entrusted to an administrative tribunal or special equity court.

   (1) Thus, Congress could create the National Labor Relations Board and direct it to decide unfair labor practice challenges and claims without a jury trial. *See NLRB v. Jones & Laughlin Steel Corp.*, 301 U.S. 1 (1937). The creation of such new public rights and their adjudication in administrative proceedings is appropriate when jury trials would be incompatible with the whole concept of administrative adjudication and would substantially interfere with the administrative agency's role in the statutory scheme.

   (2) Bankruptcy proceedings, not involving the adjudication of private rights are another area where administrative adjudication is independent of the right to jury trial.

   (3) Pure public rights, enforceable by the federal government, can still be committed to an agency free of seventh amendment claims.

c. Since *Curtis v. Loether* involved ordinary private rights of action in the federal district courts, a jury trial is required upon demand if the action is one involving rights and remedies of the sort typically enforced in an action at law. The Court found this was so for Title VIII claims, which are analogous to standard tort damage actions that were triable at law and with juries historically. The form of relief was a typically legal form of relief — actual and punitive damages. The Court distinguished the remedies available under Title VIII from those available under Title VII of the Civil Rights Act of 1964 by looking at the statutory language. Title VII's language seemingly was restricted to the award of equitable relief. Moreover, under Title VII, the award of a monetary remedy such as back pay is in the discretion of the trial judge. Under Title VIII, there is no such discretion to withhold the award of money damages on equitable grounds.

2. Two cases decided shortly after *Curtis* upheld non-jury trial of important new statutory causes of action. In *Albermarle Paper Co. v. Moody,* 422 U.S. 405 (1975), claims for back pay under Title VII of the 1964 Civil Rights Act, which forbids race or sex discrimination by employers, were held outside the scope of the seventh amendment because they were "equitable in nature." In *Atlas Roofing Co. v. Occupational Safety and Health Review Commission,* 430 U.S. 442 (1977), governmental actions to enforce duties under the Occupational Safety and Health Act were deemed to involve the adjudication of public rather than private rights despite the fact that the object of such actions is to force the defendant to pay money to the government.

3. In two very recent cases, the Court has returned to the path set out in *Curtis* and favored jury trials in connection with new statutory causes of action.

9

a. In *Tull v. United States,* 481 U.S. 412 (1987), the Court found that the seventh amendment required a jury trial with regard to the liability phase in actions instituted by the federal government seeking civil penalties and injunctive relief under the Clean Water Act. Following its approach in *Ross v. Bernhard* some 17 years earlier, the Court dissected the action and looked at its constituent elements. Although jury trial would be required on the liability phase, the Court found the discretionary calculation of the amount of a civil penalty to be one that Congress had expected would be determined by the judge without a jury. This issue was left to the judges.

b. The *Ross/Tull* mode of analysis was carried even further in the 1990 decision of *Local No. 391 v. Terry,* discussed above.

4. For now, the Court seems settled on an approach to jury trial cases that looks both at historical analogies to the modern statutory right under consideration and, more significantly, to the form of remedy specified by the statute, to decide whether it is legal or equitable in nature. Pragmatically, the Court has found repeatedly in favor of the right to jury trial whenever it would be sustained by any part of the analysis, and has moved considerably away from a strict historical search for analogies. Rather than resting its decision on the results of the historical search, the Court focuses on the form of the modern remedy. If that remedy resembles a traditionally legal remedy in almost any respect, the Court will come down on the side of the jury trial right. Contrary to the holding in *Albemarle Paper,* Title VII back pay relief may now be open to reexamination as requiring jury trial because the essence of the recovery is monetary damages payable to private parties. The public rights doctrine has been confined to cases in which the United States is the party seeking relief and has been further restricted to situations where Congress has designated administrative agencies as the appropriate factfinder in rather discrete subject matter areas, as exemplified by *Atlas Roofing.*

5. Accompanying this expansive view of the right to jury trial in searching for appropriate historic analogues to modern statutory claims, the Court has refused to consider arguments that the jury trial right should be limited in especially complex cases or actions. For a while, some lower federal courts, relying upon a footnote from the *Ross* case that claimed that the jury trial right required looking at the question of "the practical abilities and limitations of juries" as one of the factors, held jury trials unavailable in certain complex actions in which a reasonable jury would not be able to resolve complex or technical issues in a principled or rational manner. Thus, some lower courts denied or struck jury trial demands in particularly complex securities litigation. However, a complex case exception was rejected by the Ninth Circuit Court of Appeals in *In re U.S. Financial Securities Litigation,* 609 F.2d 411 (9th Cir. 1979), *cert. denied,* 446 U.S. 929 (1980). The Supreme Court's refusal to review this decision seems to have put to rest the view that some cases are beyond the rational consideration of juries.

D. **Just because there is a right to jury trial in general does not resolve the question of what that jury must look like or foreclose waiver of the right to jury trial.**

1. In federal courts today, most district courts by local rule provide for unanimous verdicts by six-person juries in civil cases. The Supreme Court approved of this practice in *Colgrove v. Battin,* 413 U.S. 149 (1973). However, it is widely assumed that juries of fewer than six, or juries of fewer than 12 in which a unanimous verdict is not required, may not pass muster as an appropriate jury under the seventh amendment.

2. Assuming that one or more of the parties to a civil action are entitled to the right to jury trial, they still may not receive a jury trial unless one or more of the parties makes a timely demand, or, if having made such a demand, the parties later waive their right to a jury trial.

a. Under Rule 38 of the Federal Rules of Civil Procedure, a party entitled to trial by jury must make an appropriate jury trial demand within ten days of the last pleading directed to that issue. The demand may be endorsed upon a pleading of the party, and common practice is to state in your complaint or answer that you demand a trial by jury on all issues triable to a jury.

    (1) If a timely demand has not been made or, having been made, there is an appropriate waiver, there is still an opportunity to seek discretionary action by the court to allow trial by jury. Rule 39(b) allows the court in its discretion, upon motion, to order trial by jury of any or all issues even though there has not been an appropriate demand. There is some indication in the cases that courts should favor jury trials and liberally allow the parties relief from inadvertent waivers of the jury trial right.

    (2) Even if there is no trial by jury either by right or with appropriate demand, the court under Rule 39(c) may, on its own initiative, try an issue before an advisory jury, although this jury's verdict will not be binding upon the court. The parties may, if they wish, make such a verdict binding.

  b. In actions removed from state court to federal court, if the parties are entitled to a jury trial, they may make a jury demand in the federal court any time within ten days after the notice for removal is filed on behalf of petitioner or within ten days after service of the notice on another party not the petitioner. An appropriate demand under state law is still valid and binds the parties in federal court; a new demand need not be made. Likewise, if no express demand is required under state law, no express demand is later required in federal court unless directed by the court. [Rule 81(c).]

E. Note on the Jury Trial Right in State Courts

  1. The seventh amendment jury trial right under discussion here has never been applied to the states. Thus states are free to experiment with their own versions of jury trial or to abolish civil jury trials altogether.

  2. The right to jury trial in criminal cases is distinct and is controlled by the sixth amendment applicable to the states through the fourteenth amendment.

  3. State courts deviate from federal practice in a number of particulars. Most states have their own constitutional jury trial guarantees. These guarantees may be either broader or narrower than that found in the federal courts. States are free to ignore or insist upon any historical basis for the jury trial right or to assign a different historical starting date for that right. For example, California requires that the action be predominately legal in order to afford the parties a jury trial right, and looks to common law practice in 1850 (when California became a state) to determine what are legal as opposed to equitable actions. This is a narrower protection of the jury trial right than that found under the seventh amendment.

III. JURY INSTRUCTIONS AND VERDICTS

A. There are three basic forms of verdict available in federal courts. The federal courts and most states have general verdict forms and forms for the most commonly used special verdicts.

  1. General verdict. The first or traditional form of jury verdict is the *general verdict*. In it, the jury returns a finding in favor of one party or the other without any explanation. For example, this may be a form which simply provides: "We find for the _____ and fix damages at _____ ." Thus the jury would either return a verdict saying "We find for the plaintiff and fix damages at $750,000" or "We find for the defendant." This is the common image of a jury verdict but obviously leaves a lot to be desired in explaining how or why the jury reached a result and leaves the jury maximum room for rewriting the law, making special arrangements to benefit one or the other of the parties.

9

2. Special verdict. The second form of jury verdict is the more specific *special verdict*. Use of special verdicts has become increasingly frequent.

   a. When using the special verdict form, the court gives the jury a series of questions to answer. These special verdicts are in the form of specific written findings on some or all of the factual issues in the case. *See* Rule 49(a).

   b. A simple form of special verdict is required in the modern comparative negligence proceeding. In this form of verdict, the jurors are asked whether or not they find each of the defendants and plaintiffs were negligent and whether or not that negligence contributed to plaintiff's injuries. The jurors then should also determine the gross amount of damage suffered by the plaintiff. Finally, the jurors must assess a percentage contribution for the negligence of each of the parties to the plaintiff's injury. Once the verdicts are assembled, the court then enters a final judgment based on those verdicts. For example, if the jury should find that in a case involving only a single plaintiff and a single defendant, the defendant was 75% responsible for plaintiff's injuries and the plaintiff herself was 25% responsible for the injuries, and plaintiff suffered $100,000 in damage, the judge should enter a judgment awarding the plaintiff 75% of the $100,000 or $75,000 as against the defendant.

3. The third type of verdict is a combination of the first two. In it, the court gives to the jury written interrogatories or questions concerning one or more of the issues of fact necessary to reach a decision together with a general verdict. *See* Rule 49(b). This allows the judge to probe certain of the actual bases for the general verdict but preserves the freedom of the general verdict, as well.

B. **It is usually a simple matter for the judge to enter an appropriate judgment following a general jury verdict. However, problems occur with each of the two specific verdicts when the jurors deliver a verdict that is in some way inconsistent, either internally or with an accompanying general verdict.**

   1. In the case of special verdicts under Rule 49(a), if the jurors' answers are inconsistent with one another, the court should not enter any judgment but return the case to the jury for further consideration of its answers to the verdicts or order a new trial.

   2. In the case of a general verdict accompanied by answers to interrogatories under Rule 49(b), two types of inconsistencies are possible. The answers may be inconsistent with one another, and the answers may be inconsistent in part with the general verdict.

      a. When the answers are consistent with each other but one or more is inconsistent with the general verdict, the court has the power to enter a judgment under Rule 58 in accordance with the answers notwithstanding the general verdict. Alternatively, the court may return the answers to the jury for their further consideration or order a new trial.

      b. When the answers are inconsistent with one another and one or more is likewise inconsistent with the general verdict, the judge is required to return the case to the jury for further consideration or order a new trial.

C. **The procedures regarding the use of special and general verdicts highlight the tension between the two.**

   1. A general verdict may be preferred for its simplicity and the likelihood that it will resolve the case, at least as far as the jury is concerned. On the other hand, it allows for covert jury nullification of the law or compromise in the case of a sympathetic party.

   2. Using special verdicts helps avoid these dangers but creates the further danger that the jury's verdicts may be inconsistent with one another or inconsistent with an accompanying general verdict, at the cost of further deliberation, a new trial, or reversal on appeal.

a. It seems a general truth that the greater the number of specific questions asked of the jury, the greater is the likelihood of confusion and inconsistency in the jury's answering of the questions.

b. The preferred practice in federal court is to attempt to have the special verdicts read harmoniously with one another if that is at all possible under any fair reading of the verdicts. Only if that proves wholly impossible will a federal court require the jury to reconsider or, as a last resort, grant a new trial.

IV. THE ROLE OF JUDGE AND JURY BEFORE AND DURING TRIAL

A. Although the jury is considered to be the ultimate fact finder, in every jury trial, the judge exercises considerable control over jury decisionmaking and over the ultimate outcome of the case on the merits.

1. At pre-trial, the court has a role in allocating the burdens of pleading and in evaluating the sufficiency of the pleadings, and, at this point, the jury plays no role. The trial judge rules on motions to dismiss, on motions for judgment on pleadings, and on motions for summary judgment before trial. Finally, the court rules on pre-trial motions and enters pre-trial orders that ultimately control the manner of proof and production at trial.

2. During trial, the court again allocates burdens of production and proof among the parties and among the particular issues in the case. The trial judge regulates the evidence produced through her considerable powers under the Federal Rules of Evidence. Upon appropriate request by a party, the trial judge may also enter a directed verdict.

3. The trial judge also instructs the jury throughout the trial on the law and how to evaluate the evidence.

    a. Under Federal Rule 51, the trial judge has now been given express authority to instruct either at the close of the evidence or at such earlier time during the trial as the court reasonably directs.

    b. The court also typically requests the parties to file written proposed jury instructions before trial, or, at the latest, before the conclusion of the trial, from which the court decides what instructions should be given or should not be given. Under Rule 51, no party can claim as error giving or failing to give a jury instruction unless the party has specifically objected to that instruction before the jury retires to consider its verdict. This process takes place outside the jury's hearing.

4. Finally, the trial judge will either enter judgment on the jury's verdict, or grant a motion for judgment notwithstanding the verdict (if appropriately requested) or grant a motion for or order a new trial. There is even provision for extraordinary relief from judgment by the trial court, and, of course, the appellate court, a panel of three judges, has a final opportunity to review the trial for errors of law and, to some extent, questions of sufficiency of the evidence.

B. Burdens of production and persuasion are allocated by the judge, and it is important to distinguish between the two of them.

1. *Burden of production.* With regard to any issue, the party who has this burden (usually the plaintiff) must present evidence sufficient to allow a jury acting reasonably to find that the element exists or is established in favor of that party.

2. *Burden of persuasion.* There is a second burden, the burden of persuasion or burden of proof or risk of non-persuasion. With regard to any issue, the party with this burden must establish that it is more likely than not that the element exists or has been established to the satisfaction of the trier of fact. This burden of persuasion itself has varying degrees.

a. In a criminal case, the party with the burden of proof — the prosecution — must prove the requisite elements of the alleged crime beyond a reasonable doubt. This is not the standard used in civil cases.

b. In some civil cases and on some issues, the party with the burden of proof must prove the existence of the required elements by clear and convincing evidence. This enhanced burden of proof applies to proving fraud and some other issues, for example, malice in a defamation action.

c. The usual burden of proof in civil cases is proof by a "preponderance of the evidence." This simply means that the jury must find that the facts favoring plaintiff (when plaintiff has the burden of proof) are more likely true than not true. It is perhaps easier to understand this burden as the burden of non-persuasion — if the jurors are undecided, that is, they cannot choose between two versions of the facts, the party with the burden of proof loses.

3. Burdens of production and burdens of proof are allocated issue-by-issue or element-by-element in the case. For example, in a typical tort case there are at least the elements of duty, breach of duty, cause-in-fact, proximate cause, and damages. Plaintiff ordinarily bears the burdens of production and proof for each of these elements, but there are cases where some of the burdens of proof shift to the defendant. For instance, the burden of proving contributory negligence is usually on the defendant, but in some jurisdictions, plaintiff must prove she is free of any contributory negligence. There are also issues on which the defending party carries the initial burden of proof, such as in connection with affirmative defenses.

a. The judge makes the initial allocations on an issue-by-issue basis with regard to pleading burdens, burdens of production at trial, and burdens of proof as between the parties, and these burdens may shift from the pleadings to the actual proof at trial.

b. The judge bases this allocation on a variety of elements, including precedent, statute, the question of who is changing the status quo, who alleges the wrongdoing, whether the defendant is seeking to avoid liability based on subsequent events, the party that is claiming the occurrence of conduct that is out of the ordinary, the question of whether facts may be peculiarly within the knowledge of one or the other of the parties, and whether there is a public policy that favors or disfavors a claim or defense.

DIRECTED VERDICTS

V. **DIRECTED VERDICTS. Under Rule 50(a) of the federal rules, the trial judge may direct a verdict in favor of a party when the opponent has failed to meet its burden of producing evidence sufficient to warrant a finding in its favor.**

A. **Typically, motions for directed verdict are made by a party at the close of the opposing party's evidence on a basic issue or portion of the case.**

1. Thus, the defendant typically moves for a directed verdict at the conclusion of plaintiff's case-in-chief, although the motion may be made as early as at the close of opening statements. The motion should be renewed at the conclusion of all evidence in the case, in order to preserve the right later to move for judgment notwithstanding the verdict under Rule 50(b). *See* Part VI.A., *infra.*

2. Plaintiff would typically make a directed verdict motion at the conclusion of the defendant's presentation of its case-in-chief. Plaintiff too should renew the motion at the conclusion of all of the evidence.

B. **Decisions on directed verdicts are highly dependent on the particular facts and elements of the case before the court. However, there are some general rules that guide the approach of federal courts in this area.**

1. **General standards.** The essence of the directed verdict is the idea that the judge should not allow the jury to decide a case, nor even submit the case to that jury, unless she finds that sufficient evidence has been introduced to warrant a jury acting rationally to return a verdict in favor of the opponent of the motion for directed verdict. It is easier to understand this in terms of a spectrum or scale of evidence.

   a. In the past, a number of courts had adopted a "scintilla rule." This is the most liberal standard possible for refusing to grant a directed verdict. Under the scintilla rule, the judge would not direct a verdict against a party with the burden of proof on an issue unless there was literally no evidence, not even a scintilla, offered by the party. This rule appears to be almost universally repudiated today, and more evidence than a mere scintilla is necessary to avoid a directed verdict motion.

   b. The general rule today is that "substantial" evidence is required in order to avoid a direct verdict. This requires not only the introduction of more than a "mere scintilla" of evidence, but also that the evidence be sufficient to allow a finding by the jury in favor of the opponent of the motion.

      (1) In deciding whether sufficient evidence has been introduced, the court is not to weigh the evidence offered by the proponent or the opponent; nor is the judge to evaluate the credibility of witnesses (except where the court is permitted to find that a witness' evidence is incredible as a matter of law); and the judge must view the evidence most favorably to the party opposing the motion and give that party the benefit of all reasonable inferences from the evidence.

      (2) Today in federal court, the general rule is that the judge is allowed to consider all evidence offered by any of the parties in determining whether there is substantial evidence in the record sufficient to allow the jury to rule in favor of the party opposing the motion.

      (3) The test is not that the judge if she were weighing the evidence would find in favor of the opponent of the motion; rather, it is whether a reasonable jury might be able to find in favor the opponent of the motion.

2. An important consideration in evaluating directed verdict motions is a distinction between direct and circumstantial evidence.

   a. Direct evidence is testimonial evidence by an observer of a fact or the thing, the item, itself, for example, an allegedly defective motorcycle tire.

   b. Circumstantial evidence is evidence offered of a fact or thing that requires the trier of fact to make an inference from the observed facts to find the critical element. For example, someone driving toward an intersection, seeing a green light indicating that the driver could proceed and observing traffic halted on the cross street, could infer that the light for the cross street was red, even though the driver could not actually see the red light. However, the evidence offered by the observer here would be circumstantial; there would be no direct evidence on this issue.

   c. In evaluating directed verdict motions, as the evidence becomes less direct and more circumstantial, it becomes more suspect. Usually, any direct evidence of a fact satisfies the requirement of sufficient evidence to allow a rational jury to decide that the fact has been established. This rule is limited when the direct evidence offered is inherently incredible or is contradicted by indisputable physical facts. Circumstantial evidence, however, involves drawing inferences, and when the non-existence of a necessary inferred fact is just as probable as its existence, then a conclusion that the inferred fact has been found calls for speculation by the jury, and this speculation is not a permissible function of a rational jury.

3. In summary: when wholly circumstantial evidence has been offered and at least two contradictory inferences are equally possible, the trial judge must grant a motion for directed

9

verdict against the party who has the burden of proof. When direct evidence has been introduced which if believed by the jury would entitle the party opposing the motion to prevail, a motion for directed verdict should be denied unless the direct evidence is wholly incredible on its face, is flatly contradicted by indisputable physical facts of the laws of nature and thus can be disregarded as incapable of belief, or (controversially) is flatly contradicted by undisputed and unimpeached contrary evidence.

Example: In *Pennsylvania R.R. v. Chamberlain*, 288 U.S. 333 (1933), a brakeman employed by the railroad was killed when he fell or was thrown from a railroad car while riding on a string of cars in the railroad's yard. The decedent was riding on two gondola cars between two other strings of seven cars ahead and nine cars behind decedent, coming down from a hump into a series of railroad tracks. After all the evidence had been presented, the trial judge instructed the jury to find for the railroad, and the circuit court, in a split decision, reversed. The argument on behalf of decedent was that the decedent was killed when the nine-car string coming from behind collided due to the railroad's negligence with the string of cars on which he was riding. Decedent's evidence consisted of the testimony of Bainbridge that from a great distance, at an extremely acute angle, and in dim light, he saw the decedent riding along with the nine-car string gaining on his string; that while looking elsewhere he heard a "loud crash" of the sort heard frequently in a rail yard, and that shortly thereafter he looked again in decedent's direction and saw the strings together, but did not see decedent anymore. The railroad's evidence consisted of the testimony of three employees riding on the nine-car string that no collision had occurred. The Supreme Court held that the district court had properly granted a directed verdict against decedent. There are at least three ways of viewing the case.

(1) The case can be viewed as a conflict of inferences from circumstantial evidence. It could be that the testimony of Bainbridge only amounts to the possible inference that the cars crashed into one another or that decedent fell off, and there is no way to choose between these two sets of inferences. The Court says, "if proven facts give equal support to each of two inconsistent inferences," neither can be taken as established. Here, the loud crash gives rise to the competing inferences of other yard activity or a collision involving decedent's string and the nine-car string of train cars. Since neither can be taken as established, the proponent must lose.

(2) The case can also be viewed as a direct evidence versus circumstantial evidence conflict. Here an inference from proven facts — circumstantial evidence — "must necessarily yield to [direct] credible evidence of the actual occurrence." In this view, Bainbridge's testimony regarding a crash is an inference at least to the extent it involved decedent's cars, and it must compete against the three employee witnesses whose testimony must prevail.

(3) In the third version, Bainbridge's testimony is "simply incredible." Given the circumstances, Bainbridge could not physically see what he claims he saw. The problem here is that the district court seemingly has made a credibility determination, in effect contradicting Bainbridge's testimony. But, given the physical arrangement, it is possible to construe Bainbridge's testimony as testimony in competition with physical facts. Under these circumstances, his testimony, which would otherwise be sufficient to get the case to the jury, cannot be credited.

VI. **POST-VERDICT MOTIONS. In the typical case in which no directed verdict motion is granted to either party at the close of the evidence, lawyers for the parties make their final closing arguments, the trial judge delivers the often-lengthy jury instructions, and the jury retires to consider its verdict. After the jury reaches a verdict, and in cases in which the jury is unable to agree upon a verdict, two motions are available to parties disappointed in the outcome of the trial. These are the motion for judgment notwithstanding the verdict (JNOV) and motion for a new trial (MNT).**

9

A. **The motion for judgment notwithstanding the verdict is in federal court merely a delayed directed verdict motion. Rule 50(b) provides "[w]henever a motion for a directed verdict made at the close of all of the evidence is denied or for any reason not granted, the court is deemed to have submitted the action to the jury subject to a later determination of the legal question raised by the motion."**

1. In federal court, the standard for judgment notwithstanding the verdict is precisely the same standard as that used in the directed verdict. The judge may grant a judgment notwithstanding the jury's verdict when the evidence offered in support of the verdict is insufficient to make out a case for proper jury consideration.

2. In federal court, a clearly made and supported directed verdict motion is an absolute prerequisite for granting a JNOV. This is a result of federal case law interpreting the re-examination clause of the seventh amendment.

   a. Cases from earlier this century held that under the seventh amendment, federal courts had no power to overturn a jury's verdict once it had been entered. Eventually, a compromise was reached in which the Court held it was permissible for the trial judge to withhold judgment on a directed verdict and grant a delayed directed verdict following the jury's verdict. This is the federal JNOV.

   b. Lawyers must be careful to specify clearly that they have made a directed verdict motion based upon insufficiency of the evidence at the conclusion of all the evidence and before the case is submitted to the jury. The cases are full of incidents in which inadequately identified directed verdicts were held not to fulfill the prerequisite for JNOV. The courts have been equally unwilling to allow other objections, such as an objection to jury instructions, to take the place of a proper directed verdict motion.

3. The absolute requirement of a directed verdict as a prerequisite to JNOV is a creature of federal law. Many states, including California and New York, allow the court to grant a motion notwithstanding the verdict without any earlier directed verdict required. This eliminates the procedural trap if parties do not make what may be unnecessary directed verdict motions, but it also prevents a party who might be able to supplement her case from introducing additional evidence in response to a directed verdict motion brought against her. Granting JNOV without the opportunity to reopen the presentation of evidence may lead to a miscarriage of justice if the failure of proof in the existing record is the result merely of oversight or technical error.

4. Since a directed verdict motion is a prerequisite to the district court granting JNOV, it is likewise a prerequisite for JNOV to be granted on appeal. Unless a directed verdict motion is made at the close of all the evidence, the verdict loser cannot on appeal raise the lack of sufficiency of the evidence as a basis for judgment by the appellate court.

5. Rule 50(b) requires that the JNOV motion be made within ten days after judgment has been entered upon the jury's verdict or within ten days after the jury is dismissed if it fails to reach a verdict. These timetables are strictly enforced. A motion for a new trial (*see* below) may accompany the JNOV and may be sought in the alternative.

6. Since the standard for a directed verdict and JNOV is the same, it may seem puzzling at first that a judge would deny a directed verdict motion and then later grant JNOV in favor

of the same party. It may be easier to understand if you consider the position in which the trial judge finds herself at the time a directed verdict motion is made following all the evidence.

    a.   If the judge grants the directed verdict motion, the jury will be dismissed and the case terminated. If on appeal, the appellate court decides the trial judge was incorrect in granting a directed verdict, the case will have to begin anew, and a full new trial held.

    b.   However, if the trial judge believes without absolute certainty that the evidence is probably insufficient to support a jury verdict in favor of the party opposing the motion for a directed verdict, it serves the system's purposes well to withhold ruling on the directed verdict and later, if necessary, grant a JNOV.

        (1) First, the jury may do the right thing and enter its verdict in accordance with the strong weight of the evidence in favor of the party seeking the directed verdict. If so, the judge has not been involved in regulating or controlling the jury, and the verdict is likely to stand on appeal.

        (2) Even if the jury makes the "mistake" of entering its verdict against the party seeking the motion, if the judge then grants a motion JNOV, and that decision is later reversed on appeal, there is a jury verdict and a completed trial in the record, and all that may need to be done by the appellate court is to reinstate the jury's initial verdict. No new trial may be necessary.

    c.   Thus, caution, economy, and protection of the jury as factfinder, all counsel in favor of judges withholding rulings on motions for directed verdict at the conclusion of all the evidence, thus preserving the right to use JNOV to correct an erroneous verdict by the jury.

    d.   Nevertheless, there remains the rare case in which the evidence is so clearly inadequate for the case to go to a jury, or where the judge is so convinced that prevailing legal rules absolutely require judgment be entered at once for one party or another, that a directed verdict is appropriate in order to avoid the wasteful expense of further proceedings.

B. **The second major post-verdict device is the motion for a new trial (MNT) under Rule 59. The modern motion for a new trial is a multi-function motion that has replaced a whole set of older motions. The standards to be applied by the trial court and on appeal vary according to the grounds upon which a new trial is sought.**

    1.   Rule 59 does not give much guidance on the basis for new trials in federal court. It states that "a new trial may be granted to all or any of the parties and on all or any part of the issues (1) in an action in which there has been a trial by jury, for any of the reasons for which new trials have heretofore been granted in actions at law in courts of the United States; and (2) in an action tried without a jury, for any of the reasons for which rehearings have heretofore been granted in suits in equity in the courts of the United States."

    2.   New trial motions, like motions for JNOV, must be made within ten days after the entry of judgment, and affidavits that might be required as the basis for the motion must be served along with the motion. A motion for new trial may also be made on the court's own initiative within that ten-day period.

    3.   The potential grounds for MNT are nearly limitless, but for the most part they fall into certain specific groups: procedural errors occurring in the course of the trial, most often errors in the admission or exclusion of evidence or instructions to the jury; misconduct of counsel; jury misconduct; newly discovered evidence; accident or unfair surprise; excessive or inadequate verdict; and the jury's verdict being against the weight of the evidence. This final new trial motion is related to, but distinct in its standards from, the motion for directed verdict and JNOV.

4. New trials based on procedural errors are among the more straightforward potential bases for a new trial. If in the course of the trial the trial judge, over objection, has erroneously admitted or excluded evidence or given erroneous instructions to the jury, after the jury has returned a verdict against the objecting party the court may grant a new trial in order to avoid reversal on appeal.

    a. The trial judge has discretion to grant a new trial if she believes that the erroneous admission or exclusion of evidence or erroneous instruction of the jury affected the jury's verdict.

    b. The appellate court reviews the determination of whether there was error in the admission or exclusion of evidence or instruction of the jury on a de novo basis. The trial judge's determination whether the error, if any, had an effect on the verdict is reviewed only for abuse of discretion.

5. New trials based on accident or surprise must be grounded upon incidents the trial judge finds are inconsistent with "substantial justice." Courts have often held that the accident or surprise in the trial must have injected a completely new issue into the case and must actually have prejudiced the opponent's case.

Example: In one such instance, the accident or surprise was the calling of a previously unannounced expert witness by the defendant. This witness was employed by the defendant but had not been listed among the experts expected to testify at the trial. The trial court eventually granted a new trial based upon the surprise evidence, and the appellate court affirmed the trial judge, holding that, although it is preferable to grant a continuance to avoid the need for a new trial, the choice was discretionary with the court. *See Conway v. Chemical Leaman Tank Lines, Inc.,* 687 F.2d 108 (5th Cir. 1982).

6. New trials based upon newly discovered evidence are also viewed quite cautiously and seldom allowed. In almost any trial, the losing side will find new evidence or reasons for needing additional evidence that counsel believes will justify a new trial. Accordingly, the standards for a new trial based on newly discovered evidence are especially high.

    a. The newly discovered evidence must have been discovered since the trial so that it could not have been presented at trial.

    b. The party relying on this ground must show that it was diligent in seeking the evidence during and before trial through discovery and other available means.

    c. The trial court must conclude that the new evidence will not merely be cumulative or impeaching but will present new issues or new materials for the jury.

    d. Finally, most courts require that the judge find it likely that the introduction of new evidence will produce a different result.

    e. These new trial requests rely heavily on trial court's discretion, certainly with regard to the weight and impact of the evidence, and counsel's diligence in seeking the evidence. But whether the evidence is, in fact, newly discovered is a matter subject to de novo review by an appellate court.

7. Misconduct by counsel or the jury also involves strong elements of discretion. Whether a lawyer in argument or demeanor has so conducted herself as to have prejudiced the result or injected personal belief into the trial is a matter of discretion to be decided by the trial court as witness to the counsel's behavior.

    a. With regard to jury misconduct, reliance on this ground is complicated by restrictive rules with regard to the kind of evidence that may be received. Under Federal Rule of Evidence 606(b), the trial judge may not receive evidence that tends to impeach a jury verdict, except to the extent that it shows that extraneous prejudicial information affected the jury's verdict. Thus, many types of juror misconduct that would otherwise provide grounds for granting a new trial may not be proved and will therefore not lead

9

to a new trial. Jurors are not allowed to give evidence tending to impeach one another to show that they improperly evaluated the evidence or took improper material into account except when that material was brought to the jury's attention outside of the trial process, for example, by some prejudicial comment to a juror by the bailiff.

b. The reason for this rule is to protect juries' verdicts. It would be the rare case where jurors do not inject some notion of their own sense of justice or life experiences into the jury deliberation, and much that is said during deliberations may not, strictly speaking, be appropriate evaluation of the evidence. However, short of bribery, jurors conducting outside experiments, or gaining testimony from their own sources, the evidence rules prevent the court from receiving evidence of less drastic misconduct.

8. More difficult to evaluate are new trials based upon a verdict against the great weight of the evidence. The standard for granting MNT on grounds of evidentiary insufficiency must first be distinguished from the directed verdict or JNOV standard. For directed verdicts and JNOVs, the trial court must conclude, without weighing the evidence or doubting the credibility of competent witnesses, that the evidence favoring the non-moving party is so insubstantial that a rational and responsible jury could not fail to return a verdict in favor of the moving party. The trial court has much greater leeway to grant a new trial on the ground that the verdict is against the great weight of the evidence.

a. First, the trial court is permitted in such a motion to weigh the evidence and to make its own independent determination as to how it would evaluate the case. No such weighing of the evidence is permitted in connection with a directed verdict or JNOV.

b. Although the standards have varied over time, and different standards are used in the states from that in the federal courts, the federal standard is one in which the judge must find that a miscarriage of justice will occur if the verdict is allowed to stand. As a federal court put it in *Aetna Casualty & Surety Co. v. Yeatts,* 122 F.2d 350, 352-353 (4th Cir. 1941): "On such a motion it is the duty of the trial judge to set aside the verdict and grant a new trial, if he is of the opinion that the verdict is against the clear weight of the evidence, or is based upon evidence which is false, or will result in a miscarriage of justice, even though there may be substantial evidence which would prevent the direction of a verdict."

c. It may be easier to understand this standard if it is contrasted with other standards employed by state courts. Some states limit new trials based on the weight of the evidence to instances in which the trial judge should have granted a directed verdict or JNOV, that is, only when the evidence is insufficient to make out an issue for the jury. Other courts have adopted a "thirteenth-juror" standard, one that lets a judge grant a new trial whenever the judge simply disagrees with the jury's verdict. The federal miscarriage-of-justice rule is designed to make judges think twice about granting a motion for new trial based on the weight of the evidence. It does not require that the evidence be so inadequate that it would support a grant of a directed verdict or JNOV on the one hand, but neither is the judge to act as a thirteenth juror. There is empirical evidence that federal judges are cautious and restrained in granting new trials on the ground that the verdict is against the great weight of the evidence.

9. New trials may also be granted on the ground that the verdict is excessive or inadequate. Often this requires a two-part process.

a. First the court evaluates the evidence to see whether the outcome of the entire trial process, including the determination of liability, is out of line with the evidence. If so, then the court ought to grant a new trial without any limitation.

b. If, however, the trial judge concludes that the jury's verdict with regard to liability is sufficiently supported by the evidence and is untainted by errors during the trial, but that the amount of the verdict is inappropriate given the evidence in the case, then the judge should grant a partial new trial based on the ground of excessive or inadequate damages.

   c. An alternative, much more frequently seen today, is for the trial judge to grant a new trial conditionally, the condition being that the party with an inappropriately excessive verdict agree to a "remittitur" of the excess amount. If the verdict winner agrees to that remittitur, then the motion for a new trial will be denied and judgment entered accordingly for the reduced amount of damages.

     (1) Some commentators view this as an extended judicial settlement device, imposing upon highly successful plaintiffs a limited or reduced verdict as a condition for avoiding new trials or potential appeal of the jury verdict.

     (2) Although a new trial ought sensibly to be granted on the grounds of either an excessive or inadequate verdict, the federal courts have held under the seventh amendment, that the process of "additur," or adding to a jury's verdict as a condition of not granting a new trial, is unconstitutional since it gives the winning party a verdict that a jury has never approved. *See Dimick v. Schiedt,* 293 U.S. 474 (1935). This has proved to be an especially unfortunate limitation on the power of federal courts to adjust inadequate jury verdicts in comparative negligence cases.

C. Post-trial Motion Procedure. Following a jury's verdict, or in cases where the jury is unable to reach a verdict, the trial court ordinarily considers motions for JNOV and new trial concurrently. This leads to a complex interplay between the two motions, their resolution at the trial court level, and their resolution on appeal in case of reversals. Under Rule 50(b)-(d), the trial court faced with both new trial and JNOV motions by the verdict loser has four sets of choices, each with its own consequences. Although the structure of Rule 50 is complicated, it ends up giving preference to the JNOV (which *terminates* the trial favorably to one side or another) over the MNT, which requires *resuming* the case, holding the new trial, and disallowing an immediate appeal. The four possibilities and the consequences follow.

1. If the verdict loser's motion for JNOV is denied and its MNT granted, then a new trial proceeds. There is no immediate appeal because there is no final judgment. Only after the new trial is held can the then-losing party appeal on the ground that no new trial ought to have been granted in the first place.

2. If the losing party's JNOV motion is denied and its MNT is also denied, then the verdict loser may appeal from the final judgment in favor of the other party, and the party who prevailed can assert grounds for a new trial as part of its position as appellee (or defender of the court's decision) because of the possibility that an appellate court may find that the JNOV ought to have been granted. *See* Rule 50(d).

3. The third possibility is that the verdict loser's JNOV motion is granted, and the court also then rules upon and grants a MNT.

   a. In this circumstance, Rule 50(c)(1) specifies that the new trial motion is conditionally granted and does not affect the finality of the judgment, which is now contrary to the jury's verdict.

   b. Under Rule 50(c)(2), the party originally favored by the verdict, who has now lost her verdict, may now move for a new trial and may likewise claim on appeal that her MNT should have been granted.

4. The last possibility is that the verdict loser's JNOV is granted but the conditional MNT is denied. Once again, the party who lost her verdict may now file a motion for a new trial with the trial court, since she is aggrieved by the court's grant of JNOV. And, on appeal, both the former verdict winner and the former verdict loser, now appellee, may assert error in the denial of their respective MNT's. *See* Rule 50(c)(1)-(2).

5. In the three of the four instances in which an appeal results, the question now becomes what action the appellate court may take in response to the motions granted or denied in the trial court and which may in part form the basis for the appeal.

   a. In the latter two cases in which a JNOV was granted, the course of action is fairly straightforward. If the appellate court reverses with regard to the JNOV, it then takes up any rulings on the MNT's. If the verdict loser's MNT was conditionally granted, ordinarily the new trial should take place, and that will happen unless the appellate court specifies to the contrary. In case the MNT was conditionally denied, the appellate court may consider for the first time the propriety of that ruling and reverse, either ordering a new trial or returning the case to the trial court for its further consideration.

   b. The greatest difficulties in practice arise when the appellate court concludes that the trial court's denial of the JNOV was in error and there has been no conditional ruling by the trial court on the appellee's protective motion for a new trial in the event of reversal on appeal. (*See* Paragraph 2 above.) In *Neely v. Martin K. Eby Construction Co.,* 386 U.S. 317 (1967), the Supreme Court held that the appellate court could enter JNOV and dismiss the case without requiring the trial court to consider a possible new trial motion by the now disappointed former verdict winner. Although the case produced a harsh result in that instance (because presumably the former verdict winner up to that time had no idea that an appellate court would have such power, and she had not sought a new trial either in the trial court or appeal), today verdict winners know that however successful they may be at trial court, both before the jury and before the judge, they must preserve any rights that they have regarding possible grounds for a new trial at every stage. They must make a clear record that there is an unresolved new trial issue by properly presenting any new trial issues to the trial court and adverting to this fact in their briefs on appeal.

EXTRAORDINARY POST-JUDGMENT RELIEF IN THE TRIAL COURT

VII. EXTRAORDINARY POST-JUDGMENT RELIEF IN THE TRIAL COURT. Most of the time, a party aggrieved by a jury's verdict or the rulings of the trial court will first challenge the verdict and rulings in the trial court by post-trial motion. If unsuccessful there, the party will assert the errors on appeal. However, there is an alternative, if unusual and more exceptional basis, for relief available in the trial court through a motion under Rule 60.

A. The first part of Rule 60(a) deals with what it terms "clerical mistakes" in judgments, orders, or other parts of the record. The trial court may note and correct these at any time on its own initiative or on motion of a party and may do so even during the pendency of an appeal.

B. Rule 60(b) deals with serious errors that might justify refusal to enforce a judgment.

   1. Under Rule 60(b) parties can obtain relief from final judgments or orders based upon: (a) mistake, inadvertence, surprise, or excusable neglect; (b) newly discovered evidence which by due diligence could not have been discovered in time to move for a new trial under Rule 59(b); (c) fraud, misrepresentation or other misconduct; (d) the invalidity of the judgment; (e) satisfaction, release, or discharge of the judgment or the fact that a prior judgment upon which the judgment was based has been reversed or otherwise vacated or it is no longer equitable that the judgment should have any continuing application; and (f) "any other reason justifying relief from the operation of the judgment." The first three grounds must be asserted no later than one year after the judgment.

   2. The first ground — mistake, inadvertence, or excusable neglect — is commonly asserted as a basis for relief from default judgments, and courts are willing to set aside default judgments upon timely application when a sufficient showing is made and a meritorious defense asserted by the party. *See* Rule 55(c).

3. In order to obtain relief on any of the grounds, it is important to show both that the ground exists as a basis for relief and that there has been prejudice so severe that a final judgment of the court ought to be set aside. Thus, the party must make a stronger showing than necessary in making an equivalent motion for a new trial within the ten days after judgment.

4. Courts have been slightly more willing to extend relief on the grounds of fraud, misrepresentation, or other misconduct of the adverse party — for example, a willful covering-up of materials subject to discovery — than they are for conduct considered intrinsic to the litigation process, such as perjury by witnesses during trial, which the courts believe ought to be remedied by effective cross-examination.

    Example: A frequently cited case is that of *Rozier v. Ford Motor Co.*, 573 F.2d 1332 (5th Cir. 1978). Rozier had sued Ford for wrongful death of her husband, who was killed when his Ford Galaxy was hit in the rear and its fuel tank exploded and burned. The trial ended in a jury verdict for the defendant. Plaintiff in interrogatories had asked Ford for any cost-benefit analyses applicable to this car, and Ford had claimed it could find no such analyses. It later was revealed that one week before trial, Ford's counsel had learned of a potentially applicable cost-benefit analysis but did not reveal that information to the plaintiff. Following the judgment, plaintiff moved under Rule 60(b)(3) — fraud, misrepresentation, or other misconduct — to vacate the judgment and for a new trial. The district court denied any relief, but on appeal the Fifth Circuit reversed, finding that the material was covered by the discovery request, Ford was guilty of misrepresentation and other misconduct, and that Ford's non-disclosure of the document prevented plaintiff from fully and fairly presenting her case because it precluded her from claiming Ford had been negligent in failing to warn owners about fuel tank dangers of which it had been aware. Had the motion been brought more than one year after judgment, relief could have been granted only under Rule 60(b)(6) and it is likely an additional showing would have to have been made sufficient to establish a fraud on the court.

5. Some of the grounds are very specialized. Relief from a void judgment requires a showing that the court lacked jurisdiction over the subject matter or the parties, or was otherwise violative of due process. *See* Chapter 2. The fifth ground may apply when a change in the law has made the particular judgment inequitable or inappropriate to continue, such as an injunction entered on a legal basis that has since been overturned in other cases.

6. The sixth ground is ordinarily limited to circumstances other than those found in the previous five that affect the substantial rights of the parties. Most courts require that the kind of error found be one that demonstrably affected the decision in the case, not one that would simply add evidence or even raise new grounds in support of one side or another in the case.

APPEAL

▶ **CHAPTER SUMMARY**

APPEAL

INTRODUCTION: Correcting judicial error is not like falling off the back of a truck. It takes foresight, skill, and persistence, with the force of inertia at all stages resisting appellate correction of trial court mistakes. We begin our discussion of the appellate process by reviewing the mechanics of appeal. There are three basic stages to a successful appeal: *contemporaneous objection* to the trial court, *timely initiation* of the appeal, and *diligent prosecution* of the appeal in the reviewing court. Even when the issue has properly been preserved and presented on appeal, a claimed error must be shown to be both *reviewable* and *reversible*.

The idea of appeal, and the widely shared intuition that we ought to have the right to at least one level of appeal from the judgments of trial courts, raise philosophical questions that affect how appeal is implemented in particular jurisdictions. We review the influence of these questions on appellate policy.

The appellate systems of American courts differ as a matter of policy on the appropriate timing of appeal. There is a spectrum of variation that ranges from an emphasis on finality of decision to an emphasis on flexibility and appellate court discretion in deciding the stage of a case at which appeal should be allowed. The two largest appellate court systems, those of the federal courts of appeals and of the California state courts, occupy opposing ends of this spectrum of variation. We accordingly use these systems as models of contrasting philosophies of appellate process and policy.

We expand our discussion of appellate policy to discuss briefly the appellate jurisdiction of the United States Supreme Court. In an important way, the Supreme Court's appellate role bridges the two models of appellate policy. The Supreme Court must both supervise the federal courts of appeals and correct errors of federal law by state courts otherwise beyond its supervision.

We conclude by examining how appellate policy has significant choice-of-forum implications.

THE MECHANICS OF APPEAL

I. THE MECHANICS OF APPEAL

A. Contemporaneous Objection. All American jurisdictions make contemporaneous objection to the trial judge a virtually absolute condition of reversible error in civil proceedings.

1. It is part of our adversarial system of justice to make the parties and their attorneys primarily responsible for the course the litigation takes to and through the court system. If the judge makes a mistake that may cause you prejudice, you must object and give the judge the opportunity to correct the error.

2. If you fail to make an objection in time to avoid prejudice, you have no right to appeal the error.

    a. In the criminal justice system there is often a lack of adversarial symmetry — the same government that pays the prosecutor also pays the judge and generally the defense attorney. One byproduct is that trial judges in criminal cases have significant duties to act "sua sponte" (on the judge's own initiative). There can be appealable error without objection when the error consists of a failure to take required judicial action sua sponte. For instance, a valid guilty plea requires elaborate judicial interrogation of the state of mind of the person who is waiving her right to trial with a presumption of innocence.

    b. In the civil justice system, however, the judge plays a more truly neutral role, especially in conventional civil litigation seeking a transfer of wealth between private parties. The judge referees the litigation, but it is your responsibility as a party to referee the judge. You do this by objecting when the judge errs and then pursuing the point on appeal, if the error has caused you harm. Very little is required of the judge sua sponte.

3. Because contemporaneous objection is such a critical precondition to an effective appeal, it is important to make sure that your objection is included in the record of the proceedings before the trial court. This is generally not a strict contemporaneous condition, and if there is a gap in the record where you did indeed object (but it went unrecorded for some reason),

the record can be corrected, provided that you can establish later the fact of the objection. That is easy to do when your opponents or the trial judge share your recollection. But since the opponents have something to lose by your pursuit of an appeal, and judges hate to be reversed, human nature makes it unwise to rely on their cooperation to establish the fact of an unrecorded objection by stipulation or amendment of the record. Take care that the court reporter makes a record of both your objection and the judge's unsatisfactory response.

B. Initiation of Timely Appeal. The next crucial step in winning an appeal is the initiation of the appeal at the proper time. With rare exceptions, such as the review of a sentence of death under the laws of some states, appeal is never automatic. It will be waived if you fail to take the initiative by asserting your right to appeal at the proper time.

1. *The notice of appeal.* In most systems you "take" an appeal by filing a "notice of appeal." Although the function of a notice of appeal in initiating an appeal is analogous to the function of the complaint in initiating the underlying lawsuit, the form of these documents is different. Unlike a complaint, a notice of appeal generally does not set forth the grounds for appeal or make any other detailed statement of the claim to judicial relief. The notice of appeal simply identifies the case, the parties, and the trial court and informs the appellate court that you (the *appellant*) are appealing the judgment or other order described in the notice of appeal. (Your opponent is called the *appellee* or *respondent*.) The specification of the grounds for appeal comes later, at the briefing stage.

2. *The time for appeal.* This is one of the trickiest aspects of appellate procedure. The time for appeal is generally quite limited and is *jurisdictional*, which means that the courts have no discretion to let you go ahead with your appeal even if it appears to have merit, and even if you tried hard to file it on time but got it in just a little bit late.

   a. Time limits for appeal are measured in days, not the months or years that you find in most statutes of limitation governing commencement of suit in the trial courts.

      (1) In the federal courts, for instance, the period for filing a timely notice of appeal in most cases is just "30 days after the date of entry of the judgment or order appealed from." [Fed. R. App. P. 4(a)(1).]

      (2) The federal courts are more generous than most in allowing a grace period within which the trial court can grant an extension of the time for appeal. [Fed. R. App. P. 4(a)(5).] But this grace period lasts only another 30 days, after which appeal is impossible.

   b. In addition to the sheer brevity of the applicable time period, the timely initiation of an appeal is made tricky by potential confusion over when that brief period begins to run. The date of the error complained of is not what counts. First, something prejudicial has to result from the error: typically an entry of judgment, but sometimes an interlocutory order such as the granting of an injunction or an order compelling a party to incur an extraordinary and irrecoverable expense. Most jurisdictions have taken care to highlight the entry of appealable orders so that litigants won't be caught napping, but problems of this sort remain endemic. Careful lawyers double-check the applicable rules of timely appeal immediately upon the occurrence of a potentially prejudicial error.

   Example: Under federal procedure, the dismissal of all claims against one of several defendants in a multi-party action is not immediately appealable absent special action by the trial court under Federal Rule of Civil Procedure 54(b). In a California state court action, Mouse sues Bird and Henson. The court grants Henson's motion to quash service of process. Mouse thinks this ruling was erroneous under modern minimum contacts analysis and intends to appeal. Meanwhile, Henson is dismissed from the action, since Mouse has no way of serving effective process under the trial court's mistaken view of the law. According to federal practice, the dismissal of Henson would not be appealable until there is a final judgment as to Bird as well. But under § 904.1(c) of the California Code of Civil Procedure, the order granting Henson's motion to quash service of process is immediately appealable, and under Rule 2 of the California Rules of Court, the notice of appeal of that order must be filed within 60 days of the entry of the order. If Mouse is more familiar with federal practice than practice in the California state courts, Mouse may fail to file a timely appeal of the adverse jurisdictional ruling as to Henson.

3. *Posting of bond.* A bond may be required to be posted incident to the filing of an appeal, in an amount sufficient to pay the respondent's costs in the event the appeal is unsuccessful. If the appeal is from a judgment that the appellant does not want to satisfy pending the appeal, a stay is ordinarily available only if the appellant posts a *supersedeas* bond (generally purchased from a surety company) guaranteeing payment of the amount of the judgment upon affirmance. The need to liquidate assets *in advance* of appellate review in order to finance a supersedeas bond (or post its cash equivalent) can impose a serious obstacle to appeal when the amount of the as-yet unreviewed judgment is a substantial proportion of the net worth of the appellant. *See Pennzoil Co. v. Texaco Inc.*, 481 U.S. 1 (1987).

C. **Diligent Prosecution of Appeal. The party taking the appeal has the burden of following through in a diligent and timely fashion.**

1. The first step required after filing the notice of the appeal is the preparation and filing of the record. It will generally be the job of the clerk of the trial court to compile a *clerk's transcript* of the pleadings, motions, orders, and other documents filed in the action. It is the job of the court reporter to transcribe his or her stenographic notes of the courtroom proceedings and to compile these transcriptions into a *reporter's transcript* of the oral proceedings in the trial court. But neither of these jobs is done automatically. The appellant must ask for the preparation of the appropriate parts of the record, and, if necessary, pay the required fees.

2. The next step is timely preparation and filing of a brief setting forth the contentions of error allegedly committed by the trial court together with a summary of the relevant facts and a careful argument of the law that entitles you on those facts to a reversal of the judgment or order in issue. The statement of facts should be substantiated by appropriate citations to the record. If you fail to file your brief on time, the appeal will be dismissed.

3. You will probably have the opportunity, at your option, to file a reply brief in answer to the brief filed by the respondent.

4. Oral argument is also generally permitted, at the option of counsel. In our view, this is an option that should almost always be exercised. In only the rarest of circumstances — where a case very strong on the briefs might become unraveled at oral argument — would competent counsel be well advised to forego the right personally to address the judges charged with decision in a client's case. In most cases, appellate courts are pleased with counsel for foregoing the right to oral argument but are likely to construe the waiver of oral argument (at least by private counsel) as a tacit admission by counsel that the client's case is hopeless.

   a. In many courts, especially among the federal courts of appeals, most cases are "screened" by the appellate court and its staff in order to restrict oral argument to cases presenting close or difficult questions of law.

   b. In some states, such as California, there is a state constitutional right to oral argument of appeal. In such states, screening is still used to sift out routine cases for "fast track" processing and summary opinions, but counsel may (and should) still insist on the right to oral argument.

D. **Standards of Review. The willingness of an appellate court to find error in the proceedings of the trial court varies according to the nature of the claimed error. It is much easier to correct errors of law than errors of fact or a questionable exercise of discretion.**

1. *Errors of law.* All appellate courts review claimed errors of law "de novo." This means that no deference is given to a trial court's determination of what the law is. A novel issue of law will be resolved by the appellate court as a case of first impression regardless of the length or detail of the trial court's statements of reasons for resolving the novel issue one way instead of another way. Of course the appellate court may choose to adopt the reasoning of the trial court, but it will do so only because it regards the trial court's resolution as the correct one, not because the trial court's resolution is in any sense presumptively correct.

2. *Errors of fact.* Although appellate courts vary in the degree of their deference to trial court findings of fact, virtually all appellate courts accord trial court fact-finding a strong presumption of correctness.

    a. Appellate courts review most trial court findings of fact under the "clearly erroneous" standard. As summarized by the Supreme Court, this means that although there is evidence to support the trial court's finding of fact, "the reviewing court on the entire evidence is left with the definite and firm conviction that a mistake has been committed." *United States v. U. S. Gypsum Co.*, 333 U.S. 364 (1948). This is a somewhat malleable standard, and as a practical matter appellate courts more frequently second-guess trial court fact-finding when the evidence consists of documentary proof rather than the live testimony of in-court witnesses whose credibility is in issue. (But note that this practical tendency is contrary to the official policy of the federal courts that the "clearly erroneous" standard applies to findings of fact "whether based on oral or documentary evidence." [Fed. R. Civ. P. 52(a).] *See Anderson v. City of Bessemer*, 470 U.S. 564 (1985).)

    b. When a challenged finding of fact is incorporated in a jury's verdict there is even greater appellate reluctance to find an error of fact. Because of the constitutional protection of the right to jury trial in federal court and the similarly sacrosanct nature of jury fact-finding under the laws of most states, jury verdicts will be set aside as factually unsupported only when there is a total lack of "substantial evidence" to support the jury's verdict. This means that the jury's verdict must stand unless the evidence is such that no "reasonable and fair-minded [person] in the exercise of impartial judgment" could have reached such a verdict. *Boeing Co. v. Shipman*, 411 F. 2d 365 (5th Cir. 1969).

3. *Judgment calls.* When the trial court is called upon to exercise its sound discretion in the conduct of litigation, for instance, in determining whether good cause exists to permit a late amendment to a pleading or to issue an order barring discovery into certain matters, an appellate court will find error in the trial court's exercise of its discretion only when the trial court's ruling is so far outside the range of the reasonable as to constitute an "abuse of discretion." While appellate systems vary in the degree of control they assert over trial court discretion, in every system review for "abuse of discretion" is highly deferential to the trial court, and in some systems the trial court's discretion is virtually immune from correction absent a showing of bias or other impropriety.

E. **Reversible Error. In addition to demonstrating error under the applicable standard of review, the appellant must demonstrate that he or she suffered prejudice from the error. Appellate courts will not lightly overturn judgments. Mere error is not reversible error. Appellant must demonstrate that the error was "prejudicial" rather than "harmless." In civil litigation this generally requires a showing of a substantial probability that but for the error the judgment would have been more favorable for the appellant.**

10

II.   THE PHILOSOPHY OF APPEAL

10

A.   **The Right to Appeal. There is no federal constitutional requirement that a party to litigation be allowed to appeal the rulings or judgment of the trial court. All states nonetheless provide a broad right to appeal both civil and criminal judgments. Congress has chosen to make all federal judgments appealable.**

B.   **The Values of Appeal. The fact that appeal is such a universal feature of American law, by dint of custom and tradition rather than any constitutional requirement, reflects a public consensus that appeal is indispensable to a decent and effective legal system. Four basic values of appeal can be identified and distinguished.**

1.   Appeal is a mechanism for *correcting mistakes* by trial courts in resolving disputes about law or fact. Society places a high value on having individual cases rightly and consistently decided. The more leisurely pace of appeal vis-a-vis trial and the sharper focus on discrete issues by both counsel and the appellate court are important guarantors of the correctness of a judicial decision that has been tested by appeal.

2.   Appeal is also a mechanism for *reviewing institutional impact*. Institutional impact takes three forms.

a.   Some trial judges may not be operating their courts properly. Appeal serves to keep trial courts on the procedural tracks laid down by the general legal system.

b.   In responding to the facts of particular cases, trial courts may propound rules likely to be applied in other cases. This is especially likely where there is a practice, as in the federal courts, of publishing trial court opinions. Lawmaking by the judicial spokes of a legal system needs to be bound by the reviewing authority of an appellate hub and its circumscribing precedent.

c.   Conversely, trial courts may reach unpublished resolutions of issues of law that should be considered and memorialized in an opinion published by an appellate court for the future guidance of other trial courts and the public.

3.   Appeal fosters a sense of *participation* by the parties in the fate of their lawsuit at the hands of the state. Adjudication of a dispute is distinctly different from settlement by executive fiat. The participation of parties in the formulation of issues and the opportunity for parties to persuade the decisionmaker according to by-and-large preexisting rules are important elements in the distinction between the rule of law and the rule of a totalitarian state. The sense of party participation in the binding but nonviolent resolution of disputes according to general rules is enhanced by placing the first-instance decisionmaker under the yoke of party-driven review and possible reversal.

4.   There is also *legitimation* of the judicial decision by a process which draws upon form and ritual to inspire a sense of duty to obey judicial decisions even when the substantive premises or outcomes of such decisions are controversial or unpopular. We all sense, by intuition or experience, that the determinations of courts in cases brought before them by others may ultimately bear on disputes in which we later become personally involved. Through precedent we are governed by law declared without our vote or participation. The integrity of the judicial process, including the important feature of appeal, thus serves to legitimate a system of dispute resolution which governs even the uninvolved, the unrepresented, and the unwitting. (Our analysis of the values of appeal is borrowed from Oakley, *The Screening of Appeals*, 1991 B.Y.U. L. Rev., No. 2 (forthcoming).

C.   **The Functions of Appeal. Derivative of these four values of appeal are the two major functions of appeal. To a degree these functions are dichotomous. A particular appellate court will likely place great importance on performing either one function or the other, but not both.**

1. *Review for correctness.* Appellate courts that emphasize this function concentrate on monitoring the performance of inferior courts to see that the rules of the game are observed.

   a. This is rather like the function of a replay official in the modern world of televised sports. The trial judge is the referee on the field, and the appellate courts exercising review for correctness are the officials in the booth who monitor and occasionally overrule the judgment of the referees.

   b. This function of appeal preeminently serves the related value of appeal that we called "correcting mistakes."

   c. Less obviously, a system of appellate review for correction also fosters the values of "participation" and "legitimation." Review for correctness helps to guarantee that the parties will be taken seriously when they assert that the facts and the law entitle them to relief. Without some degree of review for correctness, proceedings in the trial court could veer toward arbitrariness, corroding the process of claim and proof according to law into something more whimsical and personal than disciplined and official.

2. *Institutional review.* This function is forward-looking and policy-oriented, in contrast to the retrospective focus of review for correctness and its concern that the individual get her due.

   a. An appellate court exercising this function operates more like a rules committee than a referee.

   b. This function of appeal preeminently serves the related value of appeal that we called "reviewing institutional impact."

   c. Less obviously, a system of appeal organized to serve the function of institutional review again fosters the values of "participation" and "legitimation." Institutional review democratizes the law by adapting it to society as a whole, as society changes. Policy-oriented review of appellate rules of law gives reviewing courts the opportunity from time to time to overrule unjustified or outworn doctrines.

D. **The Timing of Appeal. All appellate courts — and the legislatures that create them — must confront a fundamental problem of appellate policy. At what stage of litigation should appeal be allowed?**

1. *Final judgment rule.* One common policy, identified with the federal courts, is to insist in most cases that no appeal may be taken from errors in the course of trial and the pre-trial process until the litigation has run its entire course and a final judgment has been entered.

2. *Piecemeal appeal of interlocutory orders.* In contrast to a policy that makes finality of trial court action a precondition to appeal, some states (most conspicuously California and New York) follow a policy of permitting interlocutory orders by trial courts to be appealed forthwith. This may result in several different appeals being taken "piecemeal" in the course of the litigation of a single case.

3. *Underlying issues of efficiency and fairness.* There is no free lunch anywhere in the law of procedure and certainly not in the appellate courts. There is ever-present tension throughout civil procedure between the goals of efficiency and fairness. Concern for efficiency creates pressure on the one hand to reduce the number of appeals so that the system can function without undue delay and expense, and so that those appeals that are heard are decided in a reasonably contemplative and reflective environment. On the other hand, concern for fairness argues for allowing appeal whenever there is risk of serious harm from an error in the trial court.

   a. On the efficiency side of the equation, differences in the size and distribution of judicial resources within particular jurisdictions influence local law on the timing of appeal. Jurisdictions with greater scarcity of resources at the appellate level than at the trial court level tend to limit the frequency of appeal by limiting appeals to final judgments.

10

10

Jurisdictions whose trial courts are more overburdened than their appellate courts tend to take the opposite tack, permitting piecemeal appeal in order to avoid wasting trial court time by the further litigation of a case already infected by reversible trial court error. Efficiency concerns in general will argue in favor of substantial independence for trial court decisionmaking, affording trial judges broad discretionary authority in the management of trials, and insulating findings of fact by judges and juries from appellate reconsideration.

b. On the fairness side of the equation, concern for the necessity of monitoring the performance of lower courts argues against a strict rule of finality and in favor of piecemeal appeal. The stricter a jurisdiction's doctrine of finality as a precondition to appeal, the more "institutional" and the less "corrective" will be the task of its appellate court system — at least at the level of its intermediate appellate courts. Fairness concerns also argue for reducing the independence from appellate review of trial court findings of facts by judges and juries.

THE FEDERAL COURTS AND THE MODEL OF FINALITY

III. THE FEDERAL COURTS AND THE MODEL OF FINALITY

A. General Features. The federal court system features appeal as of right conditioned on a fairly strict policy of finality prior to appeal. Close attention must be paid, however, to several pragmatic exceptions to the requirement of finality that may permit interlocutory appeal in a particular case.

B. Structural Features

1. *Review for correctness* is performed by the thirteen United States Courts of Appeals. The structure and organization of these intermediate appellate courts is described in Chapter 4's discussion of the entire federal court system.

2. *Institutional review* is performed jointly by the courts of appeals and the Supreme Court. The interpretation of legislative programs and the fashioning of federal judicial policy is ultimately the task of the Supreme Court, whose jurisdiction is discussed below. In practice, however, the limited size of the Supreme Court — most agree that nine Justices is the maximum effective size for a court whose primary role is deciding constitutional cases en banc with a reasonable degree of consistency and occasional unanimity — leaves a good deal of practical responsibility for institutional review to the courts of appeals. The Supreme Court generally reviews an issue of federal law only after a split has developed among the courts of appeals. When the first court of appeals to deal with the construction of a federal statute delivers a powerful and persuasive opinion, that will generally be adopted by all other circuits.

3. *Independence of judges and jurors.* There is a high degree of autonomy granted to both judges and juries in the federal system.

   a. Federal judges enjoy the protection of Article III's lifetime tenure during good behavior and are subject to removal only by the extraordinary constitutional process of impeachment.

   b. The "abuse of discretion" standard of review of most acts of judgment by trial judges is a highly deferential standard that makes it very difficult to establish error. In addition, the basic federal policy of finality as a condition of appeal insulates many judicial orders from any effective appeal, *e.g.*, orders granting or denying discovery or changes of venue, because of the difficulty of showing prejudice even if the broad discretion vested in the district courts could be shown to have been abused. Judicial fact-finding is subject to a "clear error" test that allows the evidence to be reweighed by the appellate court, but great deference is still accorded to the in-court judgment of the trial judge provided she makes the explicit findings of fact required by Federal Rule of Civil Procedure 52(a).

c. As noted above, intermediate federal appellate judges have a good deal of practical say in the institutional development of federal law.

d. The seventh amendment specifically mandates that findings of fact by juries be allowed to stand subject to only such exceptions as the common law permitted in 1791. This constitutional command is taken seriously. While facts found by juries must be supported by substantial evidence, federal courts show great deference to juries and strain to find substantial evidence in records that some state courts would find insufficient to support the jury's verdict. Federal appellate courts extend greater deference to juries under the federal "substantial evidence" standard than the already considerable deference to trial-judge fact-finding under the "clearly erroneous" standard.

C. Basic Requirement of Finality. The basic right to appeal is granted by 28 U.S.C. §§ 1291 and 1295.

1. Under § 1295, final decisions of the district courts in cases concerning copyrights, trademarks, most claims against the federal government, and several other specialized subjects, are directed to the Federal Circuit.

2. Under § 1291, all other final decisions of the district courts are appealable as of right to the regional circuits.

3. Effective December 1, 1990, the Supreme Court has been authorized to define by formal Federal Rule "when a ruling of a district court is final for purposes of appeal under section 1291." The Supreme Court is expected to adopt such a rule in 1991. For the present time, well-established case law holds that, in most cases, the appealable final decision will be the final judgment of the district court disposing of all claims asserted in the complaint. This general rule that no appeal may be taken prior to the entry of final judgment is subject, however, to the complex exceptions next discussed.

D. Exceptions to the Requirement of Finality Under § 1291

1. When a district court expressly so directs, a final judgment may be entered under Federal Rule of Civil Procedure 54(b) as to one or more but fewer than all the claims or parties in an action.

a. Entry of judgment under Rule 54(b) in effect severs the specified claims from the remainder of the action, and the final judgment entered as to the severed claims thus becomes appealable as of right under 28 U.S.C. § 1291.

b. This is a "one-key" exception to the generally strict federal policy of finality. Only the district court has discretion to decide that early appeal is consistent with federal policy. Once the Rule 54(b) judgment is entered, the exercise of appellate jurisdiction by the court of appeals is mandatory.

c. Trial judges are expected to exercise sparingly their Rule 54(b) power to "dispatch" part of a case for an early appeal. Any entry of a Rule 54(b) judgment must be accompanied by "an express determination that there is no just reason for delay."

2. The "collateral order" doctrine is another exception to § 1291's basic policy of finality.

a. This is another "one-key" exception to the federal policy against piecemeal appeal. In this instance, the appellate court holds the single key that opens the door to an appeal of certain issues before all issues in a case have been finally decided.

b. In its comprehensive review and regularization of early appeal of "collateral orders," in *Coopers & Lybrand v. Livesay*, 437 U.S. 463 (1978), the Supreme Court laid down an exacting "three-pronged test" for the collateral order doctrine. The order must:

(1) conclusively determine the disputed question;

(2) resolve an important issue that is completely separate from the merits; and

(3) be effectively unreviewable by appeal of the final judgment in the action.

c. **Examples** of orders *qualifying* as "collateral orders:"

(1) An order refusing under the *Erie* doctrine to enforce against a federal plaintiff a state law requiring the posting of security for costs in a shareholder derivative suit. *Cohen v. Beneficial Industrial Loan Corp.*, 337 U.S. 541 (1949).

(2) An order requiring a class action defendant to pay the cost of notice to the plaintiff class. *Eisen v. Carlisle & Jacqueline*, 417 U.S. 156 (1974).

d. **Examples** of orders *not qualifying* as "collateral orders":

(1) An order determining that an action may not be maintained as a class action. *Coopers & Lybrand v. Livesay, supra.*

(2) An order denying a motion to stay or dismiss federal litigation in deference to pending state litigation of a similar suit. *Gulfstream Aerospace Corp. v. Mayacamas Corp.*, 485 U.S. 271 (1988).

E. **Interlocutory Appeal as of Right Under 28 U.S.C. § 1292(a)**

1. The right to appeal certain interlocutory orders is granted by 28 U.S.C. § 1292(a), which is extended to cases within the jurisdiction of the Federal Circuit by § 1292(c). These are cases in which there is especially great risk of immediate prejudice that cannot be cured by the ultimate right to appeal from a final judgment. By far the most important type of interlocutory order that is appealable as of right is the grant or denial of temporary injunctive relief. [§ 1292(a)(1).]

a. At one time, some orders staying or refusing to stay federal litigation were immediately appealable as of right under § 1292(a)(1). In some federal cases, prior to the procedural merger of law and equity (upon the adoption of the Federal Rules in 1938), a stay could be granted by the equitable "side" of the federal court forbidding further litigation of "legal" issues until the "equitable" issues had been resolved. Because such stays were equivalent to the older British judicial practice of injunctions issued by courts of equity to restrain proceedings in courts of common law, orders granting or denying such stays were long equated with orders granting or denying injunctive relief and, hence, were deemed subject to immediate appeal under § 1292(a).

b. The Supreme Court recently overruled the "sterile and antiquated doctrine" that permitted immediate appeal of orders granting or denying stays of federal litigation on "equitable" grounds. *Gulfstream Aerospace Corp. v. Mayacamas Corp., supra.* The *Mayacamas* decision confirms the increasingly grudging attitude of the federal courts towards all exceptions to the general federal rule requiring finality before appeal.

2. Certain interlocutory orders relating to receiverships, admiralty cases, and patent litigation are also appealable as of right. [§§ 1292(a)(2); 1292(a)(3); 1292(c)(2).]

F. **Discretionary Interlocutory Appeal under 28 U.S.C. § 1292(b)**

1. Any interlocutory order of a federal district court that is not appealable as of right under 28 U.S.C. § 1292(a) can be made appealable under the "two-key" system of 28 U.S.C. § 1292(b).

2. The first "key" is in the pocket of the trial court. The trial court must certify in writing that the order meets all three statutory criteria for a discretionary interlocutory appeal under § 1292(b).

a. The order must "involve a controlling question of law";

b. there must be "substantial ground for difference of opinion" as to the controlling question of law; and

c. it must appear that "an immediate appeal from the order may materially advance the ultimate determination of the litigation."

3. The second "key" is in the pocket of the appellate court. The appellate court may, "in its discretion, permit an appeal to be taken." No statutory standards restrict the discretion of the court of appeals to refuse to permit the interlocutory appeal to go forward.

G. Discretionary Interlocutory Review by Extraordinary Writ

1. Extraordinary writs are permitted in the federal system under the All Writs Act, 28 U.S.C. § 1651. Their use as discretionary devices for interlocutory appellate review is strictly limited, however, to the correction of genuinely extraordinary acts or omissions by federal trial judges in the administration of their dockets. Mere abuse of discretion is generally not enough; it must be shown that the error is so grave as to amount to an *ultra vires* act in excess of jurisdiction, or to a refusal to exercise a mandatory jurisdiction.

2. **Examples** of cases in which writs of mandamus have been *granted* to correct action by federal district judges include:

a. Denial of the right to jury trial. *Beacon Theaters, Inc. v. Westover*, 359 U.S. 500 (1959).

b. Remand of a removed action for statutorily unauthorized reasons. *Thermtron Products, Inc. v. Hermansdorfer*, 423 U.S. 336 (1976).

3. **Examples** of cases in which mandamus relief was *denied*, with emphasis on the great reluctance with which the writ should be granted, include:

a. Writ of mandamus sought to review order granting discovery of sensitive material in prisoner's rights litigation without adequate in camera review; denial of writ of mandamus by court of appeals affirmed; dicta in opinion denying the writ deemed sufficient to inform discretion of the district court. *Kerr v. United States District Court*, 426 U.S. 394 (1976).

b. Writ of mandamus sought to review trial court's order granting new trial; grant of writ of mandamus by court of appeals summarily reversed with stern denunciation of dangers of permitting piecemeal appellate review via extraordinary writs. *Allied Chemical Corp. v. Daiflon, Inc.*, 449 U.S. 33 (1980).

IV. THE CALIFORNIA COURTS AND THE MODEL OF PIECEMEAL APPEAL

THE CALIFORNIA COURTS AND THE MODEL OF PIECEMEAL APPEAL

A. General Features. The California court system permits appeal as of right from final judgments and a variety of statutorily designated interlocutory orders. The hallmark of California appellate policy, however, is very liberal use of "extraordinary" writs of mandate and prohibition to give the intermediate appellate courts discretion to review virtually any trial court action that is not appealable as of right.

1. In contrast to the federal courts' fear that interlocutory appellate review will delay lower court proceedings and clog the appellate courts, the California courts welcome the opportunity to correct lower court error before it infects further proceedings and dooms them to a reversal made ever more costly by delay between error and correction.

2. Although such other states as New York and Wisconsin share California's enthusiasm for immediate review of interlocutory orders that may mine the record with reversible error, most states occupy intermediate positions on the spectrum between the federal system of

disdain for piecemeal appeal and the California system of permitting an intermediate tier of appellate gatekeepers to determine *ad hoc* when an issue is ripe for review.

3. California's enthusiasm for interlocutory appeal goes substantially beyond the recommendation of the American Bar Association that state court systems provide appellate review as of right "ordinarily ... only upon rendition of final judgment," with other orders otherwise subject to "immediate appellate review only at the discretion of the reviewing court" on a showing of public importance, a likelihood of bringing the controversy to an early conclusion, or risk of substantial and irreparable injury. [ABA Stds. Jud. Admin. § 3.12.]

   a. The catalog of orders appealable as of right in California extends well beyond final judgments to include such unusual items as orders granting new trials.

   b. Immediate appellate review in other cases is available whenever desired in the essentially standardless discretion of the reviewing court.

B. Structural Features

1. *Review for correctness.* California's intermediate appellate court (the court of appeal) reviews for correctness decisions of California's trial court of general jurisdiction, the superior court. The superior court reviews for correctness decisions of the California trial courts of inferior jurisdiction (the municipal and justice courts) and decisions of most California administrative agencies.

   a. *The courts of appeal.* There are six such courts, each serving a separate cluster of counties and formally called the "Court of Appeal for the Nth District." Most of the districts are further divided into divisions. The justices of the court of appeal are required to hear argument in panels of three and to decide "causes" by written opinion. [Cal. Const. art. VI, §§ 3, 14.] Most opinions are not published. Certification for publication of court of appeal opinions must be approved by a majority of the court according to detailed standards of public importance. [Rule 976, Cal. Rules of Court.]

   b. *The superior court.* There is one superior court in each county, along with a set of municipal or justice courts. (The variation in name of the inferior courts is anachronistic, based on the size of the judicial district served by an inferior court. There is no difference in the operation or jurisdiction of a municipal as opposed to a justice court.)

     (1) Final judgments and specified interlocutory orders of the inferior courts are appealable as of right to the appellate department of the superior court of that county. [Cal. Const. art. VI, § 10; Cal. Code Civ. Proc. §§ 77, 904.2.] Such appeals may be transferred to the court of appeal from the appellate department of a superior court. Transfer requires an order of the court of appeal after certification by the appellate department (or independent determination by the court of appeal) that transfer "appears necessary to secure uniformity of decision or to settle important questions of law." [Cal. Code Civ. Proc. § 911; Cal. Rules of Court, Rule 62.]

     (2) Superior courts may also employ the "writ review" process, discussed below, to review non-appealable action by the inferior courts. A superior court's exercise of original jurisdiction to grant or deny a petition for an extraordinary writ relating to proceedings in the inferior courts is not appealable as of right but may be reviewed at the discretion of the court of appeal. [Cal. Code Civ. Proc. § 904.1(a).]

     (3) Judicial review of the vast majority of administrative and regulatory agency orders is brought within the jurisdiction of the superior court by the comprehensive statutory procedure for the writ of "administrative mandamus." [Cal. Code Civ. Proc. § 1094.5.] A few public agencies with special legislative or constitutional status, such as the Public Utilities Commission and the Agricultural Labor Rela-

tions Board, are subject to judicial review directly in the supreme court or the courts of appeal. *See* Cal. Rules of Court, Rules 57-59.

2. *Appeal as of right versus "writ review."* The California courts of appeal exercise a conventional jurisdiction over appeals as of right from final judgments, orders granting, refusing, modifying, or refusing to modify injunctive relief, orders quashing service or dismissing on forum non conveniens grounds, orders granting new trials or denying judgment n.o.v., and the miscellany of other orders made appealable as of right by California Code of Civil Procedure § 904.1. The uniqueness of the appellate process in California lies in "writ review" of the non-appealable acts and orders of the trial courts.

    a. Article VI, § 10 of the California Constitution vests in the appellate courts "original jurisdiction in proceedings for extraordinary relief in the nature of mandamus, certiorari, and prohibition."

        (1) Under implementing legislation, the writ of mandamus or mandate is used "to compel the performance of an act which the law specially enjoins." [Cal. Code Civ. Proc. §§ 1084-1085.]

        (2) The writ of prohibition "arrests the proceedings of any tribunal ... or person exercising judicial functions, when such proceedings are without or in excess of the jurisdiction of such tribunal ... or person." [Cal. Code Civ. Proc. § 1102.]

        (3) The writ of certiorari, also called a writ of review, "may be granted by any court ... when an inferior tribunal ... exercising judicial functions, has exceeded the jurisdiction of such tribunal ... and there is no appeal, nor, in the judgment of the court, any plain, speedy, and adequate remedy." [Cal. Code Civ. Proc. § 1067.] The function of the writ of review is to command certification of the record of proceedings in the tribunal to which it is directed, and in the discretion of the reviewing court to stay further proceedings. [Cal. Code Civ. Proc. §§ 1071-1072.]

    b. These constitutional and statutory provisions, together with a liberal interpretation of the ideas of acts "specifically enjoined" and "in excess of jurisdiction," have promoted the practice of California attorneys freely seeking writs for extraordinary relief to correct unsatisfactory decisions by the trial court at any stage of the trial or pre-trial process. *See, e.g., Koch-Ash v. Superior Court*, 180 Cal. App. 3d 689 (1986) [writ sought to compel preferential trial date]; *Tyco Industries v. Superior Court*, 164 Cal. App. 3d 148 (1985) [writ sought to compel sustaining of demurrer]; *Freidberg v. Freidberg*, 9 Cal. App. 3d 754 (1970) [writ sought to prohibit discovery sanctions]. Because no clear line can be drawn between doing something that is forbidden and failing to do something that is required, the practice is to seek jointly a "writ of mandate and/or prohibition" and, where needed for an adequate record, a writ of review.

    c. The key to the success of California's system of writ review is the efficiency with which the reviewing courts exercise their discretionary jurisdiction.

        (1) As noted above, the California Constitution requires that all "causes" in the courts of appeal be decided in writing by a panel of three judges after an opportunity for oral argument. A petition for an extraordinary writ does not count as a "cause." It may be denied by summary action of the court, and the vast majority of such petitions — on the order of 90 percent or more — are dismissed summarily with no more than a postcard to counsel announcing merely "writ denied."

        (2) The odds of summary dismissal are so great that the opposing party (the "real party in interest") ordinarily files no response unless the writ is provisionally granted by the issuance of an "alternative" writ. By its terms, this writ directs the trial court to grant the relief sought by the petitioner "or in the alternative" to show cause why the writ should not be granted. The trial judge is merely a nominal party. It is up

to the real party in interest to defend the action of the trial judge by responding to the alternative writ.

(3) The issuance of an alternative writ — which occurs in only about 10 percent of all petitions for writ review — is the stage at which the petition becomes a "cause" that must receive the standard appellate disposition in writing by a panel of three judges after an opportunity for oral argument.

(a) The petitioner now files a full scale brief, generally a revision and expansion of the papers supporting the petition. The real party in interest files a responsive brief. The case is orally argued. (Waiver of oral argument is possible but quite unusual given the clear judicial expression of interest in the case by the granting of the alternative writ.)

(b) The appellate court resolves the case by written opinion. If the court decides that extraordinary relief is indeed warranted, it substitutes a "peremptory writ" for its earlier alternative writ. The respondent court is now ordered peremptorily to do or not to do whatever is specified. If the court decides, all things considered, that the trial court's action should stand, it vacates its alternative writ and issues a final order of "writ denied."

3. *Institutional review.* Discretionary review of court of appeal judgments is available from the seven-member Supreme Court of California by a review procedure modeled on the United States Supreme Court's certiorari practice. [Rules 28-29, Cal. Rules of Court.] The state supreme court can also transfer to itself, before decision, causes presenting "issues of imperative public importance" that are pending in a court of appeal. [Rule 27.5, Cal. Rules of Court.] Opinions certified for publication by the courts of appeal are often withdrawn from publication by order of the state supreme court. *See* Rule 976, Cal. Rules of Court. "Depublication orders" function as an additional means of institutional review that requires minimal expenditure of the supreme court's judicial resources. The supreme court is able essentially to "veto" the development of new law by the courts of appeal without hearing argument, writing opinions, or giving any reasons whatsoever.

4. *Reduced independence of judges and jurors.* In several structural and doctrinal respects, the judges and jurors of the California judicial system have lesser independence from political and hierarchical control than in the federal system. This is reflective of the general philosophy of the California system that actors in the judicial process need a high degree of oversight.

a. California judges hold office either by election or appointment subject to confirmation and periodic retention by majority vote. [Cal. Const. art. VI, § 16.] Three out of seven members of the state supreme court were voted out of office in the 1986 general election because of their perceived opposition to the death penalty. *See* Wold & Culver, *The Defeat of the California Justices*, 70 Judicature 348 (1987). The trial judge who ruled that the Los Angeles County Schools were unlawfully segregated — an order upheld on appeal that ultimately resulted in an extensive program of mandatory school busing to achieve racial balance — was also voted out of office. *See Crawford v. Board of Education*, 17 Cal.3d 280 (1976); Yeazell, *Intervention and the Idea of Litigation: A Commentary on the Los Angeles School Case*, 25 U.C.L.A. L. Rev. 244 (1977).

b. California judges are subject to removal by a commission process that is specifically designed to ease the removal process. *See* Cal. Const. art. VI, § 18. Judges removed from office have ranged from municipal court judges, *e.g., Geiler v. Commission on Judicial Qualifications*, 10 Cal.3d 270 (1973), to an associate justice of the supreme court, *McComb v. Commission on Judicial Performance*, 19 Cal.3d (Spec. Trib. Supp.) 1 (1977).

c. The liberal use of writ review subjects the daily conduct of business by trial judges to much more actual and potential appellate scrutiny than the "abuse of discretion" standard of review as applied by federal appellate courts in review of final decisions and occasional interlocutory orders of district courts. In judge-tried cases, appellate courts can reweigh the facts and may even take additional evidence. [Cal. Const. art. VI, § 11; Cal. Code Civ. Proc. § 909.]

d. Intermediate California appellate judges have little role in the institutional development of California law. Most court of appeal opinions are unpublished, and those that are published are, as discussed above, subject to "depublication" by unexplained peremptory order of the state supreme court.

e. California trial judges have constitutional authority to comment to the jury on the evidence, including the testimony and credibility of witnesses. [Cal. Const. art. VI, § 11.] California courts freely take issues away from jury deliberation by directed verdict even when other issues require jury deliberation, a situation in which a federal court would be likely to delay interference with the jury function until ruling on a motion for judgment n.o.v. *Compare Newing v. Cheatham*, 15 Cal.3d 351 (1975) *with Simblest v. Maynard*, 427 F.2d 1 (2d Cir. 1971). The California Constitution's guarantee of the right to jury trial in civil cases has generally been interpreted less strictly than its federal seventh amendment counterpart. *See C & K Engineering Contractors v. Amber Steel Co.*, 23 Cal.3d 1 (1978); *Jehl v. Southern Pacific Co.*, 66 Cal.2d 821 (1967); *Rankin v. Frebank Co.*, 47 Cal. App. 3d 75 (1975).

V. APPEAL TO THE UNITED STATES SUPREME COURT

APPEAL TO THE UNITED STATES SUPREME COURT

A. Discretionary Jurisdiction and Institutional Review

1. Under a long-sought statutory reform finally enacted in 1988, appeal as of right to the United States Supreme Court was abolished in virtually all cases. Review by the discretionary writ of certiorari is for all practical purposes now the exclusive means by which the Supreme Court exercises its appellate jurisdiction. [28 U.S.C. §§ 1253-1254, 1257-1259.]

2. The Supreme Court has long confined the exercise of its discretionary jurisdiction to institutional review, generally withheld until there is a split among the circuits or state courts of last resort. [U.S. Supreme Court Rules 17-18.] The Supreme Court does not review for correctness and will not exercise its jurisdiction merely to rectify a personal injustice caused by egregious lower-court error in a case without public significance.

B. Strict Finality Principles Applied to Cases From the Federal Courts

1. The Supreme Court once endorsed a "pragmatic" view of the finality required for appeal within the federal system. That pragmatism was inspired by an expedient desire to decide a case that had been briefed and argued before it became apparent that appeal had been taken prematurely. *See Gillespie v. U.S. Steel Corp.*, 379 U.S. 148 (1964). In recent years, the Supreme Court has retreated from the spirit of *Gillespie* and has consistently enforced the finality principle in exercising appellate jurisdiction over judgments of lower federal courts.

2. With great reluctance, the Supreme Court occasionally permits departure from the finality principle when that allows federal appellate courts to address issues that might as a practical matter not later qualify for appellate review or be subject to effective appellate correction. *Compare Eisen v. Carlisle & Jacqueline, supra* (allowing review under collateral order doctrine), *with Gulfstream Aerospace Corp. v. Mayacamas Corp., supra* (collateral order doctrine rarely applies). As discussed above in Part III.C.3., the Supreme Court is expected

10

in 1991 to exercise its new power to define by formal Federal Rule when a decision is final enough to be appealable.

3.   The Supreme Court's own jurisdiction to review, by certiorari, cases from the courts of appeals is contingent on those cases qualifying for appeal to the circuit courts. *See* 28 U.S.C. §§ 1291-1292; U.S. Supreme Court Rules 17-18. Although the net effect is thus to limit its own powers of review, the Supreme Court has stressed that the limited exceptions to finality enacted by the interlocutory appeal provisions of 28 U.S.C. § 1292(b) are as far as the federal courts ought generally to go down the road to piecemeal appeal. *Coopers & Lybrand v. Livesay, supra.*

C.   **Relaxed Finality Principles Applied to Cases From State Courts**

1.   In the context of its power to review state court judgments dealing with federal law, the Supreme Court has been anything but rigid in demanding finality. Despite an express statutory restriction of its appellate jurisdiction on the state-court side of its docket to "final judgments or decrees," 28 U.S.C. § 1257, the Court has shown exceptional creativity in finding finality when it wants to.

2.   Most impressive is the Supreme Court's apparent theory that its own judgment can constitute the necessary final judgment, as follows: when (important) federal rights unsuccessfully asserted in state court might prohibit certain litigation from continuing in the state court, so that the Supreme Court's exercise of its appellate jurisdiction to clarify what federal rights exist *might* result in a Supreme Court judgment ending the litigation below, that is "finality" enough. Thus finality need not attach to the judgment under review, only to the judgment *exercising* the power of review. *Cox Broadcasting Corp. v. Cohn*, 420 U.S. 469 (1975).

APPEAL AS A FACTOR IN CHOICE OF FORUM

VI.   APPEAL AS A FACTOR IN CHOICE OF FORUM

A.   **Effect of Appellate Policy on the Litigative Environment. In most instances an attorney should be able to make an informed appraisal whether the litigation of a particular cause of action is likely to benefit from a trial process in which the judge and the trier of fact have greater or lesser independence. This is really the same issue, conceived more broadly, as whether one's side of a case is favored or burdened by jury trial versus trial to the court. Even where jury trial is assured or foreclosed regardless of choice of forum, a keen eye to the comparative appellate policies of the available alternative forums may reveal significant differences in litigative environments.**

B.   **Strategic Consideration of Appellate Policy**

1.   A party with a strong factual case under the existing law would generally prefer to litigate its case in an environment in which trial judges and juries are tightly controlled and the emphasis in appellate courts is on review for correctness rather than institutional review and possible innovation.

2.   A party favored by existing law that is not particularly well-reasoned might be prejudiced by a hard look at the substantive law by an institutionally minded appellate court. Such a party would generally want to avoid litigation in a forum in which the appellate courts were particularly interested in institutional review rather than review for correctness.

3.   A party with a rather far-fetched factual case under the existing law would generally prefer to litigate its case in an environment in which trial judges and juries are barons of their own turf, with comparatively weaker review for correctness and greater emphasis on appeal as an engine for law reform.

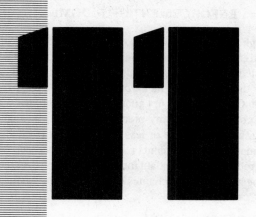

ENFORCEMENT OF JUDGMENTS

▶ **CHAPTER SUMMARY**

ENFORCEMENT OF JUDGMENTS

INTRODUCTION: Throughout this book we have emphasized that the plaintiff must always be alert to the *enforceability* of a judgment. By this we mean that the judgment obtained must be one whose enforcement cannot be resisted by a showing that the judgment is invalid. But the *enforceability* of a coercive judgment is merely the predicate to its *enforcement*. The fact that a judgment meets all of the criteria for validity set forth in Chapter 2 does not guarantee that a plaintiff who has succeeded in winning an enforceable judgment in court will gain any practical benefit from that judgment. Although some judgments are self-enforcing, operating more or less automatically to change the out-of-court positions of the plaintiff and the defendant, most judgments require the further step of proceedings to enforce the judgment in order to coerce a recalcitrant defendant into paying or otherwise complying with the judgment. In this chapter, we discuss the means and mechanics of enforcing judgments.

I. **FROM DECISION TO ENFORCEMENT**

A. **Entry of Judgment**

1. When judgment is entered as the result of a default, the procedures discussed in Chapter 8 are followed. Under Federal Rule 55, judgment enters automatically only when the plaintiff's claim is for a sum certain, the defendant has failed to appear, and the defendant is a competent adult.

   a. Before entering judgment against an infant or an incompetent, the court must appoint a representative.

   b. Before entering judgment against a party who has entered an appearance, the party in default must be given at least three-days' notice.

   c. If damages or some other aspect of the relief sought require a determination of fact, before entering judgment the court must hold a hearing on the relief to be granted. The relief granted by a default judgment cannot exceed or be different in kind from that prayed for in the defaulted claim. [Rule 54(c).]

2. When judgment is entered after a claim has been litigated to decision, judgment enters automatically only when there has been a general verdict, or in a judge-tried case, when there has been a decision that the claimant either recover a sum certain or recover nothing, with or without costs. When the jury returns a special verdict or a general verdict accompanied by jury answers to interrogatories (*see* Rule 49), or when a judge decides to grant relief other than for a sum certain, the court must approve the form of the judgment prior to its entry. [Rule 58.]

3. In federal court, two special doctrines avoid confusion about precisely what constitutes the judgment and the time of its entry (which is often crucial to the timeliness of an appeal).

   a. When there are multiple claims in an action or a claim against multiple parties, the decision of any one claim as between any two parties does not result in the entry of judgment, if other claims remain undecided between the same or other parties, unless the district court orders the immediate entry of judgment "upon an express determination that there is no just reason for delay and upon an express direction for the entry of judgment." [Rule 54(b).]

   b. In order for an entry of judgment to be effective, the judgment must be "set forth on a separate document." [Rule 58.] Entry of judgment officially occurs when the date of entry of a judgment, properly set forth on a separate document, is recorded in the chronological "civil docket" of the district court. [Rule 79(a).]

B. **Taxation of Costs**

1. Jurisdictions vary as to the details of allowable costs and the process by which they are "taxed" and added to a judgment. Federal procedure provides a well-defined and widely followed example. The prevailing party is entitled to costs as a matter of course, unless the court directs otherwise. [Rule 54(d).] Allowable costs in federal court include principally fees paid to the court, the cost of reporters' transcripts necessary for use in the litigation (such as transcripts of depositions or court hearings), and fees for court-appointed experts and interpreters. 28 U.S.C. § 1920. The greatest expense of litigation — attorneys' fees — are not ordinarily included in taxable costs by American courts, state or federal, absent special statutory provision. *See, e.g.*, 42 U.S.C. § 1988 (authorizing attorneys' fees to be added to costs in certain civil rights actions).

2. Costs are typically added to the amount of a judgment after its entry. Federal Rule 58 specifically directs: "Entry of the judgment shall not be delayed for the taxing of costs." In some jurisdictions, the prevailing party must submit a "bill of costs," with the losing party given notice and the opportunity to object. In federal court, the clerk taxes costs upon at least one-day's notice, subject to review within a further five days if the losing party objects to the amount.

3. Once costs have been conclusively determined and taxed, they become part of the judgment.

C. **Appeal**

1. The taking of an appeal does not automatically interrupt the progression from decision to enforcement of a judgment granting relief, but in the usual case the effect of the judgment will be stayed pending appeal. *See* Rules 7 and 8, Federal Rules of Appellate Procedure. Although the requirement of a supersedeas bond may sometimes be such a burden that the appellant can not obtain a stay, and may even thwart the taking of an appeal when enforcement of a judgment pending appeal will bankrupt the appellant (*see* Chapter 10), in the ordinary course of events enforcement of a judgment awaits the exhaustion of the opportunity for appeal. Our sequence of chapters reflects this normal sequence.

2. Appeal of a judgment may result in the taxation of additional costs incurred in pursuing or defending against the appeal. These costs can be substantial since they include many of the costs of preparing and duplicating the record on appeal. *See* Rule 39, Federal Rules of Appellate Procedure.

II. SELF-ENFORCING JUDGMENTS DISTINGUISHED FROM COERCIVE JUDGMENTS

A. **Self-enforcing Judgments. There are two basic categories of judgments that require no subsequent enforcement procedures (aside from the collection of costs) in order for the judgment-winning plaintiff to enjoy their benefits.**

1. *Declaratory judgments* benefit the plaintiff simply by their preclusive effect. (*See* Chapter 12 for a discussion of doctrines of preclusion.)

   Example: Suppose that Edison has sued Watt and has won a valid declaratory judgment that Edison's latest invention is not based on technology previously licensed by Watt to Edison under a royalty agreement. The judgment is no longer subject to correction on appeal. Edison can now proceed to produce and market her latest invention without fear of being sued by Watt for the payment of royalties. Edison's judgment did not grant coercive relief — the judgment declared that the new invention was not based on Watt's technology, but Watt was not enjoined from suing Edison for royalties. Nonetheless, any such suit for royalties by Watt against Edison would be immediately dismissed on Edison's motion for summary judgment. Indeed, such a suit by Watt is so clearly precluded by the compulsory counterclaim rule and general principles of res judicata that Watt would almost certainly be ordered to pay sanctions for filing a legally untenable complaint.

11

11

2. Some other types of judgments automatically benefit the plaintiff because they trigger the official action of third parties.

  a. Some such judgments are simply *variants of declaratory judgments* and may also involve some form of ancillary affirmative relief.

    Examples: The judgment in a quiet title action will generally be recorded and given the same effect as a deed of title from the defendant to the plaintiff. Judgments in other types of actions involving title to real property may be given similar self-executing effect by the recording of a compulsory transfer of title pursuant to the judgment.

  b. Other judgments may be *coercive in form but declaratory and self-executing in effect*, such as judgments awarding writs of mandate to compel ministerial acts by government officials. Although the self-executing effect of writs of mandate may analytically be the result of "voluntary" compliance by the defendant state official, this compliance is so certain that the judgment may functionally be regarded as self-executing, and in some circumstances this is formally the case.

    Example: Suppose that after a closely contested election for the Board of Supervisors the county clerk refuses to certify either Lincoln or Douglas as the winner until a court resolves a dispute over the regularity of certain votes. Lincoln sues for a writ of mandate ordering the county clerk to certify him the winner of the election. After Lincoln wins a judgment issuing the writ of mandate, state law may well entitle Lincoln to act as a supervisor even before the clerk formally certifies Lincoln to be the winner of the election.

B. Coercive Judgments. Most judgments are coercive rather than declaratory or self-executing. Some judgments are directly coercive, in the sense that they order the defendant personally to do something. Most judgments, however, are not directly coercive. They do not force the judgment-losing defendant to do anything. They merely authorize the plaintiff and others to take coercive action against a recalcitrant defendant.

1. The process of coercive enforcement of a judgment ought sensibly to be so expensive and unpleasant to the defendant that a rational defendant will find voluntary compliance to be the wisest course. It usually is much more expensive for a defendant to remain passive than to satisfy a judgment and get on with life. But not always, for two reasons.

  a. A defendant subject to a directly coercive mandatory judgment benefits from the strong American tradition of caution in the exercise of governmental power against an individual. As we shall see, the plaintiff faces considerable institutional difficulty in invoking the police power of the government to force the defendant to act in the way ordered by a judgment. Even though the plaintiff has a judgment in hand, the use of public power for private gain is very, very cumbersome in American law.

  b. The defendant may have insufficient assets to satisfy a judgment for damages. If the defendant will be "wiped out" in any event, there is no incentive to turn over assets promptly. Certainly the defendant is unlikely to be friendly to the plaintiff and anxious to reduce the plaintiff's costs of collection. Indeed, the defendant may well have a contrary incentive to use the plaintiff's costs of collection as a bargaining lever to negotiate a compromise amount that the plaintiff will accept in satisfaction of the judgment.

    Example: If *P* has a judgment for $100,000, and *D* has assets subject to execution totaling only $60,000, and it will cost *P* $7,000 to collect this amount, *P* will gain $53,000 by grinding *D* into the dust. *P* would do better by accepting $55,000, leaving *D* with $5,000 more than *D* would otherwise retain. Although *D* is the bigger loser overall if *P* grinds *D* into the dust instead of accepting *D*'s offer of $55,000 without any costs of collection (the offer leaves *D* $5,000 better off and *P* only $2,000 better off), *D* has a negotiating advantage if the value of *D*'s assets are uncertain — *D* knows better than *P* what *P* might obtain by coercive satisfaction of the judgment. Therefore, *D* has good reason not to comply with the judgment voluntarily.

2. There are two types of coercive judgments with different enforcement mechanisms.

    a. Mandatory judgments are enforced by the process of *civil contempt*.

    b. Judgments for money damages and specific relief ordering transfer of property are enforced by the process of *execution*. In some circumstances, which are strictly limited by modern constitutional standards of due process of law, assets against which an anticipated judgment may be executed can be taken from the defendant at the beginning of the litigation by the process of *prejudgment attachment*.

III. ENFORCEMENT OF COERCIVE JUDGMENTS

A. Civil Contempt

1. *Initiation by plaintiff.* A judgment may be directly mandatory or prohibitory. Such a judgment, typically an equitable judgment granting injunctive relief, speaks directly to the defendant and directly regulates her personal conduct. Despite this incorporation of a judicial command into a civil judgment, the defendant is in a sense "free" to defy the judgment. This is conceived of as defiance of the plaintiff rather than the court or the state. It is up to the plaintiff to take the additional step of requesting the judicial bite to be added to the judicial bark by initiating a proceeding for civil contempt.

2. *Civil and criminal contempt distinguished.* Unlike criminal contempt, which is a proceeding prosecuted by the government to punish disrespect for an interference with the authority of its courts, civil contempt is a private remedial proceeding litigated between adversaries. In the ordinary case, the "contemnor" (the party accused of contempt) was a defendant in the underlying civil action whose judgment is the basis for the claim of contempt. The contempt proceeding is regarded as an extension of the underlying suit and the contemnor/defendant need not be newly subjected to the court's jurisdiction.

3. *Enforcement by incarceration.* The trial court need not witness an endless chain of injunction, defiance, and renewed injunctions on pain of contempt. Upon a finding of civil contempt, the contemnor may be fined and incarcerated. Reflecting this potential for loss of liberty, some jurisdictions require proof of the contempt "beyond a reasonable doubt." *See, e.g., Ross v. Superior Court*, 19 Cal.3d 899 (1977). Incarceration for civil contempt is not imprisonment, however. "The keys to the jail are in the defendant's pocket." Performance of the required acts and payment of the fine levied in retaliation for the contempt will "cure the contempt" and result in discharge of the defendant.

B. Execution

1. *Background.* The common law writ ordering an officer of the court to give effect to a judgment was called the writ of execution. In common usage today, its meaning is equated with the execution of a judgment of death. With respect to civil judgments, coercion of the person is left to the contempt process. Civil writs of execution are directed exclusively against property.

2. *Property subject to execution*

    a. *Types of property.* Execution of a judgment seeks to replicate a defendant's voluntary satisfaction of the judgment. A judgment can be executed by seizure and sale of only such property as the defendant has the power voluntarily to alienate at the time the writ of execution issues. State laws vary on execution against property held jointly by the defendant and others. Even if the defendant has the power to alienate the entire property, the law is generally protective of the beneficial interests of non-parties.

    b. *Exempt property.* Even some of the defendant's own property is protected from execution by state statutes exempting minimum amounts of certain real and personal property. Such laws vary markedly in generosity (from a defendant's perspective). Their intent is to prevent the private gain of the plaintiff from causing the defendant and her family from becoming public charges. Congress has respected these state laws in setting up the bankruptcy process — the property that is exempt from execution of a civil judgment is the same property that a debtor gets to keep after declaring bankruptcy. Thus, a civil writ of execution means neither death nor destitution. Generally exempted are a "homestead" interest in a personal residence, up to a certain dollar amount of the homeowner's "equity" (the value of the house less the amount due on the mortgage), as well as an automobile (up to a certain value), essential household furnishings, and "tools of the trade" related to the defendant's livelihood. (Generally exempt status does not prohibit foreclosure of security interests or liens that relate specifically to otherwise exempt property.)

3. *Mechanics of execution*

    a. *Issuance of the writ.* Although there is considerable variation in local procedure and nomenclature, in general, execution of a "domestic" or local judgment entails the issuance of a writ of execution by the clerk of the trial court. The writ directs the peace officer serving the court, generally called the sheriff or marshal, to seize or assert dominion over the defendant's property. Most judgments must be enforced by execution within a specified, rather lengthy time. A judgment is subject to renewal by further proceedings, often called "scire facias."

    b. *Discovery of the property.* Although a writ of execution generally authorizes seizure of any property of the defendant that is subject to execution, as a practical matter sheriffs' departments are too busy to hunt vigorously for property to be seized in satisfaction of civil judgments. It is in the plaintiff's interest to steer the sheriff towards assets subject to execution, and sometimes this is required for issuance of the writ. (Where the judgment requires transfer of specific property to the plaintiff, the writ of execution will be limited to the specified property.) Supplementary remedies are available to plaintiffs as judgment creditors in virtually all jurisdictions to assist in the identification of property subject to execution. A debtor's examination provides discovery, under oath and on pain of contempt, of a losing defendant's assets. When assets have been transferred to avoid execution, the transfer can be nullified as a fraudulent conveyance.

    c. *Types of seizure.* The sheriff executes the judgment by seizure of property. The terminology for the seizure varies with the type of property. A levy is the seizure of property directly from the judgment debtor, *i.e.*, the losing defendant. When the seized property is in the possession of a third party, it is "attached" (the common law term) or "sequestered" (the equitable term) if tangible and "garnished" if intangible. The most frequent form of intangible property garnished in execution of a judgment is income (wages) owed to the defendant by her employer.

    d. *Sale of the property.* The levy, attachment/sequestration, or garnishment is followed by sale of the property within a specified time. The pressure of time and the general requirement of payment in cash often results in the seized property being sold at an artificially low price. If there are insufficient assets to satisfy the judgment when sold at such a deep discount, the plaintiff (who as the judgment creditor needs no cash) may buy the property at an amount equal to the judgment and attempt to resell it later in more favorable commercial circumstances. The prospect of depressed prices being realized at a sheriff's sale is a major incentive for defendants possessed of property to liquidate it themselves in order to pay off the judgment voluntarily.

4. *Foreign judgments*

    a. The full faith and credit clause of the Constitution requires interstate enforcement of judgments. The federal courts and numerous states facilitate this by providing for the registration of a "foreign" judgment from another state or, in the federal system, from a district located in another state. Absent a registration statute, the foreign judgment must be reduced to a new judgment in the state of execution by the cumbersome process of a new action to enforce the foreign judgment. In this action, the plaintiff sues in the normal fashion to collect a debt. The fact of the debt cannot be disputed, however, because it has already been reduced to judgment. By statutory enhancement of the full faith and credit clause of the Constitution, Congress requires that the state in which the defendant has assets subject to execution give a foreign judgment the *same effect* as it would be given by the courts of the judgment state. 28 U.S.C. § 1738. The only defenses available to the defendant relate to the enforceability of the foreign judgment, *i.e.*, a showing that the judgment is invalid, or that for some other reason (such as expiration of the time in which execution is allowed, or prior satisfaction of the judgment) the judgment could not currently be enforced even in the state where the judgment was rendered. Suit on a valid and enforceable foreign judgment thus results ultimately in a domestic judgment enforceable as such against the assets of the defendant.

b. Where registration statutes apply, the burden of establishing the unenforceability of a judgment is shifted to the judgment debtor. The debtor must initiate proceedings to vacate the judgment in the state or district in which it has been registered, just as the debtor would have to do if the judgment were being executed in the state that originally rendered the judgment.

C. **Prejudgment Attachment**

1. *Traditional practice.* The common law as codified by most American states traditionally allowed property of the defendant to be seized immediately upon commencement of suit and held during the pendency of suit as security for the satisfaction of any losing judgment. If the plaintiff prevailed, the seized property would then be sold in the normal fashion for execution of a judgment. In essence, the execution process was bifurcated into pre-judgment and post-judgment stages.

2. *Modern constitutional standards.* In a series of cases decided over the past twenty years, the Supreme Court has condemned prejudgment attachments as unconstitutional in all but unusual circumstances. No longer may writs of attachment routinely be issued by the clerk of a court based merely on the filing of a complaint. A judicial officer must find on the basis of facts alleged as a matter of personal knowledge that the suit is soundly based and that there is a risk of loss or removal of the assets in question. In addition, the defendant must be notified and given the chance to object *prior* to any seizure of wages, and with respect to any other type of property, must be given an opportunity shortly after the seizure to contest the grounds for seizure and to obtain a prompt return of the property if the seizure is shown to have been wrongful. *North Georgia Finishing, Inc. v. Di-Chem, Inc.*, 419 U.S. 601 (1975); *Sniadach v. Family Finance Corp.*, 395 U.S. 337 (1969).

D. **Choice of Forum Considerations Relating to Enforcement of Judgments**

1. Although frequently reduced to statute and riddled with ad hoc reforms and adjustments, the law on enforcement of judgments is largely derived from English common law as variously understood by American state-court judges. The result of common law evolution and legislative codification is a welter of state-by-state variation of basically similar procedures.

2. By and large the law governing the enforcement of judgments is state law. There is a federal statute regulating garnishment of wages (15 U.S.C. § 1673), federal bankruptcy law governs the dischargeability of judgment debts (amounts owed by a defendant held liable for damages), and, as discussed above, the federal Constitution severely limits pre-judgment attachment of assets that might later be levied upon in execution of a judgment.

Otherwise, state law is controlling even in federal court, where judgments are executed in the manner specified by local law. [Rule 69(a).]

3. In the particular case, local differences in procedure can be crucial. Thus, a forum's law on enforcement of judgments is yet another factor to be considered in the choice of the forum — at least in choosing a forum in which to enforce a judgment previously obtained. For instance, where a plaintiff can expect particularly obstinate conduct from a grudge defendant, with assets hidden or fraudulently conveyed, a forum with particularly vigorous provision for discovery of a judgment debtor's assets would be favored, as would a forum with a particularly narrow class of property exempt from execution.

4. It may appear that the location of assets should be a major choice-of-forum concern in any suit for a money judgment. This is often true in practice. But it is unwise to give overriding weight to the location of assets if that dictates a choice of forum other than the forum that will apply the most favorable law to the litigation of the merits of the cause of action. Although the enforcement of a foreign judgment is generally more complicated than the enforcement of a domestic judgment, the full faith and credit clause guarantees eventual payment wherever assets may later be found. Wise counsel will thus initiate suit in the forum that will apply the most favorable law to the dispute. Once a judgment worth enforcing has been obtained, a solid knowledge of basic enforcement procedures and good research into local variations will suffice to ensure the ultimate enforcement of the judgment.

12

PRECLUSION DOCTRINES— RES JUDICATA AND COLLATERAL ESTOPPEL

▶ ## CHAPTER SUMMARY

PRECLUSION DOCTRINES : RES JUDICATA AND COLLATERAL ESTOPPEL

INTRODUCTION: In this chapter, we take up the preclusion doctrines of res judicata and collateral estoppel, also known as claim preclusion and issue preclusion, and sometimes referred to together simply as res judicata. These doctrines, together with stare decisis and the law of the case, make up the law of prior adjudication, that is, the effect of earlier decisions or proceedings on later litigation. The doctrine of stare decisis provides generally that a court should follow its earlier decisions and will adhere to an established principle of law where the facts are substantially the same although the parties are different. Although stare decisis is a basic principle, courts publicly depart from prior decisions from time to time when they have become obsolete or bypassed by legal developments in other areas. Res judicata — merger and bar — binds the parties to an action in later litigation between them when they previously litigated or had an opportunity to litigate the same claim or cause of action. The plaintiff's claim or cause of action is said to have merged in any judgment in the plaintiff's favor, and a judgment for the defendant bars any further litigation by the plaintiff in order to establish its claim. Collateral estoppel concerns the preclusive effect of issues actually litigated and essential to an earlier judgment involving the same parties although on a different claim or cause of action. Finally, the law of the case doctrine prevents relitigation of issues of law between the parties in the same case, is restricted to the ongoing case, and has its effect in advance of final judgment.

This chapter concentrates on the two principal preclusion doctrines, looking at their constituent elements and then dealing with the mutuality doctrine and problems of inter-system (federal/state and state/state) preclusion. Res judicata and collateral estoppel are linked in civil procedure by their reliance on the finality principle. To be effective, litigation must come to an end; the parties' dispute must be resolved so that they can go on about their business. At about the time of final judgment in a civil action, the finality principle begins to be accorded even greater weight than fairness or opportunity to litigate — the dominant principles of the Federal Rules. We have already seen this principle in action in the limited scope accorded Rule 60(b) post-judgment motions for relief and in the limited appellate review of trial courts' factual determinations. When employed properly, res judicata and collateral estoppel also protect adversaries from the vexation and expense of unnecessary litigation, conserve judicial resources, and minimize the likelihood of inconsistent decisions.

Some version of these finality doctrines is found in all procedural systems, and the two elements found in American practice can be traced back to Roman and Germanic law. Preclusion doctrines developed in England and the United States (and continue to develop) principally through case law, not statutes. This common law characteristic makes them quite different from most procedural law studied so far. Although finality is essential to our procedural system, its application through res judicata and collateral estoppel creates problems when it clashes directly with the fairness principle. If a judgment is to be truly final, then it must be preserved even though later found to be "wrong" or "unfair" to the parties. Thus the central problem in this area — one that has no "solution" — is how and when we should qualify the finality of a judgment in the interest of fairness.

RES JUDICATA AS A GENERAL RULE

I. RES JUDICATA AS A GENERAL RULE MAY BE DEFINED AS FOLLOWS: A VALID, FINAL JUDGMENT, RENDERED ON THE MERITS, CONSTITUTES AN ABSOLUTE BAR TO A SUBSEQUENT ACTION BETWEEN THE SAME PARTIES OR THOSE IN PRIVITY WITH THEM, UPON THE SAME CLAIM OR DEMAND.

A. Res judicata operates to bind the parties both as to issues actually litigated and determined in the first suit, and as to those grounds or issues that might have been, but were not, actually raised and decided in that action. The first judgment, when final and on the merits, thus puts an end to the whole cause of action. *See Saylor v. Lindsley*, 391 F.2d 965 (2d Cir. 1968).

B. Although the application of res judicata requires fulfillment of each of the conditions in the doctrine, the crucial question in most instances is whether the second action between the parties is "upon the same claim or demand," that is, the same cause of action as the first.

If the claim or cause of action is the same, res judicata may apply; if the claim or cause of action is different, only collateral estoppel may be involved.

C. **The scope or definition of a "claim" or "cause of action" was traditionally highly conceptual. The leading contending definitions were the primary right theory, the single wrongful act theory, and the same evidence theory. The leading modern view espouses a transactional rather than a conceptual test.**

1. Under the primary right theory, if the defendant infringes different primary rights of the plaintiff, even by the same act, each primary right infringed is the basis for a different cause of action. Under this theory, the injury to a person and the injury to that person's vehicle or other chattels are infringements of distinct rights. Thus, personal and property inquiries as a result of a single automobile accident would lead to at least two different causes of action.

2. A second contender for defining claim or cause of action is the single wrongful act doctrine. When a single wrongful act by the defendant causes a series of injuries or infringes different rights, the injured party has only a single cause of action based on the single wrongful act by the defendant, although a variety of damages may be recovered.

3. A third conceptual theory is the same evidence theory.

   a. Under this theory, when two potentially distinct claims require for their proof the same evidentiary elements or substantially same evidentiary elements, they comprise a single claim or cause of action.

   b. The first *Restatement of Judgments* used the same-evidence test, declaring that claims are the same "if the evidence needed to sustain the second action would have sustained the first action."

4. The current *Restatement (Second) of Judgments* has abandoned the same-evidence test and uses a transactional test.

   a. Under its approach, a valid and final judgment on any given claim extinguishes all rights of the plaintiff to remedies against the defendant "with respect to all or any part of the transaction, or series of connected transactions, out of with the action arose." *Restatement (Second)* § 24(1).

   b. The *Restatement (Second)* defines a transaction pragmatically: "What factual grouping constitutes a 'transaction,' and what groupings constitutes a 'series,' are to be determined pragmatically, giving weight to such considerations as whether the facts are related in time, space, origin or a motivation, whether they form a convenient trial unit, and whether their treatment as a unit conforms to the parties' expectations or business understanding or usage." § 24(2).

   c. There is an obvious element of circularity in this definition: a transaction is what is convenient to treat as a transaction in business or practice.

      (1) But the idea is a sound one. Modern litigation allows for generous joinder of claims and parties in order to resolve all elements of what is in effect a single dispute among the parties. Where the joinder rules permit bringing a variety of distinctive legal claims or demands as part of a single case or controversy, it is appropriate for res judicata to bar a plaintiff who fails to include all the elements that might reasonably be included in the litigation.

      (2) Moreover, the definition gains coherence from its parallels in federal claim and party joinder rules that employ a transactional or logical relationship test. *See* Chapter 6.

(3) The rule is also flexible in that it allows for limitations on the scope of res judicata based upon its definition of a claim when it would be inconvenient or inappropriate to expect elements to be tried together.

(4) The approach of the *Restatement (Second)* gives greater scope to claim preclusion or res judicata than do the other, more limited theories.

(5) The trend in the lower courts today and the modern trend overall appears to be adoption of a more broadly preclusive transactional test and a movement away from the use of the more formalized "same primary right" or "wrongful act" tests. Courts today are much more willing than in previous years to invoke res judicata to ban relitigation of issues in a second suit that could have been brought in the first suit.

Example: A modern court is unlikely to allow a plaintiff to make claims of denial of due process and taking of its property in a second suit when that same plaintiff filed a series of claims objecting to the zoning laws or regulation of the use of its property in an earlier proceeding. The court's reasoning would be that the due process or constitutional claims might have been brought in the earlier action and that the plaintiff is effectively splitting her claim or cause of action and attempting to gain two bites at the apple despite the very distinctive legal bases for the claims. *See O'Brien v. City of Syracuse*, 54 N.Y.2d 353.

D. **Although the rules of res judicata are applicable to counterclaims, they raise a number of distinctive issues in this area.**

1. Most regulation of the preclusive effect of counterclaims is by rule.

   a. Federal Rule 13(a) bars a defending party from later asserting as an original claim a matter that it could have brought by means of a counterclaim and which is transactionally related to the plaintiff's original claim against it. (The doctrine of compulsory counterclaims is covered in detail in Chapter 6.)

   b. A number of states, however, do not have compulsory counterclaim rules or do not have rules as broad as the federal rule. Thus the issue arises for them whether transactionally related claims that could have been asserted defensively in an earlier action are now barred by res judicata.

      (1) Under the *Restatement (Second)* approach, a defendant who could have brought a claim as a counterclaim but who has failed to do so is precluded from later making that claim only if:

         (a) the counterclaim is required to be interposed by a compulsory counterclaim statute or rule of court, or

         (b) "the relationship between the counterclaim and the plaintiff's claim is such that successful prosecution of the second action would nullify the initial judgment or would impair rights established in the initial action."

      (2) This rule might come into play in a case involving a franchisor's suit to collect damages under its contract with a franchisee for breach by the franchisee of its obligations to the franchisor. If the franchisee in a later action brings an antitrust action against the franchisor challenging the franchisor's actions that led to the first suit for contract damages as the basis of the antitrust complaint, this antitrust claim would be barred under the approach of the *Restatement (Second)*, as it would seek to undo the effect of or undermine the judgment obtained by plaintiff in the first suit.

2. Even if there is no res judicata bar for failure to make a counterclaim, the defendant is required to raise all defenses it has to the plaintiff's claim, and, failing to do so, the defendant cannot later assert those same defenses against the plaintiff in an action to enforce the

judgment. Defenses actually litigated and decided against the defendant are precluded even when plaintiff sues on a different, but related, claim.

3. In the absence of a compulsory counterclaim rule, when facts form the basis both of a defense and a counterclaim, the defendant's failure to allege those facts either as a defense or a counterclaim does not preclude the defendant from relying on them in a later action against the plaintiff.

E. The res judicata bar operates only between the same parties to the first and second suits.

1. When new parties are involved on either side in a second litigation, res judicata will be unavailable for the new parties because of the general rule that each independent party has its own claim or cause of action. Thus, by definition, new parties ordinarily mean new causes of action.

2. However, in some instances the names of the parties are the same but res judicata will not apply, and in some instances the names of the parties are different but res judicata will apply.

   a. The general rule is well stated by the *Restatement (Second) of Judgments* § 34. It provides:

      (1) "A person who is named as a party to an action and subjected to the jurisdiction of the court is a party to the action."

      (2) "A party is bound by and entitled to the benefits of the rules of res judicata with respect to determinations made while ... a party [with exceptions];" and

      (3) "A person who is not a party to an action is not bound by or entitled to the benefits of the rules of res judicata [with exceptions]."

   b. That is, the named parties are bound by the judgment and unnamed parties are not bound, with exceptions. Exceptions occur in the following circumstances:

      (1) Where a person has more than one legal capacity.

         Example: Trustees are bound only when a they appear in both actions in the same capacity. Thus a trustee might be sued individually or in her capacity as trustee for the *XYZ* trust. The trustee individually and the trustee as trustee are two different parties although the names may be the same. *Restatement (Second)* § 36.

      (2) Nominal parties to litigation are not ordinarily bound by the judgment. Thus, in actions involving extraordinary writs, the district court or a named judge is a nominal party but is not bound in a res judicata sense by the judgment. *Restatement (Second)* § 37.

      (3) The parties' adversarial position may affect the binding effect of the judgment on them. Parties must have been adversaries in order to be bound by judgments in favor of one or the other. Co-parties are not automatically bound by a judgment in litigation between them and their actual adversaries unless a claim is made between the co-parties. They may not be bound even though they litigated adverse positions in the prior action. *Restatement (Second)* § 38.

      (4) The corollary to this rule is that the only persons who are bound by a judgment are those parties who have actually litigated the prior action as formally named parties. Due process normally limits the binding effect of judgments to the formal parties, except that:

         (a) Persons whose interests have been represented by another party authorized to act on their behalf are bound by the results of the litigation. *Restatement (Second)* § 41.

(b) This rule has been extended to situations in which nominal parties litigate on behalf of another party that actually controls the formal party. The controlling person will be bound in the litigation as well as the nominal party. *See Montana v. United States*, 440 U.S. 147 (1979).

(c) Certain substantive legal relationships that come under the general heading of "privity" bind non-parties when those non-parties are in privity with a named and litigating party.

(1) Understood practically, the privity rules translate as: To say that *X* is in privity with *P* in this context is simply to say that the relation between them is such that the judgment involving *P* may justify precluding *X* because of the relationship between them.

(2) Privity relationships are found primarily in family situations where husbands and wives may be in privity with one another or their children; in contract and property relationships; in organizational relationships; and in the indemnity-indemnitor relationship. *See Restatement (Second)* § 41.

F. Res judicata requires a final judgment. *Restatement (Second)* § 13.

1. No res judicata effect arises until there has been a final judgment resolving all of the claim or claims between the two particular parties to that piece of litigation.

2. Thus, a partial summary judgment or even verdict in favor of one party is not a judgment until the final judgment has been entered. We discuss the formal entry of judgment in Chapter 11.

3. The more interesting issue arises when the judgment is appealed. The prevailing rule is that an appeal does not suspend the finality of the judgment, although a court considering the res judicata bar may be reluctant to impose it pending appeal, which may, after all, upset the underlying judgment.

G. The final requirement for application of res judicata is that the judgment be on the merits of the claim or cause of action.

1. This requirement is related to the final judgment rule. It is easy to see that the "typical" judgment after full litigation of plaintiff's claim and a jury verdict for plaintiff or for defendant is on the merits and fully preclusive. But what about termination of the litigation before a trial of disputed facts? When is that "on the merits?"

2. Earlier code pleading systems treated judgments resulting from demurrers by the defendant and even nonsuit by motion of defendant after plaintiff's case in chief as not on the merits. The demurrer only determined that the complaint was insufficient; not that the plaintiff's claim or cause of action lacked merit.

3. This approach makes little sense today, especially in federal court with notice pleading, liberal opportunity to amend, and generous discovery. Instead, the modern federal approach begins with Rule 41.

a. Under Rule 41(a), voluntary dismissals by the plaintiff are not on the merits or with prejudice unless the court specifies.

b. Involuntary dismissals under Rule 41(b) are all on the merits except dismissals for lack of jurisdiction, dismissals for improper venue, dismissals for failure to join a party under Rule 19, and when the court in its order for dismissal "otherwise specifies."

(1) In federal court when defendant succeeds in having a plaintiff's claim dismissed for failure to state a claim on which relief can be granted [Rule 12(b)(6)], that dismissal, if granted without leave to amend, must be based on a finding by the district court that under no state of facts which plaintiff would be entitled to prove given the allegations of the complaint would plaintiff be entitled to any relief. (*See*

the discussion in Chapter 5 of the rule of *Conley v. Gibson*.) Thus involuntary dismissals in federal court, except those specified in Rule 41(b), will be effectively on the merits.

(2) A better overall approach to this requirement is one that asks: What was the basis for the court's dismissal of the case short of a fully litigated final judgment?

    (a) This should reveal whether the dismissal indeed amounted to an adjudication that the claim lacked any merit.

    (b) On the other hand, dismissals, for example, for lack of personal jurisdiction over a party, operate only to adjudicate that particular issue — that there is no jurisdiction over that defendant — and do not operate on the merits.

    (c) Likewise, federal court dismissals under other rules, for example, dismissals for failure to comply with the court's discovery orders under Rule 37(a)-(b), ought to be given res judicata effect if the appropriate sanction — dismissal of the case — is to have any real effect.

II. COLLATERAL ESTOPPEL OR ISSUE PRECLUSION

A. **A person is "estopped" or "precluded" from relitigating an issue of law or fact if the issue was actually litigated, was necessarily determined, and was essential to a valid and final judgment entered previously in litigation to which that person was party, provided the estopped party had a full and fair opportunity and adequate incentive to litigate the issue conclusively, and subject to additional fairness constraints when the party asserting the estoppel was not a party to the prior litigation.** *See Restatement (Second) of Judgments* §§ **27-28.**

1. There are some common elements to the rules governing issue preclusion (direct and collateral estoppel) as opposed to claim preclusion (res judicata). The rules for what counts as a valid and final judgment on the merits are the same for the two doctrines, as are the rules for who are regarded as parties bound by a prior judgment.

2. In other important respects issue preclusion operates quite differently from claim preclusion.

    a. Issue preclusion applies regardless whether the previous litigation concerned the same claim or cause of action (direct estoppel) or — as is far more frequently the case — a different claim or cause of action (collateral estoppel). We focus hereafter on collateral estoppel.

    b. Issue preclusion applies to issues of fact as well as law.

    c. The issue must have been actually litigated and determined as an essential part of the prior judgment. It is not enough that the issue *could have* been litigated if in fact it was not *actually* litigated or if, although litigated, there is some doubt whether it was necessarily determined.

    d. In some circumstances in some jurisdictions "mutuality of estoppel" is not required. The party to the present litigation against whom issue preclusion is asserted must always have been party to the previous litigation in which the same issue was conclusively determined, but that party's opponent in the previous litigation need not be the same person as the opponent in the present litigation who seeks to benefit from the preclusive effect of the previous litigation.

B. **In order for collateral estoppel to bar relitigation of a given issue, the same issue must have been actually litigated in the first action, although the claims or causes of action may differ. In addition, the issue must have been both necessarily decided and essential to the outcome of the judgment.**

1. Collateral estoppel is an incomplete bar. The second suit is not barred, but issues identical to those litigated in the first suit may not be relitigated. Thus, the second litigation may be simplified or disposed of in whole or in part because of the application of collateral estoppel.

2. Collateral estoppel effect may be given only to issues that were both necessarily decided and essential to the judgment.

   a. This means that issues that could have been decided differently without affecting the result of the prior judgment will have no collateral estoppel effect in subsequent litigation.

   b. This limitation is based on solid policy. A party who has gained a victory regarding an issue not essential should not be able to take advantage of that issue in subsequent litigation because it may not have been effectively and fully litigated by the opponent, especially if the opponent or the trier of fact failed to understand that it might be of consequence in another action.

   c. Sometimes the prior judgment does not establish that a particular issue was necessarily decided. The reasoning behind the judgment may be ambiguous.

      Example: P sues D for personal injuries as a result of an automobile accident involving a collision between their cars. Assume that contributory negligence is a complete defense to plaintiff's claim; there is no comparative negligence doctrine in this jurisdiction and no compulsory counterclaim rule. D answers, denying negligence and affirmatively pleading contributory negligence by P. Evidence is presented on both issues — D's negligence and P's contributory negligence. Thus both issues have been litigated. There is a general verdict for D.

      If D now sues P for her personal injuries as a result of the same accident, can D use collateral estoppel to establish any part of her negligence claim? The answer is "no." The judgment for D in the first action could have been based on either a determination that D was not negligent or a determination that P was contributorily negligent. Since we do not know which of the two determinations was the basis for the jury's verdict, neither was necessarily decided by the judgment and neither can be used for collateral estoppel effect in subsequent litigation.

   d. Sometimes the record of the prior judgment contains a finding of fact that was actually decided in favor of one party, but that finding was not essential to the outcome of the case because it was only one of two or more alternative grounds for the judgment. There is a split of authority in this situation, but the *Restatement (Second)* adopts the position that an alternative ground cannot be given collateral estoppel effect unless it was affirmed on appeal.

      Example: Suppose the facts of the previous example are changed such that the jury in P v. D returned a special verdict form indicating that the jury found both that D was not negligent and that P was contributorily negligent. Judgment was accordingly entered for D. P appealed, and the appellate court affirmed the judgment on the ground that the finding of no negligence by D was supported by substantial evidence. The appellate court did not address the issue of P's contributory negligence. According to the *Restatement (Second),* when D sues P in the second action, D still cannot invoke collateral estoppel to bar P from contesting his (P's) negligence. The alternative special verdict that P was contributorily negligent was not essential to the prior judgment, which would have been the same whether or not P was found to be negligent.

3. Collateral estoppel requires that the same issue be involved in the first and later litigations.

   a. In many instances this is a simple question because the very same issue in all regards determines the two, for example, whether the drug X is an unsafe product, whether plaintiff P drove negligently in connection with a multi-party accident, etc.

b. When it is difficult to tell if the issue in the first action is the same as in the second, courts should be extraordinarily careful to make sure that each party, and especially the party against whom collateral estoppel is sought, had a full and effective opportunity to litigate and understood the potential consequences of an adverse finding on that "issue."

c. When in doubt, courts ought to deny collateral estoppel effect to marginal issue determinations.

d. A special variant of this problem occurs when the parties in the first action were in a different adversarial relationship than they are in the subsequent action.

(1) This happened in the case of *Schwartz v. Public Administrator*, 246 N.E.2d 725 (N.Y. 1969). The parties in the second action had not been adversaries in the first action. The first action was brought by plaintiff against defendants *D1* and *D2*. There was a verdict and judgment for plaintiff versus both defendants. In the second action, *D1* sued *D2*, and the court held that both were bound by issues determined in the first case.

(2) The *Schwartz* case is the exception. The prevailing rule is that collateral estoppel does not apply between co-parties unless they are formal adversaries, that is, there is a claim (cross-claim) between them and then only as to the issues decided as part of that cross-claim action.

C. The *Restatement (Second)* makes a series of additional exceptions to the general rules of issue preclusion. Among them are the following:

1. The party against whom preclusion is sought could not, as a matter of law, have obtained review of the judgment in the initial action.

2. The issue is one of law and (a) the two actions involve claims that are substantially unrelated, or (b) a new determination is warranted in order to take account of an intervening change in the legal context or to avoid inequitable administration of the laws.

3. A new determination is warranted by a difference in the quality or extensiveness of the procedures involved in the two courts or factors relating to the allocation of jurisdiction between them.

4. The party against whom preclusion is sought had a significantly heavier burden of persuasion with respect to the issue in the first action than in the second, or the burden has shifted to its adversary, or the adversary had a significantly different burden.

5. There is a clear and convincing need for a new determination of the issue (a) because of the potential adverse impact of the determination on the public interest or the interest of persons not themselves parties in the initial action, (b) because it was insufficiently foreseeable at the time of the initial action that the issues would arise in the context of a subsequent action or (c) because the party sought to be precluded as a result of the conduct of its adversary or otherwise did not have an adequate opportunity or incentive to obtain a full and fair adjudication in the initial action.

a. At a minimum, a full and fair opportunity to litigate requires that the party have been represented in the first litigation.

b. The precluded party should not have had to labor under procedural disadvantages (for example, limited opportunities to present evidence; however, absence of right to a jury trial does not disqualify the litigation under the rule of *Parklane Hosiery v. Shore, infra*), or have too little apparently at risk to conduct a full litigation, or be at a severe practical disadvantage due to an adversary's choice of forum. This prevents an opponent from setting her adversary up, winning, and then seeking devastating preclusion effects.

c. The court considering preclusion has discretion to refuse to allow preclusion whenever the overall effect would be unfair.

D. The Mutuality Doctrine

1. At common law, collateral estoppel and res judicata required that the parties to the second action be the same or in privity with the parties to the first action.

    a. This requirement is virtually inescapable for res judicata because res judicata applies only when the same claim or cause of action is involved, and different parties almost always mean different claims or causes of action.

    b. However, this is not so for collateral estoppel. Because collateral estoppel is available when a second action is on a different claim or cause of action, it is logically possible to use collateral estoppel in the second suit even when the parties in the second suit are different from those in the first.

    c. In particular, it may seem reasonable to apply collateral estoppel *against* anyone who was a party to the first action even if the party taking advantage of collateral estoppel did not participate in the first action. After all, the "victim" of collateral estoppel would have had a full and fair opportunity to litigate the matter regardless of whether the beneficiary participated, assuming that there was an effective adversary.

    d. On the other hand, fairness and due process forbid using collateral estoppel against one who was not a party (or in privity with a party) to the first action, because such a person could not have had a full and fair opportunity to litigate the issue.

    e. Nevertheless, the common law took the view that what was good for the goose was good for the gander: if a party seeking to take advantage of collateral estoppel could not have been its victim had the action come out differently, it would not be right to let that party take advantage of the result in its favor. This is the doctrine of "mutuality of estoppel."

    Example: If *P*, the owner of a patent, sues Acme claiming Acme infringed its patent, and Acme defends on the grounds that *P*'s patent is invalid and wins on that ground, *P* can still sue Beta for infringement of the same patent, and Beta cannot (because of the mutuality rule) assert collateral estoppel to establish that *P*'s patent is invalid. Had *P* won the suit against Acme, *P* could not use those findings against Beta in the second suit because Beta had not its day in court. Since *P* could not use the first judgment had *P* won, under the doctrine of mutuality, *P* is not bound by the loss.

2. The decline of the mutuality doctrine

    a. *Bernhard v. Bank of America*, 19 Cal.2d 807 (1942), marked the first major retreat from the mutuality doctrine.

        (1) In the first suit, Bernhard as a beneficiary of the estate sued the executor of the estate for failing to include certain funds in his accounting for the assets of the estate. Bernhard lost. Bernhard then became the administratrix of the estate, and, in that capacity, sued the bank in the second lawsuit, claiming that the bank was indebted to the estate for releasing those same funds without proper authority. The bank argued that the question of whether the funds were a part of the estate had been determined adversely to Bernhard in the first suit. The bank had not been a party to the first suit, thus it could not have been bound by any determination in that suit whether in favor of Bernhard or the defendant. Since the parties were different in the second suit, the mutuality rule would have prevented application of collateral estoppel. However, the California Supreme Court held that if the bank could not take advantage of the first litigation defensively against Bernhard's claim, Bernhard would be able to continue to litigate her claim until she ran out of new potential defendants to sue. "[N]o satisfactory rationalization has been advanced

for the requirement of mutuality," and therefore the court allowed the bank to take advantage of collateral estoppel against Bernhard in the second suit.

    (2) *Bernhard* soon began to influence other states, and, by the early 1970's, a new majority had emerged that allowed at least the defensive use of collateral estoppel absent the mutuality rule. The mutuality rule's decline was hastened when the Supreme Court turned to the question in two leading decisions in the 1970's.

b. In *Blonder-Tongue Laboratories, Inc. v. University of Illinois Foundation*, 402 U.S. 313 (1971), the Supreme Court rejected the mutuality doctrine as a matter of federal practice when collateral estoppel is used in a defensive posture. *Blonder-Tongue* held that an earlier decision against the plaintiff asserting a claim of patent infringement, finding that the patent was invalid, binds that same plaintiff in a subsequent infringement action against a second defendant based on the same patent, at least where plaintiff had chosen its forum and defendant in the first litigation. Thus the defending party in the second suit could use collateral estoppel although as a non-party it could not have been bound by collateral estoppel if plaintiff had prevailed in the first suit.

c. The Supreme Court addressed the more controversial use of offensive non-mutual collateral estoppel in *Parklane Hosiery Co. v. Shore*, 439 U.S. 322 (1979). *Parklane* involved the application of collateral estoppel in a shareholders' class action brought against Parklane alleging that Parklane had issued a materially false and misleading proxy statement in connection with a merger. Plaintiffs were seeking damages or a rescission of the merger and sought to rely on a previous litigation between Parklane Hosiery and the Securities Exchange Commission (SEC). The SEC action was actually begun after the shareholders' suit was filed although it was the first concluded. In it the SEC sued Parklane on the same claims of a misleading proxy statement requesting solely injunctive relief. After a four-day court trial, the district court had found the proxy statement false and misleading as alleged and entered a declaratory judgment in favor of the SEC. Shore, one of the plaintiffs in the shareholders' suit, then moved for partial summary judgment, asserting that Parklane was collaterally estopped from relitigating the issues decided against it in the SEC action. The Supreme Court held that Parklane was indeed collaterally estoppel from denying liability to Shore.

    (1) The Court first noted that the *Parklane Hosiery* situation represented the offensive, rather than defensive, use of collateral estoppel. Parklane was not asserting collateral estoppel in order to defend itself. Rather, Shore, a plaintiff, was seeking to use Parklane's earlier defeat in the SEC action against it in order to establish his own claim. Nevertheless, the Court was convinced that it was appropriate to abandon the mutuality rule in this instance as well. The Court, relying on *Blonder-Tongue, supra*, noted that a party is not entitled to more than "one full and fair opportunity for judicial resolution of the same issue."

        (a) However, the Court recognized that offensive use of collateral estoppel did not share all the virtues that its defensive use exhibits.

            (i) There is no similar savings of time or judicial economy because there is a second suit in which collateral estoppel is used in order to establish a new claim.

            (ii) The Court also noted its use could possibly be unfair to a defendant who in the first litigation may not have asserted its claims or rights as forcefully as it could due to small stakes, unforeseeable later use, inconsistencies in judgments, or lack of procedural opportunities.

        (b) Thus the Court held that the decision to apply collateral estoppel offensively lacking mutuality should be within the trial court's discretion. In particular, its use should not be allowed where the plaintiff in the second suit seeking to take advantage of collateral estoppel could easily have joined in the first suit or when its use would otherwise be unfair to the defendant.

(2) In *Parklane* itself, plaintiff almost certainly could not have joined in the earlier SEC action; the first suit was a significant one with substantial implications foreseeable at the time; there was no inconsistency — no other intervening suits had been decided in a different manner — and there were no procedural advantages favorable to Parklane in the second suit (the Court holding that the presence or absence of a jury was a neutral factor).

(3) Thus today the rule in federal court and the predominant rule in the states is that collateral estoppel may be used both offensively and defensively by a party who would not have been bound or was not bound by the first litigation. Remember, however, that collateral estoppel may not be used against a party who was not given a full and fair chance to litigate in the first suit.

d. Currently, the availability of non-mutual collateral estoppel often turns on a case-by-case evaluation of a series of factors including: (a) which party had an opportunity to choose the initial forum and opponent, (b) possible procedural disadvantages in the first suit to the party against whom collateral estoppel will be used, (c) lack of foreseeability of subsequent litigation, and (d) whether a plaintiff seeking to take advantage of collateral estoppel has slept on her rights by failing to join in the earlier litigation.

3. Following the *Bernhard* rule, the *Restatement (Second) of Judgments* § 29 now provides: "[A] party precluded from litigating an issue with an opposing party ... is also precluded from doing so with another person unless the fact that he lacked full and fair opportunity to litigate the issue in the first action or other circumstances justify affording him an opportunity to relitigate the issue." The *Restatement (Second)* has come full circle from the first *Restatement* which had accepted in total the mutuality rule.

E. **Collateral estoppel asserted against the government, especially the federal government, also has additional limitations.**

1. In *United States v. Mendoza*, 464 U.S. 154 (1984), the Supreme Court rejected the use of non-mutual offensive collateral estoppel against the United States.

a. In *Mendoza*, Filipinos who had served in the United States armed forces in World War II sought to take advantage of a victory in an earlier suit by a similarly situated Filipino veteran who had won a judgment against the United States holding him entitled to obtain U.S. citizenship.

b. The Court rejected collateral estoppel on the ground that the government needs more flexibility on issues of substantial public importance to avoid the risk of having it bound by any particular case, especially where the government might choose not to appeal an individual instance. The government may need to change its position or reconsider it in light of later-arising events, and thus the typical use of collateral estoppel is not appropriate.

2. However, in a companion case, *United States v. Stauffer Chemical Co.*, 464 U.S. 165 (1984), the Court allowed mutual defensive collateral estoppel to bind the United States in its effort to relitigate the question of whether private investigators could constitute authorized representatives of the United States for purposes of Clean Air Act inspections.

a. The United States had lost this claim against Stauffer Chemical Co. in an earlier suit and now sought to relitigate it in a second suit between the same parties although involving a different facility.

b.   The Court thus indicated that specific fact-based decisions will retain their collateral estoppel consequences even when the government is involved, at least where the party seeking to estop the government was also party to the prior litigation.

III.   UNIQUE PROBLEMS OF INTER-SYSTEM PRECLUSION

A.   **Since the rules of preclusion are common law rules, each court system will have its own, partially idiosyncratic system of preclusion. This means that each of the states and the federal system has its own system of preclusion. Problems are relatively simple when a federal court judgment is applied to other federal court proceedings and when a state court judgment is applied to other proceedings within the same state. However, when inter-system preclusion is sought, the problems are more complex.**

B.   **Interstate Enforcement of Sister-state Judgments. The United States Constitution's full faith and credit clause and the accompanying full faith and credit statute, 28 U.S.C. § 1738, require that each state give full faith and credit to the public acts, records, and judicial proceedings of every other state.**

1.   In particular, the full faith and credit statute requires that the states give *"the same"* preclusive effect to sister-state judgments that the judgments would receive in their home states.

2.   For example, even if state *A* disagrees with *Bernhard* and does not allow non-mutual collateral estoppel, state *A* must give non-mutual preclusive effect to a judgment from state *B* which would be given preclusive effect in state *B* because state *B* follows *Bernhard* and permits non-mutual collateral estoppel. Even though state *A* is the state enforcing the judgment, the law of state *B* determines what effect state *A* must give a state *B* judgment.

C.   **Preclusive Effect of State Court Judgments in Federal Court. The Supreme Court has read the full faith and credit statute as requiring that the federal courts must enforce the judgments of state courts and give them the same preclusive effect that the states from which the judgments emerged would give them.** *Allen v. McCurry*, **449 U.S. 90 (1980). Thus the federal courts have the same duty as a state court to give effect to a sister-state judgment. The federal court applying the judgment must give it** *the same* **preclusive effect as it would have received in the place where originally rendered.** *See Marrese v. American Academy of Orthopedic Surgeons,* **470 U.S. 373 (1985).**

D.   **Preclusive Effect of Federal Judgments in State Court. This area is unregulated by statute, but the federal courts have, through a series of decisions, read the Supremacy Clause of the Constitution to require states to give preclusive effect to federal court judgments.**

E.   **Preclusive Effect of Federal Judgments in Federal Court. Federal courts must give effect to the judgments of other federal courts by virtue of the federal court registration statute, 28 U.S.C. § 1963.**

1.   This section provides that a judgment "for the recovery of money or other property" registered in a court different from the one in which the judgment was rendered "shall have the same effect" as if it had been rendered where registered.

2.   This statute is ordinarily read as allowing the federal circuit in which the judgment is registered to determine the preclusive effect of that judgment according to its own current interpretation when that interpretation differs from that of the circuit from which the judgment originated.

3.   The Supreme Court's common law preclusion doctrines require federal courts to give preclusive effect to previous federal judgments even when the previous judgment has not been registered.

APPENDIX

▶ ## CONTENTS

EXAM PREPARATION
PART 1

General Preparation: The following comments are applicable to any standard law school examination and are included by way of general preparation guidelines.

1. Good exam preparation begins with regular attendance of your law school classes, preparation for those classes, and review throughout the semester as time permits. There is no better way to understand what matters your professor believes are of primary importance or your professor's preferred approach to those matters than by attending the classes and taking notes. Outlines and study guides — even *Casenote Law Outlines* — in themselves are inadequate exam preparation. They always must be supplemented by your understanding of the emphasis of that particular course and instructor.

2. Assuming you have completed your initial preparations for the course and reviewed your outlines, do not continue to study until late the night before the examination. This only tends to increase pre-exam jitters.

3. Get plenty of sleep the night before the exam. You will do your best work if you arrive for the examination fresh and well-rested.

4. Allow for extra time to arrive at the examination site. Allow for unexpected traffic so that you don't arrive with your stomach in a knot, and/or worse yet, late.

5. Be on time. You need to maximize the time that is available. Don't put yourself at an automatic disadvantage by being late.

6. Resist the temptation to engage in last-minute conversations about the subject matter of the exam with your classmates. More often than not, you will end up convincing yourself that you don't adequately understand something for which you are fully prepared.

7. When you have received the examination, be careful to follow all of the procedural rules of the particular school and particular instructor regarding putting your name or examination number on each of the blue books or answer sheets and any other preliminary material. Be sure you understand the format of the particular examination you are about to take.

8. READ THE QUESTION. READ THE QUESTION. READ THE QUESTION. First, skim the question to get an overall sense of what is being asked. Then go back and read the question carefully. Finally, read the question a third time, jotting notes in the margin of points to cover in your answer. Students regularly lose points by failing to read the question carefully, either by addressing a non-existent issue or by failing to address a true issue. Be sure to read with great care the "call" of the question. Especially in civil procedure examinations, you are likely to receive directions to concentrate on issues involving only certain parties, or only specified rulings of the court, and not to address generally all of the issues available.

9. Very briefly outline your answer to the question. Outlining your answer will make your response more organized, will keep you on track, and will insure you don't forget to cover anything. Particularly for civil procedure questions that can cover a variety of subject matter areas, go through a mental checklist in creating your outline:

   a. Are there issues of jurisdiction or choice of forum?

   b. Are there pleading issues?

   c. Are there joinder of party and claim issues?

   d. Are there discovery issues?

   e. Are there pre-trial motion and summary judgment issues?

   f. Are there jury trial issues?

g. Are there post-trial or appeal issues?

h. Are there *Erie* issues?

i. Are there res judicata/collateral estoppel issues?

10. Write out your answer to the question, following your outline and making generous use of the facts provided. *Merely stating the rule of law is not enough.* You must *apply* the rule of law to the facts provided and explain the considerations that go into your analysis. If the result is clear, say so and explain why. If there are insufficient facts or other reasons why the result is *not* clear, say so, explain why, and explore the consequences of the alternative results.

11. Do not short-circuit your answers or analysis by reaching a conclusion that prevents you from exploring likely additional issues. For example, a question considering several jurisdictional issues could be short circuited if you conclude early in your answer that the court lacks subject matter jurisdiction over the claim or cause of action. If you reach this conclusion and then fail to discuss potential issues of personal jurisdiction, venue, or forum non conveniens, you may have discussed only one-third of the issues raised by the question. Unless you are satisfied that your instructor meant for you to stop when you reached that initial conclusion, always go on to consider the additional issues that may follow. It is unlikely that any issue can be resolved so definitively so as to cut off discussion and analysis of subjects that form important additional parts of the course during that term or semester.

12. BUDGET YOUR TIME. If your professor provides the weights or value for each question, budget your time accordingly. If your professor does not, assume each question is of equal weight. When the time budgeted for a question runs out, STOP and proceed to the next question. Achieving a perfect score on the first question will still result in a failing grade if you never begin the second question.

13. If you complete all your answers before the allotted time, review your responses and include any additional analysis you may believe enhances your answers.

PART 2: Specific Aids in Answering Civil Procedure Questions

1. Civil Procedure is full of rules, some, but not all, of which are related to one another and frequently come in discreet packages or groupings for purposes of analysis. The major groupings in the course are illustrated in paragraph 9 above. Exams at the conclusion of one semester of a two-semester course will often include a limited group of these topics, and your instructor may even rule some topics out as potential exam questions. It is useful to start by considering within which of the major groupings the question under consideration falls.

2. Within the general subject matter groupings of civil procedure, you should be careful to explore all the available alternatives. For example, within the broad subject matter of jurisdiction or choice of forum are the distinct areas of subject matter jurisdiction, personal jurisdiction over *each* of the parties, service of process and other notice issues, venue, forum non conveniens, and, for some professors, *Erie* issues. A full treatment of choice of forum or jurisdiction issues requires review of each of these subsections in answering your question. Similar distinctive sub-areas occur in discovery, which involves general topics spanning the entire discovery area — scope of discovery, exceptions to discovery and sanctions — and specific issues for each of the major discovery devices — the deposition, interrogatories, request for admissions, etc. Joinder issues raise a variety of joinder subissues. Be sure to consider joinder of parties and joinder of claims, compulsory joinder and permissive joinder, and all of the joinder possibilities available under the particular rules system; for example, in the federal system there are issues of co-parties, joinder of third parties, intervention, impleader, interpleader, and the like. The area of jury trial includes not just the right to jury trial and the question of waiver of jury trial but also issues involving the use and propriety of summary judgments, directed verdicts, judgments notwithstanding the verdict, motions for a new trial, and extraordinary relief from judgments under Rule 60(b).

3. Besides understanding each of the major groupings and sub-groupings that it contains, certain areas of civil procedure naturally work well together. Questions involving the joinder of additional claims and parties easily raise issues in the area of subject matter and personal jurisdiction. Joinder of an additional claim in federal court requires a subject matter jurisdiction basis for that claim and therefore may require consideration of the doctrines of diversity of citizenship, federal question jurisdiction, pendent jurisdiction, and ancillary jurisdiction. Adding additional parties usually requires that personal jurisdiction is available over those parties and thus raises all of the minimum contacts and notice issues involved in those areas. In the area of jury trial, the motions for summary judgment, directed verdict, judgment notwithstanding the verdict, and new trial based on a verdict against the great weight of the evidence are all joined by versions of a single standard (although it varies) for the sufficiency of the evidence and when the judge can intervene in an issue usually for the jury. These issues may even include earlier pre-trial motions, for example, the motion to dismiss and its variant of this same standard as part of the overall issue of when a claim is inadequate to support any judgment in favor of a party.

4. Some issues should jump at anyone reading a question. A long description of a given potential defendant or party's connections to the forum and scope of business dealings is an obvious invitation to discuss issues of personal jurisdiction and possibly subject matter jurisdiction and notice and, less likely, issues of joinder. If your course involves a study of the federal rules and the facts present a case in state court, very likely you're going to have to deal with the issues of removal and *Erie* questions. *Erie* questions also come up whenever the basis for federal jurisdiction is dependent upon or uses state law — especially diversity of citizenship, pendent, and ancillary jurisdiction. Pleading questions almost always require some reference, usually verbatim quotations from a complaint, answer, or other pleading, unless you are explicitly asked to draft one. Questions concerning the potential desirability of a class action are raised whenever there is a large number of potential parties on one side or another of the issue, and often allow the instructor to test on a variety of joinder devices because a class action under Rule 23(b)(3) must be superior to other available forms of relief. Finally, issues of preclusion — res judicata and collateral estoppel — are raised in questions when there has been an earlier litigation or there are two pieces of litigation involving at least some of the same parties. Although the variants can, of course, get complicated, if you keep your wits about you and your eyes open, most of the issues should be apparent, and your success or failure on the examination is more likely to be a product of your ability to marshal the facts under the law and make creative and thoughtful use of the existing materials to develop your positions or conclusions for a given question.

5. Use of the material in the *Casenote Law Outline* should help organize your material for the exam, should provide a ready checklist for considering issues under each of the questions, and in several areas provide a step-by-step analysis that can guide you through questions and some of the most difficult parts of the material. See especially the approach we advocate in considering questions of personal jurisdiction — minimum contacts; the analysis of increasing complexity in considering the issue of amendments to pleadings; and the analysis for class action issues regarding the propriety of maintaining a class action.

PART 3: Sample Questions and Answers

General introduction: This is a timed, open-book practice examination. You may use your casebook, most recent FRCP Supplement, Supplemental Materials, class handouts, your notes and your personal (non-commercial) outlines. Read each question carefully before answering. If you believe additional information is necessary to discuss any of the issues, indicate what additional information is necessary and why it is necessary.

Question I

(90 minutes)

Great Expectations ("GE"), a Delaware corporation, is a franchised chain of videodating services with 35 offices and 90,000 member-clients scattered throughout the United States and Canada. Potential GE clients make an appointment with one of the franchise offices where they are confidentially interviewed by trained counselors. If they are accepted as clients, they make a videotape which is sent to other clients who appear suitable as dating "matches." Clients pay a one-time fee of $1,500 and are charged $250 a month as long as they remain members of the service. Johnny Jones of Davis owns one of GE's franchises, "Yolo Great Expectations" (YGE), that operates in Woodland, Yolo County, California. In July 1989, Kathleen Othler, a YGE salesperson at the Woodland office, was fired by that franchise. She sued YGE and Jones in Sacramento Superior Court for wrongful discharge, claiming she was fired because she objected to an alleged GE policy that either allowed or encouraged GE employees to eavesdrop on prospective client interviewees. After limited discovery by both sides, the Sacramento judge granted YGE's and Jones' motions for partial summary judgment finding that (following California's *Foley* case): (1) Othler's discharge for objecting to GE's eavesdropping policy could not be the basis for a tortious wrongful discharge claim; and (2) her only possible remedy is breach of an implied-in-fact contract promise to discharge her only for good cause. Othler has appealed from the partial summary judgment.

Meanwhile, in April 1990, William Parker, a Woodland resident and YGE client, filed a class action lawsuit in Yolo County Superior Court on behalf of "all GE clients whose privacy has been invaded by GE employees who illegally listened to intimate details of the individuals' psychological and sexual disappointments and desires." Parker claims the eavesdropping violated California state law protecting confidential conversations. His suit seeks $3,000 for each alleged incident, plus other, unspecified damages. It also seeks a court order prohibiting GE from eavesdropping and recording private conversations with prospective clients. It names as defendants, Allen Ultimate, the founder and president of GE, Johnny Jones, YGE, and Does I-XX. Ultimate, an Ohio citizen, successfully removed Parker's action to U.S. District Court for the Eastern District of California. [Do not discuss the propriety of this removal!] In an affidavit filed in the Othler suit, Ultimate has denied that any of the practices at his franchises were illegal. In response to reporters' questions about Parker's suit, Ultimate has stated the Woodland office had listened to and recorded interviews with prospective clients but denies it is a companywide policy. He denied these practices occurred elsewhere, including the three offices he owns in Los Angeles, and he claims any such practices stopped after the Othler suit was filed.

Following removal, Parker served a discovery request on all defendants, asking them to produce: (1) all copies, tapes or transcripts of any kind of member-client interviews held at the Woodland YGE office; (2) all client records from the Woodland YGE office; (3) the names of all GE employees who eavesdropped on member-client interviews at any GE office; (4) copies of all discovery by either party in *Othler v. Jones & YGE;* and (5) any internal GE reports on the subject of eavesdropping on member-client interviews.

All defendants ignored these requests and moved instead to dismiss Parker's action for improper joinder of parties and as precluded by *Othler v. Jones & YGE.* Parker responded by requesting judgment be entered against defendants for failure to respond to the discovery requests and on the basis of *Othler v. Jones & YGE.* How should the court resolve these conflicting requests? Discuss fully.

Question II

(90 minutes)

In October 1989, Linda Paulson applied for a position as "Animal Technician — Large Animal Feed and Bedding" with the U.C. Davis Veterinary Medicine Teaching Hospital, through the Campus Employment Office. The job description stated: "($1,687-1,983 mo.) Removes animal waste from large animal stalls and replaces soiled bedding material." No special requirements were listed. She filled out a standard employment form asking her about her background and education. When asked to state any "Special Qualifications you have for this Position," Paulson, a U.C. Santa Cruz graduate who had majored in English Literature, wrote "Amateur gardener; own two large dogs."

Paulson was told she would hear about her application in two to three weeks. Four days later she received a pro forma rejection letter stating the position had been filled by someone else. Paulson thought nothing more of the matter until Thanksgiving when she got together with several former Santa Cruz classmates who were attending law school at King Hall. They asked if she knew of the allegations of discrimination concerning the Vet School and told her she should "protect her rights." Encouraged, she filed a civil action in the federal court for the Eastern District of California naming as defendants: the University of California, the Regents of the University of California, each of the Regents personally, the President of the University of California, the U.C. Davis Chancellor, the Dean of the Veterinary Medicine School, the Director of the Veterinary Medicine Teaching Hospital, the Director of the Campus Employment Office, and Does 1-100. Her complaint stated in full, after an appropriate caption:

> "On or about October 1989, Defendants and each of them violated my rights under 42 U.S.C. § 1983 and Title VII of the Civil Rights Act of 1964[1] by not hiring me for the position of Animal Technician.
>
> WHEREFORE, I pray that this wrong be remedied.

December 1, 1989

/s/   *Linda Paulson*
Linda Paulson, not an attorney
555 Elm Street
Winters, CA

> P.S. I demand a trial of my peers."

A. As University Counsel, you have just been served with a copy of this complaint and a proper summons, delivered by a U.S. Marshal. How would you respond? Discuss fully.

B. Assume that Ms. Paulson's complaint has neither been dismissed nor amended. Counsel for defendants has filed a motion for summary judgment. The substance of the summary judgment motion is the affidavit of defense counsel stating that the case has been pending for almost six months; that Paulson has conducted no discovery nor taken any other action; that in response to defendants' interrogatories asking the basis for her contention that defendants violated 42 U.S.C. § 1983 and Title VII of the Civil Rights Act of 1964, Paulson responded that when, in November 1989, she asked why she was not hired, "A Vet-Med person told me it was because I was unqualified. When I asked again in January, I was told it was because I was overqualified."

In response to the motion, Paulson filed an affidavit stating she had been told the Vet Med School discriminates against women and minorities, and that "hardly any women or minorities work there even though most of the students are women." This is all that was submitted to the court in connection with the motion. How should the court rule and why?

C. Assume Paulson's case goes to trial before a jury. Paulson introduces evidence that 90% of the Animal Technicians at U.C. Davis are men; that she applied for and was denied a job as Animal Technician in October 1989; and that a man was hired for the position. Defendants move for a directed verdict following the Paulson evidence. Defendants then admit that they gave Paulson conflicting reasons for not hiring her and that their records "just don't show" why she wasn't hired. At the close of the evidence, both Paulson and defendants move for a directed verdict. What should the court do? Discuss fully.

---

[1]42 U.S.C. §§ 2000e-2(a) provides in part: "It shall be unlawful employment practice for an employer—… to fail… to hire… any individual… because of such individual's sex…." Remedies available include "reinstatement or hiring of employees with or without back pay…, or any other equitable relief as the court deems appropriate." §§ 2000e-5(g).

OUTLINE OF ANSWER TO QUESTION I

A. Improper Joinder of Parties

1. lack of essential party under Rule 19?

   a. who would the party be? GE? Othler?

   b. are they 19(a) parties? sufficient interest?

   c. can they be joined? - even if they cannot, shouldn't be sufficient to dismiss

2. joinder of plaintiffs - Rule 23 (class action)

   a. Rule 23(a) factors - numerosity, typicality, commonality, adequacy of representation - problems with typicality, commonality, adequate representation (diverse & possibly conflicting interests)

   b. Rule 23(b) possible bases - injunctive relief vs. damages; possible basis for each subsection, but $ damages appear to dominate

   c. is the class action superior under 23(b)(3)? - why not individual suits, joinder, etc.

3. joinder of defendants - Rule 20 (same transactions/occurrences, common question of law/fact?)

4. remedies - no dismissal for misjoinder (Rule 21)

B. Discovery and Sanctions

1. relevance issues & mechanics - overbroad requests for interviews, client records, discovery in Othler; discovery from non-party (employees, reports)

2. confidentiality and protective orders - interviews may be privileged; confidential client records require protective order; reports also sensitive

3. work product - eavesdropping reports may be protected by 26(b)(3) - prepared for litigation; sufficient showing to overcome protection? (need + unavailable otherwise)

4. sanctions - possible party failure to respond, 37(d); otherwise order needed first

C. Preclusion

1. res judicata - unavailable; new parties, new claim

2. collateral estoppel - unavailable; no determined issues

OUTLINE OF ANSWER TO QUESTION II

A. Pleading and Rule 11

1. formal (notice pleading) - sufficient to put *D*s on notice? [yes] - remedy is Rule 12(f) more definite statement motion; *P* should be able to amend

2. substantive objections:

   a. no jurisdictional allegation - requires dismissal/amendment;

   b. statement of claim, statutes only - may be sufficient; relief possible; but civil rights claim

      3.   answer or preanswer motion? - try motions; but defenses could be in answer; affirmative defenses;

      4.   complaint filed without research/investigation; names everyone - *pro se* party, but Rule 11 applies; violated? sanction?

B. Jury Trial

      1.   possible damage claim (legal remedy); but equitable too (§1983/Title VII); statutes come under seventh amendment; analogous damage language *(Curtis v. Loether)*

      2.   proper demand (Rule 38(b))? timing OK; language is sufficient under notice pleading standards

C. Summary Judgment

      1.   sufficient support for motion? - is 6 months too short under *Celotex*? sufficient record?

      2.   *P*'s response - any admissible evidence or suggestion of evidence-, can disbelief of *D* count?

      3.   possible dismissal for failure to prosecute (Rule 41(b))

D. Directed Verdicts; JNOV; New Trial

      1.   directed verdict for *D*? probably yes; minimal evidence of discrimination; no cause

      2.   directed verdict for *P*? no; *P* has burden of proof; jury question

      3.   possible new trial - available after verdict - Rule 59

      4.   practicalities - wait and enter JNOV, if necessary; jury may decide for *D*; preserves jury verdict for appeal

Question III

On March 24, 1989 the oil tanker "Exxon Valdez" ran aground on the Bligh Reef in Prince William Sound near Valdez, Alaska (U.S.A.), spilling over 240,000 barrels (nearly 11 million gallons) of oil into the waters of the Sound. The oil has since spread over hundreds of square miles of ocean, fouled almost 730 miles of coastline (only four miles of which have been declared cleaned) and caused uncalculated damage to wildlife. The spill has had and will continue to have harmful effects on the local salmon, herring, black cod, shrimp, and halibut fisheries, allied commercial operations, and the Alaskan tourist trade. Exxon Shipping owns the tanker. Exxon Shipping is a wholly-owned subsidiary of Exxon Corporation, a New Jersey corporation with its headquarters in New York that does substantial business in Alaska and every state of the United States.

According to news reports, the Exxon Valdez' captain, Joseph J. Hazelwood, a New York resident, had been drinking before the accident, and was not in direct control of the tanker when it ran aground. A blood test administered nine hours after the accident found a blood alcohol level in excess of Coast Guard regulations. By late April, 17 lawsuits had been filed against Exxon Corporation and its subsidiaries, Exxon Company, U.S.A., and Exxon Shipping; Alyeska Pipeline Service Co., operator of the Alaska oil pipeline that terminates in Valdez; the State of Alaska; and a special $100,000,000 pipeline liability fund (the "Fund"). This fund, created by federal law, provides a maximum of $100 million in damages due to spills regardless of fault. Also scheduled to begin in late May are hearings by the National Transportation Safety Board (NTSB), a federal administrative agency that investigates transportation industry accidents to determine their cause(s) and suggest how similar accidents can be avoided in the future.

Davis & Davis is a wife and husband law firm in Cordova, Alaska, a town of 2,500 people some 25 miles from Valdez that is the home port for the Prince William Sound fishing fleet. Although Davis & Davis is the largest firm in town, its practice has been primarily family law, probate and real estate. Davis & Davis has filed class actions in Alaska State Superior Court and the United States District Court for the District of Alaska on behalf of a local herring fisherman, J. "Red" Poulos. The substantial allegations of each complaint are the following:

COMPLAINT FOR DAMAGES AND OTHER RELIEF

1. This action arises under federal maritime law, the Clean Water Act (33 U.S.C. § 1251, et seq.), and pendent state law.

2. This action is a class action brought on behalf of all fishermen, longshoremen, boat rental companies, tourist facilities, seafood processing companies, seafood retailers and restaurants who use the waters and products of the waters of Prince William Sound, Alaska.

3. Defendants are Exxon Corporation, Exxon, U.S.A., and Exxon Shipping (collectively referred to as "Exxon").

4. On or about March 24, 1989, Defendants negligently, recklessly, knowingly, and wantonly allowed or caused over 240,000 barrels of oil to be discharged from the vessel "Exxon Valdez" into the waters of the State of Alaska and of the United States in violation of the Clean Water Act, 33 U.S.C. § 1251, et seq., other federal maritime law, and state nuisance law.

5. Defendants' actions proximately caused devastating losses to plaintiffs and to the Alaskan and world environment in excess of one billion dollars.

6. Defendants are guilty of oppression, fraud, and malice justifying an award of damages for the sake of example and by way of punishing the defendants.

Wherefore, plaintiffs demand defendants be enjoined from further degradation of the environment; be required to forthwith remove all spilled oil from the environment and to restore the environrunent to its previous pristine condition; and to pay plaintiffs one billion dollars in compensatory damages plus exemplary and punitive damages, fines under the Clean Water Act, and costs and attorneys fees according to proof.

[signed]   *Barbara Davis*
Davis & Davis
Attorneys for Plaintiffs

INSTRUCTIONS: Now that you have carefully read the facts, answer the following questions. Make your answers full and complete. For purposes of this examination, assume that Alaska is a code-pleading state.

I

(20 minutes)

Exxon has applied in both Alaska state court and federal court for an injunction to halt the NTSB hearing on the ground that permitting the hearing to go forward will deprive it of its Seventh Amendment right to a jury trial. How should these courts rule on Exxon's request and why?

II

(60 minutes)

As attorney for Exxon, what initial response(s) would you make to Davis & Davis' complaint in both the Alaska state court and federal district court? Please explain the reason(s) for the response(s).

III

(40 minutes)

It is now March 1990, one year later. Davis & Davis' plaintiffs have made the following discovery requests in federal court:

(i) Plaintiffs want Exxon's attorneys' records of interviews with members of the Exxon Valdez crew conducted in late March 1989;

(ii) Plaintiffs want to conduct complete physical and mental examinations of the Exxon Valdez crew members (as of March 24, 1989) including full drug tests;

(iii) Plaintiffs want Exxon and its subsidiaries to produce copies of all studies done by or for the companies that in any way deal with the issues of potential damage due to oil spills on the West Coast of America.

Exxon has not responded to these requests except to object to them as "beyond the scope of proper discovery," burdensome, harassing and oppressive. In addition Exxon asserts (i) many of the crew members testified publicly at the NTSB hearings in June 1989, and they are still available for discovery; and (ii) its oil spill studies are protected "highly-sensitive and confidential proprietary information belonging solely to Exxon" or reflect Exxon's scientists' evaluation of the causes and consequences of the spill that would not be admissible as evidence. If plaintiffs make a timely and proper motion to compel Exxon to allow discovery of each of these matters, how should the federal magistrate rule and why?

IV

(20 minutes)

It is now March 1991, two years later. One of the federal court suits brought by local herring fishermen is nearly ready for trial. Exxon moves for summary judgment without producing any affidavits or other discovery material. Exxon's position is that plaintiffs have no evidence that they suffered any damages as a result of the oil spill. Plaintiffs admit they haven't been able to find any experts willing to testify that the oil is a cause of a decline in the fishery, but they claim that "everyone knows" that they used to catch 75,000 tons of herring in Prince William Sound before the spill, and in the most recent year the catch was only 39,000 tons. How should the court rule on the summary judgment motion and why?

V

(40 minutes)

a. Assume the suit in IV goes on to trial before a jury one year later (March 1992). At trial plaintiffs introduce evidence that their herring catch was: 1985 - 78,000 tons; 1986 - 56,000 tons; 1987 - 93,000 tons; 1988 - 73,000 tons; 1989 - none (season canceled by state law); 1990 - 39,000 tons; 1991 - 45,000 tons. They also introduce a stipulation (agreement) between them and Exxon that the oil spill events set out above occurred in 1989, and that each ton of herring catch lost would result in $2,000 damages to plaintiffs per year of loss. This is the only evidence plaintiffs introduce. Following plaintiffs' case in chief, Exxon moves for a directed verdict. Should the court grant the motion? Why or why not?

b. Assume the court denies Exxon's directed verdict motion. Exxon puts on its evidence: 11 experts all employed or paid by Exxon who testify the herring fishery was in decline for years before 1989 due to over-fishing and that the oil spill probably increased fish populations by wiping out the sea otters and other predators. At the close of all the evidence and again following a $129,000,000 jury verdict for plaintiffs, Exxon moves for a directed verdict or judgment notwithstanding the verdict and (following the verdict) for a new trial on the ground that the verdict is against the great weight of the evidence. How should the court rule on these motions?

c. Finally, 10 days after the verdict, plaintiffs move for a new trial on the ground that evidence introduced in another of the cases included an internal Exxon study done before 1989 that suggested an oil spill in Prince William Sound would, among other consequences, seriously harm the herring and salmon fisheries. Plaintiffs claim they didn't realize such a document existed and that Exxon had (informally) told them before trial there was no reason to seek discovery of such studies because it hadn't done any. Should the court consider plaintiffs' motion and, if so, how should it rule?

OUTLINE OF ANSWER TO QUESTION III

I. Jury Trial

    A. Right to Jury Trial in Federal/State Courts?

        1. federal court: seventh amendment applies

            a. proper demand? not made; could be made

            b. issues triable by jury? yes, damages and liability under Clean Water Act (*Tull*)

        2. state court: seventh amendment does not apply

            a. demand?

            b. state statute or constitution (probably yes)

    B. Infringement by NTSB Hearing?

        1. maybe if collateral estoppel applied (but no real judgment; Exxon not a "party"; different procedures)

        2. even if collateral estoppel applied and limited jury issues in *Poulos*, no seventh amendment violation: *see Parklane, Katchen*, even *Beacon* (and significant counter interest in discovering causes, requires administrative hearing)

II. Responses to Complaint

    A. Formal Objections

        1. state court failure to state "facts" that constitute a cause of action: allegations conclusory and too general especially regarding liability staff (¶4)

        2. federal court — only requires notice pleading — probably OK for central allegations; but more specificity required for punitive damages (special damages) and fraud — Rule 9(b) [admiralty/maritime claim? Rule 9(h)]

    B. Substantive Objections

        1. state court — cause of action? (too conclusory); forms not used

        2. federal — probably OK — sufficient *Conley v. Gibson* "claim" — Rule 12(b)(6)

    C. Motions/Demurrers [*See also* **B.**]

        1. jurisdiction — subject matter; personal looks OK, but could be raised. Rules 12(b)(1), (2), (4), (5).

        2. motion to strike? (*e.g.,* punitive damage allegation)

3. motion for more definite statement (to fill in conclusions, but Exxon probably can still respond)

4. to dismiss for lack of Rule 19 party? Hazelwood, Alaska, Fund.

    a. Rule 19(a) — no prejudice to existing parties, maybe to Fund that would be liable.

    b. order joinder — looks possible for all — even Hazelwood has many contacts with Alaska — does not affect subject matter, except Fund, Alaska on diversity (maybe)

    c. proceed without parties — yes; indemnity later

D. Attack Class Action Allegation — Certification

1. Rule 23(a) numerosity? yes; commonality? yes, spill and causes; typicality? — only for herring fishermen (and maybe Canadians; Japanese?); adequacy of representation? — real problems — small and inexperienced firm; no $ for notice; classes with antagonistic interests — competitors, etc. (subclasses)

2. Rule 23(b)?

    a. (1) (A) — risk of inconsistent adjudication? no

    b. (1) (B) — some dispose of all? possible Fund, punitive damages

    c. (2) — injunctive relief? possible, but $ damages predominates

    d. (3) — common questions predominate? events/cause, yes; damage, no. superior? — other actions pending; joinder or intervention by other parties? possible. manageable? no — too many classes, interests

E. Joinder of Other Parties/Claims

1. Rule 14(a) impleader to bring in Alaska, Fund, Hazelwood. Alyeska — derivative liability?; at least part indemnity

2. Rule 19 joinder (*see* above) and cross-claims

3. counterclaims? (dubious)

4. interpleader using Fund? who owns/controls? action limited to fund?

F. Answer — always possible: include denials, affirmative defenses (general denial proper? — in federal court, probably no)

G. Seek Sanctions Under Rule 11: complaint is obviously overbroad with baseless allegations

III. Discovery

A. Interview Records — Work Product Issue (*Hickman*)

1. within basic scope? yes

2. protected work product? Rule 26(b)(3) yes, preparation for litigation

3. otherwise unavailable? no, could have been done; had public hearing; only if members are dead, unavailable or have no current recollection

B. Physical/Mental Exams and Drug Tests

1. special scope rules (35): good cause, in issue, motion

2. are these conditions in issue? — *not* parties; "under control"? — maybe Hazelwood; but showing necessary — current drug status possibly irrelevant

C. Copies of Studies — Work Product and Experts

1. relevant? — overbroad (maybe)

2. studies done in anticipation of litigation are "work product"

3. studies done in regular course of business are freely discoverable unless within expert ("scientists" rule) (maybe for post-accident)

4. claims of "confidential, etc." — not privilege or proper objection; must seek protective order — Rule 26(c)

D. Motion by *P*s — where disclosure — allowed fees to *P*s; where denied, fees to *D*. Major sanctions? probably not — not total non-response, no willfulness or intent

IV. Summary Judgment (Rule 56)

A. As defending party — OK for Exxon to seek to attack cause element

B. Proper "Support?" yes under *Catrett*, if sufficient time for discovery (2 years); must show why no triable issue

C. Grant? probably yes — *P*s produced no affidavits or admissible evidence; what "everyone knows" is not enough and link remains circumstantial

V. Directed Verdict/JNOV/New Trial

A. Sufficient Evidence for Jury that Exxon spill was cause — no direct evidence; circumstantial evidence; is inference at least as likely as others? (no) grant motion

B.

1. if *P*'s evidence sufficed, was it sufficiently rebutted by Exxon's — no; not overwhelming contrary evidence jury would have to believe (not disinterested)

2. still grant motion — *D's* showing irrelevant

3. JNOV also proper; preceded by directed verdict motion

4. new trial — judge could grant even if directed verdict denied if verdict is contrary to great weight of evidence; reasonable if based on amount

C. *P*'s Motion for New Trial

1. can it be made? — yes, appears it must be to protect *P* — *see Neely*, Rules 50(c)(2) and 50(d)

2. should it be granted? no, *P* not diligent in seeking evidence; when was it discovered?; would it affect verdict?; probably cumulative.

EP

GLOSSARY

A

Action (or Civil Action): The formal legal proceeding whereby a party usually known as the plaintiff demands one or more forms of relief from the defendant or defendants. Federal Rule 2 states, "There shall be one form of action to be known as 'Civil Action.'" An action is the sum of a series of claims that the parties may make against one another.

Affidavit: The written statement or declaration of facts made by a party or witness under oath coming usually before a notary public.

Amendments to pleadings: Changes made to a pleading after it has been initially filed.

Amicus curiae: An outsider to the action who offers his or her position as a "friend of the Court" in an effort to convince the court to resolve a matter in that party's favor.

Answer: Under most rules systems, the formal written response by the defending party or parties to the plaintiff's complaint.

Appeal: A legal challenge made to the trial court's decision or order, ordinarily made in the "appellate courts."

B

Brief: The written arguments of law made by the lawyer or lawyers for one of the parties. In trial court proceedings, most briefs are referred to as memoranda of points and authorities.

C

Cause of action: The rule or rules of law defining the requirements for one party to obtain relief against another party. For example, the plaintiff may assert a cause of action against the defendant for negligence or intentional infliction of emotional distress.

Claim: In federal courts this term describes a right to relief entitling the plaintiff to some form of enforceable right against the defendant or other parties. Not as formal as a cause of action.

Collateral estoppel or issue preclusion: The use of issues litigated and determined in one action against one of the parties in a subsequent litigation.

Class action: An action brought by or on behalf of a large number of similarly situated parties. There may be class actions involving classes on the plaintiff's side, the defendant's side, or both.

Code pleading: The system of pleading first developed in New York as a result of the commission chaired by David Dudley Field. It is more formal than the Federal system and continues to dominate the procedural systems of major states, including California and New York.

Complaint: The initial pleading filed by plaintiff, usually in writing, in which the plaintiff formally sets out its allegations including causes of action or claims that entitle it to relief against the defendant.

Counterclaim: A claim made by the defending party or parties against the original plaintiff or plaintiffs. In Federal practice counterclaim is a part of the answer.

Court: This term is used in two ways: it may refer to a court system, for example, the Federal District Court or the Court of Appeals, and it frequently is used as a synonym for the judge.

Court trial or bench trial: A civil action in which factual issues are resolved at trial by the trial judge alone, not by the jury. The trial judge prepares findings of fact and conclusions of law, not a verdict.

Cross-claim: A claim made by one co-party against his or her other co-parties (that is a claim by plaintiff against other plaintiffs or defendant against other defendants) often seeking relief on the basis of the claims made by or against that party.

D

Damages: A form of relief, that is an amount of monetary compensation to the plaintiff as a result of injury by the defendant. Includes compensatory damages intended in some way to make the plaintiff whole and punitive damages intended to punish the defendant's conduct.

Defendant: A party against whom relief is sought in the complaint.

G

Demurrer: In code pleading, a demurrer is a challenge to the legal sufficiency of the plaintiff's cause of action. Although technically a pleading, it is treated as a motion to dismiss the claim.

Deposition: A discovery device in which lawyers may examine a party or other person with relevant information under oath outside of court.

Directed verdict: A ruling by the court that one of the parties must prevail, thus removing the matter from the jury's consideration.

Discovery: Formal investigation of the facts before trial using a set of specific devices that are usually lawyer-initiated and involve limited judicial supervision but are mandatory for the participants. The most common devices are the deposition, interrogatories, requests to produce, requests for admissions, and physical and mental examinations.

E

Equity: Formally an entire system of procedural rules distinct from the system at law, equity developed from English practice under the Chancellor. Today there are equitable remedies and equitable forms of relief in federal court but no distinct system of courts. Forms of equitable relief include injunction and specific performance.

F

Forum non conveniens: A doctrine that gives the court the discretion to refuse to hear a civil action because of its severe inconvenience to the parties and the court although jurisdiction and venue are proper.

I

Impleader: The addition of a third-party defendant by a defending party that claims the new third-party is liable to the defendant for part of the plaintiff's claim against the defendant.

In personam jurisdiction: Traditionally, the assertion of judicial power over an individual usually accomplished by personal service of process on the individual in the forum. *Compare with* in rem jurisdiction.

In rem jurisdiction: Traditionally, the assertion of judicial power over the thing being litigated. Some seizure of the thing within the forum was necessary for the assertion of in rem jurisdiction, but not personal notification of the persons claiming an interest in the thing.

Indispensable party: A party whose own interest or whose effect on the interests of other parties is so great that the action must be dismissed unless the party can be joined in the action. *See also* "necessary party."

Injunction: A court order requiring one or more of the parties to refrain from specific actions or, somewhat less frequently, requiring the party to undertake certain actions.

Interpleader: A procedural device that allows a party faced with conflicting claims against it to force the claimants to make their claims in a single action, thus avoiding the risk of multiple liability or inconsistent remedies as a result of multiple actions against the party.

Interrogatories: Pretrial discovery device in which a party sends a series of written questions to another party that must be answered under oath.

Intervention: The process in which a previous non-party formally joins litigation already underway among other parties.

J

Joinder: The rules allowing more than one party to litigate on any side of a civil action and allowing the parties to litigate more than one claim at a time against each other. There are two basic types of joinder — joinder of claims and joinder of parties. Joinder issues include the questions of permissive and compulsory joinder.

Joinder of claims: Rules allowing the parties to an action to bring more than one claim at a time against the existing parties. The federal rules allow unlimited joinder of claims by plaintiffs and other parties that assert claims.

Joinder of parties: Rules allowing more than one party to join or be joined together with regard to a single claim.

G

Judgment: The formal conclusion of the trial court's proceedings either following a jury's verdict or other determination by the trial judge that terminates the action in favor of one of the parties. Entry of judgment is the formal step necessary to start the time running for an appeal and gives the court's findings potential preclusive effect.

Judgment notwithstanding the verdict (JNOV): A trial judge's determination that judgment must be entered for the party or parties that did not prevail according to the jury's verdict. In federal court, a judgment notwithstanding the verdict cannot be entered unless the party seeking the judgment made a directed verdict motion at the conclusion of all the evidence. Sometimes referred to as "JNOV" from the Latin: judgment *non obstante veredicto.*

Jurisdiction: The power of a court to hear and determine a civil action. Jurisdiction has several elements including the requirement of subject matter jurisdiction and personal jurisdiction (*see* definitions below).

Jury trial: Civil action in which the jury determines the factual issues necessary to a judgment. The jury's decision is its "verdict." In federal court, the parties' right to a jury trial is a question determined by reference to the seventh amendment to the U.S. Constitution. *See also* "court trial."

L

Litigate: To undertake legal action either as a complaining or a defending party.

Long-arm statute: State statute that prescribes the circumstances under which the state courts will assert personal jurisdiction over persons not found in the state. This jurisdiction may not exceed that allowed by the due process clause of the fourteenth amendment to the U.S. Constitution but need not extend to the limits of due process either.

M

Memorandum of points and authorities: Legal arguments made to a court in support or in opposition to request an order or other relief.

Motion: A formal request that a court enter an order sought by the "moving party."

N

Necessary party: A party whose own interest or whose effect on the other parties' interests is so great that the party ought to be joined if possible, but whose interest or effect is not so great that the action must be dismissed if the party cannot be joined. *See also* "indispensable party."

New trial: A second or subsequent trial of the same matter ordered because the trial judge determined there were errors or mistakes in the previous trial so serious that any verdict cannot stand and the matter must be retried.

O

Opinion: The written decision of a court accompanied by the reasons given by the court for reaching its particular decision. The court's opinion may include legal and factual findings and conclusions.

P

Personal jurisdiction: The authority of a court to hear and determine a matter in a form that will be binding on a particular party or parties. If a court lacks personal jurisdiction over a given party, rendering a judgement against that party is a violation of that party's due process.

Plaintiff: The party who initiates litigation or brings a civil action against the defending parties.

Pleadings: The (usually) written claims, allegations, and defenses of the party that formally define the scope of the litigation.

Process: The formal written papers that must be formally served upon a party in order to obtain jurisdiction over that party.

R

Requests for admissions: Discovery device in which a party formally requests another party to admit certain facts or the genuineness of documents for purposes of the trial.

Requests to produce: Discovery device used by parties to inspect documents, things, and real property of other parties.

Res judicata or claim preclusion: The doctrine that prohibits a party from relitigating a claim or cause of action. A judgment in favor of the party who brought the claim "merges" the claim in the judgment, and that party may not bring another action on the claim. The losing party is similarly "barred" from pursuing the claim again or from challenging the merits of the judgment through collateral attack.

S

Sanctions: Penalties for violating a court's orders.

Special verdict: Jury verdict in the form of several individual findings of fact or issues.

Statutes: Formal acts passed by a legislature.

Statutes of limitation: The rules that limit the time in which an action can be brought to court. If an action is filed seeking relief that occurred too far in the past in excess of the limitations period, the courts should dismiss it.

Sua sponte: Latin phrase meaning "of itself" that refers to the judge's ability to take action without a specific request or motion by one of the parties.

Subject matter jurisdiction: The power of a court to hear and decide a dispute regardless of who the individual parties happen to be. The federal courts have limited subject matter jurisdiction, that is they may hear only certain categories of cases, most prominently cases involving diversity of citizenship and Federal questions.

Summary judgment: A procedural device that terminates a civil action short of trial when the court determines that there are no disputed factual issues for a jury to consider and that one or more of the parties is entitled to a judgment as a matter of law.

Summons: Official notification of the initiation of an action against a party, usually delivered by a marshall, sheriff or other official process server.

T

Territorial jurisdiction: Judicial jurisdiction (authority) over the parties and property whose legal interests are under consideration by the court, largely a function of geographic sovereignty of the government that created the court.

Trial: One of the final phases of civil litigation in which the parties through their lawyers present evidence to convince the factfinder (judge or jury) to resolve the material facts in their favor. Presided over by the trial judge, trial consists of a set of formalized stages usually beginning with jury selection (voir dire) and concluding with a judgment determining the rights of the parties among themselves. The trial result may be challenged in post-trial motions and on appeal.

V

Venue: A particular geographical area or courthouse where an action must be brought. Lack of proper venue does not invalidate a court's judgment.

Verification: Signature of a party or lawyer under oath attesting to the truth of the facts contained in the document.

G

Table of Cases
(cases cited in the main outline)

TA

TA

TA

TA

Table of Constitutional Provisions, Statutes, and Rules

TA

TA

TA

California Constitution and Statutes

State Rules of Court

Miscellaneous Provisions

TA

	Carrington/ Babcock 3rd Ed.	Cound/ Friedenthal/ Miller/Sexton 5th Ed.	Crump/ Dorsaneo/ Chase/ Perschbacher	Field/Kaplan Clermont 6th Ed.	Landers/ Martin/Yeazell 2nd Ed.	Louisell/ Hazard/Tait 6th Ed.	Marcus/Redish/ Sherman	Rosenberg/ Smit/Korn 5th Ed.
CHAPTER 1: Overview of Civil Procedure								
I. What is civil procedure and why does it seem so difficult?						1-26		
II. Why we focus on practice under the federal rules of civil procedure						26-29		
CHAPTER 2: Controlling the Choice of Forum: Jurisdiction, Process and Choice of Law								
I. Overview from plaintiff's perspective						1-3		
II. Overview from defendants' perspective						4	22	
III. Jurisdiction and valid judgments	229-350	66-305	57-240	825-1007, 1186-1192	61-224	279-522	22-24, 572-781	178-335
IV. Choice of law influences on choice of forum	458-478	343-419	241-281	218-279	225-261	464-502, 558-615	786-870	351-398
V. Other constraints on choice of forum	278-288	310-342	132-158	201, 1016-1045	225-286, 10-11, 179-193	615-627, 514-522, 427-537	700-718	335-350
VI. Attacking the choice of forum		305-310	154-158	46-51, 826-827, 909-913, 1187-1188	70-71, 80, 1001-1010	416-427	677-686, 688-715	230-232, 931-934
CHAPTER 3: Minimum Contacts Analysis								
I. Historical background		60-82	58-65	885-893, 902-904	70-82	281-295	512-592	223-241
II. The birth of minimum contacts doctrine in *International Shoe*	229-238	82-90	65-71	924-937	82-90	295-303	592-599	241-248
III. Further developments of minimum contacts doctrine	238-261	91-174	71-118	937-1003	90-174	303-415	599-672	248-335
IV. Burnham and transient jurisdiction: new questions about the future of minimum contacts doctrine							580-592	225-227, 305, 1136
V. Step-by-step guide to minimum contacts analysis								

	Carrington/Babcock 3rd Ed.	Cound/Friedenthal/Miller/Sexton 5th Ed.	Crump/Dorsaneo/Chase/Perschbacher	Field/Kaplan Clermont 6th Ed.	Landers/Martin/Yeazell 2nd Ed.	Louisell/Hazard/Tait 6th Ed.	Marcus/Redish/Sherman	Rosenberg/Smit/Korn 5th Ed.
CHAPTER 4: Federal Subject-matter Jurisdiction and Related Doctrines Affecting Choice of Federal Forum								
I. General principles of federal subject-matter jurisdiction		237-310	173-240	182-185	4-9, 193-224	15-16, 523	718-785	179-189
II. The federal court system				176-182		2-3, 15-17, 279-280, 502-513		
III. The federal question jurisdiction of the district courts	309-344	241-259	181-192	185-188, 827-834	195-201	65-66, 523, 525-526	728-748	189-206
IV. The diversity jurisdiction of the district courts	289-309	259-274	192-200	188-197, 859-867, 843-858, 1347-1348	202-209	524-525	718-726	181-189
V. Removal jurisdiction		296-305	215-222, 227-240	197-198, 867-872	219-224	526-527	775-783	219-220
VI. Supplemental jurisdiction	345-350	274-296	201-212	834-838, 843-852	210-219	528-547	748-760, 769-775	206-219
VII. Federal venue	278-285	317-330	138-144	199-201, 1025-1045, 1327-1328	179-181	615-627	700-718	335-350
VIII. The *Erie* Doctrine	458-478	346-381	240-281	218-286	225-261	558-615	786-848	354-398
CHAPTER 5: Pleading								
I. Background and overview	629-639	6-7, 420-458	283-297	35-66	347-348	66-71, 92-94	111-114	547-551
II. Code-pleading requirements — the complaint		459-471	297-304	454-455, 484, 502-520, 1201-1202	381-394	87-92	113-118	575-600
III. Notice pleading requirements — the complaint	639-650	471-477	304-316	484-486	14-16, 395-401	94-104	118-123	600-602
IV. Special pleading requirements		477-505	316-322	15-16, 35, 37, 40-41, 496-497	403-415	105-108	124-158	573-574, 577-578
V. Answers		505-526	169-171, 322-331	47-50, 537-540	434-467, 16-21	119-124	158-183	604-614
VI. Truthfulness in pleading	541-552	541-552	331-342	42-45, 526-531	13-14	110	128-137	622-624
VII. Amendment to pleadings	666-669	527-538	343-349	50, 62-66, 480-481, 490-495	21, 406-411	125-131, 116-117	188-197	614-629
VIII. Procedures for attacking the pleadings			309-315	46-55		110-117	137-143	563-574

CR

	Carrington/Babcock 3rd Ed.	Cound/Friedenthal/Miller/Sexton 5th Ed.	Crump/Dorsaneo/Chase/Perschbacher	Field/Kaplan Clermont 6th Ed.	Landers/Martin/Yeazell 2nd Ed.	Louisell/Hazard/Tait 6th Ed.	Marcus/Redish/Sherman	Rosenberg/Smit/Korn 5th Ed.
CHAPTER 6: Joinder of Claims and Parties								
I. Joinder of claims		553-556	374-382, 389-390	784-789	469-478	618-626, 705-719	207-208	412-426, 425-437
II. Joinder of parties	969-993	578-606	386-388, 390-398	207-209, 1201-1220	478-523	719-739	208-225	427-434, 437
III. Joinder of additional parties	998-1001	607-614	382-386	211-212, 1136-1137, 1172-1174	484-499	740-750	226-231	453-458
IV. Additional procedural devices	1005-1120, 993-998	556-578, 614-709	399-459	210, 213-217, 1221-1330	523-590	751-896	231-286	459-542
V. Supplement of jurisdiction		274-296	201-212	834-858	210-219	528-547	748-775	206-219
CHAPTER 7: Discovery								
I. Purposes of discovery		710-712	473-476, 514-559	66-69	28, 591-593	901-902		660-665
II. Review of the basic discovery devices	669-695	732-766	476-485	69-82	620-649	902-912	296-311	719-729
III. Outlines of the scope of discovery under the federal rules	695-732	712-732, 766-791	486-513	549-592	593-620	912-963	311-324	665-719
IV. Specific discovery devices	669-695	732-766	514-559, 473-476	69-82, 84-87, 576-580	620-649	902-912	296-311	719-729
V. The duty to supplement responses: Federal Rule 26(e)			559-560	83-84, 89	597-598	908-909, 1112		
VI. Discovery abuse and sanctions: Federal Rules 26(f)-(g) and 37		791-801		71, 73-74, 82-83, 79, 586-590		963-969	287-296, 355-363	729-748
CHAPTER 8: Pre-trial Procedures and Dispositions								
I. Alternatives to trial	216-228	1230-1280	939-1065	32, 237-238, 330-353	332-346	37-38, 175-177, 983-984, 989-997, 1255-1281	420-424, 98-100	1111-1135
II. Pre-trial conferences and pre-trial orders	132	802-819	579-589	91-97, 593-620	692-703	969-981	17-23, 408-414	813-827
III. Rule 41 voluntary and involuntary disposition	122-123	851-854	642-646	671-677, 130-132	661-679	982-983, 1134		650-657
IV. Summary judgments	744-763	820-850	616-642	99-107, 621-638	679-689	8, 134, 143-174	364-407	631-650
V. Default judgments	123	854-860	646-649	46, 61, 1054	661-670	984-989		657

	Carrington/ Babcock 3rd Ed.	Cound/ Friedenthal/ Miller/Sexton 5th Ed.	Crump/ Dorsaneo/ Chase/ Perschbacher	Field/Kaplan Clermont 6th Ed.	Landers/ Martin/Yeazell 2nd Ed.	Louisell/ Hazard/Tait 6th Ed.	Marcus/Redish Sherman	Rosenberg/ Smit/Korn 5th Ed.
CHAPTER 9: Trial and Post-trial Motions								
I. Overview of the trial process	132-136	861-873	653-655	116-161, 639-823		8-11, 997-1001	425-433	828-842
II. The right to jury trial in federal court	224-228	873-913	655-679	116-117, 775-823	703-736	1001-1059	433-480	749-780
III. Jury instruction and verdicts	420-428	871, 953-959	734-755	156-159, 700-705	781-783, 807-810	10, 999-1000, 1135, 1144-1159	553-563	41-42, 838-842, 851-872
IV. The role of judge and jury before and during trial	386-441		755-763	92-98, 280-285, 320-330, 593-619	736-756	1060-1113, 1136-1144	3-24	842-851
V. Directed verdicts	387-397	963-983	766-785	131-133, 155-156, 673-697	757-780	9-10, 1113-1118 1125-1131, 1134-1135	483-498	895-911
VI. Post-verdict motions	137	983-1014	786-804	159-161	824-834, 810-817	1118-1125, 1131-1135, 1159-1160, 1168-1169, 1170-1173	498-500	872-895, 911-918
VII. Extraordinary post-judgment relief in the trial court	138	1014-1031	804-809	744-745, 1186-1192	841-860	984-989, 1329-1341	500-510	931-943
Chapter 10: Appeal								
I. The mechanics of appeal	138-139	57-61, 1061-1138	811-831	176-182, 1352-1359	861-880	11-12, 1284-1289, 1328-1329		1038-1040
II. The philosophy of appeal	491-500, 351-353					1282-1284	872-875	1031-1038
III. The federal courts and the model of finality	62-65		831-844	176-178, 1071, 1360-1369	881-912	15-17, 1296-1310	875-923	930-931, 1046-1081
IV. The California courts and the model of piecemeal appeal						1289-1296		
V. Appeal to the United States Supreme Court	442-454	1140-1145	844-847	18-19, 181-182, 198-199, 1350, 1368	911-912	1310-1327	923-924	1081-1092
VI. Appeal as a factor in choice of forum						1327-1328		
Chapter 11: Enforcement of Judgments								
I. From decision to enforcement				162-163, 166-167, 1366-1368	884-889	1197-1202		43, 930-931
II. Self-enforcing judgments			911-936	167-173	200-201, 299-300	201-202, 1202		

	Carrington/ Babcock 3rd Ed.	Cound/ Friedenthal/ Miller/Sexton 5th Ed.	Crump/ Dorsaneo/ Chase/ Perschbacher	Field/Kaplan Clermont 6th Ed.	Landers/ Martin/Yeazell 2nd Ed.	Louisell/ Hazard/Tait 6th Ed.	Marcus/Redish/ Sherman	Rosenberg/ Smit/Korn 5th Ed.
III. Enforcement of coercive judgments	138, 1181-1193	1053-1060	936-938	174-176, 1063		177-201, 1201-1202		943-954
Chapter 12: Preclusion doctrines — res judicata and collateral estoppel								
I. Res judicata as a general rule	941-956	1148-1161	849-856	1068-1199	914-948, 983-991	628-649	947-981	955-1030
II. Collateral estoppel or issue preclusion	957-969	1166-1186	856-872	1069, 1109-1134, 1140-1172	948-983, 991-1001	649-679	981-999	978-1002
III. Unique problems of inter-system preclusion			938		1001-1014	679-705		

INDEX

ID

ID

ID

ID

ID

ID

ID

ID

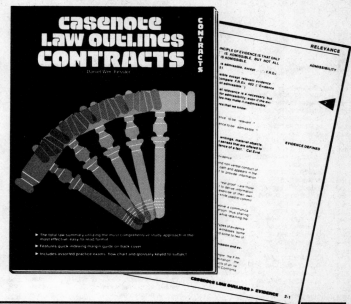

CASENOTE® LEGAL BRIEFS

PRICE LIST EFFECTIVE JULY 1, 1991 ● PRICES SUBJECT TO CHANGE WITHOUT NOTICE

Ref. No.	Course	Adaptable to Courses Utilizing	Retail Price
1380	ACCOUNTING	FIFLIS, KRIPKE & FOSTER	7.50
1265	ADMINISTRATIVE LAW	BONFIELD & ASIMOV	12.00
1263	ADMINISTRATIVE LAW	BREYER & STEWART	15.00
1260	ADMINISTRATIVE LAW	GELHORN, B., S., R. & S.	13.00
1264	ADMINISTRATIVE LAW	MASHAW & MERRILL	13.50
1262	ADMINISTRATIVE LAW	SCHWARTZ	13.00
1290	ADMIRALTY	HEALY & SHARPE	16.00
1291	ADMIRALTY	LUCAS	13.50
1351	AGENCY & PARTNERSHIP	HYNES	15.00
1350	AGENCY & PARTNERSHIP (ENT.ORG)	CONARD, KNAUSS & SIEGEL	16.00
1280	ANTITRUST	AREEDA & KAPLOW	14.50
1281	ANTITRUST (TRADE REG)	HANDLER, B. P. & G.	12.50
1610	BANKING LAW	SYMONS & WHITE	10.00
1303	BANKRUPTCY (DEBT. CRED.)	EISENBERG	14.00
1440	BUSINESS PLANNING	HERWITZ	9.50
1040	CIVIL PROCEDURE	COUND, F., M. & S	15.00
1043	CIVIL PROCEDURE	FIELD, K. & C.	15.00
1046	CIVIL PROCEDURE	LANDERS, MARTIN & YEAZEL	13.00
1041	CIVIL PROCEDURE	LOUISELL, HAZARD & TAIT	14.00
1047	CIVIL PROCEDURE	MARCUS, REDISH & SHERMAN	15.00
1044	CIVIL PROCEDURE	ROSENBERG, S. & K.	16.00
1311	COMMERCIAL LAW	FARNSWORTH & HONNOLD	14.00
1312	COMMERCIAL LAW	JORDAN & WARREN	15.00
1310	COMMERCIAL LAW	SPEIDEL, SUMMERS & WHITE	15.00
1312	COMMERCIAL PAPER (COMM. LAW)	JORDAN & WARREN	15.00
1320	COMMUNITY PROPERTY	VERRALL & BIRD	13.50
1071	CONFLICTS	CRAMTON, CURRIE & KAY	13.00
1070	CONFLICTS	REESE, ROSENBERG & HAY	16.00
1082	CONSTITUTIONAL LAW	BARRETT, COHEN & VARAT	18.00
1086	CONSTITUTIONAL LAW	BREST & LEVINSON	13.00
1080	CONSTITUTIONAL LAW	GUNTHER	15.00
1084	CONSTITUTIONAL LAW	KAUPER & BEYTAGH	14.00
1081	CONSTITUTIONAL LAW	LOCKHART, K., C. & S.	14.00
1085	CONSTITUTIONAL LAW	ROTUNDA	16.00
1087	CONSTITUTIONAL LAW	STONE, S., S. & T.	15.00
1017	CONTRACTS	CALAMARI, PERILLO & BENDER	18.00
1101	CONTRACTS	CRANDALL & WHALEY	17.00
1014	CONTRACTS	DAWSON, H. & H.	15.00
1010	CONTRACTS	FARNSWORTH & YOUNG	14.00
1011	CONTRACTS	FULLER & EISENBERG	16.00
1100	CONTRACTS	HAMILTON, R. & W.	14.00
1013	CONTRACTS	KESSLER, GILMORE & KRONMAN	18.50
1016	CONTRACTS	KNAPP & CRYSTAL	16.50
1012	CONTRACTS	MURPHY & SPEIDEL	17.00
1018	CONTRACTS	MURRAY	17.00
1015	CONTRACTS	ROSETT	16.00
1019	CONTRACTS	VERNON	15.00
1501	COPYRIGHT	NIMMER, M., M., & N.	14.50
1218	CORPORATE TAXATION	LIND, S. L & R	9.00
1050	CORPORATIONS	CARY & EISENBERG (ABR. & UNABR.)	15.00
1054	CORPORATIONS	CHOPER, MORRIS & COFFEE	16.50
1350	CORPORATIONS (ENT. ORG.)	CONARD, KNAUSS & SIEGEL	16.00
1053	CORPORATIONS	HAMILTON	14.00
1051	CORPORATIONS	HENN	15.00
1055	CORPORATIONS	JENNINGS & BUXBAUM	13.50
1056	CORPORATIONS	SOLOMON, SCHWARTZ & BOWMAN	15.00
1052	CORPORATIONS	VAGTS	12.00
1300	CREDITOR'S RIGHTS (DEBT./CRED.)	RIESENFELD	16.00
1550	CRIMINAL JUSTICE	WEINREB	13.00
1020	CRIMINAL LAW	BOYCE & PERKINS	18.00
1024	CRIMINAL LAW	DIX & SHARLOT	12.00
1025	CRIMINAL LAW	FOOTE & LEVY	12.00
1027	CRIMINAL LAW	JOHNSON	17.00
1021	CRIMINAL LAW	KADISH & SHULHOFER	15.00
1026	CRIMINAL LAW	KAPLAN & WEISBERG	13.50
1023	CRIMINAL LAW	LAFAVE	14.00
1022	CRIMINAL LAW	WEINREB	10.00
1200	CRIMINAL PROCEDURE	KAMISAR, LAFAVE & ISRAEL	14.00
1204	CRIMINAL PROCEDURE	SALTZBURG	12.00
1203	CRIMINAL PROCEDURE (PROCESS)	WEINREB	13.50
1303	DEBTOR-CREDITOR	EISENBERG	14.00
1302	DEBTOR-CREDITOR	EPSTEIN, LANDERS & NICKLES	13.00
1300	DEBTOR-CREDITOR (CRED. RTS.)	RIESENFELD	16.00
1304	DEBTOR-CREDITOR	WARREN & WESTBROOK	14.00
1223	DECEDENTS EST. (WILLS, T. & E.)	DUKEMINIER & JOHANSON	14.50
1224	DECEDENTS ESTATES	RITCHIE, ALFORD & EFFLAND	16.00
1222	DECEDENTS ESTATES	SCOLES & HALBACH	15.50
1231	DECEDENTS ESTATES (TRUSTS)	WELLMAN, W. & B.	14.00
1244	DOMESTIC RELATIONS (FAM. LAW)	AREEN	17.00
1242	DOMESTIC RELATIONS (FAM. LAW)	CLARK & GLOWINSKY	14.00
1241	DOMESTIC RELATIONS (FAM. LAW)	FOOTE, LEVY & SANDER	12.00
1243	DOMESTIC RELATIONS (FAM. LAW)	KRAUSE	18.00
1240	DOMESTIC RELATIONS (FAM. LAW)	WADLINGTON	15.00
1350	ENTERPRISE ORGANIZATIONS	CONARD, KNAUSS & SIEGEL	16.00
1341	ENVIRONMENTAL LAW	FINDLEY & FARBER	14.00
1254	EQUITY (REMEDIES)	LAYCOCK	15.00
1253	EQUITY (REMEDIES)	LEAVELL, LOVE & NELSON	16.00
1252	EQUITY (REMEDIES)	RE	19.50
1255	EQUITY (REMEDIES)	SHOBEN & TABB	16.50
1250	EQUITY (REMEDIES)	YORK, BAUMAN & RENDLEMAN	19.00
1217	ESTATE & GIFT TAXATION	BITTKER & CLARK	10.00
1214	ESTATE & GIFT TAXATION	KAHN & WAGGONER	13.00
1213	ESTATE & GIFT TAX (F. WEALTH TRANS.)	SURREY, MCDANIEL & GUTMAN	11.00
1090	ETHICS (PROF. RESPONSIBILITY)	PIRSIG & KIRWIN	10.00
1091	ETHICS (PROF. RESPONSIBILITY)	GILLERS & DORSEN	8.00
1064	EVIDENCE	CLEARY, S., B. & M.	16.50
1065	EVIDENCE	GREEN & NESSON	14.00
1061	EVIDENCE	KAPLAN & WALTZ	15.00
1063	EVIDENCE	LEMPERT & SALTZBURG	7.00
1062	EVIDENCE	MCCORMICK, SUTTON & WELLBORN	18.00
1066	EVIDENCE	MUELLER & KIRKPATRICK	13.00
1060	EVIDENCE	WEINSTEIN, M., A. & B.	16.5
1244	FAMILY LAW (DOMESTIC REL.)	AREEN	17.0
1242	FAMILY LAW (DOMESTIC REL.)	CLARK & GLOWINSKY	14.00
1241	FAMILY LAW (DOMESTIC REL.)	FOOTE, LEVY & SANDER	12.00
1243	FAMILY LAW (DOMESTIC REL.)	KRAUSE	18.00
1240	FAMILY LAW (DOMESTIC REL.)	WADLINGTON	15.00
1360	FEDERAL COURTS	BATOR, M., S. & W.	15.0
1362	FEDERAL COURTS	CURRIE	12.00
1363	FEDERAL COURTS	LOW & JEFFRIES	12.00
1361	FEDERAL COURTS	MCCORMICK, C. & W.	15.00
1510	GRATUITOUS TRANSFERS	CLARK, LUSKY & MURPHY	14.00
1371	INSURANCE LAW	KEETON	16.00
1372	INSURANCE LAW	YORK & WHELAN	15.00
1370	INSURANCE LAW	YOUNG & HOLMES	12.00
1392	INTERNATIONAL LAW	HENKIN, P., S. & S.	13.00
1390	INTERNATIONAL LAW	SWEENEY, OLIVER & LEECH	16.00
1460	JUVENILE JUSTICE	MILLER, D., D. & P.	13.00
1331	LABOR LAW	COX, BOK, GORMAN & FINKIN	14.00
1333	LABOR LAW	LESLIE	13.50
1332	LABOR LAW	MELTZER & HENDERSON	14.00
1330	LABOR LAW	MERRIFIELD, S. & C.	14.00
1471	LAND FINANCE (REAL ESTATE TRANS)	AXELROD, BERGER & JOHNSTONE	13.00
1620	LAND FINANCE (REAL ESTATE TRANS)	NELSON & WHITMAN	15.00
1470	LAND FINANCE	PENNEY, B. & C.	12.00
1450	LAND USE	WRIGHT & GITELMAN	17.0
1590	LOCAL GOVERNMENT LAW	VALENTE	17.0
1520	MEDICINE	SHARPE, FISCINA & HEAD	16.0
1600	NEGOTIABLE INSTRUMENTS	WHALEY	9.0
1570	NEW YORK PRACTICE	PETERFREUND & MCLAUGHLIN	20.0
1541	OIL & GAS	KUNTZ, L, A. & S.	13.0
1540	OIL & GAS	WILLIAMS, M., M. & W.	12.0
1351	PARTNERSHIP & AGENCY	HYNES	15.0
1560	PATENT LAW	CHOATE & FRANCIS	19.0
1431	PRODUCTS LIABILITY	KEETON, MONTGOMERY & GREEN	15.0
1430	PRODUCTS LIABILITY	NOEL & PHILLIPS	16.5
1090	PROF. RESPONSIBILITY (ETHICS)	PIRSIG & KIRWIN	10.00
1091	PROF. RESPONSIBILITY (ETHICS)	GILLERS & DORSEN	8.00
1033	PROPERTY	BROWDER, C., N., S.& W.	15.5
1030	PROPERTY	CASNER & LEACH	16.0
1031	PROPERTY	CRIBBET, JOHNSON, FINLEY & SMITH	17.5
1035	PROPERTY	DUKEMINIER & KRIER	13.
1034	PROPERTY	HAAR & LIEBMAN	15.5
1036	PROPERTY	KURTZ & HOVENKAMP	15.
1032	PROPERTY	RABIN	15.
1620	REAL ESTATE TRANSFER & FINANCE	NELSON & WHITMAN	15.
1254	REMEDIES (EQUITY)	LAYCOCK	15.
1253	REMEDIES (EQUITY)	LEAVELL, LOVE & NELSON	16.0
1252	REMEDIES (EQUITY)	RE	19.5
1255	REMEDIES (EQUITY)	SHOBEN & TABB	16.5
1250	REMEDIES (EQUITY)	YORK, BAUMAN & RENDLEMAN	19.0
1312	SECURED TRANS. (COMM. LAW)	JORDAN & WARREN	15.0
1270	SECURITIES REGULATION	JENNINGS & MARSH	14.0
1271	SECURITIES REGULATION	RATNER	13.0
1215	TAXATION (BASIC FED. INC.)	ANDREWS	15.0
1217	TAXATION (ESTATE & GIFT)	BITTKER & CLARK	10.0
1212	TAXATION (FED. INC.)	FREELAND, LIND & STEPHENS	13.0
1211	TAXATION (FED. INC.)	GRAETZ	13.0
1214	TAXATION (ESTATE & GIFT)	KAHN & WAGGONER	13.0
1210	TAXATION (FED. INC.)	KLEIN, BITTKER & STONE	13.5
1216	TAXATION (FED. INC.)	KRAGEN & MCNULTY	11.0
1218	TAXATION (CORPORATE)	LIND, S., L & R.	9.0
1213	TAXATION (FED. WEALTH TRANS.)	SURREY, M. & G.	11.0
1281	TRADE REGULATION (ANTITRUST)	HANDLER, B. P. & G.	12.0
1006	TORTS	DOBBS	16.
1003	TORTS	EPSTEIN, GREGORY & KALVEN	16.
1004	TORTS	FRANKLIN & RABIN	12.
1001	TORTS	HENDERSON & PEARSON	14.
1002	TORTS	KEETON, K., S. & S.	17.
1000	TORTS	PROSSER, WADE & SCHWARTZ	19.
1005	TORTS	SHULMAN, JAMES & GRAY	17.
1230	TRUSTS	BOGERT, O., H., & H.	15.
1231	TRUSTS (DECEDENTS ESTATES)	WELLMAN, WAGGONER & BROWDER	14.
1410	U.C.C.	EPSTEIN, MARTIN, H. & N.	10.
1580	WATER LAW	TRELEASE & GOULD	14.
1223	WILLS TRUSTS & EST. (DEC. EST.)	DUKEMINIER & JOHANSON	14.
1220	WILLS	MECHEM & ATKINSON	16.

REVISED MAY 1, 199

CASENOTES PUBLISHING CO. INC. ● **1640 FIFTH STREET, SUITE 208** ● **SANTA MONICA, CA 90401** ● **(213) 395-650**

PLEASE PURCHASE FROM YOUR LOCAL BOOKSTORE. IF UNAVAILABLE, YOU MAY ORDER DIRECT.*

4TH CLASS POSTAGE (ALLOW TWO WEEKS) $1.00 PER ORDER; 1ST CLASS POSTAGE $3.00 (ONE BOOK), $2.00 EACH (TWO OR MORE BOOKS)

*CALIFORNIA RESIDENTS PLEASE ADD 7 % SALES TAX (SERIES XXIV)